Contents • Volume 7 • Fall 2013

Editor's Note

Base Ball is back and it's bigger and better than ever. That line might have been used to describe Opening Day in any given season but it particularly describes the current number of this journal. Now in its seventh year, the semiannual publication has become an annual, with all the added heft of a book.

This year has marked the centennial of the death of Bud Fowler (1858–1913), portrayed on the front cover, a man whose playing career began in the 1870s and extended into the 20th century. Although not yet honored with a plaque in the Baseball Hall of Fame, he is the most famous baseball-playing resident of Cooperstown and the only one with a village street named for him. This pleasing development took place on the mayor's proclaimed Bud Fowler Day, April 20, 2013.

Fowler played on many integrated teams over the course of his vagabond career and was often compelled to find other employment when racism intruded upon the field. In crossing a bridge that others had built, Jackie Robinson had, if unknowingly, walked along Fowler Way.

In the afternoon before Bud Fowler Day, official Cooperstown historian Hugh MacDougall delivered an outstanding paper before the Frederick Ivor-Campbell Conference on 19th century baseball, sponsored annually by the Society for American Baseball Research (SABR). This journal provides its first appearance in print. In addition to "Bud Fowler—A Knight of the Diamond, a Knight of the Razor," MacDougall presents a stunning discovery: *The Retired Black Planter*, a play that Fowler wrote and copyrighted in 1912, the year before his death. Annotating and analyzing Fowler's humble effort, MacDougall provides an authorial doubleheader of a sort not seen in *Base Ball* before.

Having bent "the rules" in this case, the editor had the delightful opportunity to sin again, publishing two articles by the estimable Rob Edelman, a veteran contributor on baseball and popular culture. To his learned and witty contributions on Eadweard Muybridge and Frank Merriwell we have added plentiful illustration. Examining the baseball plates from Muybridge's *Animal Locomotion*, one must agree with Edelman's view that "his place in the history of moving image technology is secure."

To commend other articles—by previous contributors and newbies—would be expected here, but the best thing that might be said is: *read them*, in whatever order pleases you. Some will favor the very early settings of Richard Hershberger (1857) and Robert Tholkes (1863), others will gravitate to the early 20th century articles by Art Ahrens or Terry Gottschall.

Long, thoughtful pieces have been the special distinction of this journal, and the previously imposed ceiling of 7,000 words has here been consigned to the rear-view mirror. Charles Alexander, William Humber, and Angus Macfarlane have been encouraged to run as long as reader interest might hold, and each breaks new ground in both discovery and analysis.

Last but not least is the happy collaboration of David Nemec and David Ball, deriving from the unhappy event of Ball's death in 2011. Ball had begun an ambitious prospective book that now will see the light of day only in tantalizing fragments. One of the nearly finished chapters is offered herein as a continuing tribute to Ball, one of the contributors to *Base Ball*'s first number back in the spring of 2007 ("The Bechtel-Craver Trade and the Origins of Baseball's Sales System").

As I wrote in the Editor's Note accompanying *Base Ball*'s debut issue, "acknowledgments are tedious to read except for those being acknowledged." So while six years later I will still refer you to the masthead, I would be remiss not to mention of the individuals who have toiled in background with me to bring out this expanded number: Gary Mitchem, Mark Durr, and Layla Milholen.

John Thorn
Editor

Split Season
The National League in 1892

Charles C. Alexander

At the beginning of 1892, Nicholas Young, the mild-mannered and mostly ineffectual president of the newly amalgamated National League and American Association, exuded confidence about the coming baseball season. After two strife-filled years — a three-way war in 1890 between the National League, the American Association, and the rebel Players League and then another war the past season between the National League and the Association — peace had finally come in the form of an agreement in Indianapolis the previous December, whereby the Baltimore, St. Louis, Louisville, and Washington Association franchises merged with the eight National League franchises to form one "big league."[1]

Young said that while the $130,000 (or $118,000) buyout agreed to with the five Association franchises that were dropped might seem peace "bought dearly," in fact "the price was cheap. We will save nearly that during the next few years in salaries, with unhealthy competition removed, besides the public will pay the money by increased patronage at the games." In an effort to regain something of the interest generated by the "World's Championship Series" between the League and Association winners, played from 1883 to 1890, the owners agreed to a split-season format, with the winner of the first half (or "first season") meeting the second-half winner for the League championship. Albert G. Spalding, retired from the presidency of the League's Chicago franchise but still a potent force in League affairs, shared Nick Young's optimism about baseball's prospects for 1892 and especially the "double championship" arrangement. "The old evil of the tailender," Spalding predicted, "has been done away with by its adoption, and hope need never be dead in any city until almost the end of the season."[2]

To pay for the buyout, each National League club was to contribute 10 percent of home gate receipts to a League fund. In anticipation of an attendance surge after two lean years, the League owners voted to extend the 1892 schedule from 140 to 154 games. Rosters would be limited to 15 players. While the National League had always forbidden games on Sunday, the Indianapolis peace agreement permitted Sunday ball in those cities — St. Louis, Louisville, and Cincinnati — where the local ownership wanted it. Officially, the League retained the 50-cent base admission it had always charged, although each club had the option to charge 25 cents, the base admission in the Association.

Charles C. Alexander has written biographies of Ty Cobb, John McGraw, Rogers Hornsby, and Tris Speaker, as well as *Our Game: An American Baseball History* and *Breaking the Slump: Baseball in the Depression Era*. For *Breaking the Slump*, he was awarded the Seymour Medal in 2003 by the Society for American Baseball Research. Alexander is a distinguished professor emeritus of history at Ohio University and now lives in retirement with his wife, JoAnn, in Butler County, Ohio.

DOI: 10.3172/BB.7.5

Yet for all the rosy expectations for the season ahead, discontent still roiled the little universe of professional baseball. The Indianapolis agreement stipulated the recognition of all contracts then in force, but with the elimination of five Association franchises, dozens of players found themselves out of work. A few veteran players retired; others found places in one of the 10 lesser or "minor" leagues that started the 1892 season. The more desirable players from the Association who had signed with now-defunct clubs or were unsigned at the time of the Indianapolis agreement were parceled out among the clubs in the newly constructed National League, but in various instances club owners were unhappy at not getting this or that particular player; in other instances, players resisted going where they assigned.

Fred Pfeffer, a 10-year veteran and a Players League stalwart, returned to the Chicago National Leaguers in 1891 but never reconciled with Adrian "Cap" Anson, the domineering leader of the "Colts" (as they were now called), who had been a resolute foe of the Players League. Having signed with the stillborn Chicago Association entry, Pfeffer now refused to re-sign with Anson's team, saying he wouldn't play for Anson "under any circumstances" and wanted to be with Louisville, in his hometown.[3] A week before the season opened, he got his wish when Chicago traded him to Louisville for a nondescript infielder and cash.

Having disposed of its rivals, the NL tried a split schedule for 1892.

The previous fall, Danny Richardson , a highly regarded infielder, had signed with the Association's Philadelphia club, owned by the Wagner brothers. As part of the amalgamation agreement, the Wagners bought the Washington franchise. Richardson didn't like the idea of playing for Washington — which had been the worst team in the Association and had never finished higher than seventh (once) in either the Association or the National League — and wanted to return to the New York Giants, where he had spent his entire major league career except for his Players League season. The Giants owners wanted him back; president John B. Day threatened to seek an injunction to keep Richardson from going to Washington, while the Wagners threatened to quit baseball if Washington's claim to Richardson weren't upheld. The dispute was a bitter one, in part because of lingering resentment among the Association club owners toward the League, whose operators, they believed with considerable justification, had exploited and lied to them ever since the Association's formation in 1882. The Richardson matter ultimately led to a meeting of the League's club owners, who voted in favor of the Wagners. To placate

Richardson, the Washington owners assured him of the handsome $4,000 salary he had signed for with the Athletics and made him captain of the team variously called "Senators" or "Nationals."

Richardson joined a team that, one way or another, had acquired several capable players in the offseason. "The public can rest content," exulted the *Washington Post*'s baseball reporter after Richardson joined the local entry. "All the stars are now in line and Washington will have the greatest club in its history." Washington's manager would be Bill Barnie, who had put in a long managerial career with Baltimore and various other teams, and whom the Wagners had originally hired to manage the Athletics. "Washington last year had enough incompetent managers to last for a lifetime," wrote the *Post*'s baseball man, "so she is to be congratulated in securing a thoroughly competent one in William Barnie."[4]

But if things were looking up in the nation's capital, elsewhere players and club executives found reasons to be unhappy. The New York ownership had become increasingly factionalized since 1890, when Al Spalding, his brother J. Walter Spalding, and presidents of four other clubs canceled debts and bought enough stock in the Giants to bail out John B. Day, who had been nearly bankrupted by competition with the New York Players Leaguers. Retaining his presidency but reduced to minority ownership, Day saw his status further diminished when Edward Talcott and other investors deserted the Players League in return for stock in the New York franchise. By 1892 Day was at odds with Talcott and J. Walter Spalding, who sat on its board of directors.

All of the Giants executives were unhappy with the 1892 schedule, as were Brooklyn president Charles Byrne and his co-owners. The Giants and the cross-river Bridegrooms would have to play 63 of their 77 home games on the same dates. Byrne, moreover, wasn't on good terms with captain John Montgomery Ward, who still had the enmity of most club owners because he had been the driving force behind the Brotherhood of Professional Ball Players and its offspring, the Players League. Ward was a skilled infielder, highly respected for his leadership abilities, but the 1891 Bridegrooms had finished a distant and disappointing sixth place under his stewardship. Ward was expected to do better this season, especially with big Dan Brouthers, assigned from the Boston Association champions after leading the circuit with a .350 average, as his first baseman.

No longer having to compete with each other for players, owners in the new "big league" looked to reduce salaries. Some players were under two-year contracts, but others had to swallow big pay cuts. The new Pittsburgh owners slashed the salary of Cornelius McGillicuddy, a string bean catcher who played as Connie Mack, from $2,400 to $1,400. Addison "Ad" Gumbert, who had won 56 games in the National and Players leagues the past three years, also received a contract from Chicago president Jim Hart specifying a $1,000 cut. The New York Giants' Amos Rusie, probably the fastest pitcher baseball had seen up to that time, had won 74 games since entering the National League as an 18-year-old in 1889, and had struck out 667 batters over the past two seasons. He signed for half of what he was supposed to be paid by the Association's Chicago team.

Following a solid first-year showing with Anson's Colts, Bill Dahlen first signed again with Chicago for $1,200, then took an offer from the Association's Milwaukee club of $3,000, with a $500 advance. When the Indianapolis settlement put Milwaukee out of business, the young infielder had to sign a new contract with Jim Hart, this time for $1,500. Hart reimbursed the Milwaukee owner for Dahlen's advance—and then deducted $500 from his salary.

There was a new, forceful presence in the National League in the person of Christian Frederick Wilhelm "Chris" von der Ahe. A German immigrant who became rich through the ownership of grocery stores, saloons, and the St. Louis Browns, von der Ahe had been the most powerful figure in Association affairs. His Browns dominated the Association in the previous decade, winning consecutive pennants 1885–1888 and narrowly missing a fifth in 1889. Devastated by defections to the Players League, the Browns dropped to third in 1890 in a much-weakened Association, then, largely rebuilt, finished second in 1891 in a stronger circuit.

Speaking with a thick accent that was often parodied in the baseball press, alternately praising, rewarding, bullying, and fining his players, von der Ahe stayed in the midst of controversy. But "mein Prowns," as he called his team, would never be the power in the National League they had been in the Association. Star outfielder Tommy McCarthy and Jack Stivetts, a young pitcher who had won 33 games for St. Louis in 1891, signed with Boston. Charles Comiskey, the Browns' first baseman and captain in their glory years in the eighties, had gone with the Players League, then returned to spend an unhappy season with von der Ahe in 1891. That winter he deserted "der Boss President" for good, signing to captain the Cincinnati Reds under a three-year contract for a total of $20,000. James "Tip" O'Neill, one of the Association's best batters, followed him to the Reds. Von der Ahe also no longer had Denny Lyons, a hard-hitting third baseman whose successive drunken sprees the past season finally got him expelled from the Association. The joint Committee on Players assigned Lyons to the New York Giants. Only William "Kid" Gleason, a little righthander, and Ted Breitenstein, a young lefthander from the St. Louis sandlots who had pitched a no-hit game on the last day of last season, remained from the Browns' 1891 roster.

Another persistent object of controversy was Michael Joseph Kelly, the most popular player of his day. Thirty-two at the start of the 1892 season, the "King of the Diamond," as he was hailed in his prime, was remarkably versatile — behind the plate most of the time but also able to play the infield and outfield and occasionally go in to pitch. Poorly educated (as were most ballplayers of that time and for decades thereafter), Kelly was nonetheless considered unequaled in what, in a later time, would be called "baseball smarts" — the ability to think and act quickly and exploit any advantage the opposition gave him. Strikingly handsome, a raconteur, heavy drinker, and all-around goodtime guy, Kelly brought a special appeal to the game, even if his off-the-field behavior frequently left him unready to play.

Sold by Chicago to Boston following the 1886 season for a stunning $10,000, Kelly became the darling of New England cranks and remained so after he joined most of the game's quality players in signing with the Players League. After captaining the Boston Players to a pennant, he signed with the new Boston Association club, then was "loaned" to captain the equally new Cincinnati entry. The Association's Cincinnati venture proved a fiasco; in August 1891 the franchise moved to Milwaukee, and Kelly went back to Boston. After only four games with the Boston Association team, Kelly jumped to the Boston National Leaguers for a huge two-year contract. That act of betrayal, as the Association men saw it, served to break up peace negotiations going on in Washington. (Four months later, of course, the two organizations reached their amalgamation agreement.)

Kelly's best years were behind him. In the coming season, he would play only half the time and bat .189. He had put on at least twenty pounds and slowed considerably.

But he was still an attendance magnet, still in demand for his name and personality if not for his playing ability. John B. Day reportedly was willing to pay $10,000 for his contract and throw in catcher Jack Boyle, although J. Walter Spalding was adamantly opposed. Kelly was said to be willing; as he cheerfully told the St. Louis weekly *Sporting News*, "If they told me to play for $1.10 a day, Kel would don his little knickerbockers and do it."[5] In any case, Boston owners Arthur Soden, John B. Billings, and William H. Conant — known as the "Triumvirs" — couldn't get together on the deal. So the King remained with the Beaneaters, though not as captain. Manager Frank Selee gave that responsibility to third baseman Billy Nash.

So on Tuesday, April 12, with many new faces in many new places, the National League's "first season" got underway. Despite generally unpleasant weather, the six opening games were well attended. Boston opened defense of its 1891 pennant before the biggest baseball gathering in the history of the District of Columbia, some 6,400, with a 14–4 pummeling of a Washington team that was supposed to be much improved — but wouldn't be. John Clarkson, who had won 277 times since coming into the National League with Chicago in 1884, and in 1888 had joined Kelly at Boston for another $10,000 paid to Al Spalding, was in the pitcher's box for the Beaneaters; Kelly was behind the plate.[6] Clarkson, a better-than-average-hitting pitcher, homered and doubled; Herman Long, Boston's flashy young shortstop, hit into the spectators standing in front of the left-field fence for a home run with the bases loaded. Arthur "Hi! Hi!" Dixwell, the

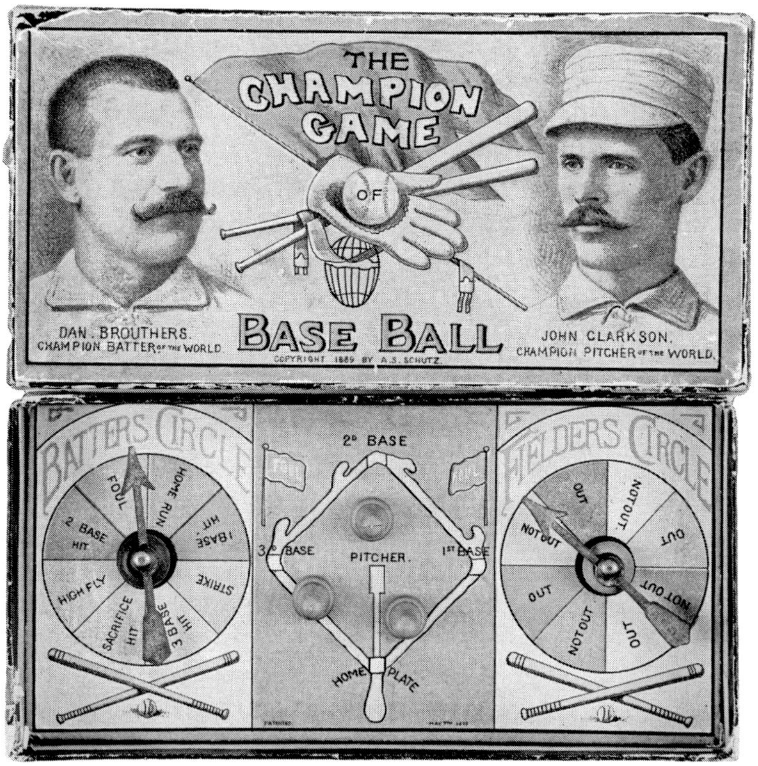

John Clarkson began the season with Boston and ended it with Cleveland, the clubs that contended in the postseason. Brouthers was with his fourth team in four years.

Beaneaters' foremost rooter (nicknamed for his piercing cheer) continued his practice of handing out cigars when the locals were victorious.

Cap Anson's Chicago Colts arrived from spring training at Hot Springs, Arkansas, to open their season in St. Louis. As always, von der Ahe put on elaborate festivities to mark the season's beginning, and 8,100 showed up to root for still another rebuilt Browns team. But the first National League game ever played in von der Ahe's Sportsman's Park ended 14–10 in favor of Chicago. Jimmy Ryan homered for the Colts; Cliff Carroll hit one for St. Louis. Gumbert had to leave the game after being hit on his pitching hand by a line drive; Bill Hutchinson relieved him and got the win. Gleason and Breitenstien pitched vainly for the Browns. In the offseason von der Ahe had signed Jack Glasscock, a 13-year veteran who had been with the Giants the previous season. Hailed as the "king of shortstops," Glasscock was among the dwindling number of men who still played barehanded. Von der Ahe made him captain, but "Pebbly Jack" had a history of fostering discontent wherever he played, and although he pleaded illness, his four errors on opening day (of eight the Browns committed) didn't win him any friends among St. Louis cranks.

In the National League's first game in Louisville, upwards of 6,000 people crowded Eclipse Park to cheer their Colonels to a 5–2 win over Cleveland, Jouett Meekin, a husky righthander, besting newcomer George Davies. In Cincinnati, Pittsburgh's Jake Beckley drove a three-run home run into the overflowed crowd in left field to win the game for Mark Baldwin, Tony Mullane taking the loss. The game was the turning point in the career of Pittsburgh outfielder Edward "Ned" Hanlon, who suffered a severe knee injury chasing a fly ball. Hanlon's playing career was essentially over, but bigger things in baseball were in his future.

Baltimore's National League debut was an eight-error, 14–3 drubbing by John Ward's Brooklyn team before 5,329 citizens of the Monument City. John "Sadie" McMahon was the victim of what would become a familiar display of incompetence by the Orioles. Skinny Dave Foutz, once one of von der Ahe's stalwarts, coasted to the win. At third base that day was 5' 6", 125-pound John McGraw, just turned 19, who had joined the Baltimore Association team late the previous season, and who was in the game only because another player was injured.

And in Philadelphia, New York's Amos Rusie outpitched Tim Keefe, 5–4, before 4,700, the smallest turnout of the day. A galaxy of men who, long afterward, would be elected to the National Baseball Hall of Fame were on the field: Harry Wright, the Phillies avuncular manager, plus Keefe, first baseman Roger Connor, and outfielders Sam Thompson, Ed Delahanty, and Billy Hamilton; among the Giants, Rusie, outfielder Jim O'Rourke, and Buck Ewing, who had moved to first base after a long career as a catcher.

Bill Barnie lasted six days into the season as Washington's manager. Barnie and George Wagner found themselves at odds on a variety of matters; Wagner traveled to Washington from Philadelphia (where he and his brother retained their wholesale meat business) to fire him personally. Wagner brought in Arthur Irwin, who had been basically a non-playing captain of Boston's Association pennant-winners in 1891, although within a few months Irwin would also be gone, and Danny Richardson would take over as both manager and captain.

Chicago's home opener was on April 23 versus Louisville, before an overflow crowd at South Side Park. (Whereas last season the Colts had alternated home games between South Side and West Side parks, both owned by Al Spalding, in 1892 they would play all their games on the south side.) The game ended in acrimony and, for many of those present, in hilarity. With Chicago ahead 4–2 in the top of the ninth inning, spectators in the grandstand began throwing cushions at customers standing on the field, prompting a cushion battle that interrupted play. Louisville captain Pfeffer demanded a forfeit; Anson argued otherwise; umpire Jack Sheridan agreed with Pfeffer and gave the game to the Colonels.

Two days earlier, Cleveland had opened at home with Cincinnati, on a field soaked by the morning's rain. Twenty-five-year-old Denton True "Cy" Young, who was coming off a 27–20 record in his first full season in the National League, held the Reds to a single run, while Elton "Ice Box" Chamberlain gave up 15 hits and 11 runs. Cleveland swept three games from the Reds, then swept another three from Chicago, with first-year man George "Nig" Cuppy, a diminutive righthander, winning the last game, 5–1.[7]

Boston's home opener at the South End Grounds, played in rain and cold, nonetheless drew 8,825, including Massachusetts governor William E. Russell, the city's mayor and board of aldermen, and about half of the state legislature, which adjourned at noon so its members could attend the game. Boston won 7–6, Charles "Kid" Nichols, a 30-game winner in 1891, outlasting Charlie Buffinton. In Pittsburgh a big parade led by the Great Western Band and 700 "newsies" who delivered for the *Pittsburgh Leader* preceded another wet game, which the local team took from St. Louis, 11–3, young Breitenstein suffering another loss, with James "Pud" Galvin, who had pitched in the National League and the Association since 1879, gaining his 308th win. On April 23, after two rainouts in New York, the Giants and Washington split a doubleheader.

At Eastern Park in Brooklyn, the Phillies' loss in the Bridegrooms' home opener occasioned some veiled criticism of Harry Wright from a Philadelphia reporter, who wondered why Wright didn't rely more on an effective field captain instead of directing his players from the bench. The 57-year-old Wright, a pioneer figure in the rise of pro-

Four figures who played large in the NL's emergence as a 12-team league were (clockwise from left) Albert G. Spalding, Abraham G. Mills, Harry Wright, and Nick Young.

fessional baseball, had led teams to four straight pennants in the old National Association and three in the National League. Universally admired and revered, he had always seemed beyond criticism. But Wright had never produced a winner in nine seasons in Philadelphia, and Phillies owners John I. Rogers and Al Reach were starting to doubt his leadership. Wright wasn't in the best of health; two years earlier he had been afflicted with an eye ailment that almost cost him his sight. Early in 1892, moreover, his wife of many years had died of a lingering illness.[8]

In his years as captain of the Browns and, in 1890, of the Chicago Players Leaguers, Charles Comiskey had often had to deal with players who were "bad actors"— men who were resentful of his authority, unserious about their work, or simply drunks. One of his problem players in 1891 was Willie McGill, a 5' 6" lefthander who had won 18 games after being transferred from the Cincinnati Association club, despite spending considerable time in St. Louis saloons in the company of Denny Lyons and Jack Stivetts. Now Comiskey and McGill, starting his third major league season but still only 18 years old, were both in the National League with the Reds.

McGill won his first start of the season, on May 1 against Cleveland, before a big Sunday home crowd, although the Reds made eight errors and Tony Mullane had to save McGill's game, which ended 11–9.[9] He lost his second start and then got drunk in Cincinnati with catcher Jerry Harrington. That was enough for Comiskey, who gave the "Boy Wonder" (as he had been known in St. Louis) train fare to return to his mother in Chicago, and put Harrington under suspension. McGill didn't return for the rest of the season (although he would be back in 1893). Harrington got into still more trouble with the Reds leader. Early in the morning of May 13, Harrington, pitcher Billy Rhines (who was recovering from a broken collarbone suffered in a wrestling match in March), and infielder Eddie Burke got drunk in Jack Paige's Saloon near Cincinnati's Fountain Square. After Rhines and Burke exchanged heated words, the trio retired to an alley outside the saloon, where the pitcher and infielder threw punches and wrestled in the mud, with Harrington trying to separate them. Comiskey suspended Rhines, continued Harrington's suspension and fined him $100, and fined Burke a like amount and subsequently released him. (He signed with New York.) While news of the Cincinnati fracas spread across baseball, Nick Young gave out a statement hailing the 12-club league as "a success, an unqualified success," adding "the players of today seem to be much steadier than those of former days."[10] Comiskey must have wondered about that.

On May 20, Ned Hanlon signed as both captain and manager at Baltimore, taking over a team buried in 12th place. Hanlon displaced outfielder George Van Haltren, who wasn't happy about giving up his captaincy and the few hundred dollars extra that went with the position. Meanwhile the owners at Pittsburgh were dissatisfied with Al Buckenberger, whom they thought should have his team higher in the standings. Tommy Burns, who had played the infield for Chicago since 1880, obtained his release from Jim Hart and Cap Anson, and signed to captain Pittsburgh under a three-year contract paying $4,500 per year. Buckenberger reverted to manager.[11]

Anson was still angry over being cheated out of the pennant the previous year (or so he believed). But after a bad start, he led a team with a payroll of less than $30,000— thought to be the smallest in the league — to a strong showing in the early going.[12] On May 20, Bill Hutchinson, winner of 102 games for Anson since 1889, pitched a 1–0 decision over Pittsburgh's Galvin for Chicago's 13th straight victory. Although the streak ended two days later, the Colts continued to play well, holding second place on June 3 with 21 wins, 13 defeats. Yet since the home opener, attendance at South Side Park had been disappointing.

Anson was unhappy with those Chicago cranks who did come to the games, and who heckled him about being old (he turned 40 that April) and slow afoot, among other things. "A Chicago crowd," he complained to the weekly *New York Clipper*, "is the worst in the world. I've stood their taunts and hisses for fifteen years, and it's beginning to weary me. I've come to the conclusion that it can't be deviltry on their part.... It's nothing more than a lack of brains. Why, I would rather face Cleveland hoodlums than play here."[13]

Although John Ward's Brooklyn club was in third place at the beginning of June with a 20–13 record, Ward's relations with Charles Byrne continued to deteriorate. Moreover, the Bridegrooms lost a solid player on May 21 when Hubert "Hub" Collins, their 28-year-old second baseman, died in Brooklyn of typhoid fever, leaving a wife and small child. Collins was buried five days later in his native Louisville, while in Brooklyn, with the approval of the League office, the Bridegrooms played a Sunday exhibition game with Cincinnati to benefit his family. Receipts from the overflow crowd of 7,136 at Eastern Park raised $2,805.

By mid–June, Anson's Colts had skidded to fourth place, behind Cincinnati, Brooklyn, and Boston, whose records, respectively, were 28–20, 30–15, and 34–13. Complaining that Boston was "outrageously strong," Reds manager Frank Bancroft advocated equalizing the strength of the League clubs before the start of the "second championship season."[14] Bancroft had a point: St. Louis was next to last at 17–31; Baltimore was dead last at 13–33. One of the few bright moments in the Orioles' otherwise dreary season came on June 10, when they trounced St. Louis 25–4, with catcher Wilbert Robinson making seven hits in seven times at bat, all singles except for one double. Little McGraw was at second base, filling in wherever and whenever Ned Hanlon needed a fill-in, but not doing much to impress his new captain-manager.[15]

George Van Haltren was an emerging star in 1892; here he is depicted some ten years later.

The "outrageously strong" Boston Beaneaters were perhaps the most talented collection of players put together up to that time. If the once-great Kelly was in decline, otherwise the Boston team was uniformly strong. (*Sporting Life*'s Cleveland correspondent attributed Kelly's low batting average to his addiction to cigarettes, which supposedly affected his eyesight, adding that Tip O'Neill, also struggling at the plate, had resorted to chewing gum to break the habit.) Whereas other captains or managers relied on two pitchers most of the time, with a third boxman used only occasionally, at the season's start Frank Selee could call on any one of four experienced starters: John Clarkson, Kid Nichols, Jack Stivetts, and Harry Staley. Clarkson was still only 30 when the season began, and his pinpoint control combined with a variety of off-speed pitches could still baffle batters. But when he had a bad day, Clarkson tended to worry and sulk. He wasn't liked by several of his teammates, in part because those who had remained loyal to the Brotherhood and affiliated with the Players League — Kelly, Staley, Hugh Duffy, Joe Quinn, and Billy Nash — still resented Clarkson for turning his back on the Brotherhood in return for a big multiyear contract from the Boston Triumvirs.

At first base for the Beaneaters was Tommy Tucker, a rare switch-hitter who had led the Association in batting in 1889 and still shunned a fielder's glove. Tucker was famous (or infamous) for standing in a coacher's box and giving out "a series of yells like that of a driver trying to start a balky team," as the Chicago reporter Joe Murphy put it. Boston's second baseman was Australian-born Joe Quinn, who batted only .218 in 1892, the low point in a 17-year career extending into the next century. Handsome Billy Nash, a native of Richmond, Virginia, and one of the few southern-born players (apart from Kentuckians), never batted .300 in a 15-year major league career but was regarded as one of the game's best at third base. But the infield star was shortstop Herman Long, who batted a solid .280 in 1892, ranged from behind second base to behind third, and fired the ball across the infield with an exceptionally strong arm. Long, by one estimate, "quietly and efficiently provided the heart and the backbone to the fine Boston teams.... Much credit must be given to their marvelous middle infielder."[16]

Tip O'Neill hit two home runs in Game Two of the 1886 World Series. By the end of 1892 he was through.

As Kelly played less and less as the season progressed, Charlie Ganzel and Charlie Bennett, both veterans at the position, ended up doing most of the catching. The usual left fielder was Bobby Lowe, who could also play second, short, or third, as needed. Right fielder Tommy McCarthy had batted as high as .350 in the Association, and while he slumped to .242 in 1891, he was the only Beaneater to appear in all of the team's 152 regular-season games.[17] The previous three years — in the National League, the Players League, and the Association — center fielder Hugh Duffy had been near the top in batting. In 1892, at .301, he was the sole Boston regular to reach the .300 mark.

The Beaneaters' everyday players

were small men by later standards; Tucker was the tallest at 5'11", Kelly by far the heaviest. Most of them were fast runners, and they were all adept at the sacrifice bunt, often executed with the flat-sided bats permitted at the time. They were also adept at the hit-and-run play, the invention of which is often credited to Frank Selee. Selee generally ran his team with a light hand, drilling his players in what to do and then assuming they knew what to do once the game was underway.

Boston's payroll, reportedly at least $56,000, was the highest in the league. Too high, in the view of the Triumvirs, whose views on players' salaries were shared around the league's front offices. Despite their splendid team, the Triumvirs claimed to be losing money in Boston, while New York, unable to rise above the lower rungs of the league, was "hopelessly behind." So "excessive salaries" had to be cut — and cut immediately.[18] Meeting in mid–June at the Fifth Avenue Hotel in Manhattan, the owners voted to reduce roster sizes from 15 to 13, thereby cutting loose 24 players. The "magnates," as they liked to be called in the baseball press, also encouraged each other to slash the pay of their remaining 13 men. And they voted to increase the per-club assessment toward paying off the debt to the dropped Association franchises from 10 to 12.5 percent of receipts.

Although Jim Hart denied pay cuts would be imposed for any of the Chicago players (who already numbered only 13), his peers left the New York meeting determined to practice ruthless economy. A number of the game's most respected players drew their releases, including Harry Stovey from Boston, Pud Galvin from Pittsburgh, George Gore from New York, and, from Louisville, Louis Rogers "Pete" Browning, who had won four batting titles (three in the Association as well as the Players League title). Those four caught on elsewhere — Stovey with Baltimore, Galvin and Gore with St. Louis (where Gore became one of five captains appointed by von der Ahe, who traveled with his team and acted as his own manager), and the hard-drinking Browning with Cincinnati (where he would be released again). Charlie Buffinton, who had won 227 major league games, quit baseball rather than accept less pay from Baltimore. Others were simply left adrift.

The Boston reporter Jacob C. Morse quoted Triumvir John B. Billings as opposing the salary cuts. "We made out-and-out contracts with these players," said Billings. "I never failed to live up to any contract I ever made in my life." Yet Morse, like other poorly paid baseball writers, had little sympathy for the players' plight. The players, he wrote, "had matters in their own hands and preferred a greedy present to a prosperous future." Billings' co-owners apparently didn't share his compunctions. While Long and Duffy weren't cut, Charlie Bennett, Kid Nichols, Jack Stivetts, John Clarkson, and nearly everybody else on the shrunken Boston roster was told he had to take less. T.H. Mathison, writing from New York for *Sporting Life*, reported that "While in this city the Boston players uttered long and loud protests against the general cut in salaries made by the Triumvirs."[19]

More than 70,000 attended the six Independence Day doubleheaders (played morning and afternoon), but the owners' austerity drive didn't slacken. New York's Silver King, who had 169 victories behind him at the start of the 1892 season, took a $750 cut, deserted the Giants, and then had to pay a $100 fine to get reinstated. William "Dummy" Hoy (so nicknamed because he was a deaf-mute), Washington's little center fielder, saw his pay slashed from $3,500 to $2,500. Cleveland players had to take cuts ranging from $600 to $200. Von der Ahe simply reduced everybody's pay by 8 percent. So it went around the league.

John Clarkson flatly refused to take a cut. That further angered the Triumvirs, who still resented having to give the pitcher so much money not to join the Players League. After Clarkson was battered for eight runs in Philadelphia, including home runs by Tim Keefe and catcher Jack Clements — the Phillies' 16th straight win — Arthur Soden wired Selee to send him home. Grumbled John Billings, "I don't want any pitchers Tim Keefe can hit for home runs."[20] The next day, while Kid Nichols ended the Phillies' run with a four-hit shutout, Clarkson rode the trains back to Boston, where his release was waiting. So far his record was eight wins, six losses.

On July 5, Clarkson signed with Cleveland, a team well down in the standings. He made his debut with the Spiders four days later, before a near-capacity crowd of Clevelanders in the second game of a doubleheader with Philadelphia, following the Spiders' 7–5 victory in the opener behind Cuppy. Clarkson received a sustained ovation as he took the pitcher's box. Again his counterpart was Keefe, but this time he held the Phillies to two runs on five hits, while the Spiders scored eight on Keefe.

Despite their disgruntlement over pay cuts, Boston's Beaneaters continued to pad their lead over Philadelphia and then Brooklyn, which recaptured second place when the Phillies slumped after their 16-game streak and an overall run of 24 wins in 26 games. Boston clinched the first-half championship on July 8 by beating Louisville, 7–2, with Stivetts striking out 10 Colonels, besides making three hits. "Hail, champions of the world," trumpeted Tim Murnane, sports editor of the *Boston Globe*, carried away with the Beaneaters' half-season triumph.[21]

A few days later the Beaneaters took the field in Chicago wearing fake beards and loud gingham and calico street attire — anything but their gray road flannels. It was a stunt meant to poke fun at Cap Anson, who the previous September had played an entire game against Boston wearing a white wig under his cap and a long fake white beard, as a way to get back at local baseball writers who liked to call him "Uncle," "Grandfather," and "Pop." (The last cognomen stuck and stayed with Anson the rest of his life.) Joe Murphy, blaming Kelly for the burlesque, wasn't amused: "Kelly, try as he may, can be nothing but coarse in anything he attempts of this kind."[22] The season's first half ended on Wednesday, July 13. Boston's record was 55–22, followed by Brooklyn (51–26), Philadelphia (46–30), Cincinnati (44–31), Cleveland (40–33), Pittsburgh (37–39), Washington (35–41), Chicago (31–39), St. Louis (31–42), New York (31–43), Louisville (30–47), and Baltimore (20–55). In the new "big league," finishing as the last team in the "first division" (the top half of the league) was considerably less impressive when a team was still looking up at five others rather than three.

The "second season" opened three days later, with Clarkson taking a tough 3–1 defeat on a muddy field in Washington before a Friday turnout of 1,979. The Spiders wrangled with umpire Charles Mitchell at such length that Mitchell finally fined captain Oliver "Patsy" Tebeau $50 and sent him to the bench, and fined first baseman Jake Virtue $10. Wrote the *Cleveland Plain Dealer*'s baseball reporter, "A few more doses of Mitchell and Cleveland will be lucky to win at all."[23] Shortly thereafter Nick Young had to give up on Mitchell, whose work drew criticism around the league. That was true of nearly all the league's frequently changing staff of six umpires, who worked alone and, despite their most conscientious efforts, couldn't possibly be in position to see everything on the field.[24] It was also a matter of learning on the job. Bill Barnie found that out when he was added to Nick Young's staff in August, after the Western League collapsed and he lost his second managing job of 1892, at Minneapolis.

In other second-half openers, Harry Wright's Phillies beat Louisville, Baltimore won from Cincinnati, New York defeated Pittsburgh, Brooklyn dealt still another loss to Anson's fading Colts, and St. Louis walloped Boston, 20–3, making 20 hits off Nichols. It was one of the worst performances in the Kid's long and illustrious career. "The Boston club," as the venerable Henry Chadwick wrote tactfully in his postseason review, "began the second division campaign in very bad form, their victory in winning the race in the first half having 'exhilarated' the team too much...."[25] The Beaneaters' listless play in the first few games of the second half encouraged the misgivings some had expressed when the split-season was adopted: that the first-half winner would let down to ensure a postseason series and extra money from the gate receipts.

Cub Stricker fought teammate Bill Halligan, ending the season for both.

But in fact Boston won nine of its first 15 games, as did Brooklyn and Philadelphia. Meanwhile Cleveland started to show a robustness missing over the first half. In his first appearance in Boston since his release, Clarkson suffered another tough loss, 3–2, to Harry Staley. But the Spiders won the next day, Cy Young defeating Stivetts, 4–1, and on August 1, Young pitched Cleveland into first place by downing St. Louis, 7–2, while Brooklyn lost to Washington and Baltimore beat Philadelphia. The Spiders were there to stay. They ran off a nine-game victory streak before losing in Pittsburgh on Charles "Duke" Farrell's three-run homer off Clarkson.

By then Pittsburgh's owners had soured on Tommy Burns' leadership. *Sporting Life*'s Pittsburgh correspondent, writing as "Circle," cited reports that Burns was lazy in his duties and stayed up into the wee hours playing cards and shooting craps with his players. Late in July, he was stripped of his captaincy and two days later notified of his release, with Al Buckenberger restored to full authority over the team. Burns quickly filed suit for $13,000, which he claimed as the balance on his three-year contract.

At Cincinnati, Comiskey's troubles continued. Having won 21 games by August, Tony Mullane wouldn't agree to the pay cut imposed on him and quit the Reds. After a short stint performing at a local theater, he rejoined the team, pitched (and lost) a game in Chicago, and then decamped to Butte, Montana, to pitch in the Montana State League. Tip O'Neill, unable to shake a season-long batting slump, played left field listlessly. After he lost a ball in the sun in Cleveland and then had a shouting match with Comiskey, the Reds' captain first docked him five days' pay, then sent him home to Woodstock, Ontario. O'Neill, who had been with Comiskey since 1884, never played another major league game. At the end, he carried a career batting average of .340. Curt Welch, a gifted centerfielder but a well-known imbiber, had signed with the Reds after Baltimore released him. He quickly showed he hadn't reformed when "he spent the Sabbath at the shrine of old Red Eye" and got himself thrown out of the Hotel Dennison in Cincinnati.[26] For that he was released again and left stranded in Cincinnati, without enough money for train fare back to his family in Baltimore. With all that going on, the Reds played poorly in the second half, winning only one more time than they lost.

At Baltimore, Hanlon's troubles also continued. On the evening of August 3, in Boston, several Orioles were sitting in the reading room of the United States Hotel. Infielder John "Cub" Stricker, 5'3" and 130 pounds, and outfielder Bill Halligan, who was six inches taller and about 35 pounds heavier, got to kidding each other. Soon the kidding turned to insults, whereupon Halligan walked over and hit Stricker in the face, breaking his jaw. Baltimore vice president George Waltz suspended Halligan for the rest of the season; Stricker's season was finished. Hanlon gimped around in Halligan's place for a few games, then had McGraw join Stovey and Van Haltren in the outfield. At the end of August, Hanlon suspended Van Haltren for indifferent play, then sent him to Pittsburgh for Joe Kelley, a young outfielder, and $2,000. Hanlon had another bad actor in Sadie McMahon. The stocky righthander was Hanlon's best pitcher, but he was one of several Orioles who liked to drink and carouse. McMahon rebelled at having his salary cut, didn't show up when he was supposed to pitch, received a $50 fine, physically threatened Baltimore owner Harry von der Horst, and drew a suspension for the rest of the season. Baltimore, according to the *Sporting News* correspondent, "seems to have had more trouble with its players getting drunk than any other club in the league this season"—which was covering considerable territory.[27]

Denton True "Cy" Young was a coming star with the Cleveland Spiders.

Out of work and needing money for his suit against Pittsburgh, Tommy Burns appealed to Nick Young, who obligingly hired him to replace Barnie on the league's umpiring staff. Like Barnie, Burns quickly learned how little he was prepared for his new occupation. Burns got bad reviews around the league; Tim Murnane wrote that in a game in Cincinnati, he "gave the Boston men a beautiful roast," and that his umpiring was so bad the local crowd hissed him.[28] Even courtly Harry Wright complained to Young about Burns' indecisiveness and general incompetence. The league's president finally decided there must be something to all the complaints and dismissed Burns.

Meanwhile Cleveland continued to win consistently, taking two of three games in Boston in mid-August. New York, with a lineup made up largely of players added during the season, made a brief surge and reached second place before fading into the lower half of the league. On August 17, Boston was in fourth place at 15–12, despite Stivetts's heroics. A couple of weeks earlier, at Eastern Park in Brooklyn, Stivetts had played left field with Bobby Lowe injured. Nichols and George Haddock pitched scoreless ball into the 12th inning, when Haddock hit Tucker with a pitch. Trying to move Tucker into scoring position, Stivetts bunted foul twice, using a flat-sided bat. Then he picked up a regular bat and drove the ball into deep right–center field, between Tommy Griffith and Tom "Oyster" Burns, for a home run. Nichols retired the side in the bottom of the ninth for the victory. The next day Stivetts pitched a no-hit game versus the Bridegrooms, but three weeks later, unhappy over his salary cut, he didn't show up to pitch in Cincinnati. The Triumvirs talked to Comiskey and Frank Bancroft about a straight trade of absentees, Stivetts for Mullane, but nothing came of it.

Mike Kelly had become more a liability than anything else. He criticized Nash's captaincy until Selee, apparently thinking to placate him, gave him the title, although as Jacob C. Morse pointed out, Kelly played only a couple of times a week; Hugh Duffy had to act as captain most of the time. On August 31, Stivetts rejoined the team, arriving in time to pitch against the Reds that afternoon. Kelly tried to catch him, but, wrote Murnane, "Kelly could not hold one ball in five." After two passed balls, the Beaneaters' new captain replaced Stivetts with Staley. According to Murnane, "Staley put no life into his work, using all slow balls, to which Comiskey's men made love." With Boston behind 6–0 in the seventh inning, Duffy doubled off Fred Dwyer; Kelly then dribbled a ball between first and second base and just walked over to the Boston bench off the first base line, as Bid McPhee tossed to Dwyer, covering first. Nash singled in Duffy for the Beaneaters' only run. Murnane called Kelly's refusal to run "rather bad work for the captain of a team."[29]

From New York, C.F. Mathison was especially hard on the onetime idol of the crowds and King of the Diamond. "Mike Kelly," Mathison wrote, "is the same man who has disgraced the game for years past.... It will be a fortunate thing for base ball when Mike Kelly finally says adieu to the game."[30] A few weeks later, Selee gave the captaincy to Tommy McCarthy, who debuted in his new role by hitting a double, triple, and two home runs in a 9–2 win over New York. By the end of August, Cleveland had built its second-half record to 29–10 and held a seven-game lead over Boston. Cy Young and Nig Cuppy pitched most of the time, Clarkson less frequently, though often with his old brilliance. George Davies was in the box for 26 games, and while his season's record was 10–16, he allowed fewer than three earned runs per game. The Spiders' only .300 batter was tubby second baseman Clarence "Cupid" Childs, whose .317 average was third-best in the league (behind Billy Hamilton's .330 and Dan Brouthers' .335). Cleveland gave up the league's fewest runs (613), in large part because of a strong infield that included Jake Virtue at first base, Ed McKean at shortstop, and George Davis at third. The outfield consisted of Jesse Burkett in left, far-ranging Jimmy McAleer in center, and in right Jack O'Connor, who the previous year had been expelled from the Association for "habitual drunkenness, disorderly conduct and insubordination."[31] With Cleveland, O'Connor generally behaved himself and did some timely batting. The regular catcher was the remarkably durable Charles "Chief" Zimmer, who two years earlier had become the first man to play 100 games at the position. In 1892 he was behind the bat 111 times.

By sweeping three games in Cincinnati at the end of September, while Boston was winning two of three from Brooklyn before dwindling crowds at the South End Grounds, Cleveland built its record to 46–17 and its lead over the Beaneaters to 7½ games. The consensus around the league was that the Spiders had all but clinched the second half.

The Boston players seemed to agree. They swept three games from hapless Washington, but in doing so made 28 errors.

By then Pittsburgh, with Al Buckenberger back in full charge, had climbed as high as third place. Mainly the improved record of the Pirates (as they were sometimes called) had to do with fine pitching by Bill "Adonis" Terry, who had started the season with Brooklyn.[32] The workhorse of the Pittsburgh staff was Mark Baldwin, but the husky righthander, who had won as many as 34 games (with Chicago in the Players League), pitched inconsistently and would end with a 26–27 record. Moreover, he got into a unique kind of trouble that September. Baldwin resided in Homestead, an industrial suburb on the left bank of the Monongahela River, east of Pittsburgh. That summer Homestead was the scene of one of the worst industrial conflicts in the nation's history, when wage negotiations between the steel workers' union and management at the giant Carnegie mills broke down. Whereupon management locked out the workers, brought in non-union labor, and hired 300 detectives of the famous Pinkerton agency. A gun battle ensued when the Pinkertons arrived by barge and tried to dock; 10 people died before the workers surrendered. Subsequently Pennsylvania's governor ordered in a detachment of the National Guard. With their union broken and their town under military occupation, those workers the company was willing to rehire went back to work.

The Carnegie mills became a regular tourist attraction for National League teams playing in Pittsburgh; John Ward, his pro-union sentiments undiminished despite the failure of the Brotherhood and the Players League, visited the strikers to express his support for their cause, as did other former Brotherhood members. Baldwin later claimed he was only a spectator in the mill yard when the workers battled the Pinkertons; nonetheless, two months later a constable confiscated two rifles from his house and arrested him on a charge of aggravated riot. Allegedly Baldwin had loaned the rifles to strikers. His father, who was a director of the Pittsburgh franchise, posted his $2,000 bond. He never came to trial, although the Pittsburgh directors—presumably with the elder Baldwin's acquiescence—briefly suspended him.[33]

Like most other National League players, Baldwin had taken a salary cut earlier in the season. But as the season ground toward its close, the club owners continued to bewail their losses. George Wagner said even with improved attendance in Washington, he would still lose "several thousand dollars," while Harry von der Horst claimed he had lost $16,000, even after salary cuts; Chris von Ahe claimed a like amount. Philadelphia co-owner John I. Rogers estimated Phillies losses at $15,000; Brooklyn had lost about $10,000. Louisville president T. Hunt Stuckey insisted players' salaries had to be slashed still further in 1892, and complained that three recent games in New York and one in Baltimore netted Louisville only $132 in the visitor's share of the gate receipts.

On October 4 the "magnates" met in New York City to discuss, among other matters, how to deal with a calculated $10,000 shortfall in the buyout money owed the eliminated Association franchises. Besides instructing Nick Young to arrange for a renewal of the league's promissory notes, they voted to abandon the split-season format and for 1893 to adopt a 132-game schedule (which would be the shortest since 1887). Most of them also agreed to cut expenses by simply releasing players wholesale. Under the standard player's contract, they would have to give 10-day notices, but inasmuch as most players were contracted to November 1 (for postseason exhibition-game purposes), the owners figured to save a couple of weeks' pay per player. Moreover, it was understood that no owner would sign anybody released by another club. Chris von der Ahe had already unloaded Jack Glasscock's salary, releasing him after he rowed with Bob Caruthers, the Browns' current captain. Pud Galvin also was released. Chatting with local players upon his return to Pittsburgh, Galvin said anybody playing for von der Ahe "deserves sympathy.... But for getting a bad name I would have smashed his tomato nose for the many insults he heaped on me. But I am not working for him any longer. Thanks."[34] By that point it had become fairly obvious that, besides releases, the autocratic Browns owner had been using suspensions and fines to save money and generate revenue.

The ownerships of Brooklyn, Cincinnati, and Chicago refused to go along with the releases program, although they also wouldn't sign released players. In anticipation of postseason play, Cleveland and Boston kept their rosters intact. But Von der Ahe eventually released everybody; Baltimore's von der Horst and Louisville's Stuckey did the same, while at Washington, the Wagners released all but three men. The New York directors gave 10 days' notice to Amos Rusie, infielders Denny Lyons and William "Shorty" Fuller, infielder/outfielder Hardie Richardson, outfielder Mike Tiernan, and 40-year-old Jim O'Rourke, who had quarreled bitterly with manager Pat T. Powers. Each of those Giants had refused pay cuts. Pittsburgh's players voted to forego their last two weeks' salaries, out of gratitude, it was reported, for being spared cuts earlier in the season. But the Pittsburgh directors told the players their 1893 contracts would specify a maximum of $2,400. One Pittsburgh player (probably newcomer Van Haltren, who was paid $3,500 in 1892) replied when asked if he would be satisfied with $2,400, "Satisfied? Well, now if a man holds you up on the street you'll give up your money before he shoots, won't you?"[35]

On October 9 front-running Cleveland went into Pittsburgh and lost 8–3, the key play being umpire Jim Gaffney's safe call of a Pittsburgh runner at first base, which led to a six-run rally on Young. The Spiders may have had the second half all but clinched, but captain Tebeau yelled at the writers in the ground-level press section to report that Gaffney made six runs for Pittsburgh. Baldwin, his suspension lifted, was the winning pitcher. Tebeau was one of the game's most volatile players, and under his leadership the Spiders had come to be known for their combativeness. As Tebeau put it, "A milk-and-water, goody-goody player can't wear a Cleveland uniform."[36]

Cleveland did clinch on Tuesday the 11th by playing Pittsburgh to a darkness-shortened tie, while Boston lost the second game of a doubleheader with Brooklyn. The Spiders were supposed to play again in Pittsburgh on Wednesday, but they returned to Cleveland for a benefit game with the Cleveland Athletic Club, the proceeds to be divided among the Spiders. About 2,000 tickets were sold; each Spider received about $150. Buckenberger wanted a forfeit to Pittsburgh, which after some hesitation Gaffney awarded. Things like that happened under Nick Young's easygoing presidency.

Everybody had assumed a postseason championship series would happen, as the owners had agreed early in the year. But when the league's club owners held a second October meeting, Arthur Soden made the surprise announcement that Boston wouldn't play. Soden believed Boston's cranks thought their team was throwing the second season, and the only way to convince them otherwise was not to play. Cleveland president Frank DeHaas Robison appealed to his peers, supported by Cincinnati's John T. Brush. After long wrangling, the owners voted 11–1 to go ahead with the series. Soden acceded, although he refused to participate in arranging the games, leaving that in the hands of the league's board of directors.

The season ended on October 15. In Washington, Boston took both ends of a doubleheader, Nichols pitching a shutout for his 35th victory, Stivetts doing the same in the nightcap for his 35th. Cleveland completed a sweep of a two-game series with Louisville — games that were scheduled for Louisville but had to be moved because a fire had destroyed everything at Eclipse Park except a section of the bleachers. It was a sad end to another dreary season for the Louisville franchise, whose teams had won only one pennant in the Association, that in the weak 1890 circuit — and would never win anything in the National League.

Final second-half standings: Cleveland, 53–23; Boston 50–26; Brooklyn, 44–33; Pittsburgh, 43–34, Philadelphia, 41–36; New York, 40–37; Chicago, 39–37; Cincinnati, 38–37; Louisville, 33–42; Baltimore, 26–46; St. Louis, 25–52; Washington, 23–52. For the full schedule, the league's breakdown was: Boston, Cleveland, Brooklyn, Philadelphia, Cincinnati, Pittsburgh, Chicago, New York, Louisville, Washington, St. Louis, Baltimore. Boston's 102 total wins were the most for any team in major league history up to that time. It escaped nobody that the four teams with the worst overall records were the four added from the Association. So much for Al Spalding's boast about no more tailenders.

Declared a Boston scribe, writing for the *Sporting News* as "Bean Blower," "never was the close of the season received with so much joy. It has been the biggest failure since the formation of the National League in 1876. Scarcely a club has made money. It was shown this year that there was such a thing as too much base ball...." From Cincinnati, "D. C. K." put it more succinctly: "Everybody, from ground keepers to magnates, are [sic] glad 1892 has passed."[37]

The Philadelphia writer Harold L. Lanigan estimated Cleveland profited about $10,000, Pittsburgh somewhat less. "To sum up," he wrote, "two clubs have made less than $20,000, and ten clubs have lost in the neighborhood of $150,000."[38] The league's total attendance was 1,822,587, topped by Philadelphia's 193, 731. Baltimore's 93,589 was the league's worst. Four teams outdrew Boston's 146,421, whose cranks, traditionally among baseball's most loyal, found little reason to care whether their team won or lost in the season's second half.

King Kelly was but a shell of himself in 1892, batting .189.

The format for the league championship series was five out of nine games: three in Cleveland, three in Boston, three in New York, if necessary. Two umpires would work each game, alternating behind the plate and on the bases each inning. Charlie "Pop" Snyder and Bob Emslie would alternate every other game with John Gaffney and Jack McQuaid. On Monday, October 17, about 6,000 people filled the seats and stood behind outfield ropes for the opening game. The spectators included Nick Young, his wife, and the imperious Soden, who made his first trip ever to see his team play in another city.

Stivetts was Selee's pitching choice; Cy Young, who had won 36 of 47 decisions, was in the box for Cleveland. It was a classic duel between two of the game's premier pitchers, featuring, wrote Charles Mears in the *Sporting News*, "so many pieces of sensational fielding that the spectators finally became accustomed to them and took them as a matter of course."[39] After 11 scoreless innings, umpires Emslie and Snyder decided it was too dark to continue. Young gave up six hits and struck out six; Stivetts allowed only four hits and struck out seven. Kelly caught Stivetts and was hitless in four at bats, but in the ninth inning he pulled the kind of trick for which he was well known, although it didn't affect the outcome of the game. When Stivetts hit a popup off home plate, Kelly, on the Boston bench, yelled for first baseman Virtue to take the ball, which was much closer to catcher Zimmer. The two collided and the ball hit the ground. Tebeau (who wasn't in the lineup) demanded that Kelly be thrown out of the game. Snyder and Emslie settled for fining him $10.

The tie was as close to victory as Cleveland would come. With Gaffney and McQuaid umpiring, Boston won the next day, 4–3, 22-game winner Staley outpitching Clarkson, whose record after joining Cleveland was 17–10, although he had lost all four of his starts against Boston. George Davis started the game at third base, but a badly bruised leg, suffered when he was hit by one of Stivetts's fastballs in Game One, forced him to leave in the fourth inning in favor of Tebeau. Boston took a two-run lead in the eighth inning when Duffy tripled in one runner and Nash singled him home. With two out in the bottom of the ninth, Zimmer followed O'Connor's single with a triple off the top of the left field fence, but Clarkson grounded weakly to first baseman Tucker to end it.

Another big crowd of Clevelanders showed up for Game Three. Charlie Ganzel replaced Kelly (who would sit out the remainder of the series). Snyder and Emslie returned to umpire. Stivetts and Young were again in the box, and again each pitched superbly, although Young, who had worked 456 innings since opening day, didn't record a strikeout and didn't have much of a fastball. Baserunning errors at critical junctures hurt the Spiders. The outcome was decided in the seventh inning on Stivetts' double, followed by McCarthy's single. That put Boston ahead, 3–2. In the top of the ninth (Tebeau had chosen to bat first, as was the home team's prerogative), Davis limped to the plate to pinch hit with McAleer at third base. He hit a broken-bat looper to Tucker, who smothered it for the third out.

October 20 was a travel day. On Friday the 21st, Selee finally started Nichols, who was matched against 28-game winner Cuppy before a crowd of 6,547 at the South End Grounds. Nichols got all the runs he needed in the second inning when Duffy sent the ball over the short right field fence, scoring McCarthy ahead of him; Quinn singled in Nash and Lowe in the sixth to make it 4–0. Cleveland made seven hits off Nichols but couldn't score. Saturday's game drew only 3,376. Clarkson went to the box in place of Young, who complained of a sore arm. Again Selee picked Stivetts. Cleveland's bats finally came alive with a six-run outburst in the third inning on Clarkson's three-run homer over the right field fence and Ed McKean's three-run triple. At that point the Spiders began yelling at the Beaneaters that they would still be playing them in New York. Not so fast. Boston came back with three runs in the next inning on three singles and two sacrifice flies, although Zimmer singled in McKean in the fifth to make it 7–3. In the bottom of the inning, Tebeau fumbled Long's grounder, the first of three errors charged to the Cleveland captain. McCarthy doubled Long to third, and both scored on sacrifice flies by Duffy and Nash. Boston blew the game open in the bottom of the sixth with four runs. Ganzel singled in one run, Duffy doubled in two, and Stivetts tripled in Duffy. In the seventh, Tucker's three-run home run over the right field fence made the score 12–7. Gaffney and McQuaid called the game at the end of the next inning. Clarkson surrendered fourteen hits, Stivetts nine.

The teams idled on Sunday, as mandated under Massachusetts law. The attendance continued to dwindle; fewer than two thousand people showed up on a chilly Monday, October 24. Selee went with Nichols; Tebeau sent Young to the box for the third time in a week. Boston took a 2–0 lead in the top half of the third inning on Virtue's wild throw over third base and Duffy's double, scoring McCarthy. Aided by McCarthy's and Charlie Bennett's errors, Cleveland scored three runs in the bottom of the inning; but Boston went ahead with two runs in the fourth on singles by Tucker, Bennett, and Nichols. Duffy singled home McCarthy in the next inning, Quinn's triple brought in another run in the seventh, Tebeau's wild throw let in another in the eighth, and Bennett's homer in the ninth made it 8–3. That finished the scoring and the series. Young "had no speed at all," according to Mears.[40] The big righthander gave up 11 hits, including two doubles, a triple, and a home run. Nichols yielded 10 hits but held Cleveland scoreless for the last six innings.

Tim Murnane was ready to put Selee in a class with the best: "Manager Selee has handled the men in a manner unexcelled by the best work of Harry Wright and Capt. Anson." Murnane described Soden, who hadn't wanted to play the games, as "the happiest man in Boston last night." But the *Sporting News* wasn't pleased with the way the Boston team had played its season. The one-sided victory over Cleveland, editorialized the St. Louis weekly, "proves to all that after the first season's flag they did not try for the succeeding empty honor, but let it go, by default as it were, and saved themselves for the more glorious struggle, if such it may be called, that came later."[41]

Although the players got nothing from the gate receipts, the Triumvirs gave their team $1,000, to be divided 13 ways. The Beaneaters also picked up a little extra from a benefit game at the South End Grounds, after which, accompanied by "Hi! Hi!" Dixwell and other followers, they adjourned to the ballpark's club room to partake of what Kelly called "the stuff that keeps some people in rags."[42] Apparently the Robison brothers thought what the Spiders received from their benefit game two weeks earlier would suffice.

Boston's cranks may have been happy with a second-straight National League pennant; those in Cleveland may have been satisfied with the best showing their teams had made in either the Association, National League, or Players League; and the Robison brothers may have been satisfied with their modest profit. But there was plenty of discontent to go around among both club owners and players. In November, while Tommy Burns was losing his suit against Pittsburgh, the owners met still again, at the Richelieu Hotel in Chicago. Out of their deliberations came decisions that would critically affect the game on the field, as well as the financial circumstances of the players.

In the past season the league as a whole had batted only .242. The general feeling among the men who ran baseball was that more offense would mean bigger crowds (a notion that would recur in periods of pitching ascendancy from then on). So, with only John B. Day of the Giants dissenting, they voted to do away with the rectangular pitcher's box, lengthen the distance from which the pitcher would deliver the ball from 55' 6" to 60' 6", and require that in delivering the ball, he must keep his back foot on a 12" × 4" rubber slab (widened to 24" × 6" before the 1895 season). Publisher Francis L. Richter of *Sporting Life* expressed the consensus: "To put him back where he should be — in the centre [of the diamond] — means the end of his baneful dominance as the King pin and controlling factor in the game."[43] The result was everything hoped for: In 1893 the league batting average jumped to .279, and to an astonishing .308 the next year. Total runs increased from 9,388 (1892) to 10,315 (1893), then to 11,680 (1894). While pitchers such as Cy Young, Amos Rusie, Kid Nichols, and Jack Stivetts gave up more runs but continued to be big winners, others such as Bill Hutchinson, John Clarkson, George Haddock, and Ad Gumbert lost most of their effectiveness.

The boost in offensive output apparently pleased the customers; by 1896 nearly three million paid to watch National League games. But whatever big numbers batters might put up, it wasn't going to get them much more money, because the club owners also voted to follow Pittsburgh's lead and impose a $2,400 salary maximum per player, beginning with the 1893 season. The average salary fell 40 percent — from $3,000 to $1,800. Given the feudalistic nature of owner–player relations under baseball's all-powerful reserve clause and the failure of the Brotherhood movement and the Players League, the players could either take it or quit the game. They took it.

The 1892 season was the first and last *scheduled* split-season at the major league level.[44] Throughout the 1890s, the National League remained locked into its 12-franchise setup, which couldn't be altered for 10 years under the Indianapolis agreement. So every year half the league's members — invariably including Washington, St. Louis, and Louisville — would be hopelessly out of the race by July. Baltimore's fortunes were different. Ned Hanlon became Harry von der Horst's co-owner and, given a free hand, made a succession of shrewd player moves, beginning with the Van Haltren–Kelley deal. The result was one of baseball's most successful and famous teams. After a seventh-place showing in 1893, the Orioles won three consecutive pennants with such acquisitions as Dan Brouthers and Willie Keeler from Brooklyn, Hugh Jennings from Louisville, and Walter "Steve" Brodie from St. Louis. John McGraw, finally settled at third base, emerged as one of the league's star players, particularly adept at coaxing walks, getting in front of pitches, and executing the hit-and-run play with Keeler, while Wilbert Robinson became one of the league's foremost catchers.

Baltimore's three pennants were indicative of the league's chronic imbalance; only two other teams won pennants in the 1890s. The Orioles broke Boston's run of three in a row (1891–1893), but the Beaneaters won their fifth and sixth championships of the decade in 1897–1898. Brooklyn closed out the century with pennants in 1899 and 1900, the latter coming after the league dropped Louisville, Washington, Baltimore, and Cleveland.[45] The Temple Cup series — a postseason matchup of first- and second-place teams, played from 1894 to 1897, with the winner gaining possession of a huge loving cup donated by William Temple of Pittsburgh — sufficed as a surrogate World's Championship Series no more than had the split-season series.

In short, the major league club owners of the late 19th century made lots of mistakes. The one "big league" was obviously a bad arrangement, and so was the unique 1892 split-season. But then such ill-advised undertakings were all too common in the doings of the all-powerful "magnates" of the period.

Abstract

In the 20th century, many of the lower minor leagues in organized baseball as well as the Negro leagues commonly played split seasons. The 1892 National League season, however, was unique in being the only *scheduled* split season in major league history. Arranged in the aftermath of the absorption of four American Association franchises to create a 12-team National League, the split season was to run 154 total games, with the first- and second-half winners meeting in a postseason championship series. Amid suspicions that Boston, first-half winners, had let down to ensure such a series, Boston dispatched Cleveland, second-half winners, in five games, with one tie. The article narrates the progress of the season, provides a critical look at the effects of the split-season decision as well as other decisions (notably in-season roster-cutting and salary slashes), and includes various episodes involving the kind of players' misadventures characteristic of what was still a raw and rowdy era in baseball history.

Notes

1. Although the official name of the new organization was National League and American Association of Professional Base Ball Clubs, from its beginning virtually everyone simply called it the National League. On the 1890 National League–Players League–American Association and the 1891 National League–Association wars, see Seymour, H., and D. Seymour Mills. 1989. *Baseball: The Early Years* (reprint); Voigt, D. 1966. *American Baseball: From Gentleman's Sport to the Commissioner System*; Burk, R. 1994. *Never Just a Game: Players, Owners, and American Baseball to 1920*; Koszarek, E. 2006. *The Players' League: History, Clubs, Ballplayers and Statistics*; Nemec, D. 2004. *The Beer and Whiskey League: The Illustrated History of the American Association, Baseball's Renegade League*; Alexander, C. 2011. *Turbulent Seasons: Baseball in 1890–1891.*

2. *New York Clipper*: Jan. 30, 1892, p. 755; Apr. 9, 1892, p. 73. The total amount of the buyout varies according to different sources.

3. Ibid., Mar. 12, 1892.

4. *Washington Post*: Jan. 10, 1892, p. 6; Apr. 9, 1892, p. 6.

5. *Sporting News*: Mar. 5, 1892, p. 3.

6. In 1892 pitchers were still pitching from the flat surface of the infield, within a 4' x 5' rectangle, the front line of which was 50 feet from home plate. But as of 1888, the pitcher had to deliver the ball with his rear foot on the back line of the box, so he was actually pitching 55 feet from the plate.

7. In keeping with the common racial insensitivity of the time, Cuppy (born George Maceo Koppe), like various other dark-complexioned players, was nicknamed "Nig."

8. Harry Wright would himself live only until October 1896.

9. Sunday ball still being illegal in Cleveland, the Spiders took the train down to Cincinnati for the game, then returned home to resume their series with the Reds. Throughout the season, the Cleveland team would make the hop to Cincinnati and also St. Louis and back for Sunday dates.

10. In the late 19th century, a few teams had bench managers, such as Philadelphia's Harry Wright and Boston's Frank Selee, who, while designating a player as captain, essentially directed their players during the game. The most common arrangement, though, was a captain (e.g., Comiskey and Anson) to have full charge of the team on the field, while a manager (such as Bancroft or Buckenberger after Burns' arrival at Pittsburgh) tended to business matters such as train schedules, hotel reservations, and ticket sales. The division of labor would become fixed after 1900.

11. *Sporting Life*: May 14, 1892, p. 1.

12. On the questionable circumstances under which Boston beat out Chicago in 1891, see Alexander, C. 2008. "Was the 1891 National League Pennant Thrown?" *Base Ball* 2 (Fall), 5–17.

13. *New York Clipper*: May 21, 1892, p. 169. Anson may have been slow afoot but not slow with his bat. In his remaining six playing years, he averaged .328. Cleveland cranks had already gained a reputation for particular rowdiness.

14. Ibid.: May 28, 1891, p. 185.

15. Later that same month, George Van Haltren, one of the top players of the period, made nine straight hits, including a double and two triples, in consecutive games with Chicago and St. Louis.

16. Alexander 2011, 168; Hubbard, D. 2008. *The Heavenly Twins of Boston: A Dual Biography of Hugh Duffy and Tommy McCarthy*, p. 88.

17. Because of rainouts, missed train connections, and other factors, late 19th century teams rarely played the full schedule of games.

18. *Chicago Tribune*: July 4, 1892, p. 12; *Sporting Life*: June 18, 1892, p. 1.

19. *Sporting Life*: July 2, 1892, pp. 8, 12; July 9, 1892, p. 10.

20. *Sporting News*: July 2, 1892, p. 1.

21. *Boston Globe*: July 9, 1892, p. 5.

22. *Sporting News*: July 16, 1892, p. 1. On the one-umpire system, see Morris, P. 2008. "'A Motion as Near Flying as Any Human Being Could Attain': The Nineteenth-Century Umpire as Sprinter," *Base Ball* 2 (Fall), 18–25.

23. *Cleveland Plain Dealer*: July 16, 1892, p. 5.

24. *Spalding's Base Ball Guide and Official League Book for 1893*.

25. *Sporting News*: Aug. 20, 1892, p. 1.

26. *Washington Post*: Aug. 17, 1892, p. 6.

27. Alexander, C. 1988. *John McGraw*, p. 29.

28. *Boston Globe*: Aug. 30, 1892, p. 12.

29. Ibid.: Aug. 31, 1892, p. 5.

30. *Sporting Life*: Oct. 1, 1892, p. 11.

31. Alexander 2011, 149.

32. The nickname derived from Pittsburgh's signing of infielder Louis Bierbauer early in 1891, when Association people insisted he belonged to the Athletics of Philadelphia. The "pirating" of Bierbauer had much to do with the Association's abrogation of the newly formed National Agreement and the onset of war between the two leagues.

33. In 1893, Baldwin made a 16–20 record with Pittsburgh and New York, then dropped from the National League. Intelligent and from a well-to-do Pittsburgh family, he eventually enrolled in Johns Hopkins Medical School, earned his M.D., and practiced for some thirty years in Pittsburgh.

34. *Sporting Life*: Sept. 24, 1892, p. 11.

35. *Sporting News*: Oct. 22, 1892, p. 1.

36. Okrent, D., and H. Lewine (eds.). 1979. *The Ultimate Baseball Book*, p. 23.

37. *Sporting News*: Oct. 15, 1892, p. 3; Oct. 22, 1892, p. 2.

38. Ibid.: Oct. 18, 1892, p. 3.

39. Ibid.: Oct. 22, 1892, p. 1.

40. Ibid., Oct. 25, 1892, p. 1.

41. *Boston Globe*: Oct. 25, 1892, p. 5; *Sporting News*: Oct. 29, 1892, p. 4.

42. *Sporting Life*: Nov. 5, 1892, p. 9.

43. Ibid.: Nov. 12, 1892, p. 2.

44. Of course the strike by the players' union in 1981, by interrupting play for fifty or so games, necessitated a split-season. In the first decades of the 20th century, the split-season format became commonplace in the lower minor leagues and was also a standard feature of the Negro Leagues.

45. The 1899–1900 Brooklyn champions were the product of a 50/50 ownership exchange in 1899 between the Brooklyn and Baltimore owners, by which Keeler, Kelley, and other first-rate players (but not McGraw and Robinson) were transferred from Baltimore to Brooklyn. On the Brooklyn–Baltimore arrangement, see Seymour and Mills 1989; Voigt 1966; Alexander 1988; Solomon, B. 1999. *Where They Ain't: The Fabled Life and Untimely Death of the Original Baltimore Orioles, the Team That Gave Birth to Modern Baseball*; Graham, F. 2002. *The Brooklyn Dodgers: An Informal History* (reprint).

The Base Ball Convention of 1857

Richard Hershberger

In early 1857, a collection of baseball clubs in and around New York City held a convention called by the senior club, the Knickerbocker, for the purpose of revising the rules of the game. This event would come to be recognized as a seminal one in the history of organized baseball, and has received the attention it is due from baseball historians. I propose here to look at it from a different direction, as a snapshot of the state of baseball, both as a social construct with clubs interacting with one another, and how the game was played on the field.

The Growth of Baseball to 1857

The earliest extant baseball code, and the direct ancestor of the modern game, is that of the Knickerbocker Club from 1845. The newly formed Knickerbockers were part of an existing baseball community in New York, and it is likely that their rules were adapted from an earlier code, but these earlier rules are less well documented and in any case the line to the modern rules runs through the Knickerbockers.[1] New York's baseball community of the 1840s collapsed, for unknown reasons, and disappears from the record following the 1846 season. The Knickerbockers were the sole organized survivor, while some individual players would regroup in the 1850s. The Knickerbockers remained active throughout this period, and even revised their rules in 1848.

A club could exist indefinitely without outside competition because its purpose was for its members to meet regularly to take their exercise together two or three days a week, dividing themselves into teams for a ballgame in a socially congenial setting. The vast majority of baseball games through the 1850s and '60s were such intramural affairs. "Match games" between clubs initially were rare highpoints to the season. They gradually grew more frequent and more important to the life of the club, with the intramural games fading away into mere practice sessions.

Baseball began a slow revival in 1851, and by the 1854 season there were about a half-dozen clubs in New York and Brooklyn. In December 1854 three of these, the Knickerbocker, Gotham, and Eagle clubs, met for a social dinner and ball, and to negotiate a common code for match games. The following spring, in a baseball first, this code was published by a newspaper.[2] That season saw an explosion of baseball activity. A vir-

---

Richard Hershberger has, in a few short years, become a leading fact-finder in our field, as he pursues his personal goal of understanding the social and organizational history of U.S. baseball from the 18th century to 1880. His recent articles in *Base Ball* include one on Philadelphia town ball (2007) and one on baseball and rounders (2009).

 DOI: 10.3172/BB.7.28

tuous cycle formed, with increased newspaper coverage encouraging new clubs, which in turn led to yet more newspaper coverage. This resulted in an unprecedented level of interest. By the end of the 1856 season dozens of clubs were active in New York, Brooklyn, and adjoining counties of New Jersey and New York.

This sets the scene for several questions about the convention: Why hold a convention at all? Why was there a need for a major revision of the rules only two seasons after the previous revision?[3] And what were the specific changes proposed, which were adopted, and why were some proposals rejected?

This Indian Peace Medal of the late 1850s testifies to baseball's rise as a national game.

The Need for a Convention

Why did the baseball community in general, and the Knickerbockers in particular, feel a need for a convention at all? Even granting that rules revisions were needed, there were other ways they could have gone about it.

The meeting of 1854 shows one possibility. This was a meeting of a limited number of clubs who played one another frequently, working the revisions out among themselves. As late as 1856 the Knickerbockers played match games only with the Gotham, Eagle, and Empire clubs. If the Knickerbockers wanted yet more changes, they could have met with just their traditional competitive partners and let the rest of the baseball community follow or not.

A more extreme possibility was that the Knickerbockers could have counted on their prestige as the senior club and unilaterally announced rules changes and only played match games with clubs willing to follow these rules.

There is a tradition of interpreting the Knickerbockers as would-be autocrats, striving to dominate the baseball community, if not on the playing field then at least institutionally. Their model, in this interpretation, was England's Marylebone Cricket Club, traditionally known in cricket circles as the "MCC." The MCC was the elite club (socially, if not necessarily competitively) of English cricket. The laws it adopted were accepted as standard.[4] It no longer holds this power, but even today it holds the copyright to the laws of cricket. A related traditional interpretation is that the Knickerbockers held themselves aloof from the rest of the baseball community. Neither interpretation is entirely fair.

The MCC analogy is based in large part on the Knickerbockers' status as a "gentlemen's club." Organized baseball began in the white collar and professional class, with a typical membership of doctors and lawyers and businessmen. In the mid-1850s working class clubs began to form. The contrast is easily exaggerated. The working class clubs were at the upper end of that range: skilled workers with the free time and financial resources to indulge in club play. The "gentlemen's" clubs were not gentlemen in the sense of the Victorian English gentry. They were "gentlemen" in the sense of acknowledging (at least in principle) standards of propriety. They were not really like the MCC by inclination, nor (as will be seen) did they have anything like the standing the MCC had within the cricket community even were they inclined to behave like the MCC.

The claim that the Knickerbockers stood apart from the rest of the baseball community is better founded. In the 1860s the Knickerbockers would conclude that competition was incompatible with the fraternal purpose of the club, and would withdraw from active competition. But that was in the future. Their five matches in 1856 against three opponents was actually more active and more varied than most that season. They, as will be discussed, favored the "fly game" and would adopt it for their internal play even after the convention rejected it. This is also sometimes seen as a withdrawal from the community, but it actually was an early stage of what would be a years-long campaign to influence this community to also adopt the fly rule. The Knickerbockers in the winter of 1856–1857 were fully engaged members of the baseball community.

The Knickerbockers in 1857 were neither would-be autocrats seeking to rule baseball, nor were they isolationists seeking to maintain a monastic purity. They were the recognized senior club. In retrospect they were not as strong on the field as in former years, but they still had a reputation as elite players. This put them in a unique position to bestow legitimacy to a convention. Their need for their imprimatur was shown the previous season, when eight clubs met in December 1855 with the intent to "make arrangements for a banquet and ball, and to establish general rules for the various Clubs." The Knickerbockers were conspicuously absent. The meeting adjourned "without taking

Baseball in the late 1850s was most often an informal, catch-as-catch-can affair. Unlike cricket, the rising American game required no manicured pitch or playing field.

definite action" with the intention to meet a week later "to give opportunity for a more general representation of the various Clubs." There is no record of this subsequent meeting taking place.[5]

The Knickerbockers were very visible in December 1856 in their call for the new convention. While they may have been necessary, this doesn't mean they got their way. The convention was run democratically. The Knickerbockers' status was duly acknowledged, but they still had to persuade the other clubs, and these attempts were often unsuccessful.

The Need for Revised Rules

In 1854 the baseball fraternity was a small group of players who knew each other personally. Things had moved past that by 1857. With rapid growth, it was no longer practical to expect that everyone knew everyone else, much less played together. The tenor of the gameplay was also changing. Match games were becoming more important, making the game more competitive. Clubs began looking for any edge they could get, including gaps in the rules that could be exploited.

The old rules were full of gaps to exploit. These had not been a problem for the games of the Knickerbockers, Gothams, and Eagles. There is a truism that games have both written and unwritten rules, with the unwritten rules filling the gaps in the written rules (and even, when there is a disagreement, superseding them).[6] These clubs understood the unstated assumptions of how the game was played. As personal contact between established and newer players grew tenuous, more of these assumptions needed to be clearly stated. Sporting newspaper columns of the late 1850s and early 1860s would be filled with queries from new clubs seeking clarifications. Often the replies had a weary tone, pointing to the applicable rule, but there also were situations requiring judgment calls. One long-term trend is the gradual closing of such gaps, with the rules getting ever-longer with provisions for ever-rarer scenarios.

The quest for any edge to win, or at least to avoid losing, is another long-term trend. This quest leads to the devising of new strategies and tactics, which in turn are judged as desirable (or at least acceptable) or an undesirable abuse. If undesirable, they are legislated away. The history of the spitball is a 20th century example of this process. By 1857 the previous two seasons had already revealed undesirable strategies requiring legislation.

The need for revision also arose because the game inevitably changed as players got better with experience. Baseball depends on a balance of pitching, hitting, and fielding. Pitching was not yet a major factor. The old assumption was that the pitcher would deliver the ball "to the bat" because the whole point was to get the ball in play. This assumption was just starting to break down at this time and pitchers would soon be attempting to induce batters to miss the ball or to hit it weakly. This would lead to four decades of rules adjustments, finally achieving stability in the 20th century. This was the future of rules discussions, however. In 1857 fielding, not pitching, was the important skill. The basic skills of catching and throwing the ball were more slowly acquired than the skill of batting against the pitching of the day. Rules written for the earlier, more primitive fielding were thrown out of balance as fielding improved and required adjustment.

The Proceedings[7]

The convention met in two sessions, the first on January 22 and the second on February 25. The first session appointed a rules committee, which met on January 28 with a mandate to present a draft to the second session. Fourteen clubs sent three delegates each to the first session. Two additional clubs joined the second session, though total attendance was lower as some earlier delegates did not return.

The first order of business for the convention was to organize itself through the election of officers. Daniel Adams, president of the Knickerbocker Club, was elected president. This acknowledged the club's status, and in any case it made sense as the Knickerbockers had called the meeting. Honors were then distributed through the election of a superfluity of officers (two vice presidents, two secretaries, and a treasurer), each from a different club, one from Brooklyn and the rest from New York. Louis Wadsworth, of the Knickerbockers, then presented a rules draft the club had prepared, but rather than take this up the convention decided to appoint a rules committee. The first suggestion was for it to have five members (which does rather suggest the Knickerbockers wanted to strongly influence it, as one of the five members would undoubtedly come from them). Other suggestions included 20 members or the convention meeting as a committee of the whole.[8] The final decision was that each club would appoint one member.[9]

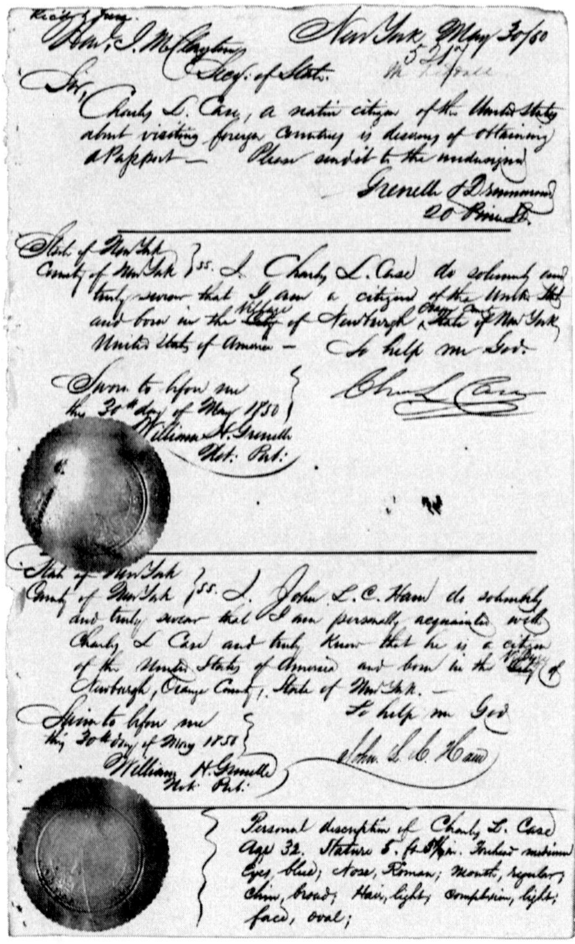
New York May 30/50
Sir,
Charles L. Case, a native citizen of the United States about visiting foreign Countries is desirous of obtaining a Passport — Please send it to the undersigned
Grenelle & Drummond
20 Pine St.

State of New York
County of New York } ss. I Charles L. Case do solemnly and truly swear that I am a citizen of the United States and born in the Village of Newburgh Orange County State of New York United States of America — So help me God.
Sworn to before me the 30th day of May 1850
William H. Grenelle
Not. Pub.
Chas L. Case

State of New York
County of New York } ss. I John L. C. Hann do solemnly and truly swear that I am personally acquainted with Charles L. Case and truly know that he is a citizen of the United States of America and born in the Village of Newburgh, Orange County, State of New York. — So help me God
Sworn to before me this 30th day of May 1850
William H. Grenelle
Not. Pub.
John L. C. Hann

Personal description of Charles L. Case
Age 32. Stature 5. ft 8¾ in. Forehead medium
Eyes, blue; Nose, Roman; Mouth, regular;
Chin, broad; Hair, light; Complexion, light;
Face, oval;

William H. Grenelle, here signing Charles Case's passport application, may have been a Knick delegate.

The purpose of the convention was then expanded by a discussion, apparently originating from the floor, on the desirability of a baseball ground in the new Central Park, with a committee of five appointed to meet with the Central Park commission to lobby for this. (They were unsuccessful in the short term, but cricket players would later complain about baseball players taking over the Central Park cricket ground.) Three balls of various size and weight were presented for consideration.[10] An assessment of $2 per club was voted to defray the costs of the convention, and the meeting was adjourned.

This committee at its meeting elected William H. Van Cott of the Gotham Club chairman and took up the Knickerbockers' draft. Some points survived the discussion, some did not, and some got through with changes. They succeeded in preparing a final draft to present to the full convention. At its second session the convention took up this draft and adopted several motions from the floor for further amendments before adopting the final version.

The following sections will consider the rules, the reasons for them, and the discussions surrounding them. They are roughly divided into clarifications stating existing practice, genuinely new rules, administrative rules, and the failed proposal for the "fly game." These divisions are a helpful tool but they are not always wholly clear and there is considerable overlap. Rather than force the analysis into this scheme, what follows will include this overlap from one category to another as it comes.

Rules Clarifications

This section will consider the rules that were not truly changes, but rather clarifications of previous ambiguities, to prevent either abuses or honest confusion.

> Sec. 2. The bat must be round, and must not exceed 2 inches in diameter at the thickest part; it must be made of wood, and may be of any length, to suit the striker.

The bats used in early baseball varied, sometimes being round and sometimes flat (often characterized as "paddles"), and sometimes sized to be swung one-handed and sometimes two-handed. A two-handed round bat was the norm in the northeastern U.S. Here for the first time the rules specify that the bat be round. Its being two-handed is not mandated, but there is no record of the smaller bat being used.

The Knickerbocker draft rules included a provision allowing a bat with one side shaved down to make a flat side. This, it was claimed, would permit for more "scientific" batting, by which was meant better-aimed hits. This proposal did not survive the rules committee. Unfortunately, there is no record of the argument against it. Cricket uses flat bats, and was the likely source of the idea. There was at least one argument made in the committee against making baseball more like cricket. The rejection of this proposal may have been part of this reaction.

The idea would resurface in the 1880s and for several years be adopted in the official rules, though to little effect. This was apparently an independent development, not inspired by the Knickerbocker proposal.

> Sec. 3. The bases must be four in number, placed at equal distances from each other, and securely fastened upon the four corners of a square whose sides are respectively thirty yards. They must be so constructed as to be distinctly seen by the umpires and referee, and must cover a space equal to one square foot of surface; the first, second, and third bases shall be canvas bags, painted white, and filled with sand or saw-dust; the home base and pitcher's point to be each marked by a flat circular iron plate, painted or enamelled white.
>
> Sec. 4. The base from which the ball is struck shall be designated the home base, and must be directly opposite to the second base; the first base must always be upon the right hand, and the third base that upon the left hand side of the striker, when occupying his position at the home base.

The previous rules had only defined the field vaguely. The distance between bases was stated as 42 "paces" from home to second and from first to third. This could be interpreted various ways. A contemporary dictionary definition put a pace at two and a half feet, which would put the bases a bit under 75 feet apart. Or "pace" might be interpreted literally, with someone stepping out the distance. If a pace is taken to be three feet, this results in almost exactly the modern distance. Some writers therefore favor this interpretation, but there is little contemporaneous support for this apart from its resulting in what is now the right answer. It is likely that actual practice allowed for a range of distances, with the convention settling on the upper end of that range. The new rules also specify for the first time the physical characteristics of the bases and that runners progress around them counterclockwise. Neither of these was a new practice.

> Sec. 5. The pitcher's position shall be designated by a line four yard in length, drawn at right angles to a line from home to the second base, having its center upon that line, at a fixed iron plate placed at a point fifteen yards distant from the home base.
>
> Sec. 6. The ball must be pitched, not jerked nor thrown to the bat; and whenever the pitcher draws back his hand with the apparent purpose or pretension to deliver the ball, he shall so deliver it. The pitcher must deliver the ball as near as possible, over the centre of the home base, and must have neither foot in advance of the line at the time of delivering the ball, and if he fails in either of these particulars, then it shall be declared a baulk.
>
> Sec. 7. When a baulk is made by the pitcher, every player running the bases is entitled to one base, without being put out.

Here we have clarifications of two points: the position of the pitcher and the definition of a balk. The position of the pitcher is specified in the 1854 as "not less that fifteen paces" from home. This in theory allowed him to be any distance to either side of center. Here his position is more narrowly restricted, probably reflecting normal practice in any case.

The rules had, as far back as 1845, prohibited balks, with a penalty of allowing the baserunners to advance a base. The reason was the same as in the modern game—to prevent the pitcher from unfairly deceiving the baserunners. But what exactly constitutes a balk is one of the perpetual mysteries of the game to this day. Here we see the first attempt to define it. There was considerable discussion in the rules committee. The Knickerbockers proposed that the pitcher be required to deliver the ball with one foot ahead of the pitching line, and that once he placed the foot ahead of the line he was required to deliver the ball to the batter, with a balk being called if he instead threw to a base. The final version was criticized for requiring the umpire to determine the pitcher's intent. Unfortunately, the argument for the final version is not recorded. One possibility arises from the practice of some pitchers of running forward as part of their delivery, like a cricket bowler. The freedom of the pitcher to range about was gradually narrowed, until he was finally tied to a specific spot, but a wide-ranging delivery was perfectly acceptable in the early years. Perhaps forcing the pitcher to complete his delivery straddling a line was considered too restrictive.

> Sec. 16. No ace nor base can be made upon a foul ball, nor when a fair ball has been caught without having touched the ground; and the ball shall, in both instances, be considered dead and not in play, until it shall first have been settled in the hands of the pitcher. When a fair ball has been caught without having touched the ground, the players running the bases shall have the privilege of returning to them.

The parts of this rule dealing with fair balls — fraught with future significance — will be discussed in a later section. Foul balls are the topic here, as this rule clarified a point of much confusion to new players of this form of baseball. Most pre-modern forms of baseball were played in the round, meaning that the ball was fully in play regardless of the direction it was hit. Foul territory was a peculiar feature of the game played by the clubs at the convention, but even within the New York metropolitan area other forms of baseball were played. When the *Spirit of the Times* first published the 1854 rules, it felt the need to insert a parenthetical explanation after the rule on fair and foul balls. As the convention's version spread further afield, many questions directed to newspaper columns were concerned with working out the ramifications of foul territory.

Foul territory is a very odd concept — a point obscured by its familiarity — with some, but not all, outcomes being disallowed on foul balls. The batter and any runners cannot advance (make an "ace or base" in the vocabulary of the time) on a foul ball. So when can they once again attempt to advance? The earlier rules did not say. With this set the language of the ball being "dead" first appears, as well as when the ball becomes live, probably without changing previous practice.

> Sec. 17. Players must stand on a line drawn through the centre of the home base not exceeding in length three feet from either side thereof, and such line shall be parallel with the line occupied by the Pitcher. They shall strike in regular rotation, and after the first innings is played, the turn commences with the player who stands on the list next to the one who lost the third hand.

Previous rules had never actually stated where the batter was to place himself. The first sentence of this rule was an addition by the second session of the convention. It prevents the batter from placing himself further back than home, which would have had the advantage of making balls weakly hit into the dirt directly in front of the batter foul. Interestingly, the first sentence of this rule was not in the draft to come out of the committee. Apparently this oversight was spotted and corrected from the convention floor.

> Sec. 19. Players running the bases must, so far as possible, keep upon the direct line between the bases; and should any player run three feet out of this line, for the purpose of avoiding the ball in the hands of an adversary, he shall be declared out.
>
> Sec. 20. Any player running the bases, who shall, intentionally, prevent an adversary from catching or fielding the ball, shall be declared out.
>
> Sec. 21. If a player is prevented from making a base, by the intentional obstruction of an adversary, he shall be entitled to that base, and not be put out.
>
> Sec. 22. If any adversary stops the ball with his hat or cap, or takes it from the hands of a party not engaged in the game, no player can be put out, unless the ball shall first have been settled in the hands of the pitcher.

The normal expectation, of course, is that the runner will head directly for his base. The addition of this rule suggests that some were starting to take evasive maneuvers and that this was perceived as an unfair tactic. The rule against the runner interfering with a fielder was present all along. The rule against the fielder obstructing the runner is new, suggesting that the tactic was also new. This is more a clarification than a new rule because it is likely that it would have been considered unfair all along, had any player thought to try it (similarly with catching the ball in a cap).

> Sec. 27. In playing all matches, nine players from each club shall constitute a full field, and they must have been regular members of the club which they represent, for thirty days prior to the match. No change or substitution shall be made after the game has been commenced, unless for reason of illness or injury. Positions of players shall be determined by captains, previously appointed for that purpose by the respective clubs.

The restriction of participation to "regular members" was new, and will be discussed in a later section. The remainder of this rule was a codification of existing practice. The standard side was nine men from the beginning of the 1850s baseball revival. It was custom rather than rule, but a firm one. A side was often referred to as a "nine" and there are no recorded instances of the New York clubs playing any other in match games. That being said, the Knickerbocker records show that even after 1857 the size of the sides in their intramural games varied. There also were occasional games outside the New York regions with different numbers, while otherwise played under the New York rules. There were occasional discussions as late as the mid–1870s of adding players, but nine players would be a fixed feature of match games from the 1850s, and by the late 1860s of all but the most informal play.

The rule against substitutions was most likely accepted practice, and would remain the rule for decades thereafter.

> Sec. 29. The umpires in all matches shall take care that the regulations respecting the ball, bats, bases, and the pitcher's position, are strictly observed; they shall be the judges of fair and unfair play, and shall determine all differences which may occur during the game; they shall take especial care to declare all foul balls and baulks immediately on their occurrence. They shall together select a referee, from whose decision — in case of a disagreement between them — there shall be no appeal.
>
> Sec. 34. No person shall be permitted to act as umpire or referee in a match, unless he shall be a member of a Base Ball Club, governed by these rules.

Clubs had long appointed umpires for their internal games. For match games both clubs continued the practice, each appointing an umpire. In theory the two umpires would reach a consensus on disputed points. In practice they often acted as partisans for their clubs, so they would refer unresolved disputes to a neutral third party. Rule 29 codifies the practice. Presumably Rule 34 was put in to ensure that the officials actually knew the rules they were charged to enforce. The following year the rules-makers would recognize the pointlessness of the two partisan umpires and would eliminate them, re-designating the referee to be the umpire.

> Sec. 32. Clubs may adopt such rules respecting balls knocked beyond or outside the bounds of the field, as the circumstances of the ground may demand, and these rules shall govern all matches played upon the ground, provided that they are distinctly made known to every player and umpire, and the referee, previous to the commencement of the game.

The 1845 Knickerbocker rules defined a foul ball as "a ball knocked out the field, or outside the range of the first or third base." The 1848 revision and all later versions omitted "out the field." So initially a ball which nowadays would be a home run was ruled foul. An explanation proposed by historian John Thorn is a desire to avoid losing balls, particularly into the Hudson River.[11] Regardless of the reason, this seems to have been the first ground rule. It seems likely that the vagaries of the various playing fields required others. Here we see this codified.

Rules Changes

This section will discuss truly new features of the game.

> Sec. 1. The ball must weigh not less than 6 nor more than 6½ ounces avoirdupois; it must not measure less than 10, nor more than 10¼ inches in circumference; it must be composed of India-rubber and yarn, and covered with leather. It shall be furnished by the challenging Club, and become the property of the winning club, as a trophy of victory.

The size and weight, though not the composition, of the ball were first set in the 1854 rules, at from 2¾ to 3¼ inches in diameter and from 5½ to 6 ounces. The convention increased both the size and weight. Ironically, the earlier specifications closely match the modern rule. Through the 1860s the larger size would be standard. On the other hand, the composition specified in the 1857 rules is essentially that used today, though nowadays the center can be cork rather than rubber. It is not clear how closely earlier balls matched the 1854 specifications. *Porter's* noted that the new rules specified "the weight and make of the ball, which has hitherto been uncertain," while the *Express* described earlier balls as "large, soft, and springy." The rise of baseball's popularity also saw the rise of baseball manufacture. It is likely that this, as much as any rule, resulted in more standardization.

> Sec. 24. If two hands are already out, no player, running home at the time the ball is struck, can make an ace, if the striker is put out.

The 1854 rules had a similar provision, but only in the more limited situation of the batter being caught out. This version would apply to a batter thrown out trying to stretch a single into a double, while if read literally it would not apply to a double play (perhaps unless the final out was the batter). What we have is an intermediate stage of refinement of an older concept, that the third out sometimes but not always precludes scoring.

> Sec. 26. The game shall consist of nine innings to each side, when, should the number of runs be equal, the innings shall be continued until a majority of runs, upon an equal number of innings shall be declared, which shall conclude the game.
>
> Sec. 31. The umpires and referee in any match, shall determine when play shall be suspended; and if the game cannot be concluded, it shall be decided by the last even innings, provided five innings have been played, and the party having the greatest number of runs shall be declared the winner.

The earlier rules ended the game when after a complete inning one side had reached 21 runs. Here we have the modern rule. This has long been recognized as one of the most important changes to come out of the convention. The provision for a winner once five innings had been played is, if anything, even more so. It eliminated from baseball the concept of a "draw." Indeed, it expunged the idea so thoroughly that the modern American sports fan finds it nearly incomprehensible.

In modern American sports, a "draw" and a "tie" are the same thing. This is not true in cricket. There, a tie means the same thing as in American sports, and is rare. A draw is similar to a tie only in that neither side can claim victory.

A cricket match, like a modern baseball game, is played to a certain number of innings: two, in its fullest form. It also has a pre-set time limit, generally measured in days. A match might last just one day, or as many as five for an international test match.[12]

For either side to achieve victory, the innings must be completed within the time limit. If they are not, then the match is a draw regardless of the score.

This concept was borrowed by early baseball clubs. Indeed, it seems to have been an unexamined assumption, never explicitly mentioned in any rule. In the baseball version, games lasted only part of one day, from the commencement of play (usually in the afternoon) up to when darkness or weather prevented further play. If at this point neither side had attained 21 runs, the game was a draw.

The possibility of a drawn game affects play, as a side finding itself lagging in scoring can play instead for a draw by, to put it bluntly, stalling. This works in cricket, and is considered a legitimate strategy. It did not work in baseball, and was abolished. To see why, one need compare the course of play of the two games.

In cricket, a batsman can be dismissed (i.e. put out) in several ways, three of them relevant here. He can be bowled, meaning the bowled ball puts down the wicket (i.e. strikes the wicket with enough force to knock off one of the horizontal cross pieces, called bails). This very roughly corresponds to a baseball batter being struck out. He can be run out, meaning the wicket is put down as he runs toward it. This roughly corresponds to a baseball runner being tagged out. He can be caught on a fly ball. This exactly corresponds to a baseball batter being caught out.

A key difference between cricket and baseball is that a cricket batsman is not forced to run on a ground ball. A cricket side stalling for a draw adjusts its strategy by batting conservatively. Rather than trying to score runs it tries to avoid outs. Balls are hit into the ground, and the players only run when it is completely safe to do so. This may not make for exciting play, but the wicket nonetheless is still being defended and skill is still required to avoid being put out. The game is still being played.

This was not true in baseball. Swinging strikes are an ancient feature of the game, but the concepts of called strikes and bases on balls had not yet developed. There was no requirement that a batter swing at a pitch, regardless of its location. This had worked in the less competitive earlier era of recreational play, as it was understood that the fun of the game was in the baserunning and the fielding and throwing of the ball. The duel between the pitcher and the batter came later. But in the heated competition of the 1850s clubs were willing to sacrifice fun in the quest for victory, or at least to avoid loss. A side stalling for a draw could simply refuse to swing at any pitches. No skill was needed, and there was no risk. But it was at the cost of actually playing the game.

This is was a major, even existential problem. A list of the season's games published in late 1856 includes 55 games. Fully one fifth of these are draws, resulting in "the disgust of parties who have gone into the field for an afternoon's recreation."[13] This had the potential to destroy interest in the game. Something clearly had to be done. One idea was that the batter "be compelled to run on such occasions, strike or no strike when three fair pitched balls had been given him, or, at most, every three fair pitched balls should be considered as one strike."[14] This was prescient, but not the path initially taken. Instead, the new rules excised the concept of the drawn game entirely.

This was only partially successful. Losing sides were no longer stalling for a draw. A winning side might in principle have an incentive to stall for darkness rather than allowing the other side the chance to retake the lead, but in practice this was not a major problem. A team might also stall for darkness if, in a late inning, the opposing side took the lead. This happened occasionally, but only a narrow set of circumstances would lead to this. What was a problem was that there were other reasons why a batter might refuse to swing at pitches, such as the hope that the ball might get past the catcher so a runner could advance. This was the infamous "hold game" of the late 1850s and early 1860s. The concept of the called strike was adopted after all. This in turn led to the concept of the base on balls, since otherwise the pitcher had little incentive to throw balls the batter could hit. But the rule change was wildly successful in removing the concept of the drawn game from the American sports consciousness.

This still leaves the question of why a complete game was set at nine innings. This is actually two questions: Why set it in terms of innings at all, and why nine? The game could have been kept at 21 runs, with draws eliminated by declaring victory to the side with the most runs if play was ended prematurely.

The switch to basing a complete game on innings rather than score seems to have been in order to more nearly standardize how long a game took. Even at this early date there was a consensus that a game ought to typically take between two and three hours. Some of the 1856 games had as few as two innings, while the longest had 12. The time spent per inning tends to be more constant than the time spent per run scored. In modern baseball a pitching duel will be quicker than a slugfest, but the variation is much less than it would be if the game was played to a fixed score. The merit of the change was summed up by the *Herald*: "This rule will prevent a game from being played out in one or two hours, or playing against time and making a drawn game, as was too frequently the case in making twenty-one runs."

There explains the switch to innings, but why nine? This is a mystery. The Knickerbockers proposed a seven-inning game. This was the version to come out of the committee, but it was amended on a motion from the floor of the convention. To add to the mystery, the motion was made by Louis Wadsworth, one of the Knickerbockers delegates. This seems to be an internal division made public, but the arguments either way are not recorded.

To add yet more to the mystery, the average game of 1856 lasted six innings. Whether seven or nine innings, the change would seem to tend to lengthen the game. There may have been an expectation that removing stalling for a draw would counter this. Better fielding would also tend to shorten the game. It is possible that the higher number of innings was favored by better clubs, or those who aspired to be better.

In the event, the nine-inning game came to be sacrosanct. Concern that the game takes too long is one of the great constants from the 1850s to this day. By 1863 match games were averaging three and a half hours.[15] The called-strike rule and relaxation of restriction on pitching technique would later shorten the game. For all the discussions about the game being too long, there has never been a serious proposal to lower the number of innings. The idea is nearly literally unthinkable.[16]

Administrative Rules

The 1845 Knickerbocker rules included administrative matters such as provisions for internal club discipline and when to allow non-members to participate. These were omitted from the 1854 code, as this version was intended for match games between clubs and such internal club matters did not apply. A new set of administrative rules was introduced in 1857, as clubs gaming the system required rules about player eligibility, and the rising popularity of the game attracted gambling interests.

> Sec. 27. In playing all matches, nine players from each club shall constitute a full field, and they must have been regular members of the club which they represent, for thirty days prior to the match. No change or substitution shall be made after the game has been commenced, unless for reason of illness or injury. Positions of players shall be determined by captains, previously appointed for that purpose by the respective clubs.
>
> Sec. 28. Any player holding membership in more than one club, at the same time, shall not be permitted to play in the matches of either club.

The nine-player side with no substitutions is discussed above. The relevant part here is the new requirement that all players be members of just one club, and that they have been a member for 30 days.

On Friday, September 5, 1856, the Knickerbockers had arrived at their ground in Hoboken for a match game against the Gothams. They were surprised to find one Mr. Pinckney among the Gotham players, as they knew perfectly well he was a member of the Union Club. Their protest was forestalled by the Gothams informing them that he had joined the Gothams the previous Tuesday, though without resigning from the Unions. This led to "the presumption ... that he entered the Gothams for the purpose of this match," but the game went on. The Unions held a special meeting to condemn this, and Pinckney resigned from the Gothams the Tuesday following the match, "expressing his conviction of the impropriety of a person belonging to or playing matches in more than one club."[17]

The 1857 rules included provisions specifically designed to prevent this happening again. Modern writers often assume that the concern was to protect the amateurism of the game. This is unlikely. The topic of professionalism would be much discussed a few years later, but it had not yet arisen in 1857. The new rules were designed to prevent

The Old Gotham Inn, a.k.a. the Gotham Cottage or Bowling Saloon, was clubhouse to the Gotham Base Ball Club. It was also the scene of the 1858 NABBP convention.

ringers, but remuneration is not necessary to explain why an enthusiastic hobbyist might jump at the opportunity to play in a first-class match, niceties of club membership notwithstanding. Nor is devotion to amateur ideals necessary to explain opposition to ringers. The practice threatened the social structure of the clubs, and led to the best players monopolizing match play. Cricket clubs allowed this, and the baseball fraternity did not think the results worthy of emulation.

> Sec. 30. No person engaged in a match, either as umpire, referee, or player, shall be either directly or indirectly interested in any bet upon the game. Neither umpire, referee nor player shall be changed during a match, unless with the consent of both parties, except for a violation of this law, and except as provided in section 27, and then the referee may dismiss any transgressor.
>
> Sec. 33. No person, shall be permitted to approach or to speak with the referee, umpires, or players, or in any manner to interrupt or interfere with any player during the progress of the game, unless by the special request of the umpires or referee.

Organized baseball has from the start had an equivocal relationship with gambling. The dangers of gambling are obvious, but so too are the benefits of the heightened interest it inspires. Early cricket matches were often explicitly played for stakes. In rule 30 we see the decision that baseball would not follow that practice, though side bets among spectators were another matter. The ban on bystanders interacting with the players or officials might be an oblique reference to gambling, but it might simply represent a recognition of the growing numbers of spectators and the absence of physical barriers between them and the playing field.

> Sec. 35. Whenever a match shall have been determined upon between two clubs, play shall be called at the exact hour appointed; and should either party fail to produce their players within fifteen minutes thereafter, the party so failing shall admit a defeat.

Tardy arrival to the field was another habit of the cricket clubs that baseball wanted to avoid. Cricket was expected to take the better part of the day, or even several days. The swift resolution of a baseball contest, by contrast, was considered an advantage of the game, so this rule naturally followed. It is not clear that it was ever strictly enforced, but the threat may have had a salutary effect upon the clubs.

The Fly Game

We have seen proposed rules not adopted, such as the flat bat, or altered, such as the seven-inning game. Here we see the discussion of the fly game, which was rejected but with a compromise, which in turn would have unexpected results.

> Sec. 11. The striker is out if a foul ball is caught, either before touching the ground, or upon the first bound.
>
> Sec. 13. Or, if a fair ball is struck, and the ball is caught either without having touched the ground, or upon the first bound.
>
> Sec. 16. No ace nor base can be made upon a foul ball, nor when a fair ball has been caught without having touched the ground; and the ball shall, in both instances, be considered dead and not in play, until it shall first have been settled in the hands of the pitcher. When a fair ball has been caught without having touched the ground, the players running the bases shall have the privilege of returning to them.

Some pre-modern forms of baseball granted an out to a ball caught on the fly or after one (or even two) bounces. This came to be known as the "bound game." Others only granted an out to a ball caught on the fly, as in the modern game. This was the "fly game." The Knickerbocker rules adopted the bound game, but at some point the Knickerbockers reconsidered this. Modern writers often assume this reconsideration was early, but this is unlikely. They would have been in a much stronger position to effect the change in the 1854 rules had they desired it, but there is no record of any such discussion. The earliest record of the idea is from 1856, when fly catches began to be praised as more "manly" and "scientific."[18]

The Knickerbockers went all-in at the convention, proposing the fly rule for fair balls, though not for foul balls. (The foul-bound rule allowed the catcher, who played much farther back than he does today, to attempt to catch foul tips into the dirt. This was considered a desirable feature, and the foul-bound rule was kept in place for two decades after the fly rule was adopted for fair balls.) This proposal was rejected by the rules committee after a lively discussion. The remnant of the proposal is seen in rules 11 and 13, which distinguish between fair and foul balls, but then treat them exactly alike. This uneconomical redundancy is explained by the proposed draft, in which rule 13 lacked the phrase "or upon the first bound."

The debate reveals the limits of the Knickerbockers' influence and divisions within the baseball fraternity. Most of the sporting press favored the change due to the ideology of manliness and scientific play. Yet the proposal would go on to be repeatedly voted down. From the start the proponents claimed that it was inexperienced and inexpert players who favored the "boyish" bound rule, yet the Gothams, the second-oldest club, voted against the fly game into 1860 while the Eagles, the third-oldest club, never voted for it; votes against it would come from some top clubs such as the Atlantics and the Mutuals. The divisions within the fraternity were more complicated than experienced and expert versus new and unskilled players. Only after a years-long concerted campaign of propaganda, demonstration matches, and arm-twisting was the rule finally enacted for the 1865 season, and it was by no means inevitable even then.

The Gotham BBC members' pin of the 1850s features three men at sea in a tub, from Mother Goose.

There also was a strange and unpredictable outcome from the debate. The rules committee of 1857 was at a deadlock until the opponents offered a compromise. The older rules allowed a runner to freely advance on a fly ball, regardless of whether or not it was caught. The compromise, intended to give an incentive to the fielder to manly catches, prohibited the runners from advancing on a ball caught on the fly. This was tacked onto rule 16, which in its draft version was concerned strictly with uncaught foul balls. A fair ball caught on the fly was to be treated the

Famous Atlantic Baseball Club of Brooklyn

The members, standing, left to right, are T. G. Van Cott, pitcher; William Burns, catcher; J. McCosker, third base; O. Teed, shortstop; Phil Sheridan, left field; R. H. Cudlip, second base; Vail, first base; Winslow, center field; Charles Comerford, right field. The men seated, left to right, are William H. Van Cott, president; G. Van Cott, umpire; H. M. Platt, game keeper.

This image, published in the Brooklyn Eagle of February 11, 1931, was misidentified as the Atlantics. It is in fact the Gotham Base Ball Club of 1855, a remarkable survivor.

same way, resulting in a dead ball until it was settled in the hands of the pitcher. This was, to the disgust of the fly ball advocates, weakened by a floor amendment allowing the runners to return to their bases at leisure.

In 1859 yet another concession was offered to the fly rule proponents, with a fair ball caught on the fly remaining live and runners subject to being put out until they returned to their bases. This was intended to create an opportunity for double plays on fly catches, but had the unanticipated effect of allowing runners to tag up on their bases and attempt to advance. After a season's play with this unplanned experiment, players decided they liked the rule and it has been kept since. In the meantime runners could still run freely on bound catches up. Eventually these bound catches were no longer outs, and therefore no longer considered any sort of catch, while runners still can advance on them.

The Aftermath of the Convention

The convention of 1857 was a watershed event in baseball history. The rules adopted are the direct ancestor of modern baseball. The following year the convention would meet again and organize itself as a permanent organization, the National Association of Base Ball Players. This would be the governing body through 1870. In the meantime professionalism entered the game. In 1871 the professional clubs split off and formed the National Association of Professional Base Ball Players. In 1876 six of these clubs, and two newly formed ones, reorganized as the National League of Professional Base Ball Clubs, which exists today as the National League. There is an unbroken chain of rules, enacted by a governing body and modifying the previous year's rules, tracing back to 1857.

Abstract

The convention of baseball clubs of 1857 has long been recognized as a seminal event in the history of organized baseball. Clubs were interacting with one another in increasingly competitive play. This article presents the convention as a snapshot of the state of baseball. It analyzes baseball both as a social construct as clubs learned to interact competitively with one another, and the resulting rules changes enacted in response to increased competition.

Notes

1. William Wheaton, a charter member of the Knickerbockers, gave an account of the earlier rules in an interview published in the San Francisco *Examiner*, November 27, 1887.
2. *The Spirit of the Times*: May 12, 1855.
3. Note that the revisions are conventionally identified as being from 1854 and 1857, but the 1854 rules were written in December and the 1857 in February, making the separation but two seasons.
4. A peculiarity of cricket is that it has "laws" rather than "rules."
5. New York *Tribune*: Dec. 10, 1855.
6. As an example, I was recently asked what rule prevented a baseman in possession of the ball from simply pushing a runner off the bag and tagging him for an out. So far as I know, there is no such written rule. The unwritten rule is universally understood and there is no need to put it in writing.
7. There are multiple newspaper accounts of the events described in this section. The best are in *Porter's Spirit of the Times*: Jan. 31, Feb. 28, Mar. 7, 1857; New York *Herald*: Jan. 23, Mar. 2, 1857; New York *Evening Express*: Jan. 23 and 31, 1857. The *Express* items merit special notice, as they have not been considered by previous baseball historians and they include details absent from the other accounts.
8. This last suggests that the convention at least tacitly adopted standard rules of procedure, though no account states this.
9. There is a minor mystery about the identity of the Knickerbocker's delegate. Some modern writers assume it was Daniel Adams, as he would be active in rules discussions several years thereafter. It is possible that he was considered an *ex officio* member as president of the convention, but he certainly was not the Knickerbocker's appointee. *Porter's* and the *Herald* name Louis Wadsworth as the member, and as these are the better known accounts this also is widely accepted. The *Express* names the third Knickerbocker delegate to the convention, William Grenelle, as the committee member. It also includes an anecdote from the committee meeting in which he deprecates his playing skill. As Wadsworth was an excellent player and had not a personality prone to self-deprecation, it is likely that it was indeed Grenelle on the committee and *Porter's* and the *Herald* (whose accounts share much verbiage in common and were probably written by the same reporter) are mistaken.
10. Sources disagree on who presented this: either Wadsworth, or Robert Cornell of the Baltic Club.
11. Cite
12. This description is of cricket in its classic form. Various other formats have been adopted in later years. Also, historically some early test matches were played without a time limit. Neither of these facts affects this discussion.
13. *Porter's Spirit of the Times*: Dec. 27, 1856; Mar. 7, 1857.
14. Ibid., Nov. 22, 1856. The word "strike" here should be understood to mean the bat making contact with the ball, not a "strike" in the modern baseball sense.
15. New York *Sunday Mercury*: Aug. 30, 1863.
16. The only exception on the professional level is that minor league doubleheaders last only seven innings.
17. *Porter's Spirit of the Times*: Sept. 13, 20, 1856.
18. The earliest known example is from *Porter's Spirit of the Times*: Nov. 8, 1856, from a report of a match played Nov. 1 between the Putnam and Excelsior clubs. It praises "several fine catches being made on the fly" and characterizes this as "an important improvement in the fielding," making it clear that bound catches were the norm.

Jimmy Callahan
He Covered All the Bases in Chicago

Art Ahrens

The list of players who performed for both the Cubs and the White Sox is more extensive than most are aware. The roll call ranges from Hall of Famers Clark Griffith, Ron Santo, and Rich "Goose" Gossage to such obscure footnotes as Vallie Eaves, Lloyd Merriman, and Taylor "T-Bone" Phillips. Not to mention author Jim Brosnan, prankster Jay Johnstone, and broadcaster Steve Stone. But there was only one player who starred for both teams and owned his own semi-pro club as well. His name was Jimmy Callahan.

James Joseph Callahan was born at Fitchburg, Massachusetts, on March 18, 1874, to Irish immigrants James and Margaret (Glynn) Callahan.[1] In boyhood, his mother nicknamed him "Nixey" for reasons long since lost to history. He received his primary education at the local public school, where he presumably practiced baseball in the playground during recess and after class. But at age 14, Jimmy lost his father and had to abandon further schooling to support his mother. He first worked at a cotton mill and was later trained as a plumber's apprentice, neither of which he especially enjoyed.[2]

James Joseph "Nixey" Callahan, player-manager of the White Sox in 1912.

It was while employed at the cotton mill that Jimmy emerged as a talented pitcher for the company team. His next stop was the semi-professional team of Pepperell, one of the best in Massachusetts. Reportedly, he won 28 games for Pepperell in 1891.[3] By 1893, Callahan was hurling for an independent professional club in New Bedford, Massachusetts.[4] It was here that he caught the eye of the Philadelphia Phillies, who signed him to a contract.

Callahan's major league debut on May 12, 1894, was hardly an impressive one, as the Orioles slugged him, 8–3, at Baltimore. The right-hander appeared

---

Native Chicagoan **Art Ahrens** has been a Cubs fan since the late 1950s. In addition to numerous articles on baseball history, he has co-authored five books on the Cubs, all with the late Eddie Gold of the *Chicago Sun-Times*. More recently he has penned two pictorial volumes for Arcadia Publishing, *Chicago Cubs, 1926–1940* (2005) and *Chicago Cubs: Tinker to Evers to Chance* (2007). Ahrens is a retired U.S. civil servant, widowed, and a member of the Society for American Baseball Research since November 1971. He resides roughly a mile from Wrigley Field.

DOI: 10.3172/BB.7.45

in eight more games that season, going 1–2 with a bloated ERA (compiled retroactively) of 9.89. His lone victory came in relief of Kid Carsey on July 9 at St. Louis, where the Phillies scored three runs in the seventh and again in the eighth to eke out an 11–10 win. Jimmy displayed some offensive skills by slapping two singles and scoring twice. He spent most of the remainder of 1894 with the Philadelphia team of the Pennsylvania State League (basically a farm team for the Phillies), where he went 10–9 and batted .320, seeing limited service in the outfield.

The Phillies apparently gave up on Callahan, as he pitched for Springfield of the Eastern League in 1895, posting a powerful 30–9 log. The following year he moved up the minor league ladder to Kansas City of the Western League, going 24–14 while playing another 32 games in the outfield, batting .314.[5] During the winter of 1896–1897, Jimmy stayed in Kansas City, making his living by doing itinerant plumbing work and (mostly) putting his pocket pool skills to use at local billiard emporiums.[6]

It was also at this time that Callahan's contract was purchased by the Chicago Colts (Cubs), earning him a permanent promotion to the majors. On January 30, 1897, the front page of *Sporting Life* noted "James J. Callahan ... has a bright future before him, as he should develop into one of the crack pitchers of the League.... He has excellent speed, good command of the ball, and is cool headed at critical stages of the game. He is also a good batsman and clever base runner."[7] The words would not be wasted.

Upon reporting to the Colts' spring training camp at Hot Springs, Arkansas, in March 1897, Jimmy met the aging superstar first baseman and manager Adrian "Cap" Anson. Although Anson was generally prejudiced against the Irish, he appears to have made an exception where young Callahan was concerned, as they took an immediate liking to each other. With his genial, outgoing personality, Jimmy also became close friends with ace pitcher Clark Griffith and center fielder Bill Lange, the team's best hitter and basestealer.[8]

Callahan hurled his first game for his new team on April 26, 1897, at St. Louis, beating the Brown Stockings (Cardinals), 9–2. The *Chicago Tribune* colorfully observed that "The first eight men who faced Callahan died natural and easy deaths by curvature of the ball" and that from the sixth inning on "Callahan had the Browns completely at his mercy."[9] It was Chicago's first win of the season following three losses at Cincinnati.

In 1913, at age 39, manager Callahan played in only six games. He had last pitched in the big leagues in 1903.

Anson had already announced that this would be his last year as a player, so on May 4 it was "Cap Anson Day" for the home opener. A warm, sunny day attracted a paid crowd of 14,968 to Chicago's West Side Grounds for almost a full house. Among those in attendance were comedian Eddie Foy, actor Maurice Barrymore and his daughter Ethel, plus alderman John Harlan. After a brass band played John Phillip Sousa's "El Capitan" in Anson's honor, he was given a silver service and other gifts to thunderous applause.

For the game, Callahan was on the mound with the 45-year-old Anson calling the pitches as his catcher. (Regular receivers Tim Donahue and Malachi Kittredge were both nursing minor injuries.) The Colts scored four runs in the second inning and one in the sixth while Jimmy held St. Louis scoreless for the first eight innings. Although he wilted a bit in the ninth, he held on to win, 5–2, for his team's third win of the season against six losses. In a special article for the *Chicago Tribune* (probably ghost written), Bill Lange stated: "After the game, Capt. Anson complimented all the players on their work, especially Mr. Callahan on his pitching. His curves were beautiful and his control almost perfect. The way he holds the men to the bases gives the club the impression that they may have found a second Griffith."[10]

Callahan felt honored that Anson gave him — still essentially a rookie — the pitching assignment on such a special occasion, and it further cemented their friendship.[11] And Anson, having already observed Jimmy's versatility, began employing him in other positions.

The captain's final season was long and frustrating as his club skidded to ninth in the 12-team circuit. But at Chicago on June 29, the Colts looked like Anson's champions of the 1880s as they set a major league record for runs scored in thrashing Louisville, 36–7. Pitcher Callahan went 4-for-7 with two doubles and four runs scored to aid in the massacre. With an obviously safe lead, all he had to do was lob the ball across the plate in later innings. Among Chicago's 30 hits were seven doubles, three triples, and two home runs, including a second-inning grand slam by Jimmy Ryan that cleared the left field fence and bounced off the wall of a building across the street. The run count was due almost as much to the Colonels' incompetence as the Colts' bats, as they issued 10 walks, hit two batters, and committed 10 errors. Only 14 of Chicago's runs were earned. The lurid headline on the *Chicago Inter-Ocean's* sports page "Colts Revel Amid Awful Scenes of Carnage" told it succinctly.[12]

NL star Jimmy Ryan joined Callahan in the AL in 1902 and 1903 with Washington.

Another milestone in Jimmy's budding career came on July 25, when he notched his first shutout in a 1–0 squeaker over Louisville, called after seven innings because of rain at Chicago. The Colts made their lone tally in the fourth when shortstop Bill Dahlen, playing his first game since suffering a spike wound to his leg on Memorial Day, stole home when Colonels pitcher Bert Cunningham and first baseman Perry Werden were arguing without calling time.[13]

Callahan's days on the slab were numbered, at least for 1897. His last pitching appearance was in relief of loser Walt Thornton as visiting St. Louis edged Anson's crew, 13–12, on August 4. From then on, Jimmy was used exclusively as a position player. By season's end, in addition to 23 pitching assignments, he had worked 30 games at second base, 21 in the outfield, 18 at shortstop, and two at third. He finished with a

.292 batting average — exactly that of the league — and a 12–9 mound log with an ERA of 4.18, slightly below the league norm. Although a competent outfielder, his infield play was below average.

Jimmy's first full year in the bigs had been a learning experience. He also liked Chicago, making it his permanent home. As soon as he had a decent amount of money saved, he became one of the best dressed men on his team, wearing expensive suits and the finest hats. Seldom was Callahan seen on the sidewalk without a walking stick, a boutonniere in his lapel, and a stickpin in his silk tie.

On February 1, 1898, Cap Anson was fired as manager and the Colts were soon renamed the Orphans by the press. Taking his place was former Chicago infielder Tommy Burns, who decided to use Callahan almost exclusively as a pitcher. It did not take long for Jimmy to emerge as the staff's number two ace behind Griffith.

Another "Anson Day" — sort of — was held at West Side Grounds on June 29, 1898. This time the celebration was for Anson's first game in Chicago at his new (and brief) job as manager of the New York Giants. In a pregame ceremony, he was presented with a huge floral horseshoe before a crowd of 12,000. Once again, the pitcher was Callahan, coasting to a 12–4 laugher over his former boss. Privately, Anson was probably happy for Jimmy, as he was already having problems with cantankerous Giants owner Andrew Freedman. He even stated in a newspaper interview, "I do not feel very disappointed about the game this afternoon."[14]

On July 6 Anson was relieved of his duties and replaced by Bill Joyce — whom Anson himself had replaced on June 11. The "hiring" had only been a publicity stunt on Freedman's part.

The Ansonless orphans turned out to be the surprise of the league. Although never in contention for the pennant, Chicago finished a strong fourth largely due to pitching. Callahan wound up the season with a flourish, winning his last three starts (including his only two shutouts, 2–0 over Baltimore on September 23 and 3–0 over Louisville on October 3) to finish at 20–10 while trimming his ERA to 2.46. However, his performance was overshadowed by Griffith, who had the best showing of his career with a 26–10 ledger and a league-best 1.88 ERA.

Fan enthusiasm was at a feverish level when the new season began, and Callahan was developing a habit of being on the hill for historic events. On Sunday, April 30, 1899, a throng of 27,489 packed its way into West Side Grounds for the largest paid attendance in baseball history up to that time. Due to the immense field crowd, it was ruled that any ball hit into the spectators would only be a single. Consequently, Jimmy weaved a 4–0 win over the Cardinals despite giving up 12 hits — all singles.

The Orphans looked like contenders until mid–July, when they started fizzling and ultimately ended in eighth place. No blame could be placed on Callahan, who went 21–12 with an eight-game personal winning streak midseason. His win total, innings pitched (294), complete games (33), strikeouts (77), and shutouts (three) were career highs. His victories included a three-hitter and three four-hitters.

The team's collapse cost Tommy Burns his position, as Tom Loftus was hired to manage the team in 1900. Over the winter, the National League contracted to eight teams as Baltimore, Cleveland, Louisville, and Washington were cast adrift. It would be the senior circuit's last structural change until 1953, when the Braves abandoned Boston for Milwaukee.

Charles Comiskey's Chicago White Sox of 1901 were led by pitchers Clark Griffith (front row, second from right), who finished at 24–7; Roy Patterson (back row, third from left), at 20–15; and Callahan (front row, far right), at 15–7.

By now Callahan had become one of the most popular players in Chicago. With back-to-back 20-win seasons behind him, expectations could not have been higher. Instead, the 1900 season was a major disappointment both for the Orphans (a fifth-place tie with the Cardinals) and for Callahan. While Jimmy was often betrayed by a punchless offense, his pitching was inconsistent and he finished with a 13–16 record, losing six of his last seven decisions with two ties called due to darkness. The worst embarrassment came in Philadelphia September 6, when the Phillies pounded him for 25 hits en route to a 20–5 slaughter. In his next start, five days later, the Giants stomped on Jimmy for 23 safeties in a 14–3 drubbing at the Polo Grounds. Both times Callahan was left in for the duration, easily the nadir of his pitching career. However, an important change in his baseball life was not far off.

The dawn of the 20th century brought new woes to the National League as it began its 25th anniversary year. The fledgling American League, founded by Cincinnati sportswriter Ban Johnson in 1893 as the Western League, a Midwestern minor league, declared itself major in 1901. When the National League refused to recognize its new competitor, the youthful confederation retaliated by raiding the older league's clubs, luring away established stars with plush contracts.

Johnson's associate Charles Comiskey had already relocated his St. Paul franchise to Chicago in 1900, taking the name White Stockings, which the National League club had discarded years earlier. On March 2, 1901, Clark Griffith signed with the White Stockings (soon to be shortened to White Sox), bringing Callahan and outfielder Sam Mertes with him shortly thereafter.[15] Thanks in part to the tight-fisted salary policies of owner Albert Spalding and his mouthpiece president James Hart, several more Orphans defected to the new circuit as well.

A broken arm sustained during spring training at Excelsior Springs, Missouri, delayed Callahan's White Sox debut until June 14, 1901. Understandably, Jimmy did not have his best stuff, but good batting support paved the way for a 10–5 triumph over the American League's first Orioles team at Baltimore. The *Chicago Chronicle* remarked that "at first it looked like he would get his bumps," but "Callahan settled down after the third and for the rest of the game shut out the Orioles."[16]

Callahan quickly made up for lost time to end the year at 15–8 with a career-best 2.42 ERA, lowest on the staff. He also aided his own cause with a .331 batting average. Highlights included a 17–3 romp over Washington (in which Jimmy drove in three runs with two singles and a triple) on July 24 and a 4–0 one-hitter versus Detroit on August 1, both at Chicago's South Side Grounds. Ironically, the Tigers' lone safety was a right field single by pitcher Joe Yeager to start the third inning.[17]

Fittingly, with Griffith as player–manager, the White Sox won the American League's first "official" pennant with an 83–53 record and a four-game lead over second-place Boston. (They had also won it in 1900 when the league was still "minor.") Griffith contributed 24 wins against just seven losses for a league-leading .774 percentage.

The championship was a case of "*sic transit gloria mundi*" as the White Sox slipped to fourth place in 1902. Seeing frequent service in the outfield, Jimmy put together a journeyman's 16–14 mark on the mound. He also pitched what were probably the two greatest games of his career — and one of them was a no-decision. On May 18 Callahan and Francis "Red" Donahue of the St. Louis Browns locked horns in a 2–2 draw that was called in the shadows after 17 innings before a Sunday assemblage of 15,819 at South Side Grounds. The headline of the Chicago *Inter-Ocean*'s sports page boasted "Callahan A Marvel." A caption beneath Jimmy's photograph read: "He pitched the game of his life against St. Louis yesterday. He struck out five men, allowed only eight hits, and made five himself in the 17 inning game between the White Sox and St. Louis."[18] Donahue proved to be every bit as tough. The *Chicago Chronicle* noted that "Donahue pitched nearly as well as Callahan" and "they had pitched magnificently, but towards the last, only their nerve was holding them up."[19] The Browns hurler squeezed himself out of numerous jams as the White Sox left 17 men on base, stranding runners in scoring position six times. As the *Chicago Tribune* observed, "It was a story of wasted opportunities for the White Sox."[20]

Saturday, September 20, 1902, was a damp, overcast day in Chicago. With temperatures hovering in the 50s, attendance at South Side Grounds was limited to 3,300 despite a rare "two for one" doubleheader with Detroit. These hardy souls witnessed history in game one as Callahan registered the junior circuit's first no-hitter, blanking the Tigers 3–0.

Relying on a low curve and occasional fastball, Callahan had a perfect game going for the first five and one third innings. Only by shortstop George Davis's throwing error did Detroit get its first baserunner, Deacon McGuire. He advanced a base on Ed McFarland's passed ball, but could go no further as the next two batters were easy outs.

Kid Elberfeld walked to start the Tigers seventh but was forced at second on Jimmy Barrett's grounder, after which Lew McAllister flied to center for out number two. Joe Yeager walked but Pete LePine grounded to Frank Isbell, who flipped to Callahan covering first base to end the would-be rally. Jimmy then was untouchable during the final two innings to preserve his gem.[21]

No-hitter or not, play was interrupted after the seventh inning for an "Amateur Day" ceremony. Headed by the *Chicago Dally News* band, 100 amateur players from five teams entered the park behind Cap Anson atop a brown horse, acting as grand marshal.[22] Charles Comiskey was given a set of fishing tackle while his wife received a bouquet of roses.[23] Furthermore, Callahan was pitching with a hangover. Jimmy was scheduled to be married soon, so some of his friends threw him a bachelor party at a neighborhood saloon the night before.[24] The second game ended in a 3–3 tie, called after seven innings by darkness.

Over the winter of 1902–1903 Comiskey released Clark Griffith from his contract so he could manage the American League's new team in New York, which replaced the struggling Baltimore franchise. On March 16, 1903, Callahan was named manager of the White Sox as Comiskey pompously proclaimed, "In my humble opinion — and mind you I have had years of experience in dealing with ballplayers — Callahan will make good both as a player and as a manager this year."[25]

While the season began with high hopes, they would soon be dashed. After splitting his first two pitching decisions, Callahan collected five hits (three singles, a double, and a triple) in a game he eventually lost to the Browns, 13–12, in 11 innings on May 8 at his home park.[26] It would be the last game he would ever pitch in the majors. Jimmy (or Comiskey) then decided he would relocate to third base. He enjoyed a good showing at the plate, as his .292 average was second on the team to Danny Green's .309 and 36 points above the league average. On the negative side, his 37 errors and .895 fielding average at the hot corner were the league's worst. And without Callahan and Griffith to lead the pitching corps, the White Sox sank to seventh place. A rash of injuries did not help either.

There were other managerial difficulties as well. According to David L. Fleitz: "To complicate things further for Callahan, Comiskey proved to be a hands-on owner, full of suggestions on running the team. Having won five pennants himself as a manager, Comiskey felt entitled to sit in the stands behind home plate at each game, make notes on the team's performance, and share his observations with 27 his field leader. He was also an impatient man...."[27]

On June 5, 1904, with the White Sox in fifth place at 22–18, Fielder Jones replaced Callahan as manager. Although the official story was that Jimmy had resigned and selected Jones as his successor, it was common knowledge that Comiskey had orchestrated the switch.

Jimmy remained on the team for the rest of that season and the next, although he was benched for several weeks in 1905 for allegedly being out of shape. He briefly tried his luck at second base, where he was no more successful than he had been under Anson, before settling permanently in left field.[28]

At Chicago on September 16, 1905, Callahan tied a club record (set by George Davis just three months earlier) by stealing four bases in a single game. With Fred Glade pitching for the Browns in the third inning, Jimmy singled and stole second. John "Jiggs" Donahue walked, after which they did a double steal. In the fifth Callahan coaxed a pass to first, then swiped second again. Donahue walked again and the pair executed another double pilfer. Since the Browns fell for the same trick twice in a row, one wonders where their brains were. To make it more bizarre, neither of the Callahan–Donahue filchings figured in the scoring. The Sox gathered eight runs in the first inning, three in the second, and one in the eighth for a 12–2 win.[29]

Semiprofessional baseball had been around in Chicago since shortly after the Civil War, and was occasionally profitable. Always the entrepreneur (and perhaps still miffed over his benching), Callahan formed his own semipro team in the Logan Square neighborhood on Chicago's Northwest Side. As expected, he was blacklisted by the National Commission for violating the reserve clause. It would be one of the most eventful periods of his career.

Callahan's Logan Squares began operation on Easter Sunday, April 15, 1906, at a ballpark on the southeast corner of Diversey Avenue and Milwaukee Avenue, close to the neighborhood's main business area. Appearing on the mound for the first time in nearly three years, Jimmy fanned nine batters and garnered two hits himself as he went the distance to beat Kenosha, 11 to 4. The *Chicago Chronicle* remarked that "Callahan showed fine control at all times and had the crowd with him all the way," and that "the new club played with major league speed." Umpiring the inaugural was Cap Anson.[30]

It soon became evident that Jimmy had one of the best semipro teams around. In addition to local talent, a handful of marginal major leaguers joined his ranks for varying lengths of time. Gus Dundon, who had played second base semi-regularly for the White Sox in 1904 and '05, spent most of 1906 with Logan Square as "Casey." Harry "Moose" McCormick, property of the Phillies, spent nearly the entire season in the Logan Square outfield under the name of "Harrison." Vive Lindaman of the Boston Beaneaters (Braves) pitched two games using the alias of "Evans."[31] Following one game, the *Chicago Tribune* observed: "'Evans' he was called on the program but he looked strangely familiar to major league fans."[32] Lou Fiene, a seldom used White Sox pitcher, hurled one game for Callahan and did not bother with a pseudonym.

During the first two weeks of July Jack McCarthy, a solid major league veteran, jumped ship from the Brooklyn Superbas (Dodgers) to join Logan Square before returning to the team that owned him. He, too, had no qualms about using his real name. The Logan Squares were given still more prestige when retired Cubs star Jimmy Ryan signed up on August 4 and remained through September 15 .[33]

With Callahan on the slab, the Logan Squares clinched the Chicago City League flag by beating a West Side team called the Athletics, 7–2, at Logan Square Park on October 14, 1906. On the same day, the White Sox shelled the Cubs in Game 6 of the World Series to capture the championship. Jimmy issued challenges to both teams, and they accepted.

On October 20 Jimmy twirled a three-hit, 2–1 nailbiter over 20-game winner Nick Altrock of the White Sox at Callahan's park. The *Chicago Inter-Ocean* described it as "no fluke" and that the Sox had "worked in deadly earnest."[34]

The following afternoon it was the Cubs' turn, again at Logan Square. Cubs ace Mordecai Brown was pitted against Chicagoan Tom Hughes, who had pitched for the Washington Senators during the season. Callahan stationed himself in left field. Hughes struck out seven of the first nine Cubs he faced, but Brown refused to be intimidated and the contest was scoreless as the Logan Squares came to bat in the last of the 10th.

The three-fingered wonder finally began to weaken, walking Nick Larson to start the inning. Callahan followed with a hard bouncer to David Brain of the Beaneaters, playing third base for the Cubs in place of Harry Steinfeldt. While Brain fielded the ball cleanly, his wild throw to Harry "Doc" Gessler at first put Logan Square runners at second and third. "Harrison" (McCormick) was then hit by a pitch to load the bags. With Charlie Reading at bat Brown's first offering went wild, allowing Larson to jog home with the only run needed.[35] Per the *Chicago Tribune*: "But for *an* error by one of the strangers in Mordecai's support, however, Brown and Hughes might have pitched a draw...."[36]

The *Chicago Evening Post* commented, "No wonder the National Commission declared Cal's Logan Squares an outlaw team. Herman[n] and Johnson and Pulliam must have had prophetic foresight." In an interview with the same paper, Callahan tweaked the noses of the baseball establishment by saying, "My only regret is that Ban Johnson, Augustus Herrmann and Harry Pulliam were not sitting in the front row to learn how it all happened."[37] Obviously, Jimmy enjoyed playing the role of curmudgeon. He was equally elated to claim city bragging rights, as he always regarded these twin triumphs as his proudest moment in baseball.

The excitement was far from over. On November 2, 1906, Callahan filed suit in Superior Court of Illinois for $3,000 in damages against Comiskey on an alleged breach of contract. However, his real target was the National Commission, whom he could get to only by suing the White Sox, as they were the party to his contract. According to the *Chicago Tribune*: "Attorney Thomas S. Kogan, counsel for Callahan, stated definitely the object of the suit is to provide in court evidence to show the national commission, which is the supreme court of organized baseball, is a worse trust than even the Standard Oil company is alleged to be." The paper then quoted the attorney as saying:

> Callahan was given a contract on March 1 last by the White Sox but was not given a position. On August 30 he was given another contract by Comiskey, who instructed the player to report at Detroit to the club. On his arrival he was informed he could not play, as Ban Johnson would not permit it.
>
> My client also asks that he be awarded his share of the $15,000 bonus which Comiskey gave to the White Sox players after their triumph over the Cubs in the world's championship series.[38]

Conveniently, Comiskey was out of town duck-hunting and could not immediately be reached for comment. American League president Ban Johnson was quick to respond, charging that Callahan "built a baseball park and organized a club which repeatedly has harbored ineligible players and violated the rules of organized baseball" and "said repeatedly that he made $12,000 out of his club this year."[39]

After additional loud-sounding posturing on both sides of the fence, the National Commission convened in Cincinnati on November 15. It resolved that Jimmy would be reinstated if he would pay a fine and divest himself of the Logan Square club, also adding that he was not entitled to any World Series money.[40] Not about to relinquish a profitable enterprise, Callahan balked at the terms, so the lawsuit died on the vine. As for Comiskey's bonus to his players, he viewed it as an advance on their 1907 salaries and acted accordingly.[41]

Callahan's next issue was what to do for an encore in 1907. The Logan Squares would not repeat as Chicago City League champions as they were bested by the Normal Parks, a South Side team. But Jimmy's bunch still performed solidly and profitably, as he drew some more aces out of his sleeve.

Callahan pulled a public relations coup in enticing the popular, hard-hitting Mike Donlin to leave the New York Giants for the Logan Squares. In addition to being a gate attraction, the colorful "Turkey Mike" led the charge to many a Logan Square victory with his broiling bat. This was especially so on June 16, when Donlin went 6-for-6 with two home runs, a double, and four runs scored in a 16–3 mauling of the Spaldings (no relation to Albert) at Callahan's home grounds.[42]

Generally appearing at first base, Donlin was with Logan Square from the start of the season through August 18, then rejoined the team for several barnstorming games in October after the regular season was over. Journeyman Jake Stahl, player–manager for the Senators in 1906, also defected to Chicago's semipro scene in '07. While he surfaced in a handful of games for Logan Square, Stahl spent most of the campaign with the South Chicagos of the city's old steel mill district. In early September Jack McCarthy decided to play hooky from Brooklyn again, linking up with Callahan for the rest of the year.[43]

Fans at Logan Square Park were given an additional treat on July 29 when Jimmy's outfit edged the South Chicagos, 2–1, in 11 innings. While the game itself was nothing exceptional, the umpire was former heavyweight champion John L. Sullivan.[44]

After being crushed by the Cubs in the 1907 World Series, the Tigers were welcomed at Logan Square Park on October 19 and 20. After the first game ended in an 8–8 draw, Detroit took the finale, 4–0, with emerging great Ty Cobb collecting a double and a triple. Although the exhibitions were well attended, they received only a fraction of the press coverage given to Jimmy's victories over the Cubs and White Sox a year earlier.[45]

The scribes did have a field day on December 18, when the sports pages of the Chicago papers were ablaze with stories about the American Association moving its St. Paul team to Chicago and turning it over to Callahan. However, there was considerable conflicting information (or misinformation?) regarding the likelihood of the proposal. The *Chicago Record–Herald* stated: "It is not at all unlikely that a third major league will be fighting for recognition ... the American Association magnates are going right ahead with their plans."[46] W.A. Phelon of the *Chicago Journal* was apocalyptic, prophesying "It will be baseball war all right, from present indications. All the peace talk sent out by the American Association was simply a blind, and the hustlers who make up their busy league were simply perfecting their plan of attack behind a curtain."[47]

The *Chicago Daily News* took a more cautious approach, noting that "The American Association, however, is not agreed on the policy of expansion.... Columbus, Indianapolis and Toledo are not in favor of the move to come to Chicago in opposition to the big leagues, but it is likely that they would favor coming to Chicago provided they could get consent from the big leagues to do so." The paper also quoted Gary Herrmann as saying, in so many words, that he did not take the threat seriously, as had a dispatch from Cincinnati in the *Journal*.[48] The *Chicago Tribune*, while conceding "there is a faction in the American Association which is secretly willing to precipitate a war," added that "the minor league would have difficulty securing a war fund even in times when money was plentiful. At present it seems impossible."[49]

The briefest summation was given by the *Chicago Evening Post*, stating bluntly: "The American Association will never establish a club in Chicago without the consent of the National and American league. The latter will refuse consent and it is known that the National League must follow the lead of the American League."[50] This analysis turned out to be correct, as all that materialized between Callahan and the American Association was his going to spring training at Galveston, Texas, in March 1908 with the Minneapolis Millers, playing a few games and serving as a correspondent for the *Minneapolis Evening Tribune*.[51]

As trivial as this seems in retrospect, it was enough to incur the wrath of the powers that were. P.D. Vroom, sports editor of the *St. Louis Post–Dispatch*, sent at least two telegrams to Garry Herrmann informing him that Jimmy was playing in exhibition games with the Millers against the Cardinals. Herrmann, in turn, contacted Ban Johnson. Johnson advised Herrmann to "proceed cautiously" and "quietly notify Mr. Robison" (Cardinals owner and president Matthew S. Robison) that his team must not play in any more games with Callahan. "I would go no further in this matter. What we want to avoid is giving this fellow too much publicity."[52]

It was also during that spring that Ty Cobb and veteran Tommy Leach of the Pirates expressed an interest in joining the Logan Squares. In all probability, they were not serious about it but were only using the threat of same as leverage in their contract negotiations.[53] Both soon came to terms with their overlords, and Cobb wound up getting twice what he had made in 1907. How Leach made out is unknown.[54]

By April Jimmy was back in Chicago getting ready for the regular league season. On April 19, 1908, Mike Donlin and Jake Stahl each paid a $100 fine and were reinstated by organized ball.[55] Donlin returned to the Giants while Stahl signed with the Yankees. On May 6 the National Commission adopted Rule 47, obviously aimed at Callahan, which enunciated:

> No national agreement player will be permitted at any time, either during the regular playing season or after or before the commencement thereof, to participate in any game with or against clubs harboring ineligible players or whose owners or managers are ineligible players. Every National Agreement player who hereafter violates this rule will be fined no less than $200 for the first offense.[56]

Although players did not always obey the new rule, there would be no more defections of any significance to Callahan from the majors. The loosely knit Chicago City League soon began having problems of its own. On June 14 the financially strapped Riverview Park team refused to open its gates for a League game versus the Marquettes. Two days later, Riverview was expelled from the circuit.[57] The City League initially announced that it would continue functioning with the seven remaining teams instead of eight, but on June 30 the magnates stated that the rest of their season schedule would be discontinued.[58] In effect, the league had disbanded, leaving its member clubs to play out the year as independents, along with the various nonleague semipro teams of Chicago. At the time of the abandonment, the Logan Squares were third in the league standings at 6–4 behind the black Leland Giants (8–0) and the West Ends (9–1). These figures did not include games between City League members and nonleague clubs, of which there were many.

With no more City League schedule, there would be no formal championship either. But league or no league, Callahan's team went on performing exciting baseball. On August 23 Jimmy had another former heavyweight titleist, Jim Corbett, umpiring his game against Cap Anson's Colts at the latter's ballpark. Callahan, playing center field, collected a double and a run scored in a 4–0 victory over his friend and former mentor.[59]

By the end of October, Callahan's barnstorming guests at Logan Square Park included the Millers, the Senators, and the White Sox. Jimmy's warriors split two with Minneapolis, while another contest was called because of darkness tied after 10 innings. Against the Senators and White Sox the Logan Squares failed to win a game as both beat them twice.[60] On October 10 Callahan found the young Walter Johnson of Washington an easy mark, gathering a single, a double, and a home run off the future Hall of Famer. Jimmy's supporting cast did not as Johnson coasted to an 11–2 cakewalk.[61]

As all of this was in defiance of Article 47 cited above, the National Commission went ballistic, naming 18 players who were to be fined the full amount and possibly blacklisted. Under the headline "Former Star of Big Leagues Now Chuckles as He Draws Magnates Into Mess," James Crusinberry of the *St. Louis Post–Dispatch* snickered, "He [Callahan] is smarter by many points than any member of the National Commission ... the commission hoped to rob Callahan of a bit of profit gained at his little ball park in Chicago."[62] Tempers cooled over the winter, the fines were reduced to $50, and all the players (excluding Callahan) regained good standing.

It was also during the winter of 1908–1909 that Callahan began supplementing his income by taking to the stage on the vaudeville circuit. He would relate humorous personal baseball experiences along with "telling Irish stories in a colorful brogue that entertained his audience and enhanced his popularity in Chicago."[63] In this capacity he met Broadway producer and baseball fan George M. Cohan. As with Anson, Lange, and Griffith, it developed into a lifelong friendship.

In 1909 the all but defunct City League was reorganized as the Chicago Baseball League with six clubs joining, including Jimmy's. While still a strong team, the Logan Squares had to be content with a second-place finish as the Leland Giants copped the city flag. Unlike the previous three seasons, this one was essentially free from controversy.[64] One of Callahan's pitchers was 21-year-old Chicagoan Eddie Stack, who later had a brief career (1910–1914) with the Phillies, Dodgers, and Cubs. Postseason competition with organized ball consisted of just two losses to the White Sox on October 16 and 17.[65]

On a more ominous note, Chicago's interest in semipro ball was now on the decline (only temporarily, as it turned out), as the Logan Squares were reportedly the only club in the new league to turn a profit. Anson's Colts had been a colossal failure in their three years of existence, forcing the old-time hero into bankruptcy.[66] Callahan did not ignore the warning signs.

The situation became more apparent as the 1910 season began. The Chicago Baseball League's schedule was trimmed by 10 games. And for the first time, the Logan Squares suffered a losing record as they finished a distant fourth behind (in order) the West Ends, Chicago Giants, and Rogers Parks. Nevertheless, Jimmy's team would make history one more time.

Comiskey Park, the new home of the White Sox, opened with fanfare on July 1, 1910. On August 27, the Logan Squares and Jimmy Ryan's Rogers Park team played an exhibition game under the lights at Comiskey's "Baseball Palace of the World" for the first night game in a major league arena. The *Chicago Tribune* enthusiastically reported:

> Night baseball played under the glare of nineteen arc lamps was tried successfully last night at Comiskey's new Sox park, Callahan's Logan Squares defeating the Rogers Parks in a well-played contest, 3 to 0.
>
> The test ... met with the satisfaction of 3,500 baseball bugs and with the leaders and

players of both teams. The game was played under exactly the same conditions as a contest in broad daylight.

The ball could be followed as readily as if thrown under natural light, and the players declared that nothing interfered with their vision.[67]

Patrolling left field, Callahan contributed a single and a double, driving in two runs. The venerable Ryan, who had purchased the Rogers Park club the previous year, had a single. The Logan Squares last played under Callahan's command on October 30, in a 3–1 barnstorming loss to the Cubs. Jimmy Callahan was not in the lineup himself, but treated the Cubs players to a banquet after the game.[68] Obviously, he was not a sore loser.

But a losing team meant diminished revenue, so Jimmy decided to quit while he was ahead. He had wisely remained on cordial terms with Comiskey after their split, and this paved the way for his return. After selling out his interests in the Logan Squares, Callahan rendered a $700 fine and was reinstated in the majors.[69] On February 17, 1911, he officially rejoined the White Sox at their departure to Mineral Wells, Texas, for spring training.

Although somewhat rusty, Jimmy enjoyed a good spring and was selected by manager Hugh Duffy as his starting left fielder. He would retain the position for two seasons.

For the first time in their history, the White Sox scored 20 runs in a game on May 11, 1911, as they crushed the Senators, 20–6, at Comiskey Park. For his part in the slaughter, Callahan knocked two singles and a home run in six at-bats. Through six and a half innings, Chicago nursed a 7–6 lead. Jimmy's home run on the first pitch in the bottom of the seventh ignited a seven-run rally to put the game on ice, after which they added six more in the eighth. Covering the game for the *Chicago American* was "Bill Bailey,"[70] the pen name of William Veeck, Sr., who later became president of the Cubs under William Wrigley.

Ed Walsh had thrown 464 innings in his epic 40–15 season of 1908.

Callahan finished the year with a respectable .281 average and career highs in hits (131) and RBI's (60). His batting average was .281 and his 45 stolen bases were fourth in the circuit. It was a remarkable comeback for a 37-year-old who had been out of the majors for six years. The White Sox climbed to fourth in the standings after a sixth-place finish in 1910.

Apparently the team had not improved enough to suit Comiskey, as he fired Duffy and named Callahan as manager in 1912. In what was his last real season as a player Jimmy remained the regular left fielder, batting .272. His second reign as the Sox field boss began with rare promise, and the pale hose were leading the league with a sizzling 26–8 record through May 25. But reality quickly set in thereafter. By July 29 they were 47–45 and had settled in fourth place, where they finished at 78–76. Once again, interference from Comiskey proved to be an obstacle, as it had during Callahan's earlier tenure as manager.

The following March Callahan was beset with

another headache — ace pitcher Ed Walsh's arm went dead. According to one story, he threw his arm out while showing off in front of a church group without warming up first.[71] A more likely explanation was that his "souper" was simply worn out from overwork. Walsh had labored (excluding 1909) anywhere from 369 to 464 innings every year 1907–1912, not counting exhibition games. He would never again be part of the regular rotation.

During the 1913 season Callahan became a bench manager. Of his six scattered playing appearances, all but one were as a pinch-hitter. Even with Walsh generally on the sidelines, the White Sox boasted the stingiest pitching in the junior circuit. Their 2.33 ERA was lowest in the league, as were their 492 runs allowed. Unfortunately, they batted only .236 as a team while scoring a mere 486 times, both at the bottom of the totem pole. The result was a slip to fifth, although they won the same number of games as in 1912 with two fewer losses. The Sox had to win their games by way of pitching, defense, and manufacturing runs. This would be a recurring pattern throughout the club's eight decades at the Old Roman's coliseum.

His playing days now over, Callahan finished with a .273 lifetime batting average and 901 hits. As a pitcher, he was 99–73 with a 3.39 ERA. He completed 169 of his 177 starts.

On November 13, 1913, the White Sox and the New York Giants embarked on a world tour to commemorate the 25th anniversary of Albert Spalding's venture of 1888–1889, following almost the same route. Callahan, Comiskey, Giants manager John McGraw, and their wives were naturally part of the excursion. The players, however, were actually a mixture of Giants and White Sox combined with selected stars from other teams. Features of the tour included a triple play in front of the Egyptian Pyramids on February 2, 1914, a private audience with Pope Pius X at the Vatican on February 9, and an exhibition game for King George V of England on February 26.[72] The party arrived at New York Harbor on March 6, then returned home to Chicago three days later.

While the papal blessing hopefully aided the pilgrims in their spiritual lives, the visit with the British monarch did not result in the teams being kings in their own realms. The Giants, after three straight pennants, were dethroned by the "Miracle" Boston Braves and finished a distant second. The White Sox started the new season with five successive wins but it was all downhill from there as they tumbled to a tie for sixth with the Yankees, costing Jimmy his job as manager.

Callahan was then kicked upstairs to the front office as business manager, tending office deals and doing occasional scouting. Comiskey finally shelled out some money for quality players in 1915, getting Eddie Collins from the Athletics and later Joe Jackson from the Indians. Suddenly, the White Sox were contenders again with a strong third-place showing. But Callahan was uncomfortable with a desk job and resigned after one season.

In retrospect, it appears to have been a mistake. First signed to manage the Los Angeles Angels of the Pacific Coast League, Jimmy canceled out when Barney Dreyfuss offered him the position of Pirates field manager.[73] Callahan inherited a club largely composed of no-names and aging veterans, including Honus Wagner, now nearing the end of his rope. Pittsburgh finished a feeble sixth in the standings in 1916.

The predicament went from bad to worse the following year. With the team in last place owning a 20–40 record, Jimmy was fired on June 30, 1917, and replaced by Wagner. Wagner did not like the job and resigned after five games, as Hugh Bezdek piloted the

Pirates from June 3 onward. Losing the position was a blessing in disguise for Callahan, for Pittsburgh remained buried in the cellar, when seventh-place Brooklyn finished 20.5 games ahead of the sunken Pirate ship. Jimmy's complete record as a major league manager was a mediocre 394–458 for a .462 percentage. In fairness, he had little top-notch talent to work with. This ended his baseball career except for some brief scouting for the Senators 10 year later.

During his post-baseball years Callahan ran a construction company in Chicago, enabling him and his family to live quite well. He was socially active, being a member of the Chicago Athletic Association, Knights of Columbus, and South Shore Country Club. Never losing his love for baseball, Jimmy was a frequent visitor at both Comiskey Park and Wrigley Field.[74]

Callahan also continued his moonlight occupation in vaudeville. He was visiting (and appearing on stage with) his old friend George M. Cohan when he died in his sleep of a heart attack at Boston's Parker House Hotel on October 4, 1934. Surviving him were his wife of 32 years Josephine (Hardin), his daughter Margaret (Mrs. Paul Barry), and two sons, Daniel and James Jr.[75]

Since it was the ballplayer's wish to be buried in his native town, Requiem Mass was offered at St. Bernard's Roman Catholic Church in Fitchburg on October 8, with burial at the parish cemetery. Father James Donahue celebrated the Mass while Father Martin Forhan conducted the graveside rites, assisted by Father P.J. McDonough of East Jaffrey, New Hampshire, and Father John Feeney of Manchester, New Hampshire. Pall bearers included Cohan, Jack Doyle of the Cubs scouting system, and Melvin Webb, sportswriter for the *Boston Globe*. Concurrently, a memorial Mass was also held at Callahan's adopted parish, St. Anselm's, at 47th Street and Ellis Avenue on Chicago's South Side. Even in death, Jimmy Callahan had covered all the bases.[76]

Abstract

Although largely forgotten today, Jimmy Callahan enjoyed an exciting and historically significant career during the late 19th and early 20th centuries. The son of Irish immigrants, Callahan remains the only person in the annals of Chicago baseball to have starred for both the Cubs (before they were known by that name) and the White Sox, *and* to have run his own semiprofessional ball club. During his stay in the major leagues, he participated in numerous history-making contests and tossed the American League's first no-hit game on September 20, 1902. As player-proprietor of the Logan Square semipro team on Chicago's Northwest Side, Callahan led his club to victories over both the Cubs and the White Sox following the 1906 World Series in which the White Sox had beaten the Cubs. Perhaps more importantly, his tenure in Logan Square helped expose the pettiness and hypocrisy of baseball's establishment.

Notes

1. *The Cherry Circle* (magazine of the Chicago Athletic Association), January 1935.
2. Fleitz. D. 2009. *The Irish in Baseball: An Early History* (p. 125).
3. *Chicago American*, Oct. 5, 1934, p. 23. Also from undated *New York Clipper* article in Callahan's Hall of Fame file.

4. *Sporting Life*, Jan. 30, 1897, p.l.
5. *Baseball's First Stars*. Society for American Baseball Research (SABR), 1996, p.20.
6. This and several other "inside stories" were told to the author by James J. Callahan Jr. (1915–1987), with whom he was a friend from 1967 onward.
7. *Sporting Life*, Jan. 30, 1897, p. 1.
8. Callahan Jr., pers. comm.
9. *Chicago Tribune*, Apr. 27, 1897, p. 5.
10. Ibid., May 5, 1897, p. 4.
11. Callahan Jr., pers. comm.
12. *Chicago Inter-Ocean*, June 30, 1897, p. 6.
13. Spatz, L. 2004. *Bad Bill Dahlen* (p. 50).
14. *Chicago Times–Herald*, June 30, 1898, p. 6.
15. Lindberg, R. 1983. *Who's On Third? The Chicago White Sox Story* (p. 23).
16. *Chicago Chronicle*, June 15, 1901, p. 8.
17. *Chicago Inter-Ocean*, Aug. 2, 1901, p. 4.
18. Ibid., May 19, 1902, p. 4.
19. *Chicago Chronicle*, May 19, 1902, p. 6.
20. *Chicago Tribune*, May 19, 1902, p. 6.
21. *Chicago Dally News*, Sept. 20, 1902, pp. 1–2, the only paper to carry a complete play-by-play.
22. Ibid.
23. *Chicago Inter-Ocean*, Sept. 21, 1902.
24. Callahan Jr., pers. comm.
25. *Chicago Inter-Ocean*, Mar. 17, 1903, p. 7.
26. *Chicago Chronicle*, May 9, 1903.
27. Fleitz 2009, 125.
28. *Chicago Chronicle*, June 6, 1905, p. 5.
29. *Chicago Daily News*, Sept. 16, 1905, p. 2.
30. *Chicago Chronicle*, Apr. 16, 1906, p. 8.
31. Unidentified newspaper clipping in Callahan's personal file, in the author's possession since 1987.
32. *Chicago Tribune*, Aug. 27, 1906, p. 8.
33. Ibid., July 2 through July 16, 1906, and Aug. 5 through Sept. 16, 1906.
34. As quoted from Schmidt, R. 1986. "The Semi-Pro Team That Beat the Champs," in *Baseball in Chicago* (pp. 22–23).
35. Ibid.
36. *Chicago Tribune*, Oct. 22, 1906, p. 10.
37. *Chicago Evening Post*, Oct. 22, 1906, p. 6.
38. Callahan Jr., pers. comm.
39. *Chicago Tribune*, Nov. 4, 1906, p. 10.
40. *Chicago Daily News*, Nov. 16, 1906, p. 5.
41. Lindberg 1983, 28.
42. *Chicago Tribune*, June 17, 1907, p. 7.
43. Ibid., Apr. 22 through Oct. 7, 1907.
44. Ibid., July 30, 1907, p. 6.
45. Ibid., Oct. 21, 1907, p. 5.
46. *Chicago Record–Herald*, Dec. 18, 1907, p. 7.
47. *Chicago Journal*, Dec. 18, 1907, p. 9.
48. *Chicago Daily News*, Dec. 18, 1907, p. 6.
49. *Chicago Tribune*, Dec. 19, 1907, p. 10.
50. *Chicago Evening Post*, Dec. 18, 1907, p. 8.
51. Callahan's *Evening Tribune* articles of March 18, 19, and 20, 1908, are part of the author's Callahan collection.
52. From telegrams and Johnson letter from Callahan's Hall of Fame file.
53. McKenna, B. "Jimmy Callahan and His Logan Squares," baseballhistoryblog.com in Callahan's Hall of Fame file.
54. McCallum, J. 1975. *Ty Cobb* (pp. 62–63).
55. *Chicago Tribune*, Apr. 20, 1908, p. 10.
56. McKenna.
57. *Chicago Tribune*, June 17, 1908, p. 19.
58. Ibid., July 1, 1908, p. 14.

59. Ibid., Aug. 24, 1908, p. 8.
60. Ibid., Sept. 20 through Oct. 19, 1908.
61. Ibid., Oct. 20, 1908, p. 3.
62. *St. Louis Post–Dispatch*, Oct. 20, 1908, p. 14.
63. Fleitz 2009, 125.
64. *Chicago Tribune*, Apr. 25, 1909, p. 2.
65. Ibid., Oct. 18, 1909, p. 6.
66. Fleitz, D. 2005. *Cap Anson: The Grand Old Man of Baseball* (pp. 294–299).
67. *Chicago Tribune*, Aug. 28, 1910, p. 2.
68. Ibid., Oct. 31, 1910, p. 2.
69. Fleitz 2009, 129.
70. *Chicago American*, May 12, 1911, p. 10.
71. Callahan Jr., pers. comm.
72. Charlton, J. 1991. *The Baseball Chronology* (p. 181).
73. *Sporting Life*, Dec. 25, 1915, p. 10.
74. *The Cherry Circle.*
75. Ibid.
76. Unidentified newspaper clipping, probably Fitchburg, in author's Callahan collection.

Eadweard Muybridge and Baseball-in-Motion

Rob Edelman

Aficionados of 19th century photography, early motion pictures—and baseball—surely will be captivated by certain still photos and moving images that populate the internet. Google the words "Muybridge" and "baseball," and you will come up with websites featuring photographic images, dating from the 1880s, that undoubtedly galled those who embraced the era's Victorian reserve. These images are of young males *sans* clothing, and who are depicted pitching, batting, catching, throwing, running and picking up a ball, and catching and dropping a ball.

The "Muybridge" in question is Eadweard Muybridge, a seminal figure in the history of the moving image in that he was the first to employ photography in a comprehensive study of the dynamics of motion. Simply put, Muybridge made a series of still photographs of his subjects. He then laid them out in chronological order to produce what in essence were moving images, which could be studied to determine the nature of motion. In so doing, Muybridge was creating a kind of motion picture several years before the actual invention of motion picture technology.

Muybridge was born Edward James Muggeridge in 1830 in Kingston upon Thames, England. He came to the United States in the early 1850s, worked in the publishing and book-selling industries, and returned home at decade's end. While in England, he became intrigued by still photography and soon came back to the United States. He eventually settled in California and, by 1867, he was calling himself "Eadweard Muybridge" and describing himself as an "artist-photographer." In subsequent years, he took countless landscape photos; one of his most successful projects was a series, titled *Scenery of the Yosemite Valley*, which was published in 1868.

A prime assignment for Muybridge came in 1872 when Leland Stanford, the railroad tycoon and former governor of California, hired him to photograph a horse while trotting. It was Stanford's belief that, when a horse trots, all four of his hooves are off the ground and in the air in certain moments: a hypothesis that only could be conclusively proven by capturing images that otherwise are imperceptible to the naked eye. Stanford had in fact placed a $25,000 bet that this was true, and hired Muybridge to help him

Rob Edelman is the author of *Great Baseball Films* and *Baseball on the Web*. His books include *Meet the Mertzes*, a double-biography of *I Love Lucy*'s Vivian Vance and fabled baseball fan William Frawley, coauthored with Edelman's wife, Audrey Kupferberg. His byline has appeared in *Baseball and American Culture: Across the Diamond, Total Baseball, Baseball in the Classroom: Teaching America's National Pastime*, and dozens of other books. He has been a juror at the National Baseball Hall of Fame and Museum's annual film festival. Edelman is a lecturer at the University at Albany, where he teaches courses in film history.

 DOI: 10.3172/BB.7.62

win the wager. Muybridge's initial photographs — the first-ever lateral images of a trotting horse — were inconclusive, but a different set he made soon afterward convinced Stanford that his theory was correct.

By this time, Muybridge no longer was content merely to photograph scenery or other still images. He became fascinated by the possibilities of serial photography, of creating groups of still images which gave the appearance of movement when placed side-by-side or in a circular fashion. With the financial support of Stanford, he began a series of experiments in which he photographed animals in motion. This project was stalled when he was arrested, tried, and acquitted for the 1874 murder of Major Harry Larkyns, who was having an affair with his wife, Flora. However, Muybridge returned to his experimentation in earnest three years later.

In image and orthography, Eadweard Muybridge was an eccentric.

His accomplishments at this juncture included the development of a camera shutter that allowed him to photograph each image in a fraction of a second. He also lined up 12 still cameras, each with an electromagnetic shutter, to simultaneously photograph trotting horses in sequence — and then repeated the experiment, only this time with twice as many cameras. The resulting images, which illustrated the horses' movements in exacting detail, were extensively printed in a range of periodicals — and brought Muybridge international acclaim. Furthermore, he concocted what came to be known as the zoopraxiscope: a device that may be the first-ever projector of images in motion. The zoopraxiscope projected onto a lighted screen a succession of still images that were affixed to slides, which then were placed on spinning glass disks. Each image depicted the subject in motion in split-second intervals, resulting in a repetitive moving image.

And then, beginning in 1884 and working at the University of Pennsylvania, Muybridge took between 20,000 and 100,000 photographs — accounts of the exact number differ greatly — of humans and animals in motion. He enhanced his image-making methodology by employing the newly available dry plate (or gelatin) technology, which simplified the photographic process. Representative images from this landmark effort were printed in *Animal Locomotion* (the complete title is *Animal Locomotion: An Electro-Photographic Investigation of Consecutive Phases of Animal Movements*), published in 1887 "under the auspices of the University of Pennsylvania." Each subject was photographed by 12 cameras, and it is noted in the prospectus for *Animal Locomotion* that "the complete movement" of each was "accomplished in about one and a half seconds." Additionally, the images "are reproduced from the original negatives by the photo-gelatine [sic] process of printing, without any attempt having been made to improve their pictorial effect, either in outline or detail; or to conceal their imperfections."

Of the 781 images in *Animal Locomotion*, 16 relate to baseball. Their plate numbers are 273–288. The first is labeled "Base-ball; pitching." Five are "Base-ball; batting." One is "Base-ball; batting (low ball)." One is "Base-ball; catching." Five are "Base-ball; catching and throwing." One is "Base-ball; throwing." One is: "Base-ball; running and picking up ball." The final plate is "Base-ball; error."

All the models are identified only by three different numbers: 25, 26, and 30. According to the prospectus, the "greater number of [human models] engaged in walking, running, jumping, and other athletic games are students or graduates of The University of Pennsylvania — young men aged from eighteen to twenty-four — each one of whom has a well-earned record in the particular feat selected for illustration." With this in mind, the most likely "baseball models" are in fact ballplayers. The most noteworthy is Thomas Love Latta (1865–1961), a catcher and captain of the varsity nine. The other two are Robert Edward Glendinning (1867–1936) and Morris Hacker Jr. (1866–1947).

Other sports are featured in the volume, with models rowing, kicking a football, tossing a spear, playing lawn tennis, performing a somersault, and swinging a different kind of bat — this one used to play cricket. Two men box, while two others fence. Other types of physical activities are featured, with models walking, climbing up and down, turning, curtsying, hopping, dancing, sitting, kneeling, or performing such simple tasks

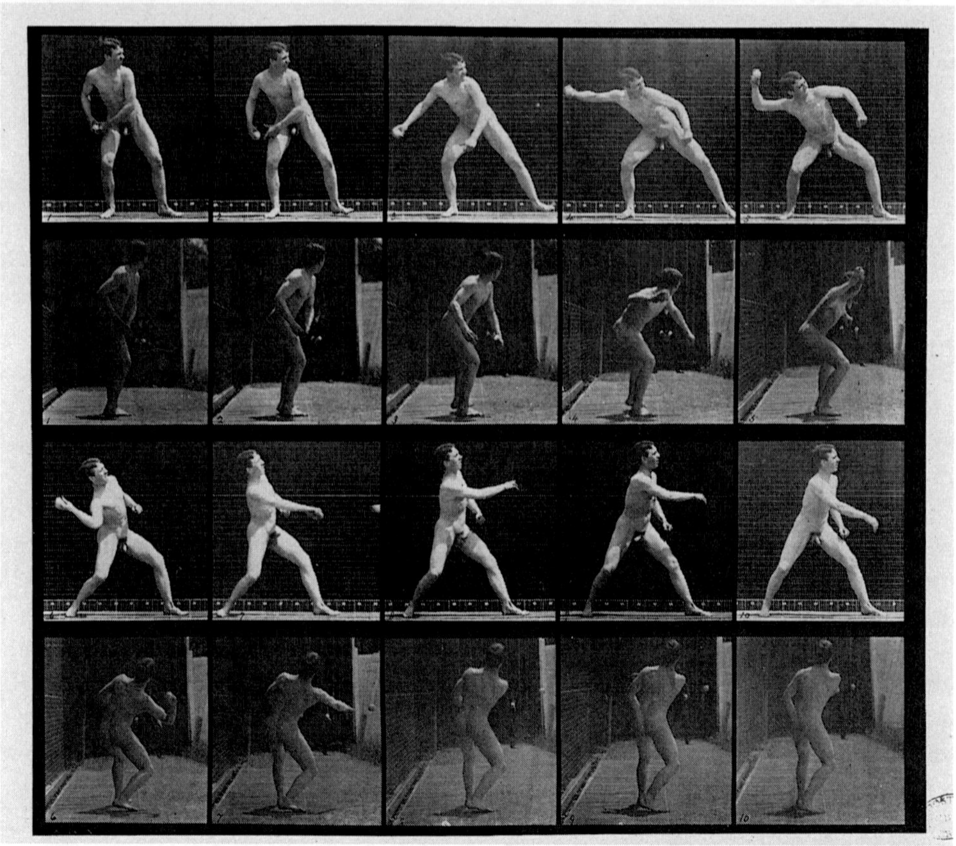

In Plate 273 of* Animal Locomotion, *Muybridge's subject exhibits the dynamics of the sidearm throw. University of Pennsylvania baseball players were models in this series.

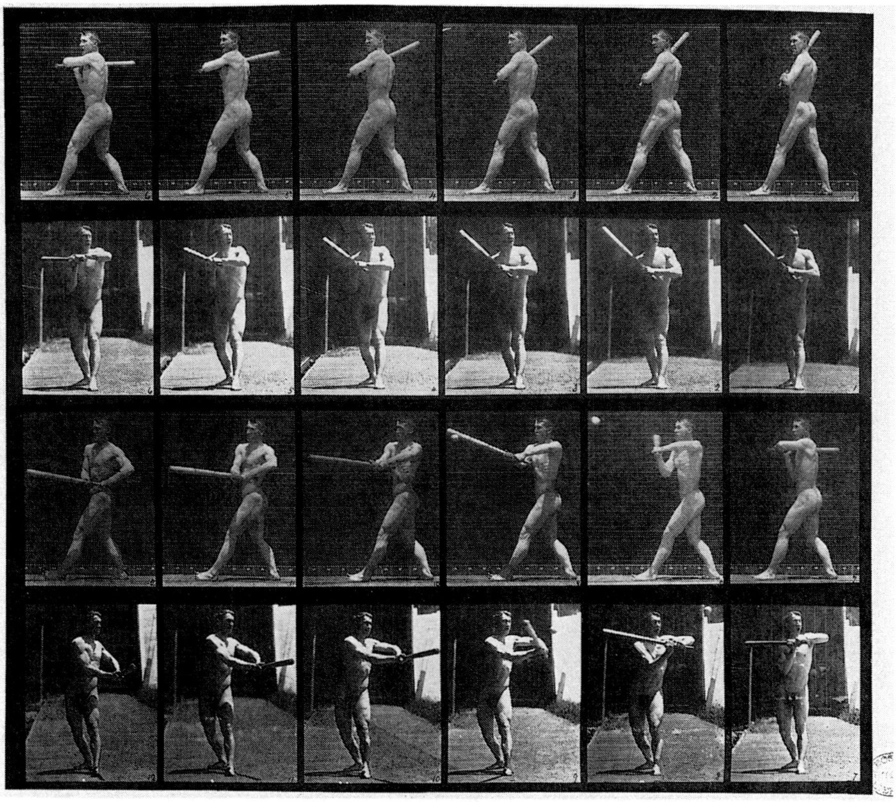

Student athletes from Penn included George Brinton, Robert Edward Glendenning, Frank Bird Gummey, Thomas Love Latta, and Morris Hacker, Jr.

In Plate 276 of Muybridge's Animal Locomotion, *the 24 frames again depict the batting sequence, as in Plate 274 above.*

In 16 images, Plate 278 above illustrates a batting form that might have made scouts wince even in 1887, even if they had not averted their eyes from prudery.

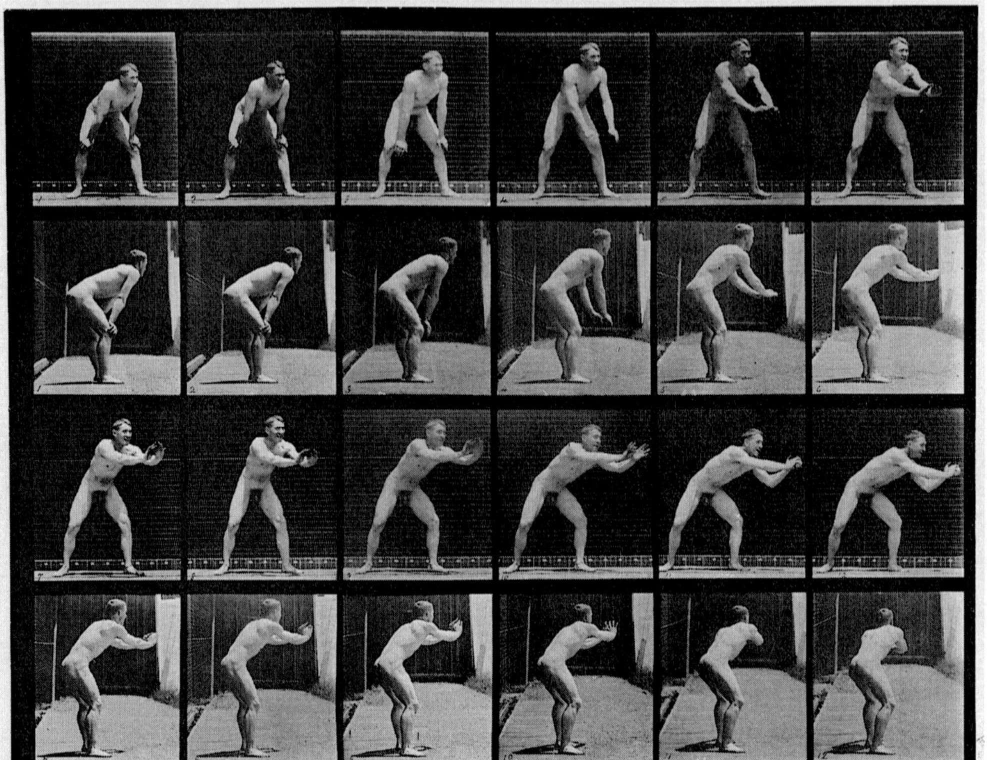

Muybridge's Plate 280 illustrates the technique of catching the thrown ball in a day when not only the hands were bare.

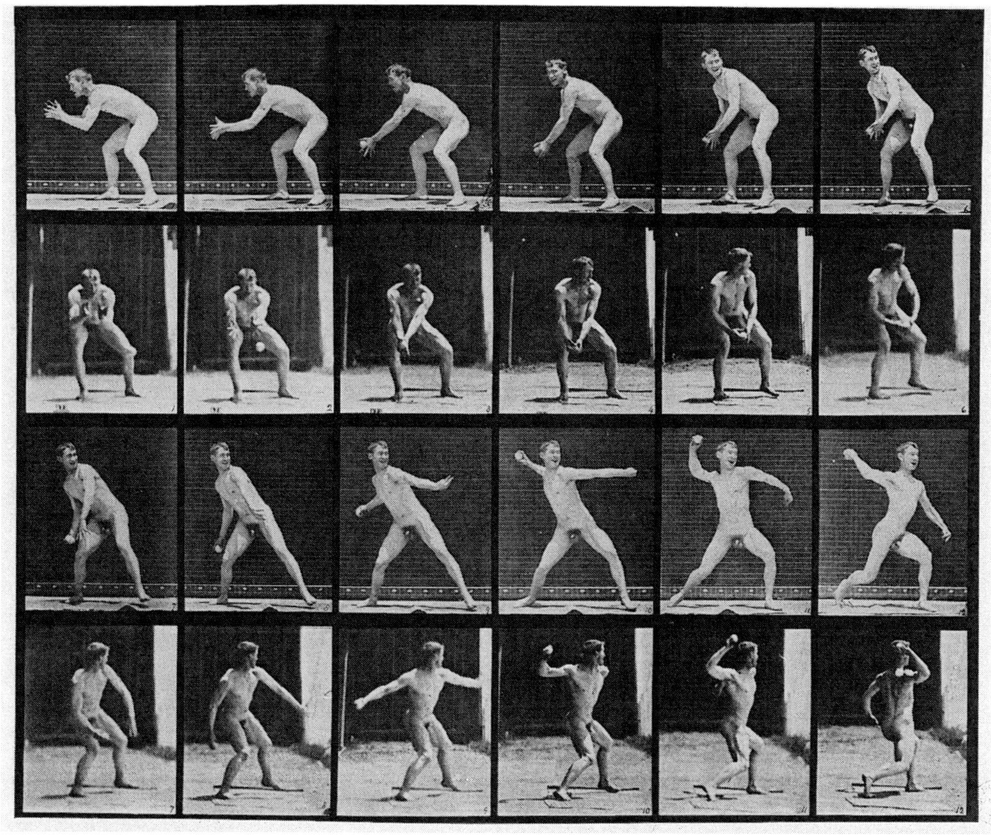

Plate 283 depicts what might have been a third baseman's technique in catching a low bounder and rising to make the throw.

Plate 285 offers what may have been a middle infielder's sidearm flip after catching a rather easy ground ball.

as emptying a basin of water, dropping and lifting a handkerchief, getting into and out of a hammock, making a bed, feeding a dog, and washing, wringing, and ironing clothes. Physically disabled individuals are photographed. Blacksmiths, carpenters, masons, farmers, miners, and bricklayers are shown plying their trades. A wide range of animals and birds are presented in motion, from baboons and buffalo to dogs and deer to goats and gnus to hawks, vultures, cockatoos, pigeons, eagles, storks. Not surprisingly, a great number of horses — saddled and unsaddled, with and without riders — are represented.

It was noted in an article printed in 1886 in *The Pennsylvanian*, the university's student publication, that "all the prominent University athletes, men and women in the various operations of every-day life, and almost every representative animal in the Zoological Garden, have been caught by the camera in every conceivable posture and active motion." But clearly, the images of athletes were the most appealing. As proof that ballplayers held the same fascination in the 1880s as they do today, the paper added that

> ... the part most interesting to University men is the delineation of the athletic sports, foot-ball and base-ball, running, jumping, vaulting and wrestling. Nearly every well-known University athlete of the past two or three years has served as a model in the nude, many of them showing magnificent physiques, and exhibiting exquisitely the play of every muscle. The facial expressions in successive intervals of some feat of skill and strength, is a study in itself.

Of the images taken of a ballplayer catching and dropping a ball, *The Pennsylvanian* quoted Muybridge: "See how curiously ... and yet how perfectly, this plate illustrates the occurrence of an error in catching." The publication continued, "True enough. In the successive pictures the ball is muffed, strikes the player's thigh, runs up under his arm and across his back, while he is looking eagerly on the wrong side for it."

11. Athletes. Base Ball; Batting.

A rendering from* Descriptive Zoopraxography, or the Science of Animal Locomotion Made Popular, *1893.

At the very least, *Animal Locomotion* served to redefine the movement of living things, not to mention the manner in which this movement was recreated in paintings and sculpture. And then, at the 1893 World's Columbian Exposition in Chicago, visitors paid an admission fee to view Muybridge's moving images. He also offered talks on his work and published a monograph, the complete title of which is *Descriptive Zoopraxography; or, The Science of Animal Locomotion Made Popular*, which was available "as a memento of a series of lectures given by the author under the auspices of the United States Government Bureau of Education at the World's Columbian Exposition, in Zoopraxographical Hall, 1893." In its preface, it is noted that the zoopraxiscope "is set in motion, and a reproduction of the original movements of life is distinctly visible to the audience.... By this method of analysis and synthesis the eye is taught how to observe and to distinguish the difference between a true and a false impression of animal movements." But animals are not the sole living creatures featured in *Descriptive Zoopraxography*. The reproduced images are drawings, rather than photographs. One is of a ballplayer swinging a bat. For the sake of propriety, this hitter is clothed.

Muybridge eventually returned to England, where he passed away in Kingston upon Thames in 1904 — just as the motion picture was beginning to advance beyond its baby steps. Nonetheless, his place in the history of moving image technology is secure. For after all, before such pioneers as Thomas A. Edison, W.K.L. Dickson, and Auguste and Louis Lumière, there is Eadweard Muybridge. Before the earliest baseball films — the 50-foot-long *The Ball Game* (1898), for example, or *Casey at the Bat* (1899), which runs the same length — there are Muybridge's ever-so-brief moving images that are labeled "Base-ball; pitching," "Base-ball; batting," "Base-ball; catching and throwing," and "Base-ball; error."

Abstract

Eadweard Muybridge is a pivotal figure in the evolution of moving image technology in that he was the first to employ photography in a comprehensive study of the dynamics of motion. Beginning in 1884 and working at the University of Pennsylvania, Muybridge took thousands of images of humans and animals in motion, with each subject simultaneously photographed by 12 cameras. Some were college baseball players; as a result, Muybridge created split-second-long moving images of ballplayers pitching, batting, catching, throwing, and running.

Works Cited

Books

Muybridge, E. 1887. *Animal Locomotion: An Electro-Photographic Investigation of Consecutive Phases of Animal Movements.* Philadelphia.

_____. 1893. *Descriptive Zoopraxography; or, The Science of Animal Locomotion Made Popular.* Chicago.

Muybridge's Human Figure in Motion. Mineola, N.Y. 2007.

Articles

Millard, C. 2013. "Running Through His Mind: 'The Inventor and the Tycoon,' by Edward Ball." *New York Times*, Jan. 25.

"Topics of the Time. Muybridge and the Athletes," *The Pennsylvanian*, vol. 2, no. 13, 1886.

Web

Chicago Magazine: www.chicagomag.com/Chicago-Magazine/The-312/July-2011/Chicago-Home-of-the-Worlds-First-Movie-Theater/

Library of Congress Online Catalog: http://catalog.loc.gov/
National Gallery of Canada: www.gallery.ca/en/see/collections/artwork.php?mkey=24720
UCR/California (University of California, Riverside) Museum of Photography: www.cmp.ucr.edu/collections/permanent/object_genres/photographers/muybridge/index.html
University of Pennsylvania: The University Archives and Records Center: www.archives.upenn.edu/faids/upt/upt50/muybridgeeguide.pdf http://www.archives.upenn.edu/histy/features/muybridge/muybridge.html

Bud Fowler

A Knight of the Diamond, a Knight of the Razor

Hugh MacDougall

The speech upon which this article is based was delivered at the 2013 Fred Ivor-Campbell 19th Century Baseball Conference in Cooperstown.

This year, 2013, marks the centennial of the death of John W. Jackson, better known by his playing name of Bud Fowler, who is generally considered as the first professional African American baseball player. He grew up here in Cooperstown, and as you know, our mayor will later today be formally designating a small and hitherto unnamed street leading from Chestnut Street to Doubleday Field as "Fowler Way."

Bud Fowler's 30-year career in baseball has been summarized in every recent book on early baseball, and in many recent articles. Some of them cover his whole career, like that of the Baseball Biography Project of the Society of American Baseball Research,[1] others concentrating on specific periods in his long and complicated life.[2] The first book-length biography, Jeffrey Laing's *Bud Fowler: Baseball's First Black Professional*, is scheduled to appear in July.[3]

I shall not today try to go over Fowler's baseball career in detail. Much of it has already been told, mostly from contemporary newspaper stories. Rather, I want to consider Bud Fowler as the human being, whom we are honoring in Cooperstown today.

Childhood

Bud Fowler was born on March 16, 1858, as John W. Jackson, in the Mohawk Valley town of Fort Plain. As an infant he was brought by his parents to the overwhelmingly white community of Cooperstown. In 1860 it had only 28 African Americans, and only six children under 18, out of a population of about 1,600. In 1870, 13-year-old Bud was one of only six black children attending the local public school.[4] A schoolmate — James Fenimore Cooper, the grandson of the famous author — would later recall: "There played with us a little black boy, Johnnie Jackson, who felt his color so much that he used to

A retired American diplomat, **Hugh MacDougall** is the official Village historian of Cooperstown, New York, and an avid researcher into history. In 2012 and 2013 he presented to the Frederick Ivor-Campbell Conferences on 19th century baseball, held in Cooperstown, papers on the life of Abner Graves, whose 1905 letters first led to Cooperstown's identification as "the home of baseball," and on "Bud Fowler," the first professional African-American baseball player, who grew up in Cooperstown.

DOI: 10.3172/BB.7.71

say that, if it would make him white, he would willingly be skinned alive. What became of Johnnie ... I don't know—[he] just faded out of life."[5]

Ironically, perhaps, this James Fenimore Cooper would in 1936 become the first President of the National Baseball Museum.[6] However accurate Cooper's recollection may have been, the anecdote reflects something important about Bud Fowler: He had grown up with white companions—and for the rest of his life he wanted to live as an equal among America's majority racial group.

Bud Fowler said he learned to play baseball, undoubtedly with white companions, on the grounds of the Cooperstown Seminary on Chestnut Street,[7] which in 1869 would become the Cooper House Hotel.[8] A hotel poster, printed after 1879, shows young men playing a very informal game of baseball in a field to the left of the hotel.[9]

A Knight of the Razor

What lay behind this unusual man? Everything written about Bud Fowler notes, if only in passing, how he continued to practice the barber trade he had learned from his father. Many contemporary newspaper stories mention it.[10] But what baseball writers have overlooked is that this made him a Knight of the Razor—a black barber who shaved white customers. Like his ancestors, Bud Fowler was a member of a unique fraternity—almost a medieval guild—in 19th century African American culture.

This is one of only two known images of Fowler. Here he is, age 27, with the Keokuk Hawkeyes of the Western League in 1885.

His father—John Henry Jackson—was a barber who practiced his trade in Cooperstown and Oneonta for at least two decades. His mother was the daughter of a barber, and they had many barber cousins in towns like Fort Plain along the Mohawk Valley.

What was this guild of barbers, who dominated the barbering trade during much of the 19th century, competing successfully against whites, and forming a great percentage of the small African American middle class? How did they succeed in a nation filled with racial discrimination? In the words of one modern scholar: "Barbering was servile. White customers felt comfortable being shaved by a black barber. The proprieties were preserved. The black man was in deferential attendance on the white man. African-American men who were careful to show they "knew their place" could do well as barbers."[11]

And they did. The Knights of the Razor became a tightly knit community of men, organized along traditional trade-craft lines, and often closely related by family ties. They formed a network around the country, in which traveling black barbers like Bud Fowler could count on finding colleagues and work.[12]

After the Civil War, black barbers faced increasing competition in big cities from white immigrants, especially Italian barbers who brought their craft with them to America.[13] Some turned to serving black customers in the rapidly growing black parts of those cities. Others moved to smaller communities in the interior.

Baseball Beginnings

Sometime after 1870 Johnnie left home, and in 1877 we find him playing baseball in a Boston suburb for the amateur Chelsea Franklins, under the name of John Fowler.[14] He pitched several games against the professional Lynn Live Oaks, a team belonging to the International Association, and *The New York Clipper* gave him his first review, writing of one game that "the pitching of both clubs was excellent."

Why he left Cooperstown, what brought him to Chelsea, and why he permanently adopted the last name of Fowler all remain mysteries today. Because John Fowler routinely addressed fellow players as "Bud," he was given that nickname, and after about 1890, as in modern baseball writing, he was usually called just Bud Fowler. That is how he signed his public letters, and what I call him in this paper.

Then on April 24, 1878, Fowler pitched for a so-called "Pickup Nine" team, largely chosen from the Chelsea Franklins, against the professional Boston Red Caps—a National League team that would eventually become today's Atlanta Braves. Its more experienced and older pitcher, Tommy Bond, was already a rising baseball star.[15] Nevertheless, the amateurs defeated the Boston Professionals 2–1, with Fowler on the mound. Perhaps as a result, when the Lynn Live Oaks' regular pitcher developed a lame arm,[16] Fowler was asked to join that team as pitcher for at least three games. This made him the first African American to play professional baseball in America—the title he has borne ever since.

Local newspapers were impressed.[17] The next year Fowler pitched for the Malden team of the Eastern Massachusetts league,[18] and then disappears from the papers for a time. His entry into baseball was written up in some detail last year, in SABR's *Nineteenth Century Notes*, by his current biographer Jeff Laing.[19]

Throughout his playing career Bud Fowler proved himself a gifted pitcher and catcher, and a superb second baseman. As *Sporting Life* put it in 1885: "With his splendid abilities he would long ago have been on some good club had his color been white instead of black. Those who know say there is no better second baseman in the country; he is besides a good batter and fine base-runner."[20]

The list of white teams on which Fowler played includes, more or less in order, teams in Niles, Ohio; Keokuk, Iowa; Stillwater, Minnesota; Pueblo, Colorado; Topeka, Kansas; Binghamton, New York; Montpelier, Vermont; Laconia, New Hampshire, Crawfordville, Indiana; Santa Fe, New Mexico; Greenville, Michigan; Galesburg, Illinois; Burlington, Iowa; Lincoln, Nebraska; Findlay, Ohio; Lansing, Michigan; and Lima, Ohio.

For over twenty years Fowler's skill as a baseball player was the object of praise.[21] As he neared the end of his playing career in 1908, he could be called "the greatest colored ball player who ever lived."[22]

But Bud Fowler was also a polite, courageous, and above all persistent human being both on and off the baseball field. It would be hard to find a baseball player of any time or place who devoted himself to America's game more thoroughly or for a longer time.

Baseball Manager

After 1894 Fowler concentrated on organizing touring black baseball clubs, beginning with the Page Fence Giants, sponsored by a wire fence company and a bicycle manufacturer.[23] The Page Fence Giants travelled in a special parlor car bearing its name in gilt letters, and with comfortable quarters for the players, including a kitchen, and

> a [large] apartment which is the dining, sitting, and sleeping room combined.... There are twelve upholstered chairs. The berths—20 in all—swing in toward the wall, so that they look like panels in the side of the car. The floor of the dining room is covered with a pleasing design, and the sitting room is carpeted.... Double windows prevent any dust from getting in and also keep out the cold and damp air more effectively.[24]

At each stop, the players mounted bicycles for a parade through the streets leading to the playing field. With this arrangement, Bud Fowler had solved three problems: He provided his team a comfortable place to sleep and eat in an America where hotels were rarely open to African Americans; he provided an entertainment show that made white residents willing to accept the game as something more than an athletic contest; and he advertised his sponsors.

Bud Fowler left the Page Fence Giants after one season, apparently caught up in a repeated dream—which never quite materialized—of leading a black baseball team to the Pacific Coast, or even to Europe or Australia. The rest of his active baseball life was a mixture of playing, organizing, and managing baseball teams.

In 1899 Bud Fowler organized the Black Tourists Colored Base Ball team, intended to provide white audiences with both sport and entertainment. Fowler advertised that: "A feature of this club will be daily parades, which will be made in full dress suits, black pants, white vests, swallow-tailed coats, opera hats, silk umbrellas. The club will play its games in full dress suits."[25] A Denver paper patronizingly promised that: "The darkies

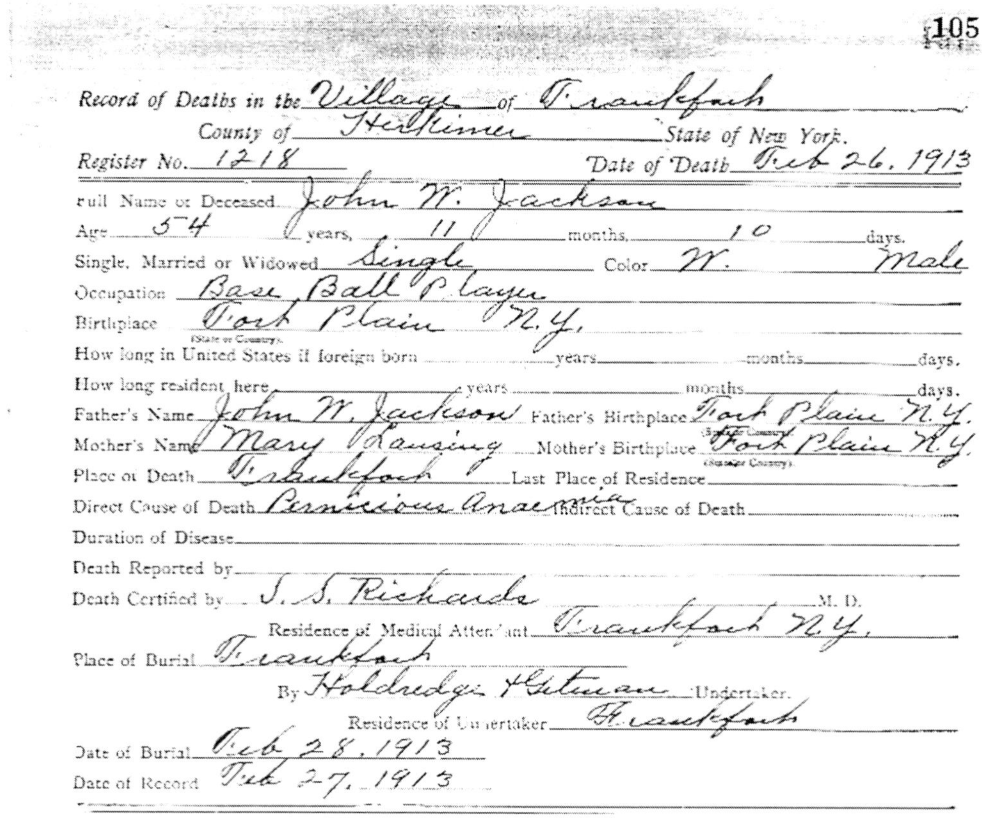
105

Record of Deaths in the Village of Frankfort

County of Herkimer State of New York.

Register No. 1218 Date of Death Feb 26, 1913

Full Name of Deceased John W. Jackson

Age 54 years, 11 months, 10 days.

Single, Married or Widowed Single Color W. Male

Occupation Base Ball Player

Birthplace Fort Plain N.Y. (State or Country.)

How long in United States if foreign born ____ years ____ months ____ days.

How long resident here ____ years ____ months ____ days.

Father's Name John W. Jackson Father's Birthplace Fort Plain N.Y. (State or Country.)

Mother's Name Mary Lansing Mother's Birthplace Fort Plain N.Y. (State or Country.)

Place of Death Frankfort Last Place of Residence

Direct Cause of Death Pernicious Anaemia Indirect Cause of Death

Duration of Disease

Death Reported by

Death Certified by S. S. Richards M. D.

Residence of Medical Attendant Frankfort N.Y.

Place of Burial Frankfort

By Holdredge & Getman Undertaker.

Residence of Undertaker Frankfort

Date of Burial Feb 28, 1913

Date of Record Feb 27, 1913

Fowler's death certificate states his occupation as "Base Ball Player," but he was more than that. A century after his death, his pioneering path shines more brightly than ever.

are a funny lot and the games will furnish a combination of skill and frolic."[26] Though its continuity is not clear, Fowler continued to run versions of his Black Tourists team on and off through 1911. And while his dreams of America's far west continued, he never got farther than western New York.

It remains difficult to untangle the complete story of just where Bud Fowler played, what teams he actually organized or managed, and how much was just journalistic rumor and speculation. But for many reasons, financial and otherwise, few of his further dreams came to fruition.

Discrimination

We shall never know more than a fraction of what Bud Fowler faced from the racial animosity of fellow players, of opposing teams, of owners and managers, or of baseball fans. Like a good barber, a true Knight of the Razor, he had learned how to keep his mouth shut, and usually did so. But in 1895, he is said to have summed up his real problem, allegedly telling *Sporting Life*: "My skin is against me. If I had not been quite so black, I might have caught on as a Spaniard or something of that kind. The race prejudice is so strong that my black skin barred me."[27]

Twice Fowler was summarily dismissed from teams when they discovered his race. In 1881, the Guelph Maple Leafs of Ontario released him on arrival when some team members objected. A local paper was openly critical: "Fowler is a well-behaved young man and it is not at all to the credit of the Maple Leafs to treat him as they have done."[28]

It was the same in 1888, when a team in Lafayette, Indiana,[29] fired him as soon as he showed up. This time, Fowler made his anger known. As reported by *Sporting Life*, "He claims that he asked for his release on account of the prejudice he found to exist in the board of directors and patrons of the game against his race."[30]

And at least twice Fowler was dropped from teams after playing with them for some time. The Binghamton Bingos "released" him in 1887, with the stipulation that he never play for a member of the International League.[31] In a public letter, Fowler insisted he had left voluntarily to accept a "flattering offer from the management of the Cuban Giants," and thanked the Binghamton public "for their kind and courteous treatment of me at all times."[32]

He did not, in fact, join the Cuban Giants, the then very popular black baseball team — with nothing to do with Cuba — but moved north to captain the baseball team of Montpelier, Vermont, where he not only played well but "seemed to be the favorite with the spectators and was greeted with applause every time he stepped to the plate."[33]

Fowler drifted from Organized Baseball to the Findlay, Ohio, semipro club of 1894.

Years later, Fowler told what had happened: "Did you ever hear the story of the way the negro ballplayers were sidetracked? ... There were six of us in the International, back in '87, and the white players sent in a protest to the League Directors, who passed a rule that in the future no colored players other than those then under contract should be signed.... That is how the color line was sprung by a lot of boot-legs."[34]

In 1894 and 1895, Fowler had successfully directed and played on an independent white team in Findlay, Ohio. But, when he returned there in 1899 it turned on him. As the press put it: "The white members of Findlay's ball club have drawn the color line, and have demanded ... that Bud Fowler, colored, be ousted from their team. They will quit if their demand is not heeded."[35]

Only two photographs of Bud Fowler seem to exist. The most familiar is a team picture of the 1885 Iowa Keokuks,

Besides Fowler, the Findlays also featured Grant (Home Run) Johnson. The club was strong enough to play the Cincinnati Reds and the Cuban Giants.

where Fowler stands, arms at his sides, between and lower than four white men, looking very much the outsider. Another is with the Ohio Findlays in 1894. It is commonly said that white players often refused to appear in photographs showing their team's lone black member.

Some white players sought deliberately to injure Fowler. An anonymous baseball player told the *Sporting News* in 1889:

> I could not help pitying some of the poor black fellows that played in the International League. Fowler used to play second base with the lower part of his legs encased in wooden guards. He knew that about every player that came down to second base on a steal had it in for him and would, if possible, throw the spikes into him.... About half the pitchers try their best to hit these colored players when [they are] at the bat.[36]

Bud Fowler made an eloquent public protest against racism on February 12, 1908, following a rambling, two-hour public speech in Binghamton by the notoriously racist South Carolina Senator Benjamin Tillman.[37] Tillman had asserted that "the Negro is but slightly removed from the baboon," and that black children were "as far below the Asiatics as earth is below heaven." A believer in "America for the Americans," he rhetorically asked whether his Northern audience had "ever thought what it means for a white man to work under a negro's heel?" A newspaper account said he also "calmly announced that it had been decided that it would be necessary to kill some negroes." Part of the Binghamton audience hissed and walked out, including some African Americans who were present. Others applauded.

Bud Fowler's response appeared the day after Tillman's talk was reported in the press, suggesting that he may have attended Tillman's lecture. In what seems a mixture of anger and despair, Fowler agreed with Tillman that Northerners were ignorant of the race problem — but only because they "never had the experience of dealing for years in that disgraceful traffic [in] slavery." Tillman had spoken of eight million African Americans, but Fowler reminded him that this failed to include some 7,000,000 others of mixed ancestry "who are body, flesh, soul and blood of the Senators' ancestors."

Senator Tillman had quoted from a French nursery rhyme. Bud Fowler countered with two of his own:

> He's good enough among his race,
> And that alone is his true place,
> I don't regard him for his skill.
> He's nothing but a negro still.
>
> If Jim should take my little farm
> And make it yield just like a charm,
> From it my empty pockets fill.
> Why Jim is just a negro still.

And Fowler concluded with the unfinished thought: "The bravery the negro possesses through which our armies have been successful.... But why discuss that? He's nothing but a negro still."[38]

Fowler's letter is sprinkled with half a dozen Bible citations, including one from Galatians: "There is neither Jew nor Greek, there is neither bond nor free, there is neither male nor female: for ye are all one in Christ Jesus."

Ending

I wish I could say that Bud Fowler, who had devoted his life so fully to baseball, and to the equality of African American players, could have had a happy old age, supported when needed by the sport to which he had contributed so much. It was not to be.

In September 1908 *Sporting Life* reported that Bud Fowler was dying of consumption, destitute, and living with his sister Harriet in Frankfort, New York, on the Mohawk River some 25 miles west of the Fort Plain where he was born.[39] In its next weekly issue, it quoted a maxim it attributed to Fowler: "Fewer flowers to the dead, and a little more charity to the living would help some."[40]

In the spring of 1909 an effort was launched to hold a benefit game for Fowler in Brooklyn,[41] but nothing came of it.[42] Nor did a second effort in November.[43]

For a time Fowler's medical condition apparently improved, the *Sporting Life* writing:

> "Bud" Fowler, the veteran colored player ... writes us from his home in Frankfort, N.Y. that he has not consumption at all. An X-ray examination has revealed the fact that he has for six years been suffering from an injury sustained while stealing a base in Indianapolis. He broke the lower left rib, which bent inward, growing on the end hard flesh which pierced a kidney. Fowler has had the rib removed by an operation and is now

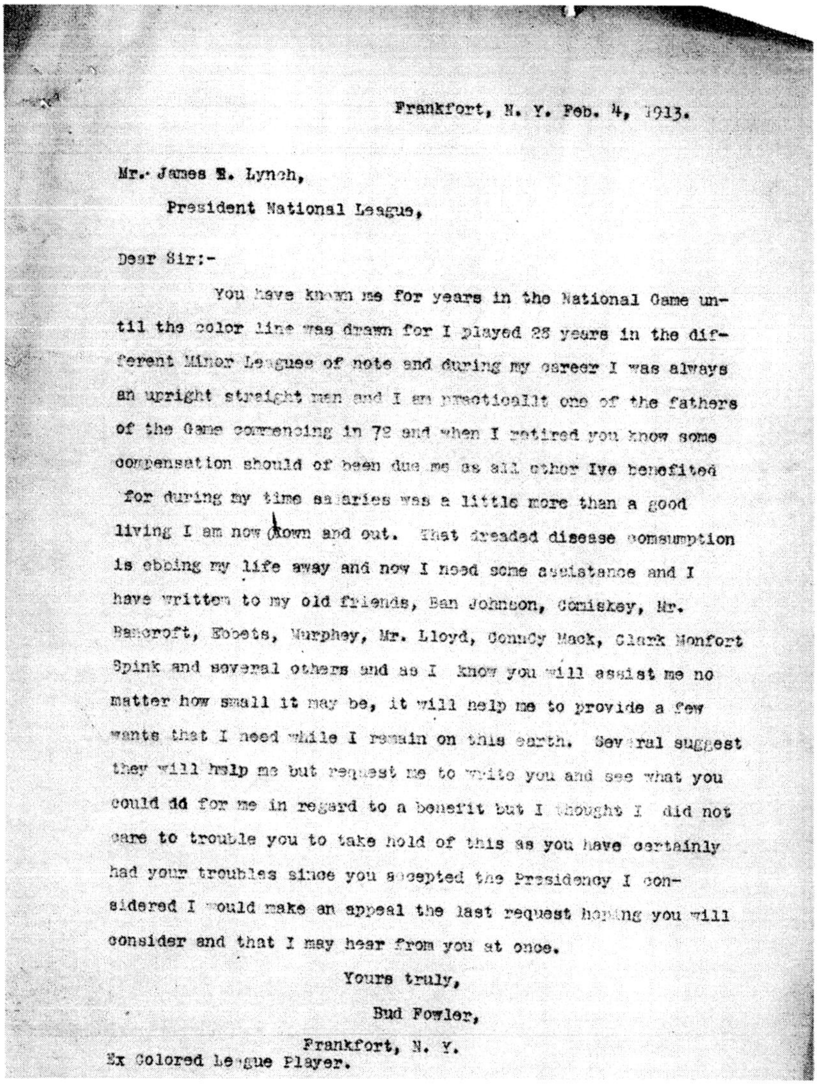

Frankfort, N. Y. Feb. 4, 1913.

Mr. James E. Lynch,

President National League,

Dear Sir:-

You have known me for years in the National Game until the color line was drawn for I played 25 years in the different Minor Leagues of note and during my career I was always an upright straight man and I am practicallt one of the fathers of the Game commencing in 72 and when I retired you know some compensation should of been due me as all other Ive benefited for during my time salaries was a little more than a good living I am now down and out. That dreaded disease consumption is ebbing my life away and now I need some assistance and I have written to my old friends, Ban Johnson, Comiskey, Mr. Bancroft, Ebbets, Murphey, Mr. Lloyd, Connie Mack, Clark Monfort Spink and several others and as I know you will assist me no matter how small it may be, it will help me to provide a few wants that I need while I remain on this earth. Several suggest they will help me but request me to write you and see what you could dd for me in regard to a benefit but I thought I did not care to trouble you to take hold of this as you have certainly had your troubles since you accepted the Presidency I considered I would make an appeal the last request hoping you will consider and that I may hear from you at once.

Yours truly,

Bud Fowler,

Frankfort, N. Y.

Ex Colored League Player.

In the year of his death, Fowler sent this plaintive letter to National League President James Lynch. Note that he states the year of his onset in baseball as 1872.

> rapidly recovering his health and strength. He has just composed a base ball song which he has dedicated to the National Commission. It deals with Cooperstown, N.Y., where the game was first named.[44]

Unfortunately, I haven't located the song.

Bud Fowler's last years were summarized, after his death on February 26, 1913, in a newspaper from Gloversville, New York—another small city in the Mohawk Valley:

> John W. Jackson, the one time famous baseball player, known as "Bud" Fowler, died a few days ago at the home of his sister, Mrs. John Odom of Frankfort, N.Y. Jackson was well known in this city having spent some time in this vicinity two years ago. He camped at Vandenberg's pond ... and had a number of boats which he rented to fishermen. During the cold weather he came to this city where he worked at the barber shop of Adelbert

> Dana.... He left here for New York, where he was taken ill and later left the metropolis for Frankfort, where he died.... [He] was for about a year a resident of Amsterdam [New York], conducting a barber shop ... at the corner of Market and Shuler streets. While there he organized a colored ball team for a tour of the western states, but owing to ill health was obliged to sell his interest in the team.

The Knight of the Diamond had completed his course; the Knight of the Razor had returned to his old trade. But his health continued to deteriorate. Early in February 1913, he wrote a despairing letter to James Lynch, president of the National League: "I am now down and out ... and now I need some assistance."[45] He had written to many old friends, he said, and while some had promised help, most had evidently referred him to Lynch. "I know you will assist me," he concluded, "no matter how small it may be, it will help me provide a few wants that I need while I remain on this earth."

President Lynch sent him back a two-line response, suggesting that he apply to the Ball Players Fraternity. Three weeks later John W. Jackson, alias Bud Fowler, was dead.[46] Buried in Fort Plain, he didn't have a tombstone until SABR provided one in 1987.[47]

Abstract

Bud Fowler (1858–1913), real name John W. Jackson, grew up in Cooperstown, New York, and in 1877 became America's first professional African American baseball player with the Lynn (Massachusetts) Live Oaks of the International Association. In a baseball career that lasted more than 30 years, he became a superb second baseman on otherwise white teams, and—as racial discrimination in baseball increased—a manager of innovative touring black teams. His success in the game he deeply loved was made possible in part by his alternate profession as a black barber—a member of a professional fraternity which dominated the shaving of white customers during much of the 19th century. This assured him employment in communities throughout the United States.

Notes

1. McKenna, B. "Bud Fowler." http://sabr.org/bioproj/person/200e2bbd
2. See, e.g., in more or less chronological order: Robertson, C. 2012. "Bud Fowler Childhood Home Research," a paper prepared for the Cooperstown Graduate Program; Laing, J. 2012. "Bud Fowler's Big Break," SABR, Nineteenth Century Notes; Tholkes, B. 1993. "Bud Fowler and the Stillwaters," in D. Anderson, ed., *Before the Dome: Baseball in Minnesota When the Grass Was Real* (pp.79–82); White, R. 1992. "Baseball's John Fowler: The 1887 Season in Binghamton, New York," *Afro-Americans in New York Life and History* 16.1; Laing, J. 2011a. "Bud Fowler in Santa Fe (1888): The Myth of the West for 19th Century Baseball's First African American Baseballist," *Base Ball* 5.2, 52–62; Laing, J. 2011b. "Bud Fowler's Coming of Age: The Making of an African American Baseball Pioneer in 1889," *Black Ball* 4.2, 5–16; Heaphy, L. 2011. "The Page Fence Giants: Nineteenth Century Champions," *Black Ball* 4.2, 76–83; Morris, P. 2009. "Bud Fowler's Lost Years," *Black Ball* 2.2, 10–23; Simkus, S., ed. 2012. "Bud Fowler's Last Appeal," *Outsider Baseball Bulletin* 3.45.
3. Laing, J. 2013. *Bud Fowler: Baseball's First Black Professional.*
4. See my compilation of African American census information in Otsego County at: http://theusgenweb.org/ny/otsego/aacensus/aacensus.htm
5. Cooper, J. 1921. *The Legends and Traditions of a Northern County* (p. 101).
6. *A History of Cooperstown*, New York State Historical Association, 1976, p. 51 (hereafter cited as "History of Cooperstown"). This is a chronological compilation of village histories and chronicles mostly based on the weekly *Freeman's Journal* newspaper.

7. It had been built in 1854. *History of Cooperstown*, 251.

8. *History of Cooperstown*, 66.

9. Poster in my possession, bearing the name of Simeon E. Crittenden, who became the Hotel's proprietor in 1879.

10. *Sporting Life*, Sept. 23, 1885, p. 5; *Denver Rocky Mountain News*, Jan. 17, 1887, p. 2; *Santa Fe New Mexican*, Sept. 28, 1888, p. 4; *Lincoln Evening News*, Nov. 21, 1892; *Adrian Daily Telegram* (Michigan), Aug. 30, 1894, p. 3; *St. Paul Globe*, Nov. 14, 1904, p. 5; *The Gloversville Morning Herald* (N.Y.), Mar. 3, 1913, p. 2.

11. Winch, J., ed. 2000 (orig. 1841). *The Elite of our People: Joseph Willson's Sketches of Black Upper-Class Life in Antebellum Philadelphia* (p. 20).

12. Bristol, D. 2009. *Knights of the Razor: Black Barbers in Slavery and Freedom.* A perhaps similar book—*Shaving Men, Grooming Race: A History of Black Barbers and Barber Shops, 1830–1970*, by Quincy Mills—is forthcoming.

13. Boyd, R. "Ethnic Competition for an Occupational Niche: The Case of Black and Italian Barbers in Northern U.S. Cities During the Late Nineteenth Century, *Sociological Focus* 35.3, 247–266. http://dx.doi.org/10.1080/00380237.2002.10570702.

14. The 1877 game is the first known reference to Fowler as a baseball player; previous accounts have always given 1878.

15. See: http://en.wikipedia.org/wiki/Tommy_Bond_(baseball); http://en.wikipedia.org/wiki/Major_League_Baseball_Triple_Crown

16. *Boston Daily Advertiser*, May 18, 1878, p. 1; *Boston Daily Globe*, May 20, 1878, p. 4, and May 25, 1878, p. 1. This was probably a George Price, born about 1850, a single man who in 1880 was working in a shoe shop in the shoe-manufacturing Boston suburb of Marlborough, and living as a boarder. See US Census, State of Massachusetts, Middlesex County, Town of Marlborough, p. 47, 294–461. Baseball accounts simply identify him as "Price" or, occasionally, "G. Price."

17. *Boston Daily Advertiser*, May 18, 1878, p. 1; *Boston Daily Globe*, May 18, 1878, p. 4.

18. *Boston Herald*, May 22, 1879, p. 4; July 11, 1879, p. 2.

19. Laing 2012.

20. *Sporting Life*, Dec. 30, 1885.

21. *The New York Clipper*, May 18, 1878, p. 61; *Muskegon Chronicle* (Michigan), May 23, 1884, p. 3; *Springfield Daily Illinois State Journal*, May 14, 1885, p. 8; *Santa Fe New Mexican*, Sept. 28, 1888, p. 4; *Saginaw News* (Michigan), Nov. 7, 1889; *Omaha Daily Bee*, Feb. 1, 1891, p. 8; *Adrian Daily Telegram* (Michigan), Aug. 30, 1894, p. 3; *Sporting Life*, May 17, 1902; *Indianapolis Freeman*, Mar. 11, 1905, p. 7.

22. *Sporting Life*, Sept. 19, 1908, p. 2.

23. Wikipedia, Negro League Baseball.

24. *Adrian Daily Telegram* (Michigan), Apr. 1, 1895, p. 3.

25. E.g., *San Antonio Daily Light*, Aug. 16, 1899.

26. *Denver Post*, Sept. 22, 1899, p. 9.

27. Allegedly from *Sporting Life* in 1895, and often quoted—but without specific citation. I cannot find it in the online files of *Sporting Life* at: http://search.la84foundation.org/search?site=default_collection&client=default_frontend&output=xml_no_dtd&proxystylesheet=default_frontend&proxycustom=HOME/

28. *Toronto Globe*, July 4, 1881 (reprinted from the *Guelph Mercury*). When Fowler then moved on to the nearby Petrolia Imperials, his new teammates there so harassed him that he had to quit. At least this last Canadian stint eventually brought him recognition: In 2006, he was posthumously inducted into the Black Hockey and Sports Hall of Fame in Dartmouth, Nova Scotia.

29. *Logansport Pharos Tribune* (Indiana), Mar. 27, 1888.

30. *Sporting Life*, Apr. 18, 1888, p. 2.

31. *Harrisburg Patriot* (Pennsylvania), Aug. 9, 1887, p. 1, and many other papers.

32. *Binghamton Daily Leader*, c. July 2, 1887, quoted in Burgos, *Playing America's Game*, p. 57.

33. *Rutland Herald*, Aug. 24, 1887. Quoted from Bob Davids.

34. *Cincinnati Post*, Jan. 20, 1905, p. 6.

35. *Fort Wayne News*, July 22, 1899, p. 3.

36. *Sporting News*, Mar. 23, 1889, quoted in Malloy, J. 1982. "Out at Home," *The National Pastime* 2.1, p. 28.

37. *Binghamton Press*, Feb. 11, 1908, p. 2.

38. *Binghamton Press*, Feb. 12, 1908, p. 6.

39. *Sporting Life*, Sept. 19, 1908, p. 2.

40. *Sporting Life*, Sept. 26, 1908, p. 4.

41. *Sporting Life*, Dec. 19, 1908, p. 9.

42. *The New York Age*, Apr. 22, 1909.
43. *Brooklyn Daily Eagle*, Oct. 24, 1909.
44. *Sporting Life*, Mar. 27, 1909, p. 3.
45. Reproduced in Simkus 2012.
46. His death certificate states his "direct cause of death" as "pernicious anemia."
47. See Davids, B. 1987. *Memorial Observance for John (Bud) Fowler, Black Baseball Pioneer*. Frankfort, N.Y. (SABR).

Bud Fowler
Playwright

Hugh MacDougall

A Discovery

I spent much of last spring researching the life of African American baseball player Bud Fowler, while preparing a paper about him for the annual Frederick Ivor-Campbell 19th Century Base Ball Conference, held in Cooperstown, N.Y., April 19–20, 2013. I was attracted to him for many reasons. He is credited with being the first African American professional baseball player, whose career with otherwise mostly white baseball teams began in 1878 with a minor league in Massachusetts. He is the only baseball player of note to have grown up in Cooperstown. And his 30-year career in professional baseball was marked with unusual determination in the face of enormous racial discrimination. It was only after presenting my paper that I discovered that Bud Fowler had in 1912 also written, and copyrighted, a play entitled *The Retired Black Planter*, also published—for the first time—in this volume. This is the story of that discovery, and of that very amateur but sometimes fascinating play.

Bud Fowler—A Black Barber Who Loved Baseball

Bud Fowler (1858–1913) was born as John W. Jackson in the Mohawk Valley town of Fort Plain, New York, and was brought as a baby to the almost exclusively white community of Cooperstown, some fifty miles away on Lake Otsego, at the head of the Susquehanna River. His father, as well as his mother's father, were black barbers, members of a unique and almost forgotten group of African Americans that flourished during the 19th century. It was, indeed, as a black barber that Bud Fowler often earned his real livelihood in a day when even professional baseball rarely paid a living wage.

Throughout most of the 1800s the craft of shaving and cutting the hair of white customers in America was dominated by African Americans—first often as slaves, and

---

A retired American diplomat, **Hugh MacDougall** is the official Village Historian of Cooperstown, New York, and an avid researcher into history. In 2012 and 2013 he presented to the Frederick Ivor-Campbell Conferences on 19th century baseball, held in Cooperstown, papers on the life of Abner Graves, whose 1905 letters first led to Cooperstown's identification as "the home of baseball," and on "Bud Fowler," the first professional African-American baseball player, who grew up in Cooperstown. He subsequently discovered and tracked down a copy of the never-produced play copyrighted by Bud Fowler in 2012, which is here printed for the first time.

DOI: 10.3172/BB.7.83

later as free men with a specialized trade that raised them into the tiny African American middle class. White men of means welcomed being shaved by polite and deferential blacks, the "knights of the razor" as they came to be called — despite the sharp, open razors with which they plied their trade. And the African Americans who shaved them learned to be polite — even when insulted; calm — even when angered; persistent — even when life grew difficult; and above all apparently subservient — even when they felt themselves superior to those they served. These were lessons that Bud Fowler learned, and which served him well both as a baseball player and a barber.

Black-owned and operated barber shops became scattered throughout American cities and large towns, where they served only white customers, often in surroundings of greater luxury than they could find at home. African Americans were either too poor to pay for barbering services, or were excluded by racial prejudice and segregation. And since each barber shop must serve a large number of customers, black barbers worked and often lived in otherwise white neighborhoods or communities. Their dominance in big cities gradually diminished after the Civil War, as Italian and German barbers brought their crafts with them from Europe, and as racial prejudice increased in America. They were forced to shift to serving the growing African American populations in big cities, or move for a time to smaller, white, interior communities like Cooperstown and towns in New York's Mohawk Valley. Between 1850 and 1900, the number of black barbers in New York's rural Otsego County rose from zero to 11, and then declined back to zero.

Thus it was with Bud Fowler, who grew up and attended public school in the virtually all-white Village of Cooperstown, where his parents had moved about 1859, and where he learned the barbering trade from his father. He also learned to play, and to love, the baseball he played with his young white companions. Then in his late teens, under circumstances we still don't know, he left Cooperstown and made his way to Chelsea, Massachusetts, outside Boston, where by 1877 he was playing the baseball he loved with the amateur Chelsea Franklins team. He had adopted the name of Fowler, under which he played for the rest of his life. In the following year, 1878, he was briefly drafted to pitch for the nearby Lynn Live Oaks, a small team in the International League — thus becoming America's first professional black baseball player.

In a Mathew Brady photograph, abolitionist Gerrit Smith frowns.

From then until the mid–1890s, Bud Fowler played for otherwise white teams, many in minor leagues, all over the United States. He became known as an excellent pitcher and catcher, and then as a superb second baseman who deserved to be in the major leagues. All too often, however, Fowler was ejected from teams because of racial prejudice by fellow players, by owners, or by fans. Newspaper reports suggest he was sometimes deliberately assaulted by white players, who would slide into second base feet-first — not then a common practice — in an attempt to injure Fowler's legs with their cleats; Fowler is said to have learned to armor his legs with wood in an attempt to protect himself. But he continued to persist.

After about 1895, as formal segregation was adopted by professional baseball, Fowler turned instead to organizing, managing, and often playing for touring black baseball teams — most notably the Page Fence Giants, which was co-sponsored by wire fence and bicycle companies. For it, he arranged a private railroad car for his players, to save them from being excluded from racist local hotels, and provided entertainment as well as good ballplaying by parading his players around town on bicycles and in fancy costume.

Bud Fowler persisted in organizing such touring companies, though often without much financial success, almost until his death in 1913, when — after several bouts of illness — he died at his sister's home in Frankfort, a town in New York's Mohawk Valley some twenty-five miles from his birthplace in Fort Plain.

Thus was the life of John W. Jackson, alias Bud Fowler, an African American who insisted on playing baseball for over 30 years, despite enormous difficulties, and who is recognized today as the first of his race to be a professional player. He was a reticent man, who never married and left no descendants. We know about him almost exclusively from brief newspaper accounts, including a very occasional interview and one letter to editors.

Bud Fowler — Playwright

This was the story of Bud Fowler that I presented at the 19th Century Baseball Conference in Cooperstown last April. But I continued to look for information about this enigmatic but fascinating man, repeatedly searching out references to his name on the internet. And I stumbled on a series of index entries to a play copyrighted in 1912 — a play entitled *The Retired Black Planter*, submitted by somebody named Bud Fowler. At first I didn't think much about it — there must be many people in America named Bud Fowler. But then I suddenly found the complete copyright entry. The play called "The Retired Black Planter" had been registered to Bud Fowler of Frankfort, New York! And Bud Fowler the baseball player had been, in 1912, living in his sister's home in Frankfort. This was too close to be a coincidence — I was convinced that the usually reticent African American baseball player I had been studying for so long had actually written and copyrighted a play. But could I find that play? I decided to give it a try.

According to the copyright entry, *The Retired Black Planter* had been registered on the basis of a single typewritten copy. When I contacted the Copyright Bureau, I was informed that old copyrighted documents, after copyright protection had expired, were usually not retained — but that sometimes they were passed on to the Library of Congress.

The Play

After several inquiries to the Library of Congress I was on July 3, to my surprise and delight, very kindly emailed a scan of Bud Fowler's play, by Joseph Jackson, a Manuscript Reference Technician at the Library of Congress's Manuscript Division. A handwritten cover page, at the beginning of the 21-page typewritten document, reads, in somewhat awkward capital letters:

DRAMATICO-MUSICAL.COMPOSITION
AUTHOR.BUD.FOWLER
THE.RETIRED.PLACK.PLANTER
COPYRIGHT.APPLIED.FOR
JANUARY 3rd 1912

The typewritten play, with dialog in black and other instructions lighter (perhaps originally red from an old-fashioned two-color ribbon), occupies just 16 pages, but is preceded by five preliminary pages, including a list of characters, a (partially illegible) description of the setting for each of its six scenes, and a synopsis of the plot. The action takes place first at a lumber plantation near Ticonderoga, New York, and then at a plantation in Galveston, Texas. The play is divided into four acts, the last of which contains three scenes, for a total of six scenes.

The Retired Black Planter has 10 characters, some of them in brief cameo roles. There is General Marqueze (described in the list of characters as "rich, Nicaraguan, banished from his country") and Charles Marqueze ("his son, a civil engineer and adventurist"). The General has become wealthy cutting and selling timber near Ticonderoga on land obtained from the well known New York State abolitionist Gerrit Smith, who in real life did sell Adirondack properties to both black and white buyers.

Marqueze's general manager is Colonel Brown (described as "A runaway slave, the retired Black planter"), with his wife Madam Brown ("Loving mother, always silent"), their daughter, Maud ("Closest daughter, Madam's favorite), and—in cameo roles—Lucretia ("Youngest daughter, always busy") and Miss Graves ("Colonel's niece, his favorite. A musical entertainer").

Also in the cast are Sir Brainard ("Wealthy Port [sic] Rican, his Secretary"), Little Sammy ("Adopted son of Charles Marqueze, gifted with a wonderful voice"), and finally the Minister ("Loved by all").

The son, Charles Marqueze, has gone to Nicaragua to seek his fortune in the mining business, and has not been heard from since by his father the General. As we later learn, however, he has paid one visit to the United States, during which he became engaged to Maud Brown, and they had set a date for their marriage.

While the son is away, General Marqueze is killed by a falling tree, but before dying leaves half his property to Colonel Brown and the other half to be kept for his son Charles, should he ever return from Nicaragua.

Colonel Brown has but one aim in life—to buy back the plantation of his former master in Galveston, Texas, and so become "the retired Black planter." With his share of the General's estate, he succeeds in buying that plantation from the widow of his former master. However, greed gets the better of him, and he uses the property he is supposed to save for Charles Marqueze to invest in sugar in Puerrto Rico. When this investment is wiped out by a hurricane, he has mortgaged his newly purchased plantation in Galveston, and faces ruin when that investment also turns sour.

At this point a wealthy Puerto Rican named Sir Brainard, a part of the General's entourage, has agreed to finance Colonel Brown in return for being allowed to marry his daughter Maud. Although Maud has (unknown to her father) become engaged to Charles

Fowler organized but is not depicted here with the Page Fence Giants of Adrian, Michigan, in 1895, when he also played with the Adrian club in Organized Baseball, for whom Honus Wagner played.

Marqueze when he made a brief visit back to America, she has agreed to marry Sir Brainard in order to save her father from fiscal disaster, and a date for their wedding has been set.

On the day set for this wedding Charles again returns to America — now a rich man. He learns by happenstance what has occurred, and instructs his adopted son Sammy to deliver a message to Colonel Brown during the wedding ceremony. It begins, and just as the Minister asks if anyone objects to the marriage, Sammy shows up with a message from Charles stating that he is engaged to Maud.

Nevertheless, Maud insists that the wedding ceremony with Sir Brainard continue, as it does. A second time the Minister asks whether anyone objects to the marriage. Charles Marqueze now appears himself to object, saying that he and Maud had become engaged a year before, when he had seen her in Boston, and that their engagement had never been broken.

Maud faints and is carried out, and Colonel Brown's wife — supposedly known for her silence — suddenly speaks, and in a long oration, insists that Maud must be allowed to choose the husband she really wants. Charles Marqueze follows this up, denouncing Colonel Brown for his evil deeds, and demanding that he let Maud choose freely between Sir Brainard and himself. Colonel Brown suddenly repents, confesses his sins, and says Maud may marry as she chooses.

Maud re-enters, and after quoting extensively from several psalms, chooses Charles to be her husband. The marriage ceremony is now begun the third time, and is carried through to the union of Maud and Charles.

An angry Sir Brainard, thus jilted, threatens to foreclose instantly on the mortgage to Colonel Brown's plantation. But all turns out well. Charles — now wealthy from his gold mines in Nicaragua — hands Colonel Brown a check for $15,000, and tells him to "pay off the mortgage and now by right of law, you will be the Retired Black Planter." A chorus sings as the curtain falls.

Did Bud Fowler Really Write This Play?

Was this play — such as it is — really written by Bud Fowler the African American baseball player? Aside from his name and address on the copyright listing, there are several indications that he did. One is that Bud Fowler had lived in Galveston, Texas, in 1897, managing the Galveston Flyaway baseball club. Another is that Fowler was an active Christian, probably — like his father — of the Methodist persuasion. Early in 1908 Fowler wrote to a Binghamton, New York, newspaper bitterly complaining about a speech given the night before in Binghamton's Methodist Church by South Carolina's blatantly racist Senator Benjamin Tillman. In his letter, Fowler — who was probably one of the African Americans who attended Tillman's address — larded his remarks with five specific biblical citations. In the play, Maud Brown quotes extensively, if not always accurately, from the 27th and 31st Psalms of David, and the Minister recites the opening of the Christian wedding ceremony no less than three times.

The Retired Black Planter is introduced as a "Dramatico-Musical Composition," and each of the four acts ends with instructions for music and a chorus — though where these musical interludes are to be found is not stated. But Fowler did have some musical background. According to press reports, he composed a song in 1895 called "The Page Fence Giants," after a touring baseball team he had just organized. And in 1909 he is said to have composed a song about Cooperstown, dedicated to the National Baseball Commission. Neither song, however, has been located.

Despite Bud Fowler's long professional involvement with baseball, his familiarity with written plays seems wholly amateur. Indeed, Fowler may never have actually seen a printed play. Thus, he introduces each and every piece of dialog by quoting the last word or two of the previous speech, follows it with "cue for" the name of the next speaker, and then the word "speaks." Exits and entries are included as needed in these bits of instruction. This rather strange formula is surely unknown in the theatrical world.

The typewritten text includes numerous unlikely phrases and grammatical errors, suggesting that Fowler was not accustomed to writing dialog, though his spelling is usually fairly accurate. Except for one short speech by Sammy, Charles Marqueze's adopted son, there is no attempt at racial dialect. There are a number of handwritten interpolations in the script. The titles ascribed to some of the characters — notably those of Colonel Brown and Sir Brainard — are both improbable and never explained.

And, finally, the plot rushes along at breakneck speed, except for the final scene with its three-times repetition of the marriage ceremony, and includes unexplained gaps in time, not to mention characters who appear suddenly out of nowhere, and disappear just as quickly.

Is There a Mixed Marriage?

Moreover the plot leaves unanswered one significant question: Did Fowler consider the Marqueze family to be white or colored? In short, was his play intended to depict an interracial marriage between the Nicaraguan Charles Marqueze and the African American Maud Brown? Nowhere is this overtly stated. The play was presumably written sometime in 1911, when the Central American nation of Nicaragua was much in the public eye, as America prepared for a lengthy military involvement in a continuing Nicaraguan civil war. To many white Americans, particularly just before the First World War when American racial prejudice reached something of a peak, Central Americans as a group were certainly assumed to be of at least mixed racial origin. What the African American Fowler thought we do not know.

During the period of Fowler's long baseball career, it was not uncommon for light-skinned African Americans to claim Spanish or Latin American origins in order to escape increasingly stringent racial discrimination. A number of black baseball teams, including the Cuban-X team with which Fowler played briefly in 1898, called themselves Cuban only to disguise their actual racial makeup.

On the other hand, everything we know about Bud Fowler, who grew up in the overwhelmingly white community of Cooperstown, and who played on white baseball teams so long as he was allowed to do so, suggests that he wanted to participate as an equal in an interracial society. Perhaps, despite its title of *The Retired Black Planter*, Fowler's amateur effort at writing a play was intended to portray a mixing of America's two main races. We shall probably never know. In any case it adds a new dimension to our knowledge of a very important early African American baseball player.

DRAMATICO — MUSICAL COMPOSITION
AUTHOR BUD FOWLER
THE RETIRED BLACK PLANTER
COPYRIGHT APPLIED FOR
JANUARY 3rd 1912
[D28365]

DRAMATICO-MUSICAL COMPOSITION
IN FOUR ACTS, SIX SCENES
AUTHOR — BUD FOWLER
THE RETIRED BLACK PLANTER.

CAST OF CHARACTERS.

GENERAL MARQUEZE
A RICH, NICARAGUAN, BANISHED FROM HIS COUNTRY.

CHARLES MARQUEZE
HIS SON A CIVIL ENGINEER AND ADVENTURIST.

COLONEL BROWN.
A RUNAWAY SLAVE, THE RETIRED BLACK PLANTER

MADAM BROWN.
LOVING MOTHER, ALWAYS SILENT

MAUD.
OLDEST DAUGHTER, MADAM'S FAVORITE.

LUCRETIA.
YOUNGEST DAUGHTER, ALWAYS BUSY.

MISS GRAVES
COLONEL'S NIECE, HIS FAVORITE, A MUSICAL ENTERTAINER.

SIR BRAINARD
WEALTHY PORT [sic] RICAN, HIS SECRETARY

LITTLE SAMMY.
ADOPTED SON OF CHARLES MARQUEZE,
GIFTED WITH A WONDERFUL VOICE.
THE MINISTER.
LOVED BY ALL.

SCENERY.

FIRST ACT—DRAMA.

A piece of land extending out into Lake Champlain just across from Fort Ticonderoga. The fallen walls of the old fort in the distant, water between on the point of land a fine old fashion home just outside the door an old bucket well, raised with a pole, at the water's edge, a small dock, two small boats in the back ground, roads through the big trees, and a sawmill in the distance.

SECOND ACT.

A sawmill standing in the woods, running and sawing a log, pieces of logs and sawed boards scattered around back of mill woods, a roadway and a raceway back of the mill.

THIRD ACT

Picnic grove in woods on the Lake Boats at dusk

FOURTH ACT.

Library in the interior of Villa on the Plantation on the Bay of Galveston, Texas.

FIFTH SCENE—DROP CURTAIN.

Sand beach, Galveston Bay sand piled up, small hole inside of the curtain, to the distant Plantation, Cotton, sea, horses, mules, cattle, people in cotton fields, Villa back from beach.

SIXTH SCENE

Parlor arranged for wedding in the Villa.

SYNOPSIS DRAMA.

GENERAL MARQUEZE

A rich Nicaraguan, a widower, with one son banished from his country comes to New York State, goes into the northern part of State, buys a large tract of lumber lands from Garrett Smith, the famous Abolutionist [sic] of the Military Tract, near Fort Ticonderoga. Erects saw mills and a fine home, his general manager a runaway slave, his wife, Mistress of Wanders Rest. Name of his residence. General Marqueze' son is a civil engineer, after graduating. For a vacation goes to Nicaragua, his native home for a visit of six months, he organizes a prospecting party They go into the interior of Nicaragua to search for gold. They discover a rich mine but are all lost in the jungles, for a year and a half during his absence his father General Marqueze is killed by a log in the woods no communication can be gotten to his son his will he names Colonel Brown as his Administrator to settle up his affairs, giving him one half of his possessions. The other half he to reserve for his son should he return. Colonel settles up the estate buys his old master's plantation in Texas, becomes dishonest, takes young Charles Marqueze share of the estate, invests in Fruit lands in Porto Rico. Through a hurricane his crops are destroyed, mortgages his plantation to again replant his crops, makes the young, rich, Port Rican is in love with his daughter, by mutual agreement Maud will become his wife to save her father although Maud is engaged to Charles Marqueze after returning from Nicaragua to find his father dead, and all his possessions sold, the Colonel gone and his whereabouts unknown. Meets his daughter in Boston at school, love at first sight he will return to Nicaragua with his mining machinery return in one year. Maud will be his wife. Maud receives no communication from him in six months, he is in the mountains at the mines, Maud discouraged, no hopes of his ever returning. Will marry the Port Rican the wedding, objections why they should not be xxxx made man and wife. Telegram to Maud from Charles Marqueze. Will arrive at Galveston in time to be married on the appointed time two days later Too late. Maud will marry at once to save her father disgrace. He then must deal with Charles Marqueze for his donhesty [sic]. Charles Marqueze enters the reception room where the wedding is taking place. Madam after silence all her life, Maud must choose her choice between the two men. Chooses Charles Marqueze being a rich man now, forgives the Colonel for his dishonesty, gives him a check to clear the mortgage, retains all that his father left in his care for him, and now he is by right of law the Retired Black Planter.

DRAMATICO MUSICAL COMPOSITION
THE RETIRED BLACK PLANTER.4 Acts — 6 Scenes
Author — Bud Fowler.

FIRST ACT.

GENERAL MARQUEZE *Enters, Speaks.*

God, how can I repay you for this nature's gift (Water), that I am now enjoying? Why can not the great numbers of human beings see alike? Without it nothing can be made and nothing could exist.

Could exist. Cue for Charles Marqueze, enters — speaks.

Good evening, Father! You seem to be in deep thought about something. Are you worrying about anything?

About anything. Cue for General Marqueze — speaks.

No Son, thoughts of happiness instead of worry. I was talking to myself casting my eyes over the blue waters of Lake Champlain. I discovered that old Historical Fort Ticonderoga, its fallen walls still standing. The hearts and thoughts of the American people will always remember. Just above it I see that mysterious orbit, the Sun. I remember reading when a boy the past history of men. It was their pastime to watch its daily course through the heavens, but why should this be such a surprise, it gives us sunshine, draws waters from the ocean, and lakes into the clouds which produces rain, irrigates the land, dampens the soil, which produces all earthly wants, which we need to exist. A noble gift from him, the Lord. For years I have been his servant. He has been my guiding star. I have accumulated a large fortune! banished from my country Nicaragua, for trying to serve my people, but through others unloyal to their subjects. I came to America, this great, and glorious country, where all now breathes the air of freedom, and pursuit of happiness, established this thriving industry, all for you. Sent you to college, you have graduated, mastered a profession that fits you to take up this work, a Civil Engineer, seek the Lord as your guide, be honest good and upright and in years when you get old you can look back and see what use you have made from the Light, Darkness, Land, Water and the benefits of your fellow man.

Fellow Man. Cue for Charles, speaks.

Father, as you have given me this advice, this lesson I will always remember which means success being a young man having new ideas through education, but lack of practical experience. I will work out the problems laid out for me during my summer vacation. I have not been idle, traveled the streams, valleys and mountains which you possess, surveyed the surroundings, found streams of pure water from the mountains that will flow perpetual, minerals in the mountain of valuable price, unknown to anyone but to myself. The land is rich and fertile, will produce the wants for the people, at present to export these wants is slow and costly, but in time, railroads and waterways will be improved; then I will be able to transport these things to market quicker and cheaper. I always remember the words Mother taught me when a little fellow, "Keep the Lord in sight, all roads are plain or they run up or down, sheep tracks, highways to town, by even that little one beneath the hedge where seldom shines the sun.["]* My arrangements to leave this evening to go to Boston, there sail for my native home, Nicaragua to be gone six months, then to return home and take up this industry you have built up for me.

For me. Cue for General Marqueze, speaks.

Yes, as you have filled your contract with me, graduated. My promise was that you should return to your birthplace for a six month visit. Here is a draft for four hundred pounds, should this not be sufficient after hearing from you, I will supply you with more. Communicate with me as often as possible should anything happen we can get in touch by the quickest way possible.

Way possible. Cue for Colonel, enters, speaks.

General, the Madam requests me to inform you and Charles that supper is waiting; as you wish to hail the Captain of the tug as he passes with the tow of logs, and shingles down to Whitehall They will round the point in about twenty minutes.

All Exit.

Cue 20 minutes. steam boat whistles, passes

Enters: General Marqueze speaks.

Hullo, hullo Captain

Captain. Cue for Captain, speaks.

Hullo General, whats the orders.

The orders. Cue for General, speaks.

While you are at Whitehall after discharging your cargo, have what repairs needed, take on our supplys [sic] for two weeks. Good night, hoping you and the crew a safe trip down the Lake.

Down the Lake. Cue for chorus, sings. Curtain ends first Act/Drama.

SECOND ACT — DRAMA.

Curtain, Enters General & Colonel. General speaks.

Henry, Today is a beautiful one.

Beautiful one. Cue Henry speaks.

Beautiful day, everything is moving well.

Moving well. Cue for General speaks.

No shutdown, Henry. Keep the saw going the rest of the day and on all night. All the men who wish to make tonight's shift, will be paid double time.

That large order for Kimble & Co. New York must be delivered in fifteen days to fill it the mill must run three days and nights. Divide your men in shifts to fill the nights. Colonel and myself are going into the woods among the big timbers, which you shall [?] cut from some 12 × 14 trees.

Exit—General, Colonel, working, singing in mill. Messenger arrives, speaks.

Men, shut down the mill and come with me, a big tree fell and the General could not get away. It caught him and maybe he is killed.

Mill shut down, all exit.

Return with General, speaks.

Colonel, notify my son by cable. Not hearing from him in three months, I fear you cannot communicate with him. Send one of the men for Justice Smith. I will make a will

**Lizette Woodworth Reese (1856–1935), "At Cockcrow" (from* The Congregationalist*).*

should I die. I will leave all in your charge, but look after my son's interest. Hurry me to the house so I can receive medical aid.

Exits, General. Mill starts singing, General is Dead.

Curtain ends second act — Drama.

THIRD ACT — DRAMA.

Curtain — Enters Colonel and Madam. Speaks Colonel.

Madam seated. Madam for several days since my return from Texas, I will explain all to you. After arriving in Galveston I went immediately to the Old Plantation Saw Old Mistress; the Old Master dead several years and the Plantation for sale. I at once returned to Galveston, bought the old Homstead [sic] through a Real Estate dealer, and in the future years we will live and dwell where we were born; the daughters will remain in Boston, graduating next spring. While in New York, I sold and disposed of this property. They will take possession in thirty days. Those of the employers [sic] who wish to go can do so.

Do so. Cue for Madam, speaks.

Then you have at last fulfilled your wishes, that some day you could be in a position to return to Galveston, purchase from your master the old Plantation and villa, and be the Retired Black Planter, but Colonel it is nearly two years since any communication has been received from Charles Marqueze He must be dead. The part of the country he and his associates penetrated to seek gold is the most deadly on earth. The General was good, noble and honorable. Have you in settling up the Estate made arrangements for his son's part of the Estate should he ever return? I hope so.

Hope so. Cue for Colonel, speaks.

Yes, I have nearly settled the affairs. In New York, I met a young, rich Port Rican, and purchased from him part of his fruit lands in Port Rico, and made him the secretary and Treasurer, myself President of the company. Looking over the Morning World in New York I saw this article, which you may read.

Madam reads paper.

Twenty months in the river bottoms, jungles and mountains of Nicaragua. Charles Marqueze and a party of five, a prospecting party went into the interior of Nicaragua in search of gold, was lost for twenty months, was rescued by party of men sent to search for them by the Government of Nicaragua. All well and working a rich mine, said to be the richest ever discovered in the country. Three of them returned with the rescuing party to purchase supplys [sic], and Charles Marqueze whose father is one of the largest lumber men in New York State, will return there for a visit and purchase mining machinery to develop their mine.

Madam speaks after reading.

Thanks be God, his is found and rescued at last.

At last. Cue for Colonel, speaks.

Madam, all these long years of silence you have now spoken. You must remember the conditions of the people are strange circumstances. Corruption is everywhere involved by man. The power to do wrong in the minds of the people are weak, to become great and rich. This I fear will be my mistake.

Enter Employes, Colonel speaks.

Servants, to day is Emancipation Day! A day of happiness, pleasure and freedom. The pursuits of all happiness and liberty in America. The surroundings of this beautiful grove, the last place for us to join together in New York. I hope will be a day of jollification. I have purchased in Texas my Old Master's Plantation and Villa, and am now the Retired

Black Planter Those who choose to go there and still remain under my employe [sic] can do so, those who will go, speak so. I make arrangements for transportation, it will be a new industry to you young men, but willing and honest, so success will be yours. The rest of the day enjoy yourselves as you wish with pleasure.

Songs, Musical, dancing, chorus on tug boat at the Picnic

End Third Act. Curtain drops.

FOURTH ACT — DRAMA.

Colonel seated—Reception room. Enters Miss Graves embraces Uncle—

Dear Uncle, what seems to be the trouble, are you not happy? This day Maud's marriage.

Maud's marriage. Cue for Colonel, speaks.

Miss Graves I must acknowledge I am not feeling the best, and today should be my happiest moment, but at your arrival, if you will render some of your choice selections, and sing for me, you will refresh my memory.

My memory. Cue for Miss Graves, speaks.

Certainly, Uncle your wishes shall be granted. I hope it will comfort you. Music has its charms, and refreshes the memory and mind. When the brain is overtaxed with trouble, it brings moments of feeling and happiness, social meetings of members of a family.

Playing, singing.

Singing cue for Colonel, speaks.

Miss Graves, Dear Niece you have demonstrated often, when my mind is not at rest, that your playing, and singing those old familiar songs. They fill my heart with joy, and I forget the thoughts that are so straining to my mind. Thank you, thank you.

Thank you. Cue for Miss Graves, speaks.

Uncle, I assure you always when you request me to play, makes me happy, and tonight I will surprise you all. The wedding march that I have selected to play for Maud tonight, will be new to you all, and quite appropriate. I must now leave you Uncle to arrange some small matters for tonight. Good night. *Exit.*

Good night. Enters Maud and Madam. Madam speaks.

Colonel, today is a beautiful one, but has been so long. Maud and I are tired working all day.

All day. Cue for Colonel, speaks.

No doubt you are, but many a day during your life, have been in that condition, but hereafter you may live without hard work.

Hard work. Cue for Madam, speaks.

Colonel, not only work but my heart has been nearly broken. We have been man and wife for years in slavery and in freedom; after drifting through Canada we came to New York with our two daughters, found a home and a friend General Marqueze, but by God's calling he departed. In his will he left you enough to be a wealthy man. You promised him by oath to look out for and protect his son. This you have not done. God forgive you. He had confidence and trusted you. What have you done? You greed for money, your ambition to someday buy your Old Master's Plantation. You committed a sin before God, and man. Stole and absconded, bought land in Porto Rico. Through misfortune lost nearly all and today mortgage debt upon the old homestead that you will never be able to repay to one, who you have wronged. Why did you not tell me the truth? Maud has told me all; tonight she will marry Sir Brainard, not her choice to save you from disgrace. The man of her choice is Charles Marqueze. They have been engaged for over a year and tomorrow was to be their wedding day, but no communication from him in six months. They met in Boston. He has known your whereabouts for over a year, so it comes to man, when they gather to plot, they command, but not always do they govern. A woman knows because her instincts never fail I warned you about the Estate. You were silent but there is one you will have to face, Charles Marqueze. *Exits.*

Charles Marqueze. Cue for Colonel, speaks.

This is all true. May God protect me some way.

Some way. Cue for Maud, speaks.

Father cheer up. I have sacrificed my future life for you. Remember where there is a wrong lane in life time, there is always a chance for one to make it right, but Mother always silent. I am afraid now, silence will be her motto until the grave is her resting place.

Resting place. Cue for Colonel speaks.

We doubt this is so. Why did I commit this crime? Until late have I considered my condition. It was not the greed for money, wealth or honor, that I committed the deed. It was the wish of my heart, that after these years in slavery, should freedom reach my people, that I would accumulate money enough to come here, buy this Old Homestead, and spend the remaining days on earth in happiness.

And [In] happiness. Cue for Maud, speaks.

May God find some way to make the wrong done right. Come lets [sic] forget, dinner is about ready.

About ready. Enters Lucretia, speaks.

Father, you are looking happy. Your mind is on this wedding tonight. I am so awfully tired. I have worked hard, made all arrangements for the reception, done all the cooking.

The cooking. Cue for Colonel speaks.

Daughter, you are a noble girl. When you see and find the man you love, and get married, I will do all the work and the cooking.

The cooking. Cue for Lucretia, speaks.

Yes, I believe you will, but I am afraid this will never be. Cares of a married life is not always happiness. Now as things exist I am always happy, no cares, no troubles, suits me. Dinner is now ready. *Exits Lucretia and Colonel.*

Ends fourth scene. Drop curtain.

SCENE FIFTH.

Enters Colonel and Brainard speaks.

Colonel today is the happiest in my life, and to night I will take unto myself a wife, one that I love and in the future will protect. A change of life from leisure to one of many cares. You have all these years provided yourself with a lovely home, where daily, and nightly, you breathe the pure and healthy air from this bay; coming from this great Gulf of Mexico. Through speculation you have lost nearly half your Plantation and Villa, but the mortgage I hold I will invest it in this property, but you will hold a controlling interest.

Interest. Cue for Colonel[,] speaks.

Yes, you will from tonight be my partner, and I hope you will never regret it. Not feeling so well of times I stroll along the beach for miles and I thought you would like the exercise.

The exercise. Cue for Brainerd [sic], speaks.

Yes, I have enjoyed the stroll as it is getting along in the day, we had better return for I have some little matters in the city this afternoon to arrange.

To arrange. Cue for Colonel speaks.

Well we will stroll along back.

Exit Colonel and Sir Brainerd [sic].

Along back Enters Marqueze. Sammy enters from sand dugout.

Marqueze speaks.

Well Sammy where did you come from.

Come from. Cue for Sammy speaks.

Every day I come out on the beach, dig a hole, and have a fine sleep.

Fine sleep. Cue for Marqueze[,] speaks.

You still love to sleep, yet, I see. Sammy I have been gone a long time. Then there is where Colonel Brown lives, fine place, and Maud is to be married tonight; to Sir Brainerd [sic], does she love him?

Love him. Cue for Sammy, speaks.

No, dere is no love in Maud's heart for him, always been dere for you. I am so glad you come down. Will be something doing now.

Doing now. Cue for Marqueze, speaks.

He saw these men that were here? I saw them from the distant [sic].

The distant. Cue for Sammy, speaks.

Dat was Colonel Brown and Sir Brainerd [sic] talking about the wedding tonight.

Tonight. Cue for Marqueze speaks.

I see it all, after the Colonel has sacrificed nearly all by speculation, now it remains for him to give his daughter to one she does not love to retain his possessions. They were here planning, but Sammy, I fear they are working a losing game. The Colonel must settle his affairs with me before this wedding takes place. The ceremony will be performed at eight o'clock, so Sammy you meet me outside the Villa at half past seve [sic]. I have a message I want you to deliver.

To deliver. Cue for Sammy, speaks.

I will shore be thar, do anything for you, Mr. Marqueze.

Exit, Sammy and Marqueze.

End Scene fifth.

THE WEDDING.

Scene Sixth. Last Act.

Guests enter for wedding. March played. Wedding ceremony.

Dearly beloved, we are gathered here in the sight of God, and in face of this company to join together this man and woman in Holy Matrimony, which is commanded by St. Paul to be honorable among all men; and therefore is not by any to be entered into unadvisable or light; be reverently discreetly soberly in the fear of God, into this Holy State. These two persons present come now to be joined; if any one can show just cause why they may not lawfully be joined together, let him now speak or hereafter forever hold his piece [sic].

Piece. Cue for Sammy, enters, Note, Sammy exits

Maud reads, hands to families [?].

Galveston, Texas

To Miss Brown: arrived in Galveston this noon, will arrive at Villa tomorrow day of the engagement. Charles Marqueze.

Telegram handed to Minister, speaks.

What say you all to this objections [sic].

Objections. Cue Maud speaks.

Elder, I request you to fulfill your duty, perform this ceremony.

This ceremony. Cue Minister presides.

Dearly beloved, we are gathered here in the sight of God, and in face of this company to join together this man and woman in Holy Matrimony, which is commanded by St. Paul to be honorable among all men; and therefore, is not by any to be entered unadvisedly or lightly, but reverently discreetly, soberly in the fear of God, into this Holy State. These two persons present come now to be joined if any one can show just cause, why these may not lawfully be joined together, let him now speak, or else hereafter forever hold his piece [sic].

Piece. cue for Marqueze. Enters, speaks.

I object to this marriage.

This marriage. Cue minister speaks.

What is the objection, have you why this marriage shall not take place.

Take place. Cue for Marqueze, speaks.

That I am Charles Marqueze engaged one year ago in Boston to Maud Brown. Have arrived in time; tomorrow was the day set, the engagement has never been broken.

Maud faints, exits.

Never broken. Cue for Madam, speaks.

Colonel Brown, as Maud's mother, I have my rights in this land of freedom, silent, I have always been, but your acts and deeds of the past has given me courage and strength to demand Maud's rights at this wedding. Maud must be granted the privilege of choosing between these two men for a husband, and you must consent to it. It is wrong for humanity to go against nature's laws. Man should remain the symbolic head of a nation and family, but woman should have her choice of a husband, woman's chief mission in life is to be a romantic wife, and an ideal mother, a patriot [sic] of Art and beauty. This she can not be by being dissatisfied with her future surroundings, force and power of man is wrong, if a person fails to love, how wonderful is this will of power, but if one loves, no law cannot stop the thoughts; how gracious has the Lord been in his provisions for nature's paradise for humanity. The importance that we attach to life is dear, is a thing beyond our comprehension. We hold our life and freedom valueless when forced to do against our will. This is Maud's condition, but it will never be, for the willing and obedient. The image of God in flesh is to be rewarded.

Be rewarded. Cue for Marqueze, speaks.

Ungrateful man, Colonel Brown, you betrayed you trust in time of need, and distress. You was given shelter and work by one who in his heart loved you as his brother. Your business dealings of lumber, experience, and practical financial qualities made you a man of wealth, through one General Marqueze, my father. Not satisfied with enough to provide and take care of you and your family during your life time, your sound judgment failed. Rational as you were, all your life to do right, stupidly and selfishness as Kings who ruled centurys [sic] ago, you lived to ruin your daughter [illegible insertion], but your time has been wasted. Until you settle the affairs with me, or I prove my manhood with you; two years ago, you planned your future life's ambition. Came to Texas, bought your Old Master's plantation and Villa, invested in other business ways, a failure was your fate. You were nearly ruined, to save yourself from disgrace and ruin, you at this hour rule as a King, and demand your daughter to obey your wants, be generous give to your daughter her liberty, and freedom.

And freedom. Cue for Colonel speaks.

My thoughts and memory has changed! my past station in life was limited through the command of men. God saved these burdens, made me free. I sinned against his gifts! at present in the eyes and hearts of my beloved friends, I am considered nothing, the good book says, "Do unto others as you wish to be done by." My daughter may choose the husband for her future happiness.

Future happiness. Cue for Maud enters, speaks.

What have I done! The Lord is my light and my salvation. Whom shall I fear? The Lord is the strength of my life. "Then the wicked, my enemies, and my foes come to eat up my flesh, they stumble and fall. (O Lord), do I put my trust let me never be ashamed; bow down thine ear to me, deliver me speedily, be my strong rock, save me," Pull me out of the net they have laid for me! have mercy upon me, for I am in trouble. Mine eyes are consumed with grief, yes, my soul and belly, my time is in thy hand; deliver me from the hand of mine enemy's and from those who try to persecute me. Make thy face shine upon thy servant; save me for mercy's sake. Allow me to choose Charles Marqueze. Father be of good courage and he will save you also.

You also. Cue for Minister, procedes [sic] with Matrimony, speaks.

Dearly beloved, we are gathered here in the sight of God, and in face of this company to join together this man and woman in Holy Matrimony; which is commanded by St. Paul to be honorable among all men, and therefore is not by any to be entered into unadvisably [sic] or light [sic]; to be reverently discreetly, soberly in the fear of God into this Holy State...

These two persons present come now to be joined. If anyone can show just cause why they may not lawfully be joined, together, let him now speak or else hereafter forever hold his peace. Wilt thou have this woman to thy wedded wife? To live together after God's ordinance in the state of matrimony. Wilt thou love her, comfort her honor and keep her in sickness and in health, so long as you both live?

Both live. Cue for Marqueze, speaks.

I will.

Minister speaks.

Wilt thou have this man to live together, after God's ordinance in Holy Matrimony? Wilt thou obey him, serve him, love and honor him in sickness and health, to love and cherish and forsake all others? Keep thee only unto him so long as both you shall live.

Shall live. Cue for Maud speaks.

I will.

Will. Cue for Minister.

Who gives this woman to this man. I thee wed and with my worldly goods I thee endow in the name of the father, and of the Son, and the Holy Ghost, Amen.

Ame., Cue for Sir Brainerd [sic], speaks:

Colonel Brown tomorrow the mortgage on this property is due, and if not raised I will foreclose.

Foreclos., Cue for Marqueze,

Sir Brainerd [sic]remain. Colonel Brown you have after your dishonesty proved yourself a man, and you shall be rewarded for such. The one half interest my father left for me I present to you as a present. Here is a check for Fifteen thousand dollars, pay off the mortgage and now by right of law, you will be the Retired Black Planter.

Chorus, ends drama. Curtin [sic].

RETIRED (The) black planter; play in four acts and six scenes, by B. Fowler. 21 p. fol. Typewritten. [4799 © 1 c. Jan. 17, 1912; D 28362; Bud Fowler, Frankfort, N. Y.

***Copyright bureau listing, 1912, for* The Retired Black Planter.**

Abstract

Bud Fowler (1858–1913), real name John W. Jackson, was an African-American who grew up in Cooperstown. He devoted 30 years to baseball, as a player in mostly professional white teams and then as an organizer and manager of touring black ones, while practicing his alternate trade as a black barber. Shortly before his death in 1913 he copyrighted a long-forgotten play entitled "The Retired Black Planter." A successful search of the Library of Congress turned up a typewritten copy, which though amateur in style, illustrates Fowler's fight against racial discrimination, ending with an interracial marriage. This first publication of the lost play adds to our understanding of Fowler's long and unique career in baseball.

William Shuttleworth
The Father of Canadian Baseball

William Humber

By rights we should be cautious of titles such as the above. They imply the creation of something out of very little and, in this case, a paternity that might be more aptly described as the status of a near relation. In William Shuttleworth's case, however, the designation seems appropriate. For this is Canadian baseball we are talking about — not the game's ultimate origins.

Baseball has roots in old European customs surrounding the arrival of spring and a more or less direct heritage from bat-and-ball games with a multitude of names including the two-worded "base ball." They arrived in North America in the 18th century (possibly even earlier) as the less successful bat-and-ball variations from the United Kingdom where cricket had attained the place of prominence.

While some English to this day dismiss baseball as little more than a game of rounders played by young girls at the beach on bank holidays, there was less "turning up of one's nose" in North America accompanying the playing of bat-and-ball games other than cricket. Those whose bat-and-ball skills were too primitive for cricket could partake of the then easier play of games resembling baseball. In many versions runners could be retired if plunked with the thrown ball while off a base.

The game grew in American soil and appears to have been a widely popular recreation, given the past decade's almost daily discovery of new accounts. It was not, however, what we think of as a formal, organized game until well into the 19th century; reporting of the game in its own right, rather than as the accidental accompaniment to some other news event, does not occur until the 1840s.

Early "bat and ball" in Canada is less an example of Americans commanding the playing of games north of the border and more reflects their disorganized, carefree character, and a passage directly, in some cases, from the United Kingdom. In other cases it arrived as a barely digested regurgitation of something that had passed from the United Kingdom through the United States to Canada, much like a letter sent from Liverpool and arriving in New York on its eventual journey to York (today's Toronto). Finally, in some cases it was a Canadian reinterpretation of what had been modified and refined in the United States.

In Canada we have multiple references with varying degrees of validity to early bat

---

William Humber is a Canadian sports historian with five baseball titles to his credit. He has been a SABR member since 1978, and is currently a member of the selection committee for the McFarland-SABR Award, given annually to the authors of the best articles on baseball history and biography. From 1982 to 1983, he served on SABR's Board of Directors.

 DOI: 10.3172/BB.7.100

and ball play. These include "ball" in an early 19th century diary account from York (Toronto); some form of "bat" being played in Manitoba in the 1830s; ball playing in Quebec in the late 1830s; a news reference to "games of ball and bat" in Dartmouth, Nova Scotia in 1841; restrictions on "ball" in legislated encumbrances in 1845 preventing the disturbance of the Sabbath in Upper Canada (today's Ontario); and rounders in British Columbia by the 1850s.

The Central School, Hamilton, about 1860. The Young Canadians played north of this site.

There is a famous account almost fifty years after the fact of a game played in Beachville, Ontario, on June 4, 1838, which some have questioned as willful fiction on the part of its teller, and others have argued is a commingling of things seen and played from several different times. I support the latter opinion and suggest that while the surrounding details of the Beachville story ring true in terms of its date, surrounding events, and the soldiers in attendance, its rules look a lot like something played in Ontario in the 1850s with four bases and a home plate.

However, we do know a distinct Canadian game was being played throughout the 1850s and here our story begins.

Formal teams with rules, club organization, and intentional news accounts, as noted, began to appear in the United States in the 1840s and such momentum carried into the 1850s with increased regularity and geographic spread; always, however, against the apparent rising tide of cricket whose English immigrant-playing partisans were often superior players to their American and Canadian brethren. Whether this drove those with weaker bat-and-ball skills to baseball is open to speculation, but it should be stressed that such choice owed very little to considerations of national origin, as much because baseball-type games had come, like cricket, from the same country. If national origin had meant anything in this period, it's almost certain Canadians would have opted for cricket as the more skillful and successful demonstration of English identity.

Here's what we know. The first organized baseball team in Canada was the Young Canadian of Hamilton established in 1854 and playing their games on the grounds north of that city's Central School and in a site proximate to today's City Hall. In 1865 William Shuttleworth claimed to be that team's "paternal head" and there never was any dispute of this. He was toasted with cries of being a jolly good fellow for his role. In several other places he notes the team's growth from its beginnings in 1854, making reference in one instance to 14 years of play. The pages of the *Hamilton Gazette* reviewed from 1854 and 1855 make no mention of baseball, but, given that the game was new and the club as formed was likely only for intrasquad purposes, the lack of reporting either directly or incidentally is not surprising.

William's birthplace is uncertain though several sources say Brantford, most likely in 1834. He grew up here and we can only speculate that he played some version of early baseball in Brantford. Primitive versions of baseball were being played in nearby Ontario places, and his later enthusiasm and skill speak to at least some grounding during his boyhood. His parents James and Eliza (Elizabeth) were not prominent persons in town like another Shuttleworth family, though it's possible the two families were related. By the age of 18, as reported in the census released in 1852, William was living in nearby Hamilton. Later directories of the decade show him working as a clerk (possible salesman) for Colin McRae in his dry goods business in the Lister Block.

William, it appears, was a strong proponent of the two-inning, 11-a-side Canadian game (with the additional positions of fourth baseman and back-up behind the catcher), but by the end of the decade there was a desire to play other teams including those in nearby Buffalo, along with a perception that the New York rules of the game (essentially, though not completely, those of today) were more exciting. For instance in the Canadian game all 11 batters had to be retired before the other team came to bat, unlike the New York rules requiring only three outs, thus providing greater exchange between offensive and defensive roles.

We must infer much, not only about how those Canadian-rules games must have looked but how many were played in Canada in the 1850s, and this goes for William's role as well. Organizing and playing the game in this period, however, are both consistent with the age of a young man in his early twenties. He enjoyed a modest occupation but one with some degree of personal freedom, unlike that for laborers, and finally on the basis of accounts near in time (though in the 1860s) we can conclude that he was the driving force behind the sport. Confirming this is his decade-long role as President of the Maple Leaf club, the organization that emerged out of the Young Canadian in 1861. Why and how this process occurred is only partially clear, but there seems to have been a minor tussle in Hamilton regarding the merits of the Canadian versus the New York game. Though apparently opposed to the New York rules, William quickly acquiesced to the change.

In his decade-long role as club president, he was also vice president of the first fledgling Canadian baseball organization in 1864 (if by Canadian we are content with a geography stretching from Ingersoll to Hamilton, that ignores the rest of the country!). He was the skillful catcher of the team at least well through the 1860s, and he also umpired some of the most important matches including one between Woodstock and Guelph in 1868 that turned into a mini-riot.

Why, then, has William Shuttleworth had such a limited acknowledgement for his role in Canadian baseball history despite having formed and managed its first successful club? First, he took a disparate, uneven, and carefree game and gave it permanence and structure in an era when the game did not have media prominence in Canada. Records of those early days are sparse. Second, his initiative soon spread by the early 1860s to other places in southwestern Ontario including Ingersoll, Woodstock, and Guelph (his influence on London, where there was a club in 1856, is less certain), and those towns soon surpassed Hamilton as ones with superior baseball teams. Third, there is a paucity of photographic evidence from those early days. To date we have found no photo of

William either as a player (photos were taken at the 1867 Detroit tournament at which William participated so these might still exist) or in his later years, though one may appear once his significance is fully proclaimed. Finally, he was neither a wealthy nor prominent Hamiltonian in his later years in comparison to what became of at least some of his teammates; consequently, little biographical research has been undertaken until now. John James Mason (b. 1842) for instance was a future mayor and an important military man. Like Mason, Shuttleworth was a member of the 13th Battalion, which marched off to contest with the invading Fenians in 1866, but his highest attainment was color sergeant, unlike Mason's level of major.

His family and employment obligations gradually overtook his baseball leadership. In 1869 his younger brother James (b. 1840), also a fellow player, died, but we have no record of its effect on William. We do know that he umpired a game a few weeks later, and a day after his daughter was born. Additionally, his employer Colin McRae's company had gone into receivership in 1868 following McRae's death. William appears to have been self-employed for some time before eventually working as an upholsterer and salesman with James Reid's furniture company in the 1880s. Upon his marriage to Matilda, his family reached five children in 1874. By that year he was 40 and thus past his ball-playing days. Most devastating was undoubtedly the death in 1881 of Matilda. She was only 44. At least two of his children went to live with their older brother (also a William) and our William lived as a boarder in a hotel.

At some point he left Hamilton to live with son James in Geneva, New York, and the two worked as upholsterers. William died in 1903 and his body was returned for burial next to Matilda in the Hamilton cemetery. Twenty years after his death, H.F. Gardiner penned a brief account of the man he called the father of Hamilton baseball, "Billy" Shuttleworth. It's a familiarity of name never used in formal places, including the newspaper accounts, during William's lifetime, but perhaps captures the friendliness, joy, and good spirit associated with the game he played.

The Hamilton city directory account of 1862–1863 records his presidency of the Maple Leaf (noting that they were originally the Young Canadian) club and their playing location. The executive listed, however, is from 1862–1863, and not from their organizational structure of 1854. We should not, from this sketchy account, have assumed he was the team's originator. It was a mistaken "leap of faith" I made in my books on Canadian baseball and which hopefully I have now corrected in more detailed and continuing research on the life of William Shuttleworth. This subsequent examination confirms, to my satisfaction, his seminal role, as well as the 1854 startup of the first organized club.

In 1866 the Maple Leaf moved into grounds on Upper James Street, kitty-corner to Robinson Street, a location almost certainly that of the Burlingtons, a team the 1862–1863 directory showed had started in 1855. There was an amalgamation of these early teams at some point before 1866 (Mason for instance is shown on the executive of the Burlington team in 1862–1863 but by mid-decade, was a leading member of the Maple Leaf) and a decision was made to move to the Burlington's grounds.

As baseball reached greater heights of popularity by the 1870s, as the rules and scores began to look more like our own, as professionals upgraded the quality but also incited the following of the game in that decade, as the increasing organization of the sport led to the establishment of a Canadian league in 1876 and more significantly the National League south of the border, the old pioneers were soon forgotten. *Bryce's Cana-*

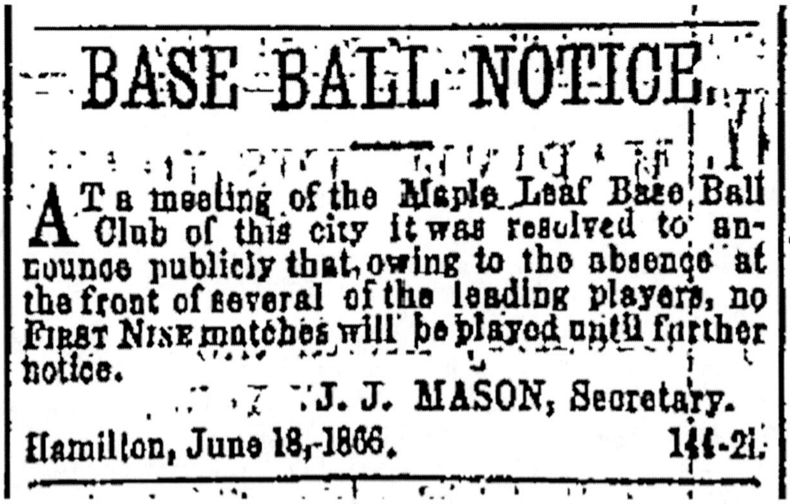

BASE BALL NOTICE.

AT a meeting of the Maple Leaf Base Ball Club of this city it was resolved to announce publicly that, owing to the absence at the front of several of the leading players, no FIRST NINE matches will be played until further notice.

J. J. MASON, Secretary.

Hamilton, June 18, 1866. 144-2i.

The Fenian raids of 1866 interrupted the schedule of the Maple Leaf Base Ball club. Three players went to the front with the Thirteenth Battalion.

dian Base Ball Guide of 1876 briefly mentions the passing from the stage of the old Hamilton Maple Leafs and their long established heritage but there was nary a word about Shuttleworth. Hamilton baseball had moved by this time to the Crystal Palace Grounds and by the 1880s the city was playing in the highest echelons of minor league baseball.

George Sleeman's Guelph Maple Leafs dominated Ontario baseball in the first half of the 1870s followed by the London Tecumsehs in the latter half. Toronto finally took notice and by the 1890s that city would be the leading remnant of south central Ontario's one-time Canadian baseball hegemony. By then the game was popular throughout Canada, having started in Montreal and Atlantic Canada as early as the 1860s, but now flourishing on the prairies and as far west as Victoria.

William Shuttleworth did not create this cross-Canada enthusiasm but he did lay the foundation on which all future baseball organization in Canada would grow. He played the game at what, for the time, was a high level of skill; helped organize the first formal though geographically limited Canadian organization; and umpired meaningful games as a respected arbiter.

As the "Father of Canadian Baseball" he should no longer be forgotten.

* * *

Brantford, Ontario's baseball fans received the treat of their spectating lives on the last day of June 1874 as the respective best teams of the United States and Canada met at their town's tournament. The Boston Red Stockings with three future Hall of Famers — Harry Wright, Al Spalding, and Jim O'Rourke — bested brewer George Sleeman's Guelph Maple Leafs 26–6, taking home a $150 prize in gold.

Boston was the dominant team of the era in the National Association, the predecessor to the National League formed in 1876, but they could make as much money barnstorming even to relatively small venues like those in Brantford and Guelph, Ontario. A year previously in the latter town it is recorded that a livelier ball than usual was inserted into the game, facilitating Boston's victory.[1] Bob Addy, a player with that 1873 touring team, has been identified as a Canadian from Port Hope,but apparently he didn't object to the visitor's hijinks at the expense of his "fellow" Canadians.[2]

The story of the ball was told for years and most likely inspired Zane Grey's short story in *The Redheaded Outfield and Other Stories* about a barnstorming team undone by such a maneuver in a game in Guelph, whose citizens were described by Grey in a manner perhaps comparable to how Americans might have imagined a similar crowd in Brantford:

> Some 500 men and boys trotted curiously along with us, for all the world as if the bus were a circus parade cage filled with striped tigers. What a rustic, motley crowd massed about, in and on that ball ground. There must have been 10,000. The audience was strange to us. The Indians, half breeds, French Canadians, the huge hulking, bearded farmers or traders or trappers whatever they were, were new to our baseball experience.

For Guelph's part the 1874 games with Boston were just before they left for Watertown, New York, where they won what was described as a "world tournament" but whose teams were below the top level of the day. Amongst those they beat was the Ku Klux Klan club of Oneida, New York. *Harper's Weekly* included an image of the Guelph team in a later issue that summer.

It is not recorded if Brantford's own most famous baseball "krank," as supporters of that day were known, attended his former hometown's tournament in June. It would have been a shame, however, if William Shuttleworth was either unable to do so or was not aware of the game. No one deserves more credit for advancing the game's play in Canada from its informal roots to a level of organization such that the game's best teams would visit the place where he grew up.

Multiple sources claim Shuttleworth's birthplace as Brantford in 1834 but census information of that era is often misleading, inaccurate, or missing, still there seems little doubt that he spent his youthful days in that town. His father and mother, James and Elizabeth (or Eliza) Shuttleworth, were Brantford residents as listed in the 1851–52 census of Canada East and West, with children, Ellen (16), James (12), Mary Jane (10), and Eliza (9) though they were significantly less prominent than the neighbouring family of Joseph Shuttleworth.[3] The latter Shuttleworth had begun his employment after immigration in a distillery but went on to own a farm and establish a canning and fruit business notable for its exports.[4] His sons, George and James, would eventually represent the company's interests as far away as England.

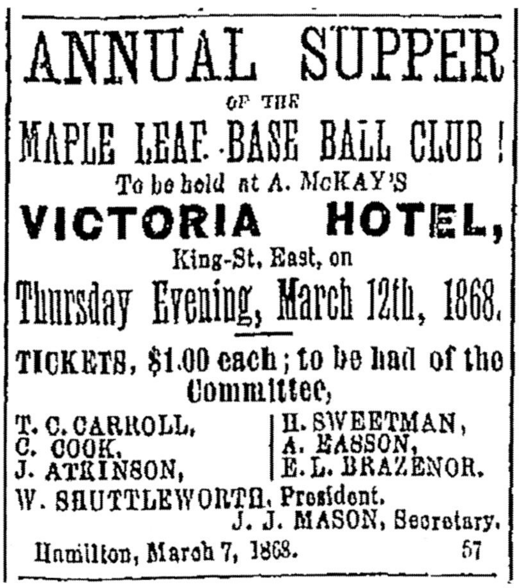
ANNUAL SUPPER
OF THE
MAPLE LEAF BASE BALL CLUB!
To be held at A. McKAY'S
VICTORIA HOTEL,
King-St. East, on
Thursday Evening, March 12th, 1868.
TICKETS, $1.00 each; to be had of the Committee,
T. C. CARROLL, H. SWEETMAN,
C. COOK, A. EASSON,
J. ATKINSON, E. L. BRAZENOR.
W. SHUTTLEWORTH, President.
J. J. MASON, Secretary.
Hamilton, March 7, 1868. 57

At this supper the Maple Leaf club proudly displayed the trophy ball it won at the Detroit Tournament in August 1867.

Joseph Shuttleworth is mentioned in Brantford's assessment roll of 1847 and in the Canadian Directory of 1851. William's father, James, is in neither of these and though it's not as yet ascertained that Joseph and James were related it seems likely they were brothers given that they were the only Shuttleworths in Brantford, lived in the same part of town (the North Ward), were of similar age, and both seem to have worked initially in the distillery business likely under Joseph Mawbey.

The Canadian census of 1851–52 lists a William Shuttleworth (18) living in Hamilton.[5] The scene greeting him on arrival was probably not too different from that below.

He appears to be living as a boarder (or "inmate" as the census described such residency!) with D. McRae, a merchant, and Mrs. M. McRae. Shuttleworth's listed birthplace (Brantford) and age (born 1834) match up with the known history of our William Shuttleworth. Like so much of our attempts to reconstruct the time and place however certain facts raise questions.

William Shuttleworth's religion is shown as Methodist despite James and Elizabeth and their family's listing as Church of England. How to explain this anomaly? Is this our William Shuttleworth? I'm certain it is. Firstly Hamilton was a town of just over 10,000 and to suppose there was a second William Shuttleworth also from the same town and of the same age stretches credulity. And our William is not shown in the census with the rest of his family in Brantford. Where else was he most likely to be but in nearby Hamilton? As well, later city directories only account for one William Shuttleworth — ours! We know Joseph Shuttleworth's family were leading Methodists and many conclusions can be drawn.

- William could have taken his "uncle's" affiliation.
- There existed a Methodist Episcopal Church in this period, perhaps overlapping the two affiliations.
- William was the child of, or was raised by James and Elizabeth, but had an unknown connection to Joseph's family.
- The census takers simply listed the information incorrectly.
- The McRae family with whom he boarded, and who were Methodist, either converted him or listed him as such.
- In an act of youthful rebellion William temporarily forsook his own family's religious affiliation.

We don't know but an incorrect listing seems the most likely explanation, particularly since he chose the Church of England for his later census affiliation (1861, 1871, and 1881) and as the place for his 1862 wedding to Matilda White. He appears in several city directories, in 1856 as a clerk with P. McRae, in 1858 as a clerk with Colin McRae and boarding at the Burlington Hotel, and in the 1862–1863 directory once again as Colin McRae's clerk but now living on Elgin near the Gore, no doubt with his new bride.

By 1858 younger brother James, now about 18, is described as a shoemaker living with J. Quirk. John Quirk is listed in *Sutherland's 1868–1869 Directory for the City of Hamilton and County of Wentworth* as a "varnisher," almost certainly in the role of a burnisher in the shoemaking industry of the 19th century. Further research reveals a Helen Quirk, who died in Wingham, Ontario, in 1914 as originally born in 1835 in Brantford and who listed her father as James Shuttleworth and her mother as simply "Bobier," no doubt a maiden name. Her age, the father listed, and the Brantford location line up perfectly with William's sister who is listed in the 1851–1852 census as Ellen. Ellen and

Helen, being so similar in nomenclature, we can conclude tare the same person. There were as well Quirks listed as being from Brantford in the same records maintained for the 1862 marriage of William and Matilda, though whether this was how Helen (Ellen) and John met is pure conjecture. The conclusion drawn is that James was provided with an occupation and a place to live by his brother-in-law John Quirk and John's wife, Helen (Ellen), James's sister.

There is no record of John Quirk having played baseball but the shoemaking profession was a perfect fit for an aspiring ballplayer like James.

Bryan D. Palmer quotes a reminiscence from that period:

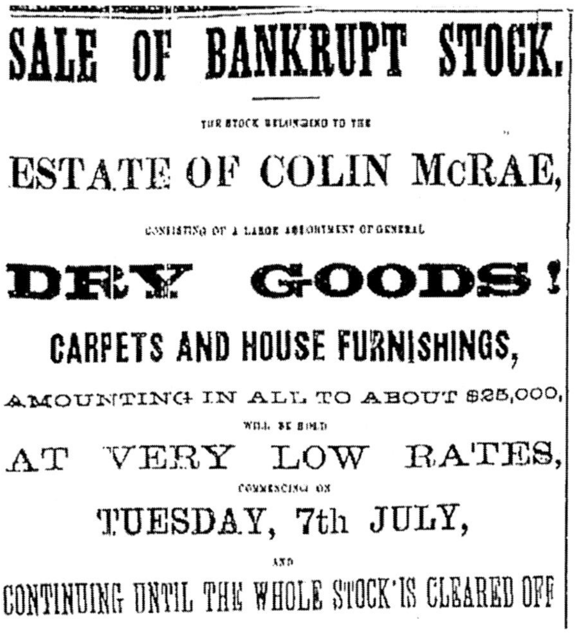

SALE OF BANKRUPT STOCK.

THE STOCK BELONGING TO THE

ESTATE OF COLIN McRAE,

CONSISTING OF A LARGE ASSORTMENT OF GENERAL

DRY GOODS!

CARPETS AND HOUSE FURNISHINGS,

AMOUNTING IN ALL TO ABOUT $25,000,

WILL BE SOLD

AT VERY LOW RATES,

COMMENCING ON

TUESDAY, 7th JULY,

AND

CONTINUING UNTIL THE WHOLE STOCK IS CLEARED OFF

With Colin McRae's bankruptcy in 1869, a job change was in the offing for William Shuttleworth.

> I would tell what I know about team shoe making. The men are a jolly set and have their own little rackets. A team is composed of a laster, healer, burnisher, and finisher. The best thing is to get a steady team, for unless you have that luck you are never sure of a full weeks work. Shoemakers have more "uncles" and "aunts" than any other mechanic. If in the summer the day be fine, some one of the team gets the "flem," and the others cannot work without him, so they are obliged to stop, and as a rule, they get the "hines."[6]

So this places both William and his younger brother James in Hamilton in the 1850s. What is lacking, however, is an account of their ballplaying during that time. Our information is recorded in at least three places.

Thomas Hutchinson's 1862–1863 directory for Hamilton (p. 224) contains the following:

> Maple Leaf Base Ball Club (late Young Canadian)
> Organized April 1854
> The following are the officers for 1862—
> Wm. Shuttleworth, President;
> Chas. Waugh, Vice President;
> David Davies, Secretary;
> Thomas Carroll, Treasurer.
> Field directors—John Dicker, Samuel Coulter and Henry Wooly,
> Grounds, facing Central School, between Bond and Bowery streets.

It also lists:

> Burlington Base Ball Club
> organized 1855

The following officers for 1862-
J.C Davis, President
P.W Dayfoot, Vice President
J.J Mason, Secretary
Geo. Black, Treasurer
Directors — D.McCraney, W.H Reid, A. Ecclestone
Club grounds, Upper James street cor Robinson. Field days, Mondays, Wednesdays and Fridays, No. of Members — 50

The *Hamilton Gazette* of 1854 and 1855 however contains no accounts or references to these two clubs forming, or playing. There is one account of a cricket match in 1854 between teams from Paris, Ontario, and London, Ontario, but that's as close to a bat and ball game as we get. The lack of a baseball reference, however, is not unusual. Baseball or "base ball" was still in its embryonic evolutionary stage, moving from casual and informal encounters towards a more formal status as a recognized, organized, and reported sport.

A brief history is necessary, recognizing however that this is my belief, but that others abound. The rise of cricket in England in the 18th century as the preferred and dominant "bat and ball" game with a set of agreed upon rules, formal organization, and media accounts condemned all other "bat and ball" games in England to wither and fade away as serious adult recreations. These other games might have continued to be played as a warmup for the truly serious game of cricket, or been stunted in their growth, becoming the plaything of children, or these other games might have languished in out of the way locales which hadn't got the message, or didn't care, that a more modern age of cricketing prominence was upon them.

A reduced "ballplaying" snobbery however, or even in some cases an outright rejection of cricket's bat and ball dominance, followed the transfer of these apparently "failed" bat and ball games to North America (and this applied to Canada as well as the United States). Even in North America cricket had the head start as the preferred high level bat and ball sport, but often the skill levels required to excel were missing in homebrews who had trouble competing with recent English immigrants, or who welcomed the ability to tweak, and in some cases overhaul, baseball's rules. This was unlike cricket, whose essential refinement had largely been completed by the 19th century, and whose rules authority was under the strict and conservative control of the Marylebone Cricket Club located atLord's Cricket Grounds in London.

The bat and ball styles of play we associate with baseball-type games in North America went by many names. In some places rounders, in others townball, in others "ball" or "bat," though the "baseball" description continued and this was so even in England as evidenced by its appearing in such unlikely places as Jane Austen's late 18th century novel *Northanger Abbey.*

Some observers of this period bemoan the absence of sources for the game and note that where they do occur it is usually a one-off, almost accidental mention without accreditation. The problem, however, is not enough sources but too many. They are found in diverse, unconnected and unpredictable places, and new ones continue to turn up in the unlikeliest places. Accounts or mention of baseball-type activity are found in random diaries, town proclamations, public regulations, stories, and even accidental news accounts but seldom is baseball the focus of these stories as it would later become. More often it is cited because it was a public nuisance or a casual exercise recorded in an almost by-the-way sort of mention without any importance or significance attached to it.

Only in the 1840s does the game creep formally — and in its own right rather than as an inadvertent piece of some other occurrence — Into the public recordkeeping of news journals. Along with this is the beginning of regular team organization and an attempt to provide some level of agreed upon, though still evolving, rules. This happens first in the United States and particularly in the New York City region, though Boston, in the form of the Massachusetts Game, and Philadelphia are also developing unique interpretations. Likewise a Canadian version has taken shape by the 1850s.

The diversity of early baseball-type activity in Canada is remarkable, more so because as a British colony and a setting for cricket's dominance one might have thought an Americanized game would have had little chance of success. The key, however, is that baseball would not be thought of as "American" until long after it had sunk its roots into Canadian playas something distinctly Canadian.

The varieties of early baseball-type activity in Canada suggest that while we have no record of childhood play in Brantford during William Shuttleworth's youth in the 1840s (unless an unlikely, but always possible, reminiscence turns up, or a third-party account appears) the probability of informal but unrecorded play, by him and his friends, is high. It's the best explanation of why and how a young man would have developed both the skill to play and desire to organize a more formal structure in 1854. The second reference to the organization of baseball in Canada was found in the *Hamilton Spectator*'s account of December 4, 1865 regarding the Maple Leaf Base Ball Club Dinner, as follows:

> Last evening the members of the Maple Leaf Base Ball club held their first Annual Dinner in their room on John Street, the President Mr. W. Shuttleworth, occupying the Chair and Mr. Thos. Carroll the Vice-Chair. About 30 persons sat down to the spread, which was provided by T. Young, saloon keeper and was got up in the best style. The usual toasts of the Queen, the Royal Family, the Governor General, the press, etc. were drunk with all the honors and songs appropriate to these were sung by several members of the Club. The toast "Prosperity to the Maple Leaf Base Ball Club" having been proposed, the President replied in suitable terms, *giving a short sketch of the Club, its organization in 1854,* [emphasis mine — BH] since which time it has been steadily increasing up to the present time. Toasts and speech making was kept up till a late hour, all apparently enjoying themselves.

Neither account, however, places Shuttleworth at the start of baseball in Hamilton. The *Hamilton Times* report of the Maple Leaf Base Ball Club Supper in its February 23, 1867, edition appears however to clinch the matter.

It is particularly puzzling therefore that the first media mention of baseball in Hamilton in 1859 with a box score and writeup and which appears in the New York *Clipper*, the leading sports and entertainment journal of the age, has no mention of either Shuttleworth brother. A game on May 24, 1859, is described as having been played under the New York rules of baseball between the Young Canadian club of Toronto and the Young America of Hamilton.

None of the players however are mentioned in later accounts of baseball in Hamilton, leading one to surmise that they were either visitors to the town (given the arrival of the Great Western Railway between Buffalo and Hamilton five years earlier this is not far-fetched), were representatives of junior teams, or were cricketers playing baseball as a sidelight. It is a mystery still being examined.

We do have one somewhat helpful piece of information however. In the early 1980s a researcher, Eves Raja, provided the author with his notes on early baseball. Unfortunately sources were not provided, but those pieces of information in his notes that have been sourced by the author at a later date have generally proved to be accurate so it is likely similar validation will follow for these comments, which include the following:

> May 24 1859 First game of BB [baseball] played using the 9 man team (N.Y. BB Association Rules) played in Hamilton, Ont. Veteran players such as W. Shuttleworth and A.S. Feast refuse to have anything to do with the new game.

What was being played by Ontario teams of that period was something that the *Clipper* would later describe as "the game played in Canada," and the "Canadian game." The August 4, 1860, *Clipper* notes in its description of a game between the Young Canadian Club of Woodstock and the Rough and Ready Club of Ingersoll, "The game played in Canada differs somewhat from the New York game, the ball being thrown instead of pitched, and an innings is not concluded until all are out, there are also eleven players on each side." Additional positions included a "back stop" behind the catcher, and a 4th base which we assume was removed from what we would think of as home plate. Only the runs in this, and a subsequent game between those two clubs that season, are shown so there was no indication of innings played. Other accounts referenced below however say, that as in cricket, two innings was the norm. It should be noted as well that James Shuttleworth is the Woodstock shortstop.

This description may go a long way to explaining the debated circumstances surrounding an account of the game alleged to have been played in Beachville, Ontario (outside Woodstock) on June 4, 1838, and as described by a Dr. Adam Ford in a letter published May 5, 1886, by the *Sporting Life* magazine. Ford's account recalled from a childhood when he was about seven years of age is almost too good to be true. He names the players, recalls the June day — hich was in fact a public holiday in the British Empire for the mustering of militia — and even mentions the presence of spectators: Scotch volunteers likely off in pursuit of rebels from the previous year's Upper Canada Rebellion. Ford's described field was as shown in the accompanying figure.

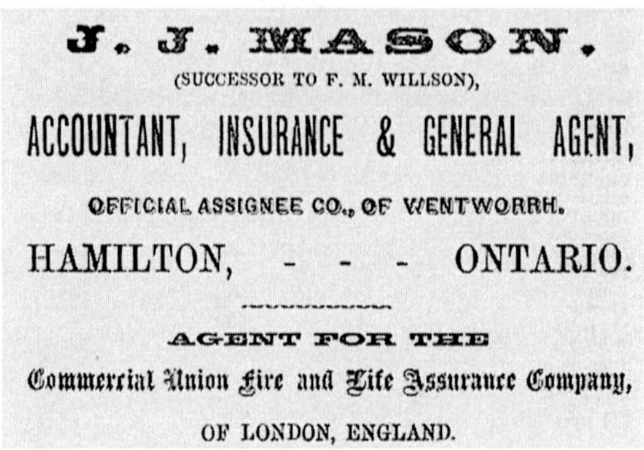

Testament to J.J. Mason's prominence: an ad in the 1868–69 Sutherland directory.

What is less convincing is his recollection of distances between bases and the game's rules, suggesting as some have said that he was mixing together remembrances from different eras. This point of view has significant merit in my mind, and given Ford's recall of having played the game as a young man in his twenties in the St. Marys area, I would suggest that his description of a four bases game follows our understanding of the "Canadian Game" —

though other features of his description, such as number of players who needed to be retired, do not. Once again this speaks to the muddled character of the story, but its detail, the time of its submission long before the Cooperstown myth had been broached, and his refusal even to suggest this may be the game's lost evolutionary link, satisfy me not only as to its attempt at authenticity, but also as its confirmation of what was something distinctly Canadian being played in Ontario in the 1850s.

A brief history of the game in Canada appeared in the *New York Clipper* of September 10, 1864:

> The American game [one assumes by this they mean the New York rules] was adopted in Hamilton for the first time in the spring of 1860 and by the Young Canadian Club of Woodstock in the season of 1861. About six weeks afterwards the Y.C.s gave a challenge to their seniors of Hamilton, whom they beat in a well-contested game, by a majority of three runs.

The reference to the "seniors" of Hamilton appears to confirm Hamilton's place as both the older of the two in organization but also refers to the age of their players.

How this came to be may be explained again in Raja's notes. In "1860, James Shuttleworth moved to Woodstock and organized a home and away series against the cricketers from Ingersoll. Woodstock took both games 83–59 and 100–58 [the two games referenced above]. The second game, on August 24, would be the last 11-man game to be played in Canada." (Just to be clear: though the men from Ingersoll may have been cricketers, and this has not been verified, it was the Canadian version of baseball that they were playing.)

The source for this appears to be a 1915 reminiscence by J. Henry Brown in the *Woodstock Sentinel Review* of April 12 that year, and as transcribed by Raja, "James Shuttleworth of Maple Leaf of Hamilton club came to work in Woodstock as a shoe maker [presumably in 1860 since he was in the games played that year against Ingersoll] and helped organize the team on a lot on Reeve St. back of the Post Office. Later a man named Wood came to Woodstock and the old-style game was given up and the regular American game adopted." The small problem with this chronology is that the Maple Leaf moniker would not be associated with Hamilton's team until 1861, but this may be due to a later confusion as to the timing of the club's naming. James's residence, however, is not in doubt. He appears in the 1861 census in Woodstock, though the name is misspelled as Suttleworth.[7] On the basis of his Upper Canada birthplace, religious affiliation, and age, it is most certainly James Shuttleworth, but here is one more reason to be suspicious of that day's recordkeeping.

James had left Hamilton not because of a "Johnny Appleseed" desire to spread baseball throughout Canada but because of a major economic downtown in the city. Amazingly, the 1860s would be a raucous and highly successful period for baseball in Hamilton. Perhaps citizens needed something to take their mind off the calamities surrounding them.[8]

James's primary influence was his older brother William. And if James was the supporter or perhaps instigator behind Woodstock's playing of the 11-a-side Canadian game, it follows that this was the game played by the original Young Canadian of Hamilton. Supports for this point of view oddly come from London, Ontario. That city's London Base Ball Club, according to George Railton's 1856 city directory, consisted of 22 players, a number perfectly suited to two teams playing the Canadian game, suggesting that the Canadian interpretation of 11-a-side baseball of four bases in which all had to be retired, as in cricket, before the other team batted, was extensive in this part of Ontario.

And according to researcher Craig Waff, an early game was described in "Base Ball in Canada," from the *Clipper* of September 27, 1856:

> London [ON], Sept. 15, 1856. Editor Clipper: Within the past few months several Base Ball clubs have been organized in this vicinity, and the first match game was played between the London and Delaware clubs, on Friday, the 12th inst.

The box score reveals that the 34–33 score eventuated when the clubs stood at 26–23 after the first inning, and then London outscored Delaware 11–7 in the second inning.

Confirming the essence of a Canadian interpretation of baseball is a June 1, 1861 *Clipper* description of the Woodstock Young Canadian club's election of officers for the year, it was noted that "The club was organized last June and during last season played six matches, winning them all. At the last meeting of the club it was resolved that they should practice the New York game for one month, and if at the end of that time they like it better than the Canadian game, they would adopt it altogether."

The June 22, 1861 *Clipper* confirmed the conversion in its description of a game between the Young Canadian club of Woodstock and nine players picked from the town of Woodstock. The Young Canadian prevailed over nine innings 10–7 and the Clipper said, "This is the first match that has ever been played there on the New York system."

James Shuttleworth had played in both the 11-man Canadian game of 1860 and now the New York system of nine men to the side of 1861. He occupied the high skill position of shortstop, attesting to his reputation and ability. As well, he was listed as one of the club's three Directors below the executive positions of President, Secretary, Treasurer, etc.

In Hamilton, meanwhile, on August 18, 1860 the Burlingtons of Hamilton lost to the Queen Cities of Buffalo 30–25 in what historian Joseph Overfield, in *Niagara Frontier* magazine, Summer 1964, described as the first international baseball match. In late August 1860 the Young Canadian Club of Hamilton were humbled in their first cross border match with the Niagara Club of Buffalo 87–13 (a score possibly explained by the Young Canadian having just switched from the "plugging Canadian Game with its softer ball to the harder ball, and faster pace, of the New York Game). At a return match in Buffalo the Young Canadians lost by a more respectable 45–13 score.

By the next season the interest in further meetings between Canadian and American clubs was noted in the same June 1, 1861 issue of the Clipper describing Woodstock's conversion to the nine-man game. Common rules were essential for such meetings.

On July 20, 1861 a baseball club was organized in Hamilton known as the "Maple Leaf" and with no mention of William Shuttleworth on the executive. Had he objected too strenuously to the move towards the New York system the previous year? Had there been a falling out with other players? Had the result of the game with Niagara caused other players to question the existing leadership?

Researcher Eves Raja argues that Arthur Feast, a stonemason, (though the Hamilton Directory of the period lists only an Alfred Feast, a marble cutter — the names being close enough however to suggest they may be the same person)) who was to popularize the game in Guelph, had supported William Shuttleworth's defense of the Canadian game; however, Charles (C.L.) Wood, a young innkeeper from the United States, eventually won the day with his support of the New York version, and the newly named Maple Leafs of Hamilton essentially assumed direction of the "Young Canadian" organization that had been started by William Shuttleworth.

I have not yet been able absolutely to substantiate the above process but several developments appear to support its general outline. Significantly, for instance, the Maple Leaf lineup 10 days later, on July 30, 1861, lists William Shuttleworth as the catcher of the Maple Leaf team playing the New York game against the Burlington club (also of Hamilton) before 800 to 900 spectators. All was apparently quickly forgiven if such was in fact necessary. Shuttleworth's play was described as "very good." The Burlington players included J.J. (John James) Mason, also from Brantford, though of an age closer to William's brother James. Born in 1842 in England, Mason's family came to Brantford in 1850 and five years later he started as a junior clerk with an auctioneer in Hamilton. He was a major player in Hamilton sports for the rest of his life.

The Shuttleworth brothers confronted each other on the diamond on September 3, 1861, in Hamilton as the Young Canadians of Woodstock scored three in the top of the ninth to outlast the Maple Leaf of Hamilton 24–22. Notably C.L. Wood acted as official scorer for Woodstock. Several sources including Raja credit him with introducing the New York rules into Woodstock. At their annual meeting in April 1862 he was elected President of the Woodstock Young Canadian baseball club while James Shuttleworth continued as a director.

One of the more intriguing pieces of sporting news that year was the appearance in Toronto of the Maple Leaf name for one of its clubs — not however for baseball or

The Young Canadians, later the Maple Leafs, played on the grounds on the north side of Central School until the end of the 1865 season. The bird's eye view shows the general area.

hockey (which wouldn't formally take off until the late 1880s), but for cricket. Of baseball Toronto was largely silent in comparison to those nearby cities of southwestern and south central Ontario (J.F. Jameson was in the Toronto lineup for the first New York rules game of May 1859 and a few months later was listed by the *Globe* newspaper as president of a new Toronto-based Canadian Pioneer club. This was largely it, however, for Toronto baseball news for many years.)

On May 24, 1862, William Shuttleworth (listed as 26 but probably 28), described as the son of James and Elizabeth, and Matilda White (24), described as the daughter of David and Aley White, were married by Rev. Dr. Blackman at St. Thomas Church, Hamilton. William's brother James was the best man.

As noted in the 1862–1863 city directory, William was also back in the leadership position with the Maple Leaf, having been appointed president with two of last year's executive, David Davies and Thomas Carroll supporting him as secretary and treasurer, respectively. Claiming overconfidence and accidents as the reason for their loss the previous season to Woodstock they mounted another challenge and this time were well-beaten, 41–14, but blamed the condition of Woodstock's grounds.

Lengthy procedural squabbling preceded the two teams' return engagements in 1863. According to Raja, James, perhaps having new opportunities, or eager to reunite with his older brother, returned to Hamilton. McCann, the Maple Leaf pitcher who "sends in the ball with lightning speed," was certain of success but two losses of 41–25 and 26–12 confirmed Woodstock as the leading Canadian team. It was a triumph repeated in 1864 as the Young Canadian of Woodstock squelched any last sense of Maple Leaf supremacy by crushing them 30–2. William's brother James, at what should have been his career peak, instead was the Maple Leaf's official scorer. Was he ill, injured, not good enough? We don't know.

Shortly thereafter the Young Canadian of Woodstock beat the Victoria of Ingersoll 37–12 to claim the champion Silver Ball. On such a positive and perhaps overconfident note they moved on to Rochester, where on Thursday September 22 they took the field against one of America's leading clubs, the Atlantic of Brooklyn. The *Clipper* report of October 1, 1864, provided a brief history of the Canadian club including, "They defeated the oldest club in Canada — the Maple Leaf of Hamilton—In three games, the last one by a score of 30–2." They were no match for Brooklyn, however, succumbing 75–11. It would eventually dawn on Canadian teams that they could only compete against the best American squads if they abandoned their solely amateur and local Canadian lineups for professionals from either side of the border, but those developments were almost a decade away. The exciting news for baseball in Canada that year was the formation of the Canadian Base Ball Association. William Shuttleworth of Hamilton was named vice-president.

Meanwhile James Shuttleworth was kept busy as an umpire. Baseball in Hamilton wasn't limited to the Maple Leafs and the Burlingtons. The Flamboro and Barton clubs were but two of a remarkable flourishing of teams in the second half of the 1860s. James was saluted with cheers after umpiring a match between the two teams on September 15. Also, once in August and then later in September Flamboro beat the Maple Leaf club of Guelph, whose lineup included some of the future stars of its rise to the pinnacle of Canadian baseball in the 1870s. Baseball had been introduced into Guelph a few years before by A.S. Feast but its greatest days lay ahead under the leadership of the Guelph brewer George Sleeman, discussed above.

An all-star game of sorts, the first of its kind in Canada, took place at the end of September. Representing the "East" were three players each from the Flamboro, Barton, and Hamilton Maple Leaf clubs, while Guelph (Maple Leafs), Woodstock (Young Canadian), and Ingersoll (Victoria) made up the West. J.J. Mason, Angus Secord, and Thomas Carroll represented the Hamilton Maple Leafs while James Shuttleworth of the same club umpired the game won by the West 19–15.

A renewed golden age for the Hamilton Maple Leafs was awaiting the team and in 1865 William and James Shuttleworth were both significant players in the team's lineup for what in retrospect would be the last extended time. In early April William was reelected to the presidency with Thomas Carroll his vice-president; W.H. Reid, in the throes of bankruptcy hearings, was named secretary and John Stoneman was treasurer.

Dundas and Ancaster met early in the season as the sport's popularity in the Hamilton region showed no signs of abating. An intrasquad game of Maple Leaf members was also played with William leading off for one team and James umpiring the affair. A reorganization of both the West Flamboro club and the Star Base Ball club was announced.

A Queen's Birthday celebration intrasquad game in May on the team's grounds by the Central School[9] near Main was characterized by the raising of a flag (likely the Union Jack); William Shuttleworth captained one team, and the baseball played in this "manly game" was described as "scientific." In June William and James led their Maple Leaf team to a 34–11 victory over West Flamboro. "Mr. [William] Shuttleworth of the Maples, was particularly agile on the occasion, making six runs and only losing one hand. The attendance of spectators was very large." Box scores of the day contained only two categories: H.L. for hands lost (i.e., the batter was retired at the plate or on the base paths), and R. for runs scored. James's total was 4 H.L. and 3 R.

The Mechanics Independent of Dundas was an emerging rival to the Hamilton Maple Leafs. A team of former cricketers, with obvious bat and ball skills, they extensively advertised the July match of the two organization's second teams in which Dundas won in ten innings. The Maple Leafs scorer was listed as a "Mr. P. Shuttleworth," raising questions as who this might have been. In mid–July both William and James played on the Hamilton team which beat their Maple Leaf namesakes from Guelph 25–15.

Bat and ball fever was now part of fraternal order and working class celebrations and picnics. The Sons of St. Crispin annual holiday featured a cricket ball tossing contest won not surprisingly by a Maple Leaf ballplayer, John Stoneman. Significantly for Hamilton's future sports history a football match was played between the married and single men, though it is not clear whether this was similar to soccer as we know it or the gridiron rugby type popular to this day in the city. Football and baseball games would also be featured at the Hibernian Society picnic later in the summer.

An early August public holiday saw Hamiltonians heading into the country, east to Toronto, or in company with the Maple Leaf baseball club travelling on the Great Western Railway to Niagara Falls. The day featured picnicking by the Falls, visiting the historic Lundy's Lane "War of 1812" battle site, touring the "wax figgers [sic]" museum, and later in the day watching a high wire walker cross between the United States and Canada. At 2 P.M. in conditions described as excessively hot, William and James along with J.J. Mason, pitcher Thomas McCann, Thomas Carroll, and Angus Secord, of the Maple Leafs defeated Niagara 30–17.

William and James were both in the lineup in mid–August when the Maple Leaf bettered the Newcastle Beaver, the first time they had played a team from east of Toronto. In late August competition resumed at the highest level of Canadian baseball when the Maple Leafs, with both Shuttleworths playing, narrowly beat Ingersoll 26–24 and now pointed towards a renewal of their rivalry for supremacy with the Young Canadian of Woodstock at the Provincial Exhibition in London.

The deadly seriousness of these matches was never better demonstrated than in the chaotic disagreement which led to the match not being played despite Hamilton having travelled all the way to London. In our distance in time from the circumstances, the squabbling seems trivial. Each side had provided a preferred ball. Hamilton as the challenger claimed the right to designate the ball. Woodstock objected on the grounds it was a second class ball palmed off on Canada as if it were first class, and argued for use of a ball manufactured by Harvey Ross of Brooklyn, New York.

Neither side would give and as Hamilton prepared to leave, Woodstock apparently relented but by then the damage was done. The game was cancelled despite umpire Stephen Rymal (of Hamilton's Barton club) ruling that the Maple Leafs as the challenging party "were bound to provide the ball": "I decide that it was a first-class ball [the one

The Corktown neighborhood of Hamilton, undated but pre-1900. The boxed area shows the general location of the Maple Leaf playing grounds.

provided by Hamilton], and by the Young Canadians refusing to play, the Maple Leaves [sic] of Hamilton have the right to claim the game."

The Maple Leafs held their annual dinner on December 1, 1865, in their club rooms on John Street and boasted of their having won "handsomely" eight of ten matches with other teams, and, those two losses being against combinations of other clubs.

> Their defeat cannot be recorded to the credit of any single club in the Province. The Maple Leaf club has been established a term of years, and is virtually the parent of all other organizations of the kind in Western Canada, as it most assuredly is the first in science of the game.

It was at this gathering the team announced it was moving from its "old grounds upon Main Street" to new playing grounds upon [Upper] James Street.

In conclusion the revelers noted that, "For their efficiency in the game, and the general prosperity of the Maple Leaf, much is due to the President, Mr. William Shuttleworth, who has always manifested a deep interest in the same, and his encouragement of such manly recreations reflects creditably upon the character of the gentleman," and they concluded with a rendition honoring a "jolly good fellow."

Unfortunately the next season was marred by events outside of baseball. Irish agitation for independence from Great Britain, and the conclusion of the American Civil War, brought many Irish Americans of both Catholic and Protestant persuasion together in an uneasy alliance known as the Fenian Brotherhood.[10] Raids into the British colony of Canada began in 1866. The Fenian raids have been largely forgotten today but the threat they posed was a factor in speeding up the ultimate unification and confederation of the new country of Canada one year later.

Such was the temper of those days that a parliamentarian from Canada West, Joseph Rymal, described the Fenians as "half human hyenas" and proposed (apparently tongue in cheek) to offer a reward of five dollars for each of their scalps. At a time however when conflicts between natives and settlers in the American West were being regularly reported, the humor was lost on a Detroit newspaper which attacked Rymal's bad taste and brutality. Hamilton's response to the Fenians was the arming of the Thirteenth Battalion. J.J. Mason was one of at least three Maple Leaf ballplayers with the Battalion, the others known being John Stoneman and William Shuttleworth (who at his eventual discharge would be listed as Color Sergeant). Fears of an invasion appeared to have subsided in April but then a raid commenced in early June and the Battalion marched off to repel the invasion. It saw action at Ridgeway, and in response to the continuing conflict the following notice appeared in the *Hamilton Times* of June 18, 1866:

> BASE BALL NOTICE.
>
> At a meeting of the Maple Leaf Base Ball Club of this city it was resolved to announce publicly that, owing to the absence at the front of several of the leading players, no FIRST NINE matches will be played until further notice.
>
> J.J. MASON, Secretary.

Images of two of the Maple Leafs, Mason and Stoneman are offered herein. I'm uncertain whether their titles as shown were those of 1866 or ones later attained. I have yet to find an image of William Shuttleworth.

Some degree of normalcy was returning in August as the Maple Leafs booked passage on the steamer, *Passport*, for their game with Newcastle. Not only did the "Maples" as the *Times* reported on August 9, 1866, lose 75–44, but William Shuttleworth, "...one of the best players of the Maple Leaf club was disabled by an accident and obliged to withdraw from the game at the third innings which circumstance may account to some extent for the disparity exhibited.

The Hamilton player returned home today by the steamer *Champion.*" It's possible the injury caused Shuttleworth to remain an extra day. He bounced back quickly, however, resuming his leadoff spot against the Victoria club of Ingersoll in mid–August, collecting three runs in eight at bats as the Leafs humbled the visitors 45–17.

Once again an all-star game was held at the end of the season and J.J. Mason was one of three Maple Leafs named to a squad which also had players from Flamboro and Dundas. They beat the "West" team with players from the Victoria of Ingersoll, the Young Canadian of Woodstock, and the Guelph Maple Leafs, 25–21. The Hamilton Maple Leafs took home the silver cup which they themselves had donated as the prize.

While it might be thought that William Shuttleworth would have begun reconsidering his baseball commitment in light of his injury, as well as his advancing years as a ballplayer (now into his thirties) and his obligations as the breadwinner for a family with young children, such does not appear to be the case.[11] Nor did the apparent withdrawal of his brother James from the baseball scene, whether because of illness, occupational uncertainty, or changing interests, play into William's decision.

Historian Michael Katz's academic study of Hamilton in midcentury confirms that while the nuclear family was as important in Shuttleworth's day as we think of it today, so was the associational life and its social gatherings which some modern critics such as Robert Putnam (*Bowling Alone*) claim are in decline in the 21st century.

For William Shuttleworth the primary activities of 1867 seem to have been in his role as Color-Sergeant of the 13th battalion, organizing excursions and social activities, as well as providing the grounds of the Maple Leaf Base Ball Club on upper James Street for a series of athletic sports for the visiting Toronto Field Battery.

The other great event was the grand assembling in mid–August at Detroit for what was boldly called the World's Base Ball Tournament, on the city's new grounds at the terminus of the Woodward avenue street railroad. Seating was available for 2000 spectators. The Maple Leafs were entered in the First Class level of the tournament and at the conclusion of Hamilton's 19–10 win over the Welkin club of Port Huron, in which William Shuttleworth crossed the plate twice,"a grand parade of the several clubs in uniform took place on the grounds. A photograph of the entire company was taken. There being more than 20 clubs in attendance the turn out in the variegated uniforms made no mean exhibition."

The Unknown Club of Jackson, Michigan, won first prize, the Alleghany near Pittsburgh the second, and the Maple Leaf finished third. J.J. Mason accepted the trophy, a gold ball valued at $100. The hollow ball of silver, covered with a heavy sheet of gold, bore the inscription, "Won by the Maple Leaf B.B. Club at the Detroit Tournament August 1867." The trophy was displayed for several days in the window of Stevenson and Attwood's Hamilton jewelry store. In celebration the next March, the team placed a large ad in the *Hamilton Times* for their annual dinner at which the "magnificent" gold ball was on display.[12]

By the 1868 season Hamilton was awash in baseball clubs. John Stoneman had jumped to the Active club. The Star club was preparing for a major tournament in

Niagara Falls in June. Other teams included the Sunshine, the Golden Leaf, the Oak Leaf, the Ontario, the Barton, the Defiance, The Fearless, and the Excelsior, as well as workingmen's teams including the "Unknowns" of the Canadian Hat Factory, the "Well Knowns" from the Pop Factory, the Cigar Makers, the Tobacconists and the Iron Moulders.

The Young Canadians of Woodstock, described as the champions of Canada, replayed their ill-fated 1864 encounter with the Brooklyn Atlantics at the Niagara Falls tournament. Supported by three additions from the Hamilton Maple Leafs, they suffered less embarrassment this time, losing 30–17 in a five inning game, abandoned in the sixth because of a torrential downpour.

The Maple Leafs, according to an account from the June 27, 1868, *Hamilton Times*, "the champion club of the city," fell to the Star club by 10 runs. Neither Shuttleworth was in the lineup. Sporting affections in town were now being challenged by lacrosse, which was moving west from strongholds in Montreal and Toronto. A game advertised for July 11 includes an admission charge (ten cents!), the performance of the Band of the 13th Battalion, and a contest between the local club and the nearby Six Nations.

Only bits and pieces of William's personal life are known. For instance, what became of his father, mother and siblings other than James? The Sutherland's Directory of 1868–1869 shows what appears to be either his mother or sister living in Hamilton. The "Mrs." implies she was more likely a widow than a divorcee, since death was far more common. However the abbreviations listed in the Directory include that for a "widow" and such is not appended to Eliza Shuttleworth's name. Additionally, William is now described as a salesman, though the distinction from his previous description as a clerk may be minor.

We do know however that a job change was in the offing for William Shuttleworth, as his old retainer's company was in its last days. The local paper announced the disposition of Colin McRae's remaining stock.

Compounding that trauma for William and other Hamiltonians was the extraordinary heat wave blanketing the entire northeastern part of Canada and the United States. Multiple deaths from sunstroke were reported. In those days before air conditioning, one's only defense was walking in the shade, avoiding unnecessary activity, and sponging one's skin all over in the morning. Yet on a Friday afternoon when the temperature nudged 95 degrees the Maple Leaf, with William Shuttleworth back in his leadoff position, outscored the Star team who had bested them earlier in the year, 67–34. William crossed the plate five times but the hero of the day was Thomas McCann with ten runs. Illness, no doubt due to the prolonged heat wave, caused the Fearless and Excelsior clubs to postpone their match a few days later.

William Shuttleworth appears to have been undaunted by the end of the McRae business, the heat, or the challenge of lacrosse. Instead he was in Woodstock in early August to umpire the Canadian championship match between the Young Canadians of Woodstock and the Maple Leaf club of Guelph. Woodstock won 36–29 before over 2,000 fans entertained as well by two bands. It was later reported that while Shuttleworth kept the game on the field under control such was not the case in the stands where players and spectators engaged in a "general row." Several Guelph men "were unmercifully beaten" and that town declared its unwillingness to "go visiting to Woodstock again."

The *Guelph Mercury* condemned Woodstock for its wide-eyed reputation for being the headquarters of many pugilists, gamblers, and 'light fingered gentry' in general, who are not kept in proper subjection." Countering that on August 15 was a *Hamilton Times* comment that "juvenile depravity at Guelph is appalling." A purse of $200 was raised for a return match between Woodstock and Guelph to be played on Hamilton's neutral grounds. Ironically however the *Hamilton Times* reported in an August 5, 1868, article on "baseball" problems in their own city:

> "Every Sunday afternoon, between the hours of three and six o'clock, on the commons directly opposite the corner of Mary and Lind streets, may be witnessed an exciting game of base ball, jumping etc. inaugurated by the juvenile banditti of the locality, and who vary their diversions by a raid on the neighboring orchards. These, with numerous other disgraceful scenes, are a terror to citizens residing in that quarter, and the police would do well to make their appearance in that direction."

A match on August 21 between the Actives led by John Stoneman and William Shuttleworth's Maple Leafs at which he was back as catcher, saw the Actives defeat what was described as the "parent club" by ten runs. Meanwhile the Stars were charging ten cents to see their match on the grounds of the Maple Leaf against a visiting Buffalo team. It is the first known charging of admission for a baseball game. It did not deter a large crowd, as the Star beat the "Frank Perew of Buffalo" team 54–34 with William Shuttleworth umpiring. At the end of the month the Maple Leaf finally defeated the Actives, to whom they had lost twice previously, but William was not in the lineup.

Throughout that summer Ingersoll (dubbed the mushroom champions) had beaten Woodstock to claim Canadian honors but had in turn been beaten by the Tecumseh Club of London. Challenge matches, rather than a formal league structure, made it hard to determine who the best team was. Though William was back in the lineup for the Maple Leafs visit to London, they were crushed by the Tecumsehs 69–15. The *Hamilton Times* called it "Humiliation of the Maple-Leaf Club." Members were asked to attend the Maple Leaf regular meeting at their John Street club rooms.

There was now so much sporting activity in Hamilton it was unrealistic to expect the Maple Leaf ascendancy or hold on its members to continue forever. A broader sense of baseball's popularity was found in a column from an ex-Hamiltonian now living in Rochester, New York. His description of baseball fever in that city could have been applied equally to Hamilton. By the 1869 season baseball had been flourishing not only in southwestern Ontario but throughout most eastern regions. Prescott in eastern Ontario was a hotbed, and Ottawa was emerging as such. The game had been in Montreal throughout the sixties, and a team from that city played against one from Atlantic Canada's Saint John, New Brunswick. This was unusual given the strong north-south pull of nearby American markets for Canadian teams seeking games outside their own local region.

The *Clipper* (May 29, 1869) headlined one Canadian box score with the title, "Ball Tossing Across the Border," and in a 14 August commentary quoted a London Ontario correspondent's refrain that,

> The American national game is spreading rapidly in this section of the Queen's domain, and will ere long completely obliterate the "Hould Henglish" [sic] game of cricket. The masses see that it is a more exciting game than cricket; that more skill has to be displayed by the players and that it is not near as tedious to witness.

Nevertheless in 1871 cricket retained its supremacy in some places as the British colony of Newfoundland played an international match of sorts with the Canadian province of Nova Scotia in Halifax.[13]

A major tournament of the province's best teams in Woodstock in late June and early July resulted in victory in the first class for the Victorias of Ingersoll, followed by the Maple Leaf of Guelph and the Young Canadians of Woodstock. Despite a neat uniform of white cricketing flannel and scarlet hose, the Tecumseh of London finished out of the running.

The Hamilton Maple Leafs did not participate and the Independents of Dundas now appeared to be the area's superior team. William Shuttleworth and his teammates were increasingly a reminder of what had once been. Nothing represented this more poignantly than the following two notices in the *Hamilton Spectator*. First from 28 August 1869 under the heading "Respect for the Dead":

> The members of the Maple Leaf Base Ball club are requested by the Vice President T.C. Carroll to assemble at the Club's room on John St. this (Friday) afternoon at 2:00 o'clock for the purpose of attending, in a body, the funeral of their late comrade, James Shuttleworth.

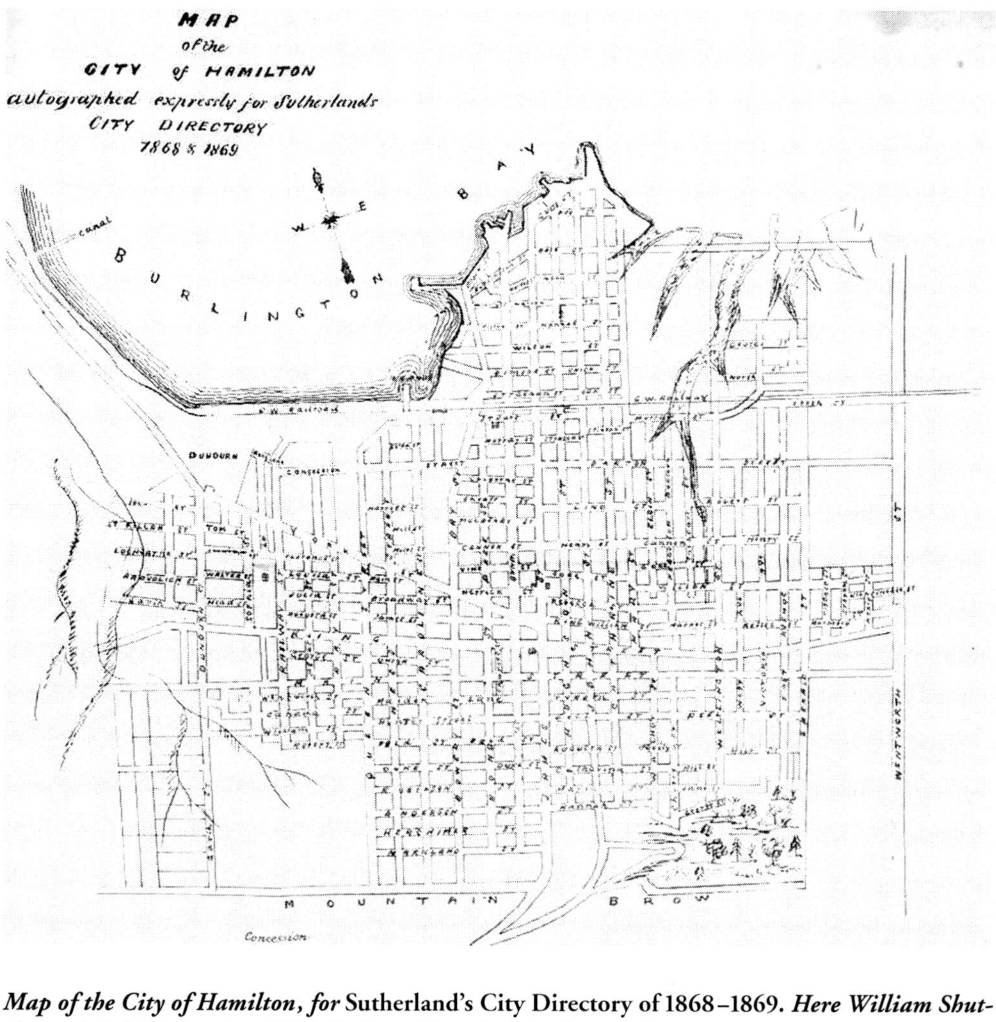

Map of the City of Hamilton, for Sutherland's City Directory of 1868–1869. *Here William Shuttleworth left his mark as "The Father of Baseball in Canada."*

And then a few days later on Monday, August 30, 1869, also in the *Spectator*, under the heading "Funeral":

> A large number of the members of the Maple Leaf Base Ball Club accompanied the remains of the late Mr. James Shuttleworth to the grave. The deceased gentleman was an enthusiastic admirer and promoter of the game of Base Ball and his loss will be severely felt by the various clubs with which he was connected.

There is no doubt more to learn about these events. James had not been publicly active in Maple Leaf games for some time, and though he is described as an admirer and promoter, it is notable that "player" is not said. More details about the cause of death are yet to be uncovered and the grave to which he was escorted has not as yet been found. Even though Ontario law required official recording of deaths beginning in 1869 no such record has yet been found. Given the precarious income status of many Hamiltonians in this period and the transiency of occupation for those either clerking (as William was doing) or shoemaking (James' profession) it is perhaps not surprising that a more formal grave site was not identified and mounted with a tombstone. Two weeks after his brother's death in 1869, William was back on the diamond umpiring a match on September 15 between the Ontarios of Hamilton and the Queen City of Buffalo.

Of long term significance for local sport, the Hamilton Foot Ball Club, from which have descended today's Canadian Football League Ti-Cats, was formed on November 3, 1869. According to Football Canada's Timelines this happened over George Lee's Fruit Store, as the club adopted a black and orange color scheme. Their first game on 18 December 1869 was on the Maple Leaf base ball grounds against the 13th Battalion. William Shuttleworth's role, if any, in arranging this fixture is not known.

The May 7, 1870, *Clipper* reports William's return as president of the Maple Leaf Club with Thomas Carrroll his vice-president. Toronto's belated participation at the higher levels of baseball was recorded that year in the appearance of the Dauntless Club.

Guelph Maple Leafs had continued their winning ways from their late season championship victory over London in 1869 and then with a similar triumph in August 1870 over Woodstock. J.J. Mason umpired a match around the same time in which Dundas Independents easily beat the Hamilton Maple Leaf without William Shuttleworth in the lineup. I have found no further records of William playing in a game but it is possible he did. The *Clipper* of April 15, 1871 reported his continuing role as president for another term of the Maple Leafs with Carroll also re-elected as vice-president. That same year William and Matilda's fourth child, a son, was born and likely in memory of his brother was named James. Another Shuttleworth appears in the Directory that year and although not definitive may be William's sister Mary, approaching or having reached her 30th birthday and appropriately living on Maiden Lane.

Since it is likely that William was self-employed, it was not surprising that a year later (1872), with a wife and four children to support, approaching the age of 40 and recognizing the importance of his own health and the time required for his employment, his name was missing from the executive of the Hamilton Maple Leafs. Thomas Carroll was named President.

Harry, a fifth and final surviving child, was born to William and Matilda in 1874. The city they lived in had changed significantly. William's world, however, was to be altered permanently in 1881.

Catastrophe struck in that year with the death of William's wife Matilda on October 7 at the age of 44, leaving him a widower and father of five children. We might wonder with Matilda's death how William "senior" looked after his young family, three of whom were twelve and under. The answer appears to be that by 1885–1886, William "senior," our father of baseball in Canada, was living on his own as a boarder at the Walker House, while William "junior" had assumed responsibility for his younger brothers.

William "senior's" employment history is unclear through this period, though Raja, likely referencing a news article that Gardiner only partially quoted, claims that Shuttleworth continued in his dry goods business until retiring from it in 1883. A city directory of 1885–1886 lists two William Shuttleworths — father and son.

William "senior" apparently worked for James Reid, the famous furniture man, at some point, so we might conclude that the "Wm." listed was William "senior," appropriately described as an upholsterer likely with that company. William, "junior" would thus be the salesman living at 16 Grove. Supporting these conclusions is our knowledge that the elder William went by Wm. in the 1900 United States census and his occupation at that time was listed as upholsterer.

The 1891 census shows William "junior" working as a clerk in a furniture store, almost certainly a salesman, but ultimately clinching the above conclusion is the listing in that census of William "junior's" two brothers, James (20) and Harry (16), living with his family (Harry was still living with William "junior" in 1901).[14] In William "junior's" case he married Jennie Vassie (b. 1863) in 1888. A daughter Marion, born the year before (1887) is listed as a family member in the 1891 census. Her parentage is uncertain. By the 1901 census however William "junior's" wife is listed as Mable (b. 1868).[15]

William "senior" entered the upholstery business with his son and daughter-in-law in Geneva, New York.[16] It was here he died on March 31, 1903. There was a small notice of such in the *Geneva Advertiser* and a few other local papers. He was not as significant a person in that world as he had been in Hamilton. His body was returned to Hamilton to be interned alongside his late wife Matilda.[17]

Baseball in Hamilton as elsewhere had long since moved far away from the easier fraternity and amateurism of William's day towards increased professionalization and the building of a more substantive ball grounds. As Hamilton's mayor in the mid–1880s J.J. Mason, while at the same time attempting to help the victims of a downturn in the economy, was also part of the changes in baseball. He supported new facilities and an enhanced profile for the game which would see Hamilton and Toronto abandon their one-time affiliation with other Ontario towns to enter the emerging professional and commercial world of "organized baseball" with its models of major and minor leagues. As noted by one observer, Hamilton could not exist on baseball friendship with Guelph. Hamiltonians would soon discover that likewise Toronto would not be content with the baseball friendship of their city. Mason followed William (senior) to the grave a few months after his fellow ballplayer's passing, succumbing to tuberculosis.

An account in the *Herald Scrapbook* (Vol. G1 part 1, p. 99–100) titled the "Father of Baseball," by H.F. Gardiner, dated September 8, 1923, summarized William Shuttleworth's life. In it he is referred to as "Billy" Shuttleworth, a familiarity that does not appear in those accounts of his life from the period in which he lived (nor is the name "Bill" used to describe him). Perhaps the use of "Billy" is meant to suggest the playfulness of the project he started. Gardiner wrote:

Do the baseball enthusiasts of 1923 ever talk of/about Billy Shuttleworth? When looking through the papers of 1903, I came upon the notice of his death, which occurred at the residence of his son, James, at Geneva N.Y. 31st of March 1903. The body was brought to Hamilton for burial. Mr. Shuttleworth was 70 years of age. He had been with the old Lister firm in Hamilton, then with Colin McRae, and afterward with James Reid, the famous furniture man. He was color sergeant in the Thirteenth battalion at the time of the Fenian raid in 1866, and he was regarded as the father of baseball in Hamilton, having been president of the original Maple Leaf club.

Yet while he is undoubtedly Hamilton's father of baseball, he was much more. In taking the game from its informal roots and formalizing it into an organized sport for young men with a team structure and eventually a well-developed network of teams throughout this part of Ontario, where the game reached its highest level of play, he deserves the title, "The Father of Baseball in Canada." A final direct connection to William appears in 1946. The accompanying photos located in Hamilton's Public Library show Harry, Harry, William Shuttleworth's fifth and final surviving child, now in his seventies, with the famous ball from the 1867 Detroit tournament, no doubt given him by his father. Where the ball went from here is not known, but its location, if it still exists, and more information about the Father of Canadian Baseball, William Shuttleworth, is now the task for today's researchers.

Abstract

The first place in which the modern institutional and organized structure of baseball appeared in Canada was Hamilton, Canada West (today's Canadian province of Ontario), in 1854 with the establishment of the Young Canadian baseball organization, followed a year later by the Burlington club, also in Hamilton. We can confidently say that William Shuttleworth of that city was, from the game's earliest organized days in Canada, baseball's leading proponent and premier pioneer, and deserving of the title "The Father of Canadian Baseball." A somewhat distinct Canadian interpretation of baseball was played throughout the 1850s featuring 11 men to the side, and two-inning games in which "plugging" a runner between bases was allowed. By the 1860s players of this era, including Shuttleworth and his Hamilton teammates, had switched to New York Rules, but not before William's brother James had introduced the old game to Woodstock, a community that would surpass Hamilton as the best team that decade.

Notes

1. Box score from an undated news account of 1873 Boston–Guelph game with reference to lively ball.
2. Box score from the New York *Clipper*, August 24, 1861, from a game between Bowmanville and Port Hope appears to show Addy (though the name is spelled Addie), playing as a teenager in a local game. He is described as a fine player and "a very powerful batter."
3. Joseph Shuttleworth's census data for 1852 is also problematic, listing him as being age 40, making his birth year 1812, not the 1807 date shown in his biography. Other facts, however, such as the name of his wife Ellen Duckworth, line up with both census and biographical information confirming that this is the one and same Joseph Shuttleworth despite the discrepancy in age.
4. JOSEPH SHUTTLEWORTH (deceased), was born in Lancashire, England, in 1807, and spent his younger days in his native land. In the year 1830 he came to Canada, settling in Brantford, where he was

engaged in the distilling business for some years with Mr. Mawby. By trade he was a baker, and was proprietor of a bakery and general confectionery for several years. Subsequently he was engaged in the butchering trade for many years, and then moved on to a farm. In 1867 he came to Brantford where he died on December 24th of that year. Mr. Shuttleworth was a member of the Methodist Church, and one of its charter members. He married in Brantford Ellen Duckworth, also a native of Lancashire, England, by whom there was a family of six children —five living. The mother is also living, and enjoying good health in her sixtieth year. James R. Shuttleworth, canner of fruits, Brantford, was born August 7th, 1848, and received his early training in Brantford. When quite a young man he engaged in the grocery and fruit business, and when nineteen years of age bought out E. Sims & Son. This business he carried on for twelve consecutive years, when he entered the wholesale foreign and domestic fruit trade and canning industry. In 1875 his brother Joseph M. entered as a partner, and in 1878 went to England in connection with the business and became a member of the firm of Simonds & Co., fruit brokers, Liverpool, England, for which firm he acts as agent. In June, 1882, another brother, George, became associated in business. Shuttleworth Bros. enjoy an excellent trade in Ontario, and have established an agency in Chicago.

James R. is a member of the A.O.U.W. Lodge, a reformer in politics, and, with his wife, is an adherent of Brant Avenue Methodist Church. He married October 1881, Martha, daughter of Wesley Howell, by whom he has one child, Hugh R.

5. William's listing in the 1851–1852 census .
6. John Swinton's paper, February 1, 1885 from Palmer, B. *Culture in Conflict*, (p. 36).
7. James Shuttleworth, Ontario Census, 1861.
8. Population is always a revealing portrait of a city's success or calamity. The figures below speak for themselves.
9. Central School's location in the 1862–1863 Directory was listed as Bond and Bowery. Today it should be noted that Park Street was *Bond Street*, and Bay Street South was *Bowery Street*.
10. The Catholic–Protestant and "international" identity of the Fenians was shown in the June 4, 1866, issue of the *Hamilton Times* listing those arrested.
11. The 1881 Canadian census shows the extent of William Shuttleworth's family.
12. The dinner was described on March 19, 1868, in glowing terms.
13. An international cricket match reported in the *Clipper*, 1871.
14. The 1891 census shows both James and Harry living with William "junior" and his family. James (20) is described as an upholsterer and Harry (16) as a message boy.
15. William Shuttleworth "junior's" 1901 household reported in the census.
16. 1900 U.S. census lists an 1836 birth (almost certainly it was 1834) and his occupation as an upholsterer. Father and son are both listed as upholsterers.
17. Cemetery records for William and Matilda Shuttleworth.

The Sam Barkley Case

David Ball *with* David Nemec

The disbandment of the Buffalo and Providence clubs in the spring of 1886 ended the epidemic of club buyouts that had begun with the conclusion of the trade war with the Union Association following the 1884 season. The next years would see some buyouts of entire teams, but increasingly the focus turned to transactions more familiar to us involving small numbers of players sold or traded by clubs, generally as a part of normal business. Regularized by the elimination of the 10-day rule and the creation of the waiver system, trades and sales became increasingly routinized.

Even before the dispersal of the Providence and Buffalo players was finalized, however, the American Association gave the new waiver rule its first test, and it was a severe one. Before the sale of second baseman Sam Barkley was finally straightened out, a league president had lost his job, a club was impelled to desert the Association and join the National League, and it became glaringly apparent that the new rule did not begin to solve all the problems of transferring players from club to club.[1]

Barkley had been one of the players to come to the St. Louis Browns in the purchase of the disbanding Toledo franchise's best players after the American Association pared from 12 to eight teams once the Union Association ceased operations. Also included were outfielder Curt Welch and pitcher Tony Mullane. A member of the Browns in 1883, Mullane signed a contract for $2,500 with St. Louis's Union Association club, but then, apparently concerned that the UA might fail and render him blacklisted by the established major leagues, he agreed to tear up his new contract and return to the AA for the same $2,500 the Unions were to pay him. Browns president Chris Von der Ahe did not bring Mullane back to his own team, however, probably because of legal complications if he were to try to play in St. Louis. Instead he arranged to sign Mullane to a contract with the new Toledo club, thereby assuring that he would not bolster a serious rival of the Browns for loop championship honors. Since a player still could not be compelled to sign with a team that had purchased his release, Von der Ahe therefore procured written

David Ball was, before his untimely death in 2011, employed in the library of the University of Cincinnati, where he had received a doctorate in Roman History. He compiled a register of 19th century interclub transactions and wrote a biography of O. P. Caylor that appeared in the *Dictionary of Literary Biography* volume "American Sportswriters and Writers on Sport." He was a frequent contributor to SABR publications and this journal.

David Nemec is the author of *The Great Encyclopedia of 19th Century Major League Baseball, The Beer and Whisky League, Early Dreams* and many other novels and works on baseball. *This Day in Baseball: A Day-by-Day Record of the Events That Shaped the Game*, was co-written with Scott Flatow. *The Union Association: An Unexpected Last Stop* includes excerpts from his compilation of the biographies of every player, manager, owner, league official and regular umpire that took part in the creation and development of major league baseball in the nineteenth century. His latest book is *The Rank and File of 19th Century Major League Baseball Biographies of 1,084 Players, Owners, Managers and Umpires.*

 DOI: 10.3172/BB.7.126

promises from each player to sign a contract after the then mandatory 10-day waiting period had expired before giving Toledo a down payment on the purchase price, with the remainder to follow when the players were signed. But the players' promises were not binding. When midnight arrived on the 10th day and all the other players assembled to sign, Mullane was in a hotel room with representatives of the Cincinnati Reds, who were counting out 20 $100 bills as an advance against the $5,000 in salary they had agreed to pay him in 1885. Barkley, who may have had a falling out with Mullane over personal issues, sharply denounced Mullane's repudiation of his promise to Von der Ahe, urging that the pitcher be permanently blacklisted.[2] He played a strong game at second base for the Browns in 1885 but was unhappy nevertheless. Joe Pritchard, *Sporting Life*'s St. Louis correspondent, would later remember that "Sam Barkley, when he played second base for Von der Ahe's team, used to tell the people in every town the Browns visited that he would like to get away from the Browns and play elsewhere."[3]

If Barkley did not wish to play for the Browns, Von der Ahe was happy to rid himself of a malcontent while finding a place in the lineup for his excellent utilityman Yank Robinson and putting some money in his pocket. In December 1885 when the American Association came together in Philadelphia for its annual meeting, president William Nimick and manager Horace Phillips of the Pittsburgh club offered Von der Ahe $750 for Barkley's release. Von der Ahe replied that Barkley's release had "cost me $1,000 when I got him, that I thought Robinson was just as good good a man at second, and that if they would give me $1,000 for Barkley they could have him if he was willing." Billy Barnie of Baltimore at first thought Von der Ahe was joking, but when he realized Barkley was really on the sales block he told the Browns' president that if he could wait while Barnie telegraphed his board of directors, Baltimore would probably be willing to meet his price. By December 14 Barnie had agreed to Von der Ahe's proposal and Baltimore's acquisition of the infielder was announced as accomplished fact. Nimick and Phillips went home disgruntled over their failure to get their man, but they soon informed Von der Ahe they were willing to pay his price. The St. Louis president announced he would consult Barkley himself and let him choose the purchaser, or remain in St. Louis if he preferred."[4]

Barkley was spending the early winter in New Orleans, a popular spot for professional players to play winter ball during the 1880s. During a game there Barkley had a clash with his enemy Mullane, flinging his bat at Mullane after the pitcher threw at him. He soon left town, traveling up the Mississippi River to St. Louis where he met with Von der Ahe, who explained that Barkley could choose between Pittsburgh, Baltimore, or the Browns.

Billy Barnie's Orioles had risen to the first division in 1884 after finishing in the Association cellar their first two seasons, but then had dropped back into last place in 1885. Baltimore's fans had supported their unsuccessful team quite well, but Barnie feared falling attendance at the end of the season might be an indication that the city's patience might be wearing thin. The always excitable Barnie had been complaining loudly about his Association colleagues' unwillingness to help him strengthen his team either by selling him players or by loosening the rules that restricted player movement. At the joint meetings in the fall, he had railed against the new waiver rule that forced him to keep his hands off the Providence and Buffalo players, threatening that he might jump to the National League in order to get a share of the bounty that was being distributed there unless the other Association clubs helped him out. But everybody else needed all the good players they had; as Louisville manager Jim Hart would remark wryly, "Since his team has been a loser Billy seems to think that the Association ought to give him a winning team; he seems to forget that the other clubs have their own troubles as well as he and that the giving of players to the weak teams has not been very well introduced yet in the association." As a result, Barnie was offered only benchwarmers the other teams intended to dispose of anyway. In Barkley he now had the prospect of a player who was no castoff.[5]

Although Von der Ahe allowed Barkley to choose his own purchaser, he said he preferred to send the star second basemean to shore up the weak Baltimores, and when it began to look as though it would turn out that way, he was praised, sometimes in rather extravagant terms, for his generous willingness to help the Orioles out. Said one Baltimore writer:

> Mr. Von der Ahe's action in giving Barkley for a Christmas present seems to be prompted by a very kind and sympathetic heart and is refreshing to hear of in these days of scramble for players. Nothing seems impracticable to him in the line of assisting a weak club, and if there were more to follow his example the business of base ball would run along smoothly and the receipts and profits would be greater.[6]

A *Sporting Life* article reported that Von der Ahe, "one of the biggest hearted men in the American Association," was giving Barkley to the Orioles *gratis.* More jaded observers thought Von der Ahe was giving the Orioles Barkley only because he himself owned a piece of the Orioles, but events would show this was certainly not the right explanation.[7] On the other hand, it would become apparent as well that, while Von der Ahe may perhaps have genuinely wanted to give Barnie a hand, he expected to be paid, and his primary concern was probably getting his $1,000. Nor was Von der Ahe's willingness to let Barkley choose his own purchaser an act of generosity. If he wanted to be rid of the disgruntled but marketable player — he almost certainly did, and probably knew that Barkley would distain the option of staying with the Browns — then he had no choice but to let Barkley go where he wanted. According to the new waiver rule, when more than one club in a league indicated a desire to accept the services of a released player, the man himself could choose which club to join.

Sam Barkley with the St. Louis Browns, Buchner Gold Coin card, 1887.

So it was left to Pittsburgh and Baltimore to woo Barkley. Barnie had already contacted him in New Orleans by telegraph, but Barkley refused to commit himself, and he reportedly told others he preferred to go to Pittsburgh.[8] Barnie then requested that Von der Ahe contact him when Barkley returned to St. Louis, but Von der Ahe told him he had already left to go to his home in Wheeling and

"If you want him go for him quick."[9] Barkley had hardly arrived in Wheeling before Pittsburgh's president Nimick and manager Horace Phillips appeared in town. It was Christmas Eve, but they wanted to talk contract. Barkley refused to accompany them to Pittsburgh, since he had already agreed to meet with Barnie in Wheeling, but said he would come to Pittsburgh after seeing the Orioles' boss. Barkley was asking $2,250, and Phillips later claimed that he and Nimick had met Barkley's terms, and "Barkley as good as promised to accept the offer, accepting a railroad ticket to Pittsburg [sic], where he was to have gone to sign." Another version of the story had it that the Pittsburgh officials refused to illicitly surpass the newly implemented $2,000 salary limit, and Barkley himself claimed that he had put the Pittsburgh officials off without any definite agreement.[10]

There was no rest for the weary club official. Wheeling lies close enough to Pittsburgh that Nimick and Phillips presumably enjoyed Christmas at home, but Billy Barnie spent it in a strange city, visiting a man whose attraction for him lay neither in social graces nor family ties, but simply his ability to play second base. The fullest account of the meeting is Barnie's. The two met at the McClure House in Wheeling, where Barkley told him frankly that he preferred "for personal reasons" to play in Pittsburgh — perhaps Barkley wanted to be close to his Wheeling home, or it may be he did not relish the idea of going from the Association champions to an Orioles team that even the acquisition of a Sam Barkley could hardly lift far out of last place. He was "after the most money," however.[11] Barnie, who prided himself on faithful adherence to the rules and never had enough cash to cut many corners anyway, was not among the owners willing to violate the new $2,000 salary limit, but he nonetheless told Barkley he would pay as much for his services as any other club. The limitation rule allowed exceptions for players paid extra money to act as team captain, and Barnie offered to pay an additonal $250 for that service, then ran his offer up to a total of $2,450 when Barkley raised his price. Barkley himself then suggested, according to Barnie, that for just 50 more dollars he would sign a written statement promising to contract with the Orioles once his release was finalized. After some reflection Barnie agreed, and the two men visited the shop of Barkley's tailor, where they found witnesses for Barkley's signature of a simple agreement pledging to "sign and play with the Baltimore B.B. Club for the season of 1886" when Von der Ahe had released him, and an undated standard player contract as well. Barnie insisted he had been careful to act in the most scrupulous manner, making sure first that Barkley had not committed himself to any other club and then admonishing Barkley's witnesses not to let him sign anything if he were not completely satisfied with the terms. Barnie handed Barkley a check for $500, the two had dinner and Barnie returned to Baltimore.[12] Barkley himself later applied a caveat in his description of the agreement he had signed: "I signed with him conditionally, said condition being that he would secure my release, he stating at that time that he had virtually secured it, and would have it when formally declared when he forwarded the bonus of $1,000, *which was to be remitted immediately.*"[13] And of course it was true that his agreement must be conditional in the sense that it could not take effect until Von der Ahe had released him.

Within a few days Barnie was on the road again, returning to Philadelphia where another Association meeting was about to convene. He arrived on December 28 and showed off the documents signed by Barkley to various club officials, including those from Pittsburgh, whom he accused of meddling in his deal with the result that he had had to increase his offer to Barkley. Barnie had pleaded for help for his weak team.[14]

> This is a sample of the way they help me. At the first chance I have to get a really good man, one of the clubs pledged to give me a lift steps in and tries to rob me of the fruits of my enterprise, compelling me to spend a large amount of money to secure a man whom I could have gotten without trouble and at much less trouble if Pittsburg had stood aloof. D-n such friendship. Hereafter I'm going to look out for Barnie and the Baltimore Club, and depend upon no one but my self. I'm tired of professions of friendship without performance.

Most importantly, of course, Barnie displayed Barkley's documents to Von der Ahe as a sign that the sale could take place. Both officials were pressed for time, however, so Barnie delegated Gus Abell of the Brooklyn club to talk to Von der Ahe while he himself went back to Baltimore. Those two met the next morning and agreed that Barnie would send the thousand dollars to St. Louis and Von der would then forward Barkley's release to Association secretary–president Denny McKnight. With the 10-day rule no longer complicating matters, the exchange of money, the player's release, and the signing of the new contract could now take place almost simultaneously.

According to the *Sporting Life* account, Abell and Von der Ahe expected the payment would be sent by wire and would arrive very quickly. On December 30, Barnie, not considering the payment a matter for hurry, put a check in a registered letter instead. The next day he wired Von der Ahe to let him know the money was on the way.[15] In the meantime, on their way home from Philadelphia, the Pittsburgh club officials and American Association president Denny McKnight had taken the train west from Philadelphia in company with Von der Ahe, who no doubt discussed the Barkley situation with them. Von der Ahe got back to St. Louis and did not find Barnie's promised money awaiting him, nor had Barnie's telegram yet arrived, so he telegraphed Nimick, saying Pittsburgh could still have Barkley if they would send the money immediately. Nimick and Phillips accordingly put one thousand dollars at Von der Ahe's disposal and wired Barkley in Wheeling, telling him Barnie's deal had fallen through and they still wanted him. Barkley got on the train to meet them in Pittsburgh, where he told them he regretted signing the written agreement, but he remained leery of embroiling himself in trouble of the sort Mullane had gotten into, so to reassure him the Pittsburgh officials took their man to the office of Denny McKnight.[16]

By a coincidence—fortunate at least for Phillips and Nimick—McKnight was in easy reach because he was a resident of Pittsburgh. In fact, he had become the first president of the Pittsburgh club as well as the Association itself when both were formed in the fall of 1881. He had severed his connections with the team only the previous spring and at the annual meeting in December, President McKnight had added the Association secretaryship to the presidency he already held, with a healthy increase in salary to cover the increased administrative responsibilities. The election had not been without opposition, in part because some of the Association men, notwithstanding his separation from the Pittsburgh club, suspected he remained a partisan of his old team. Nevertheless, he was elected by a vote that was unanimous, even if the sentiment behind it was not undivided.

With manager Phillips as well as Barkley listening, Nimick explained to McKnight what had happened and asked him for an opinion. McKnight would later say he had explained to Barkley that American Association and National Agreement rules left him free to sign with Pittsburgh, since the papers he had signed for Barnie were without force because he was still held by St. Louis. However, McKnight reminded Barkley that, having taken Barnie's money and given his word, he had committed himself to the Orioles and was contemplating a dishonorable action McKnight could only warn him against taking. That, at least, was how McKnight recalled the conversation months later when it had become a matter of controversy. If McKnight remembered accurately, then only the first part of his advice to Barkley made any impact, for Barkley wired both Barnie and Von der Ahe, telling him he had reconsidered his agreement with the former and desired to go to Pittsburgh, and McKnight himself wired Barnie to the same effect. Barnie replied, pleading that McKnight hold off until he could write full details. The next day McKnight wrote Barnie more fully. His letter, although mildly conciliatory, gives no sign of concern over Barkley's moral obligation to honor his original agreement:

Baltimore manager Billy Barnie in the Old Judge card series.

> *My dear Barnie*: I do not see any help for you in this Barkley matter. The document which you showed me, with his signature, is simply an agreement between you and him, as far as our rules are concerned, binding him by his *honor* to sign with you. He has been here talking to me, Nimick and Phillips also, and I am compelled to agree with them that nothing in our rules or the National Agreement gives you any hold on them. Barkley now expresses his intention of signing with the Allegheny Club, and I cannot refuse to accept his contract with them. My own friendly feelings toward yourself cannot be considered in the question. If Von der Ahe releases Barkley under our rules and resolutions of Dec. 8 he can sign where he pleases.
>
> Yours truly, H.D. McKNIGHT, Pres.
>
> P.S.—You know, I think, that I sincerely hope you get a good team and do good business next season. I have argued to Mr. Nimick your case of getting a good team, but he argues, in what you cannot deny is a sensible manner, that he also must have a good team and must strengthen where he can. It cannot be called selfishness in his case any more than in yours. It is simply business carefulness. It is easy for me to ask him to let you strengthen, but how can I reasonably ask him to weaken himself? That is what this whole matter comes down to.
>
> Barkley says that he regretted signing that promise with you, and has notified you that it is called back; you must, therefore, see that, no matter how much I would like to see you get this fine player, I cannot do anything to help you.[17]

In the interim Von der Ahe received Barnie's telegraphed assurances that the money was coming, and he informed Nimick that Pittsburgh's acquisition of Barkley was off again. But the letter from Barnie did not arrive in the next several days and Von der Ahe concluded it never would. Since he was now holding Pittsburgh's money, without contacting Barnie again on the afternoon of January 4 he telegraphed the Pittsburgh officials they could sign Barkley and McKnight an official notice of the player's release. Having sent these missives, Von der Ahe went to his office, where he sat down to write Barnie a letter. Before he could finish it, the registered letter sent by Barnie, having escaped some limbo in the the postal system, was delivered. It was too late now to stop the train of events, and that evening Barkley signed with Pittsburgh. An embarrassed Von der Ahe could only start a new letter to accompany the return of Barnie's check, expressing his perplexity at how long the letter had taken to arrive, although he noted the letter had in fact been registered a day after Barnie said it had been sent and added that "if you had even mentioned in your telegram that you had sent the money by registered letter I might have made inquiry at the post office as I did this morning at every express office in the city, but it seems you adopted the slowest method to get the money here. You can not blame me for this disappointment, although I am very sorry on your account."[18]

How had Von der Ahe landed himself in so awkward a situation? Suspicions were not lacking that he was in cahoots with Pittsburgh, and his train ride home with Nimick and Phillips was singled out as an opportunity for conspiracy. Moreover, Barnie claimed that on January 3, aware that Pittsburgh was tampering with Barkley, he had wired Von der Ahe to send the release directly to him but Von der Ahe had remained "strangely silent" until he released Barkley to Pittsburgh the next day.[19] Von der Ahe himself never alluded to the telegram of January 3. No one ever claimed that Pittsburgh had raised its offer for Barkley although it is certainly imaginable Von der Ahe may have favored that club as a matter of Association politics, since he and Horace Phillips had both felt disgruntled over their omission from the important schedule committee.[20] The likelier explanation, however, is that the sale of Barkley to Baltimore went off the rails in large measure out of a misplaced sense of delicacy on Von der Ahe's part and the peculiar situation of the Baltimore club.

All in the service of alliteration, William Barnie called himself Billy, went bald, and ran baseball clubs for lengthy periods in Baltimore and Brooklyn. A journeyman catcher–outfielder who had turned to organizing minor ball clubs, at the start of the 1880s Barnie had attempted to revive professional baseball in Brooklyn under the famous name Atlantic. Barnie's Atlantics were one of a number of independent clubs trying to get a foothold as the game revived during the doldrums of the late 1870s. When the American Association organized in the offseason of 1881–1882, the Atlantics were expected to be one of the members, but Barnie backed out at the last moment, leaving the Association to bring in a hurriedly formed, undercapitalized team in Baltimore. Barnie's withdrawal may have been a fortunate stroke for the Association, because his Atlantics collapsed in midseason of 1882, but while the Orioles lasted the year they were a hopeless last-place team. In the fall the

Ambidextrous pitcher Tony Mullane, "The Apollo of the Box."

Baltimore management threw up its hands and pulled out, leaving Barnie to take over the club. In addition to some financial support from brewer Harry Vonderhorst and his father John, Barnie had a partner, a theater manager named A.T. Houck; the two revamped the Orioles on a capital of $400, and after Houck withdrew two years later, Barnie operated on his own as the manager, the president, the owner, and in fact the entire Baltimore baseball club.[21]

Although he is said to have been the son of a prominent New York builder and to have given up a career in an investment company to become a baseball player,[22] Barnie never showed any signs of having a personal fortune at his disposal, and with the Vonderhorsts unwilling to plow more than a modicum of money into the club's operation he had nobody to answer to — not entirely an unenviable position in a day many a club was backed financially by a large coterie of meddleseome small stockholders — but also nobody to provide sufficient funds when they were needed suddenly in a game known in 1880s with good reason as "the National Uncertainty."[23] Albert Mott, who wrote the Baltimore correspondence in *Sporting Life* for many years under the pseudonym "T.T.T.," remarked in 1888 "Barnie has always been consistent in one thing, and that is to deal in cheap goods. That will explain the career of the Baltimore Club to a large number of people." In a sympathetic review of Barnie's career when he finally severed connections with the Orioles in 1891, T.T.T. observed that he had "struggled on under financial difficulties with no money to offer under the sales system and in a generally crippled condition. That he was able to run that club at all and compete with the other strong teams in the American Association is a grand tribute to his managerial abilities. He was actually making bricks without straw."[24]

Barnie's lone wolf situation was no secret in the baseball world. A St. Louis reporter who suspected Von der Ahe was presenting Barkley to Baltimore thought that Von der Ahe had given the game away when he mentioned Barnie's having said he must consult his board of directors before committing to the purchase, "for it is known the country over that the full directory of the club is made up of Barnie alone."[25] The deduction proved faulty, but Von der Ahe himself undoubtedly understood the truth behind the premise as well as anyone. When Barnie spoke about consulting his directors, Von der Ahe must have assumed this was a face-saving way of saying Barnie would have to go back to Baltimore and carry his hat in his hand to businessmen from whom he might hope to borrow the funds necessary to pay for Barkley's release. Von der Ahe probably never had complete confidence that Barnie would find the money to pay him, and may well have told Nimick and Phillips as much on the railroad trip west. When Barnie's money did not arrive, as he tactfully wrote the Baltimore chief, "I came to the conclusion that some friend of yours had promised you to send the money but had changed his mind about the time you sent your first telegram."[26] Of course, Von der Ahe did not mean that someone had taken the money from Barnie and then chosen to hold on to it; he meant that Barnie's source of funding had fallen through. Never having had faith in Barnie's ability to deliver, and interested above all in getting his thousand dollars for Barkley, Von der Ahe then turned to Pittsburgh, refraining from contacting Barnie again perhaps because he felt it indelicate to confront the latter with his impecunious situation.

Be that as it may, as *Sporting Life* editorialized, the whole affair did much to take the shine off Von der Ahe's "reputation as big-hearted Chris, always ready to do friend a good turn."[27] The greater share of criticism however went to the Pittsburgh club and Barkley, neither of whom found many defenders outside Pittsburgh. Instead a parallel was instantly drawn to Tony Mullane's nefarious behavior a year before, which triggered his suspension for the entire 1885 season. Barnie pressed home the point that when he dined with Barkley after they had made their agreement, the player had expressed his contempt for Mullane's contractual shenanigans and said that "a man like Mullane should be debarred forever from playing ball." As for the Pittsburgh officials, their conduct seemed all the more shameful in that they themselves had taken the lead in urging Mullane's punishment for breaking an agreement with Von der Ahe not then strictly prohibited by the rules after showing the Association board of directors a letter from pitcher Ed Morris indicating that he and his catcher, Fred Carroll, were waiting for the outcome of Mullane's hearing to decide whether to honor their agreements to sign with Pittsburgh after obtaining release from Columbus. Now, they were taking the opposite position. Moreover, with slick-fielding Charlie "Pop" Smith holding down second base, the Pittsburgh management was seen as a dog in the manger signing a player far more important to Baltimore than to its own team.[28]

Under the headline "A MEAN ACT," *Sporting Life* wrote that "the lesson of the Mullane case has apparently lost effect and needs repeating," and the *Brooklyn Eagle* weighed in, urging that "something will have to be done by the American Association ... to put a stop to the conduct of professional players who, like Mullane the pitcher and Barkley the second baseman of the St. Louis Club team, seem to be devoid of all honorable influences in their way of making engagements with clubs." In the Cincinnati *Commercial Gazette*, Opie Caylor wrote that the Mullane precedent must be followed, or else "the country will see that Mullane was punished simply to hamstring the Cincinnati team, and not because he had offended against any base ball laws." In Louisville, Barkley was remembered as the spokesman for a group of Toledo players who, before the deal with Von der Ahe had been bruited, had promised to sign with the local club only to back out when Barkley claimed a grievance on the flimsy grounds that they had not been invited on a postseason barnstorming tour with the holdover Louisville players.[29] Brooklyn and the Athletics also lined up very quickly in favor of Baltimore.[30]

Sam Barkley with Pittsburgh, 1887, in the Old Judge card set.

Barkley's fate was to be decided by the Association's Board of Directors at the spring schedule meeting, which was to convene on the first day of March in Louisville. After some preliminary business, the Board heard another multiple-signing dispute over Ernie Burch, an outfielder claimed by the Metropolitan and Brooklyn clubs, the Association's two representatives in the New York City area. The testimony indicated that Brooklyn's case was so strong that the Mets had no claim at all. Therefore, "the Metropolitan delegates, although somewhat disappointed, acknowledged the justice of the Brooklyn claim, and accepted the decision with grace and dignity," later meeting with Charlie Byrne of Brooklyn to bury the hatchet. They buried it in the back of Denny McKnight, in fact, for not only Byrne but Major George Williams of the Mets agreed that McKnight had incited the dispute by leading the Mets to believe they had a case when in fact they had none. "His idea seemed to be to try and please everybody, and the natural result was that he pleased nobody," complained Williams.[31]

The Board now turned to the main event, the Barkley matter. Zack Phelps of Louisville and Lew Simmons of the Athletics were the only board members capable of considering the matter, however, for a majority of the members — Barnie, Von der Ahe, and McKnight — had to recuse themselves from voting, although McKnight presided at the meeting.

The Pittsburgh side had brought along an attorney, but the Association declined to let him argue, and so he returned home, leaving Nimick and Phillips to present their case against Barnie. Barkley was not present, but Pittsburgh presented an affidavit from him. Testimony continued from late morning until 4:00 P.M., at which point Simmons and Phelps announced they would announce their decision the following morning.

On the morning of March 2 Simmons and Phelps reported their decision in an opinion that no doubt was the work of Phelps, a prominent Louisville attorney. Phelps began by noting the argument that Barnie's agreement with Barkley had been invalid because Barkley was still under reserve by St. Louis at the time it was made. Barnie's claim that the "the agreement between the St. Louis Club, Barkley and the Baltimore Club was tantamount to a release" was rejected as plausible but not supported by the rules of the Association, which stated unequivocally that players were bound to their clubs until formally released. Barkley's Christmas Day agreement was therefore set aside as invalid.

The opinion then turned to McKnight's testimony concerning his conversation with Barkley in Pittsburgh.

> On that occasion President McKnight properly advised Barkley that his contract with Baltimore was irregular, and he had the legal right to repudiate it; but at the same time that, since he had accepted the money of the Baltimore Club, and given his word to play there, such a course as he contemplated would be in bad faith and dishonorable, and advised him against such action.
>
> This association has taken steps in advance of other associations in discouraging duplicity, trickery and dishonor among the managers and players by severe penalties, as evidenced by its action in another case [Mullane's]. It is contended, however, this case is not parallel to that, because of the fact that the player went to President McKnight, the head of the association, and asked his advice, upon which occasion the President adivsed him of the right to repudiate the contract, which was irregularly made. If these were the only facts in the case we would be disposed to agree with this position, but it appears further that President McKnight very properly remarked to Barkley on the impropriety and dishonesty of such a course, and advised against the doing of a dishonorable thing. For this reason we are unable to see any material difference between this and the precedent referred to. It is therefore ordered that S.W. Barkley be and he is hereby suspended for a period of

> one year and fined $100 for duplicity and dishonorable conduct, which is calculated to bring the American Association into disrepute.
>
> In view of the fact that the Pittsburg [sic] Club also purchased the release of the player, they shall have the right to reserve him when this penalty shall have been satisfied.

McKnight's report that he had warned Barkley he was acting in bad faith was therefore taken as the basis for placing the decision on exactly the same terms as that in Mullane's case, although a fine was substituted for the much larger share of his advance money that Mullane had been required to repay Cincinnati. Simmons, Phelps, and many of their colleagues may not really have believed McKnight's story. They probably remembered the letter from McKnight that Barnie had published in *Sporting Life*, which made some mild show of sympathy for Barnie's position but gave no indication that he thought Barkley's position questionable. Now he was speaking differently, but as George Williams of the Mets would shortly tell a New York reporter, McKnight seemed to be trying to please everybody, and in the process he had failed to please anyone.[32] How impartial a presiding judge many of the delegates considered him is illustrated by Opie Caylor's account of the aftermath of Phelps report. When Jim Hart, the Louisville manager, moved that the two directors' recommendation be approved, Nimick sprang to his feet to object. McKnight said "Mr. Nimick's point of order is well taken," to which someone, quite possibly Caylor himself, replied that Nimick had not actually made a point of order. Nimick promptly took the cue McKnight had given him and made one, and McKnight not surprisingly ruled in his favor. The delegates promptly voted by a 5–2 count first to overrule the point of order and then to accept the report. Pittsburgh was joined by the Mets in the minority, on the ground that Barkley himself had not been heard, and St. Louis abstained in the absence of Von der Ahe.[33]

Barnie, at first disappointed, soon decided that, unlike the mother of the baby in the famous story of King Solomon, he was satisfied to see Barkley sit out a year rather than allow Pittsburgh to have him. The Pittsburgh delegates went away angry, and threatening to sue. A common reaction was that the club officials, themselves the guiltiest parties, had arranged to let one another off the hook, leaving the unfortunate ballplayer as the only sufferer.[34]

It soon became clear that Pittsburgh indeed intended to back Barkley in seeking an injunction to prevent his suspension. McKnight telegraphed the Association clubs urging a meeting in Pittsburgh to consider the situation, but they suspected the invitation was a ruse to get the issue within the jurisdiction of the Pennsylvania state courts.[35] Nevertheless, aware that Barkley had received no opportunity to speak for himself, McKnight was instructed to call a special meeting at Cincinnati on March 20, at which time Barkley was to be formally charged under an accusation drawn up by Barnie. McKnight reportedly complied only two days before the meeting, after no fewer then four clubs had made the request.[36]

When the delegates arrived for the meeting, however, they found Barkley absent and, more astonishingly, McKnight himself had wired Caylor that he would be unable to attend due to illness. His absence came as a surprise even to Al Scandrett, the club secretary who represented Pittsburgh at the meeting, who had expected to meet McKnight at the station in Pittsburgh and then to find him already in Cincinnati when they arrived there.[37] Worse yet, McKnight had sent none of his official papers to a meeting he himself had called.

The champion Browns' greyhounds pictured here first belonged to pitcher "Egyptian" Healy—so named because he was born in Cairo, Illinois. Owner Chris von der Ahe then bought them.

This was the last straw for the Association men. At best, it seemed McKnight was admitting to incompetence; at worst, he had deliberately dragged his heels in the interest of a dishonest ballplayer and the club whose interest he had favored all along. As George Williams of the Mets said, "It was a clear case of duplicity, and an effort to assist Pittsburg [sic]."[38] A telegram was therefore sent demanding McKnight's resignation, and when he refused to comply, more charges were drawn up and he was deposed from office. Unsure whether the deposition should be voted on by the Board of Directors or the full membership, the Association did it both ways, just to make sure it would stick.[39]

Barkley had not shown up either, and in the meantime it had begun to occur to the Association men that he might never have been advised of the charges against him. McKnight himself informed them from Pittsburgh that he had received Barnie's letter containing the official charges, but in his illness he had negelected to open what he had assumed must merely be Barnie's Association dues. Barkley therefore had never received official notification of his hearing. At 2:00 a long telegram was drawn up, notifying Barkley directly that Barnie had filed charges of disreputable conduct against him and asking that he appear in Cincinnati on Monday March 22 to answer to them. Nimick had telegraphed asking whether Barkley might be represented by Major Edward A. Montooth, the attorney Nimick's club had procured to represent him, and the Association replied affirmatively.[40] On March 22, the Cincinnati *Enquirer* ran a dispatch from Pittsburgh stating that Montooth and Nimick had left for Cincinnati, but in fact neither Montooth nor his client Barkley appeared there that day. Two days, with time out for a railroad journey, would hardly have given them adequate time to prepare a defense; more important, Montooth must have seen quickly that there was little purpose in coming to

Cincinnati and providing legitimacy to a hearing whose outcome was a forgone conclusion, especially when the short notice offered an opportunity to question its legitimacy. The Association accordingly spent another two hours taking testimony and then for a second time inflicted upon Barkley in absentia the penalty of a one-year suspension and a hundred-dollar fine.[41] An angry McKnight told a reporter he did not want to force his services where they were not wanted and would go quietly if asked "in a civil and gentlemanly way," but promised to drag the matter out in court if he were treated in a hostile manner. He can hardly have settled doubts about his impartial conduct as Association president when he told Wikoff that the whole affair demonstrated their "intense hatred" for the Pittsburgh club. Meanwhile, Barkley's attorneys were proceeding with a request for an injunction against the Association, placing the Pittsburgh club in the anomalous position of being one of the defendants although everyone understood it was actually the motivating force behind the complaint. In a hearing on April 2, barely over two weeks before the start of the baseball season, the complainants argued their case on the ground of the inadequate notice given Barkley of the Cincinnati meeting; they also argued that the American Association constitution authorized clubs to discipline players but did not allow the organization as a whole to do so. The Association's attorneys denied Barkley was entitled to relief and argued that jurisdiction was lacking, as the court's decision would not hold against clubs outside Pennsylvania, but Judge Stowe observed that an injunction could prevent any Association games from being held in the state, where not only the Pittsburgh club but the Athletics were located. Stowe believed the Association had the right to discipline its players provided it adhered very closely to its own rules. Stowe seemed to take the issue of inadequate notice seriously. The Association men, of course, believed that Barkley had failed to receive timely notice because of the inaction of a man who was effectively acting as the agent of Pittsburgh, not the organization as a whole, but Stowe naturally took the view that Barkley simply must be given adequate notification, and the Association, having chosen McKnight as its chief executive, remained responsible for his actions prior to his depositon from office. Stowe announced he would take the matter under consideration and deliver a decision in a week. He seemed to "look kindly towards Barkley," according to the *Sporting Life* correspondent, but the Association men promised a protracted fight.[42]

No sooner had the court adjourned than Nimick and Charlie Byrne sat down together in the office of the American Association's counsel. Byrne, the Brooklyn club president who had gained steadily in influence during the scant two years his club had spent in the Association, was authorized to reach a settlement with Nimick, and in fairly good time the two hammered out a compromise. Within a few days all the clubs had agreed to lift Barkley's suspension on condition that his fine be increased to $500, a sum that was no doubt paid by the Pittsburgh club. Pittsburgh also agreed to release Milt Scott, the journeyman first baseman who had figured in Fort Wayne's sale of its players and then been picked up by Pittsburgh after the Indianapolis buyout, while the other clubs kept hands off in order to let Barnie have Scott. He was hardly full compensation for the loss of Barkley. Even though he filled one of the holes in the Orioles' lineup in 1886, he produced arguably the least offensive production in history by a regular first baseman.

It was not a complete backdown on the Association's part; but to cover an agreement balanced toward Pittsburgh's interest, Byrne emphasized that Nimick had taken the initiative to settle in order to avoid antagonizing its partners further, and his own authorization to act on the other clubs' behalf had been subject to the requirement that Barkley's punishment not be dropped altogether. Simmons and Phelps released a statement saying that they had refused requests to modify Barkley's punishment in order to "have the Courts say, if they can, that an employer cannot discharge an employee who has so conducted himself as to lose confidence or respect." But now, since they had had their day in court and since "the main cause of this and other disputes has been got rid of," they would heed the unanimous request of the Association clubs to settle the differences between Baltimore and Pittsburgh and start the post–McKnight era in harmony. With this final kick at Denny McKnight's rear, the deal was settled and Barkley was in a Pittsburgh uniform in time to play in Pittsburgh's opening game.[43]

Chris Von der Ahe of the St. Louis Browns, Buchner Gold Coin card, 1887.

McKnight had now agreed to step down from the presidency and hand over his papers and records, with Scandrett and Nimick appointed a friendly auditing committee that he could be assured would not seek reprisals.[44] By late May, *Sporting Life* was writing that "with every week Barnie becomes more convinced that Scott is worth two Barkleys."[45] But Scott, although a fine fielder, was so atrocious a hitter that by the end of the season he was released, ending his brief major league career. Ernie Burch, whom Brooklyn and the Mets had tussled over, lasted a little longer, but likewise was released and departed from the majors in July 1887; at the end of that season a Brooklyn commentator characterized Burch as the team's "supreme failure.... Utterly without ambition, energy or pride in his work, here was a good player who went to seed through sheer laziness."[46] As so often, the players who were the object of the fiercest struggles proved not to be worth the trouble. Even Barkley fell from his perch as one of the outstanding infielders in the game. He proved something of a malcontent in Pittsburgh as he had been in St. Louis, suffered arm problems and gained weight, and was moved to first base. Sold to Kansas City in the spring of 1888, he failed as a player–manager and by July 1889 had been sold to minor league Toledo, this time passing through waivers without even one Association club claiming him.

As a final coda to the Barkley affair, Pittsburgh accepted an offer to jump to the National League in the fall of 1886. When the Association came together for its annual meeting in December, Pittsburgh representatives requested a refund of four hundred dollars, on the grounds that the club had agreed with Charlie Byrne in April to lift Barkley's suspension and retain the one hundred dollar fine originally inflicted, but at Byrne's request they agreed to allow the Association to save face by raising the fine to five hundred dollars, with the addition to be refunded later. Now Byrne insisted he had only promised to bring the matter before the Association, which, as it turned out, had no intention of doing its recalcitrant former club any favors. Much commotion was roused over the possibility that Pittsburgh might sue for its money, but the matter was finally dropped, and with it the Barkley affair passed into the history books.[47]

By the end of 1886, many Association officials must have been happy to rid their organization at last of the Pittsburgh club, but the Alleghenys' jump was to be the first of several that would contribute greatly to sapping the Association's strength, until it was finally subsumed by the League after the 1891 season. The Barkley affair demonstrates the remarkably self-destructive conduct the Association men were capable of when the mood was on them, but, more important, it revealed that the new rules governing player movement between clubs generated by the Mullane incident, among others, might, generally speaking, facilitate player sales, but they could not absolutely prevent horrendous complications under the right—or wrong—circumstances. Making the baseball world completely sanguine for transactions between clubs would require still more rules changes, and even before that, club officials would need to arrive at an irrevocable consensus in favor of the view that other teams must keep their hands out of a deal arranged by two of their number.

Abstract

Before the institution of the Reserve Clause after the 1879 National League season, players were free to change teams at will upon the expiration of their contracts (usually extant for only one year). Yet the first version of the Reserve Clause was only a baby step in regulating player movement from team to team. In the early 1880s player trades were still not a feature of the game, in part because no player could as yet be compelled to go to another team against his wishes. A player's right of refusal often also stymied player sales as well as so-called "waiver" deals in which one team would try to steer an unwanted player to a rival, sometimes out of simple generosity but more often in exchange for future considerations.

In a book begun before his untimely death, 19th-century baseball historian David Ball set out to track the painstaking evolution of the present-day rules regarding player movement from team to team. David did not leave an introduction to his book or notes explaining its proposed scope, but we believe he planned to carry his work only to the conclusion of the 19th century. Among his fully developed sections is the story of the remarkably complex Sam Barkley case, in which the St. Louis Browns endeavored to sell their disenchanted second baseman to the highest bidder in the winter of 1885–1886, on the heels of rule revisions prompted by the nefarious Tony Mullane case of the previous winter. Upon its final settlement, major league owners and officials arrived at the rude recognition that their work to achieve movement of a player from one team to another that was equitable and acceptable to all had only just begun.

Notes

1. Harold Seymour and Dorothy Seymour Mills give a brief account of the Barkley affair in *Baseball: The Early Years*, pp. 217–218.
2. *Sporting Life*, Jan. 13, 1886, p. 1,; *Cincinnati Enquirer*, Apr. 21, 1886, and May 10, 1886. Mullane and Barkley are said to have had a falling out over a woman in Toledo.
3. *Sporting Life*, Jan. 19, 1887, p. 2 col. 6.
4. *New York Times*, Dec. 14, 1885; *Sporting Life*, Dec. 23, 1885, p. 2 col. 2; Dec. 30, 1885, p. 3 col. 5; Jan. 6, 1886, p. 1 col. 4; and Jan. 13, 1886, p. 1 col. 3.
5. *Sporting Life*, Oct. 28, 1885, p. 2 col. 5 and p. 4 co. 22; Jan. 13, 1886, p. 2 col. 3; *Baltimore American*, Jan. 24, 1886. Among the unsatisfactory lot of players Barnie was offered at the October meeting was George McGinnis, St. Louis's third pitcher, who wound up signing with Baltimore after Von der Ahe released him during the 1886 season.

6. *Sporting Life*, Dec. 23, 1885, p. 2 col. 4.

7. *Sporting Life*, Dec. 16, 1885, p. 2 col. 4; *New York Times*, Dec. 21, 1885. Barkley himself subsequently released a statement in which he said he had not known of the deal before meeting Von der Ahe in St. Louis on Dec. 22 (*Sporting Life*, Jan. 13, 1886, p. 1 col. 5); but other accounts, especially the *Times* article, contradict that claim conclusively. Cf. *Sporting Life*, Dec. 30, 1885, p. 1 col. 1, which states that Von der Ahe was Barnie's creditor but did not own any share of his ball club, besides confirming that he had sold Barkley rather than giving him away (a fact that would soon be unquestionable).

8. *New York Times*, Dec. 21, 1885; *Sporting Life*, Jan. 13, 1886, p. 1 col. 5.

9. *New York Times*, Dec. 21, 1885; *Sporting Life*, Dec. 30, 1885, p. 2 col. 5; and Jan. 13, 1886, p. 1 cols. 3–5.

10. *Cincinnati Enquirer*, Jan. 5, 1886; *Sporting Life*, Jan. 6, 1886, p. 3 col. 3; Jan. 13, 1886, p. 1 col. 5.

11. *Sporting Life*, Jan. 13, 1886, p. 1 col. 5.

12. *Baltimore American*, Jan. 10, 1886; *Sporting Life*, Jan. 13, 1886, p. 1 cols. 3 and 5.

13. *Sporting Life*, Jan. 13, 1886, p. 1 col 5 (italics in original).

14. *Sporting Life*, Jan. 6, 1886, p. 3 col. 3.

15. *Baltimore American*, Jan. 10, 1886; *Sporting Life*, Jan. 13, 1886, p. 1 cols. 3–5; Jan. 20, 1886, p. 4 col. 1.

16. *Cincinnati Enquirer*, Jan. 5, 1886; *Sporting Life*, Jan. 13, 1886, p. 1 col.5; *Baltimore American*, Jan. 17, 1886.

17. Quoted from *Sporting Life*, Jan. 13, 1886, p. 1 col. 4; see also *Cincinnati Commercial Gazette*, March 2, 1886.

18. The quote is from *Sporting Life*, Jan. 20, 1886, p. 4 col. 1; see also *Cincinnati Enquirer*, Jan. 5, 1886 and *Sporting Life*, Feb. 3, 1886, p. 2 col. 5.

19. *Sporting Life*, Jan. 13, 1886, p. 1 col. 3.

20. Von der Ahe alluded to his anger over the matter in *Sporting Life*, Feb. 3, 1886, p. 2 col. 5, and Phillips was quoted (*Sporting Life*, Jan. 13, 1886, p. 2 cols. 2–3) as saying that in order to secure election to the combined job of AA president and secretary, McKnight had made so many promises of seats on the committee that his supporters from Pittsburgh and St. Louis were left off.

21. *Baseball's First Stars*, p. 6; *Cincinnati Enquirer*, Mar. 14, 1882; *New York Times*, Nov. 6, 1882; *Baltimore American*, Jan. 5, 1886; *Sporting Life*, Oct. 3, 1891, p. 10 cols. 1–2. For the first Baltimore club, see *Sporting Life*, Feb. 10, 1886, p. 2 col. 2.

22. *Baseball's First Stars*, p. 6

23. Vonderhorst eventually took over full ownership of the club from Barnie as repayment of a debt: *Sporting Life*, Oct. 3, 1891, p. 10 cols. 1–2. Vonderhorst is usually said to have been a part owner very early, and his role as concessionaire and even creditor may have begun as early as 1882, but he did not take much interest in the Orioles' fortunes until about the time the Barkley case was decided: *Sporting Life*, Mar. 24, 1886, p. 3 col. 3

24. *Sporting Life*, Mar. 24, 1886, p. 3 col. 3; Oct. 3, 1891, p. 10 cols. 1–2.

25. *New York Times*, Dec. 21, 1885.

26. *Sporting Life*, Jan. 20, 1886, p. 4 col. 1.

27. *Sporting Life*, Jan. 20, 1886, p. 4 col. 1.

28. *Cincinnati Enquirer*, Jan. 10, 1886; *Sporting Life*, Jan. 20, 1886, p. 2 cols. 3–4. Pittsburgh reportedly intended to move Smith to third base, supplanting Willie Kuehne, a move the *Enquirer* thought would be a mistake because Smith was a better second baseman than Barkley.

29. *Cincinnati Commercial Gazette*, Jan. 10, 1886; *Sporting Life*, Jan. 13, 1886, p. 1 col. 3. For Barkley's dealings with Louisville, see above.

30. *Cincinnati Commercial Gazette*, Jan. 10, 1886; *Sporting Life*, Jan. 13, 1886, p. 1 cols. 3 and 5; Jan. 20, 1886, p. 1 col. 2.

31. Where not otherwise noted, the following account is from Opie Caylor's report in *Sporting Life*, March 10, 1886, p. 3 cols. 1–4. The reactions of Byrne and Williams to the outcome of the Burch case are given there and in the *New York Times*, Mar. 22 and 25, 1886.

32. *New York Times*, Mar. 25, 1886.

33. *New York Times*, Mar. 25, 1886.

34. *Sporting Life*, Mar. 10, 1886, p. 3 col. 2 and p. 5 col. 1.

35. *Sporting Life*, Mar. 31, 1886, p. 1 col. 3.

36. *Sporting Life*, Mar. 31, 1886, p. 1 cols. 3–4.

37. *New York Times*, Mar. 25, 1886.

38. *New York Times*, Mar. 25, 1886.

39. *Cincinnati Commercial Gazette*, Mar. 21, 1886; *Sporting Life*, Mar. 31, 1886, p. 1 cols. 3–4. Wheeler

Wikoff, who had lost his position as AA secretary the previous December, when the loop voted to consolidate the offices of president and secretary in the hands of President McKnight, now succeeded McKnight in the combined office.

40. Montooth was a former Pittsburgh district attorney who practiced law in partnership with his brother Charles, with whom he was associated on Barkley's behalf in subsequent litigation. Reports of the Barkley case sometimes mistakenly refer to "Moontooth" or "*Mayor* Montooth." See *Pittsburgh Legal Journal*, Feb. 23, 1898, p. 261.

41. *Sporting Life*, Mar. 31, 1885, p. 1 col. 4.

42. *Sporting Life*, Apr. 7, 1886, p. 1 cols. 4–5.

43. *New York Times*, Apr. 12, 1886; *Sporting Life*, Apr. 14, 1886, p. 1 col. 5; Apr. 21, 1886, p. 1 col. 3.

44. *Sporting Life*, Apr. 14, 1886, p. 1 col. 5.

45. *Sporting Life*, May 26, 1886, p. 5 col. 5.

46. *Sporting Life*, Oct. 5, 1887, p. 5 col. 6.

47. *Sporting Life*, Dec. 22, 1886, p. 1 cols. 1 and 5; Jan 12, 1887, p. 1 cols. 2 and 5; and March 23, 1887, p. 5 col. 5. Although everyone knew the club had paid Barkley's fine, the N.Y. *Clipper*, quoted by St. Louis *Post–Dispatch*, Jan. 10, 1887, suggested that, since the penalty was officially Barkley's, Pittsburgh had no formal claim to a refund.

A Permanent American Institution
The Base Ball Season of 1863

Robert Tholkes

Fittingly, the first to be noticed playing the New York Game in 1863 were Union soldiers stationed at Port Royal, South Carolina, according to a note in the *New York Times* of January 9: "New-Year's day was observed by the soldiers in a few of the camps here and at Beaufort by target-shooting, games of base-ball, and the usual amusing sports of climbing a greased pole, wheelbarrow races, sack races, &c."

On the 11th, the *Sunday Mercury* published details received about a hotly contested match at Fort Pulaski, Georgia, which had been captured in April 1862 to close the port of Savannah. The match featured two teams from New York's 48th Regiment, eight to a side.

Quoting several newspaper items and soldiers' diaries, Kirsch reported ball play, whether New York Rules, Massachusetts Rules, or townball, to be endemic in both armies, including prison camps. Worsening prison-camp conditions in 1863 and thereafter, abetted by the breakdown of the custom of prisoner exchanges, substantially reduced play among prisoners.[1]

Those awaiting the coming of spring to the north of the fighting could pass the time gnawing the bones of the 1862 season: The sporting press in New York published the statistics of 16 area teams, indicating that more clubs were compiling such numbers, despite the decline in the number of active clubs caused by the war. Henry Chadwick had published only nine such sets of numbers for 1861 in the 1862 *Beadle's Dime Base Ball Player.*

In Philadelphia, at least, the death in October 1862 of the still-mourned Jim Creighton notwithstanding, the game could still gain ground as beneficial exercise for young men. On January 19, the *Public Ledger*, noting baseball's increasing popularity, opined (in a remark that hopefully escaped the million or so milquetoasts serving in the army), "Our male citizens were becoming too effeminate, and the influence of field sports will do much to improve their physical powers."

In March, the *New York Clipper* inaugurated a future staple of baseball coverage: the player profile. The *Clipper* had for several years published profiles of eminent boxers and stars of the stage, two pastimes it had long covered in depth. Its March 7 issue

---

Robert Tholkes of Minneapolis is a veteran contributor to SABR publications and to *Base Ball*, concentrating on the game's amateur era. Bob's past activities include several years as an officer of SABR's Halsey Hall Chapter (Minnesota), biographical research on major leaguers with Minnesota connections, and service as newsletter editor for SABR's Origins of Baseball Committee. Bob's article continues his series of seasonal sesquicentennial commemorations.

DOI: 10.3172/BB.7.143

turned the spotlight on Atlantic stalwart Dickey Pearce. The description by the author, who remained anonymous, of Pearce's style at shortstop indicates that the elements of competent play at the position were already in place:

> If it was a grounder, he would first stop, pick it up fearlessly, encourage by his deliberation and movement the poor fellow running the base, with the hope of reaching it, and then away went the ball like a rifleshot, straight into Price's hands at first base, just a second before the player put his foot on the base. "Judgment," Dickey would cry, and "out on the first base," would be the reply of the umpire, invariably.

Attention finally turned to the prospects for the coming season. The *Sunday Mercury*'s Philadelphia correspondent reported on March 8 that a "brilliant" season was anticipated in that city, with much action at the celebrated Camac"s Woods playing ground. The action that would overshadow it in July—125 miles due west at Gettysburg—was not yet anticipated. The Athletic had just held their annual meeting, and planned to open their season by hosting the first prominent collegiate team, the Nassau, of Princeton. Trips were planned: to Altoona, Pennsylvania, in May, and to the New York City area in June. Their progress was hampered somewhat, first by an April snowstorm, and then, as reported by *Fitzgerald's City Item* on May 2, because Camac's Woods had been made unavailable for baseball games; it had been sold, and would become a brickyard. This left the clubs scrambling for new sites. The Athletic found new grounds at 17th and Masters. *Wilkes' Spirit of the Times* noted on March 28 that the New York Base Ball Club, which played only intramurally, would rent out its grounds at 63rd Street and Third Avenue ("now about the only ones on Manhattan Island") for two days in the week, and the *Brooklyn Daily Eagle* noted on March 24 that in addition to the Union Grounds, another Brooklyn skating pond, the Capitoline, would host baseball.

Dick McBride, pitcher of the Athletics, **Sporting Times, *June 13, 1868.***

Starting Play

The *Daily Eagle* had on March 24 also provided a count of the number of days the various ponds had been open for skating in the past winter, by way of emphasizing how mild the weather had been; thus encouraged, apparently, Brooklyn clubs opened their seasons in April. The Star Club played an intrasquad game on April 6, though this was exceptional; most started play on Fast Day, April 30. This was, as the *Sunday Mercury* noted on April 19, a month earlier than in 1862.

Fast Day was reported as a success. The *Sunday Mercury* noted on May 3 that the throngs at the initial intramural practice games were larger than in any previous year,

Athletic Clubhouse detail, from a larger image in* Harper's Weekly. *Depicted was a game between the Athletics and the Atlantics of Brooklyn.

especially at the Atlantic's grounds. On May 9, *Wilkes' Spirit of the Times* printed reports from both Hoboken and Brooklyn noting the large turnout of spectators and clubs, including a lively session by the Knickerbockers. Practice games had also begun in Philadelphia, the *Clipper* noted on May 2, and announced that in addition to the Athletic, the Keystone were planning on visiting New York. Altogether, the *Clipper*'s correspondent gushed, "if things go on as they have already commenced, and the same spirit is manifested throughout, we shall no doubt have to record the season of 1863 as the most eventful in the annals of the game."

May then turned rainy, keeping even the most spirited off the diamonds, but inter-club matches began in Philadelphia on the 22nd, when the Athletic hosted the Nassau, and in the New York metro when two second-tier clubs, the Mohawk and the Juniata, played on the 23rd. By then, planning was underway to host the first intercity visit of the year, by the Athletic to New York, and only a few matches appeared for early June on the *Sunday Mercury*'s usually comprehensive list of "Matches to Come Off."

The season did kick off in Boston on May 31, when the Lowell Club of Boston scaled the Tri-Mountain Club, also of Boston, 37–1. The Lowell had youth on its side. When they again defeated the Tri-Mountain in a championship series held in the fall of 1864, the *Boston Herald* noted on October 5 that while the Lowell were aged 18–21, the Tri-Mountain "were considerably more advanced in years." The Lowell's second nine followed that up on June 1 by defeating the Shawmut Club, apparently a one-nine outfit,

34–11. The Lowell did not take the field again in 1863; perhaps no further challenges were received. The Excelsior's visit of 1862, which had been at the invitation of the Bowdoin Club (apparently inactive in 1863) was not repeated. The few other baseball items in the Boston press for 1863 concern intercollegiate play, such as the Harvard frosh's win over Brown's sophomores, at Providence on June 22, 27–17, to the accompaniment of the offerings of a brass band. The *Boston Daily Advertiser*'s remark of June 30, "If we cannot have cricket, by all means let us have base ball" must stand as expressing the attitude of Beantown journalists. By the time the Champion Club of New York played in Boston on a September tour, their opponent was the Union Club of Lowell.

Intercity Visits

The Athletic's program for its second New York visit was ambitious: an unprecedented six games in six days. Three substitutes would accompany the announced nine. The 1863 visit would be unprecedented in another way: Despite the desire expressed in their press release (reprinted in *Wilkes' Spirit of the Times* on June 20) to "renew associations they have found most delightful," the visitors announced in advance that they would accept no social invitations — banquets, late suppers, and the theater were out. The postgame "sandwich and lager business" (as the *Sunday Mercury* termed it on June 6) aside, this trip would be all baseball. The emphasis in the Philadelphians' 1862 letter on mixing with the New York baseball fraternity socially would take a back seat; their stated purpose for 1863, as printed in the *Philadelphia Press* on June 15, was "to acquire all the new fine points of the game." All the charms of the early game had not yet fled, however; the same issue of the *Mercury* noted that on June 2 the turning point in a game between the Henry Eckford and Empire clubs at Hoboken had occurred when an errant throw to first base had sent the ball into the river, allowing three runs to score.

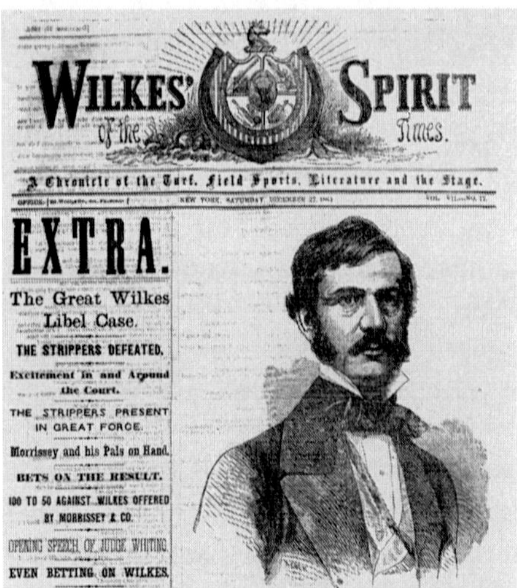
WILKES' SPIRIT of the Times.

A Chronicle of the Turf, Field Sports, Literature and the Stage.

EXTRA.

The Great Wilkes Libel Case.

THE STRIPPERS DEFEATED.

Excitement in and Around the Court.

THE STRIPPERS PRESENT IN GREAT FORCE.

Morrissey and his Pals on Hand.

BETS ON THE RESULT.

100 TO 50 AGAINST WILKES OFFERED BY MORRISSEY & CO.

OPENING SPEECH OF JUDGE WHITING.

EVEN BETTING ON WILKES.

BILLY MULLIGAN SHOWS UP.

Testimony for the Defence.

JUDGE WHITING'S GREAT CLOSING SPEECH.

CHARGE OF THE COURT.

VERDICT OF THE JURY.

VICTORY!!

***George Wilkes was a journalistic pioneer here shown in his self-named* Spirit.**

The Athletic detrained at Jersey City on June 15, and were immediately transported to Brooklyn for a game with the Excelsior, who were playing their first game since the death of Creighton. The visitors got everyone's attention by defeating their hosts in 10 innings, 18–17. *Fitzgerald's City Item* (the newspaper published in Philadelphia by Athletic president Col. Thomas Fitzgerald), in its lengthy report on June 27 of the trip, attributed the result to the "indifferent throwing" of Excelsior captain and catcher Joe Leggett. A loss to the Mutual at Hoboken followed on the 16th, 17–11 (Boss Tweed, the *City Item* noted, gave

Underneath these boards must lie the warning, "Post No Bills." These were the Broadway offerings of mid-summer 1863. Note Tom Thumb and troupe at Barnum's.

one of the speeches at the postgame feasting), and another to the Eckford on the 17th, 10–5, in a game shortened to six innings by rain. The Union Grounds, the *Brooklyn Daily Eagle* noted in its story the next day, was "covered with small white clover, no more than an inch high," which in the *Daily Eagle*'s opinion didn't interfere with play. The Athletic had lapsed in their determination to avoid side entertainments, taking a morning whirl in coaches and carriages around Central Park with the Mutual on the 16th and accompanying the Eckford on the morning of the 17th on a tour of the Continental Iron Works ("birthplace of the *Monitor*," the *Daily Eagle* noted) and the Brooklyn Navy Yard. The Atlantic then handed the visitors a third loss, 21–13, on the 18th. The Philadelphians' visit closed on the 19th with a victory, 37–17, over the Star Club of Brooklyn. They then entrained for Newark for a game against the Eureka Club, on the 20th, which ended with the unusually low score of 8–6, in favor of the Eureka. The result afforded Henry Chadwick, in his report published in the New York *Clipper* on June 27, an opportunity to editorialize on the importance and superiority of games marked by good fielding rather than heavy batting. Batting, he proclaimed, any "muffin" could learn. Reported attendance for the games had varied from 2,500 to 8,000 spectators. The *City Item* on July 4 pronounced itself satisfied, considering the heavy schedule and unfamiliar fields, with two wins out of six.

Fancifully describing the Athletic's peregrinations on this trip in terms of a military campaign, *Harpers Weekly* on July 4 boasted, "The Base-Ball Club has this great value at the present moment, that it is the 'school of the soldier' in vigor, endurance, and agility." Not everyone was yet enthralled. In the column adjoining its June 27 report on the games, the *City Item* printed one of its regular letters from a New York correspondent, who both panned the Athletic's play and opined that baseball was too violent, and "could be replaced by other and better games."

"Take 'Em on the Fly"

The returning gentlemen of the Athletic entered Pennsylvania only a few days ahead of the less polite troops of Confederate General Jubal A. Early, who was in search not of trophy balls but of supplies for the advancing Army of Northern Virginia, for which the rebels scrupulously paid, in good CSA currency. Proper attention to the baseball season was suspended as the Emergency of 1863, as the invasion was dubbed locally, unfolded. "A DULL WEEK," a *Sunday Mercury* subhead complained on July 5, due to "the war excitement, the going off of militia regiments," so that there "was little of interest during the past week in base ball playing." Two years of war had evidently taken the edge off the patriotism and self-sacrifice of the sporting press. Among the Athletic of Philadelphia, the *Sunday Mercury* noted on July 12, 18 had gone off with the militia, including, the *City Item* noted, seven of the first nine. Their field captain, DeWitt Clinton Moore, was also captain of a militia unit, and, the *Press* noted on July 1, was recruiting volunteers with a broadside entitled, "Take 'Em on the Fly." Though incensed with the trouble caused the season by "this Pennsylvania invasion," the *Sunday Mercury* was optimistic: "As soon as that trouble blows over, our players will be found at their posts again, eager for the fray." The *Clipper*, on July 18, was in a wistful mood: "The great game of iron and lead ball, between the loyal and rebellious States, is now engrossing all attention.... We hope the last innings will soon be played."

Another milestone in the game's march toward professionalism nonetheless was marked at this time: Tom Pratt, the 19-year-old star pitcher of the Athletic, had, the *Sunday Mercury* diplomatically explained on July 12, "been offered a good situation" while with the team in New York, and had resigned from the Athletic Club upon its return to Philadelphia. He would move to Brooklyn, and, since he had "had his name proposed as a member of the Atlantic Club," become that club's pitcher. The *Clipper* saluted the news on the 18th with the observation that his new post (as pitcher) was "an honor no doubt that he was exceedingly ambitious of obtaining." Pratt's onset with his new club was delayed when he marched off with Captain Moore and the other Athletics to do his bit in turning back the rebels. Further evidence that the top clubs, at least, were considered professional appeared in *Wilkes' Spirit of the Times* (August 29 and September 12) and the *Clipper* (September 19) when both listed games between teams of newspaper employees under the heading, "Amateur."

The Championship Season

The New York championship season kicked off in July, featuring the same contenders as in 1862: the Eckford, defending champions; the Atlantic; the Mutual; and the Union of Morrisania. The Eureka, of Newark, was also mentioned as a contender, but it absorbed narrow defeats by the Atlantic and Mutual early on, and scheduled no further championship matches. The Eckford opened defense of its crown on July 22 by holding off the Mutual in Hoboken, 10–9, a chore that consumed three hours and 40 minutes, and then took another low-scoring game at Morrisania, dropping the Union by 8 runs to 4 in a four-hour affair on July 30. The *Brooklyn Daily Eagle* huffed in its coverage on the 31st that the low scoring in the Union game was "sufficient evidence that the game was pruned down so as to take away many of its most conspicuous beauties."

The first match between the Atlantic and Mutual at the former's home ground in Bedford on August 3 proved contentious — as the *Daily Eagle* subheaded in its coverage the next day, "Almost A Row." The game was played in oppressive heat. The *Sunday Mercury* claimed in its coverage on the 9th that it was "95 in the shade" at gametime, 3:00 P.M. More than three hours later, the home team, which had batted first, took an imposing eight-run lead into the bottom of the ninth. Seven batters later, the Mutual had seven runs, and after two outs, the tying run scored. The sun being within minutes of setting, the specter of "playing off" — delaying the finish of the game to throw the result back to the last completed inning — reared its ugly head. According to the *Eagle*, a protracted, confused discussion of whether sufficient light remained for play ensued; *Wilkes' Spirit of the Times*, in its coverage of August 15, estimated that 25 minutes were thus lost. The umpire finally determined in the affirmative, the next Mutual stood in, swung and missed three times, and on the third miss took off for first base. The catcher, Dickey Pearce, made no effort to catch the ball. With Pearce continuing to ignore the situation, this runner circled the bases with the winning run, which under the rules did not end the game; a third out was required. Sunset had now occurred, but the umpire, John Grum of the Atlantic's archrival, the Eckford, remained unwilling to call an end. The next batter followed suit, and walked around as far as third base before Charles Smith of the Atlantic consented to tag him, for which, reportedly, the Mutual gave him three cheers.

The *Daily Eagle* commented that the blame for such disgraceful behavior in the upper reaches of the baseball "fraternity" lay with the effort to crown a champion: "The bitter rivalry that ensues, the objectionable efforts that are likely to increase the playing strength of the contesting clubs, and the general discord that is thereby introduced, to say nothing of the evils arising from the encouragement of the gambling spirit ... afford sufficient proof of the injurious effect they have on the welfare of the game." The *Sunday Mercury*, after prophesying gloomily in its coverage on the 9th that 1863 would likely become the last season where the clubs would engage in a series of championship matches, called on August 16 for the majority of right-thinking club members to control the beast, lest the game fall to the level of "low trotting matches" under the control of "degraded gamblers." Meanwhile, it announced on August 30, gametimes would be moved up to 2:00 P.M. to prevent waning daylight from affecting the outcomes.

Whatever measures were taken privately by the clubs, a month elapsed before championship matches resumed, and the Atlantic, the Eckford, and even the spectators were reportedly on their best behavior when the Eckford spoiled Tom Pratt's Brooklyn debut on September 2, routing the former champions 31–10 on their home grounds at Bedford, and defeating them in the return match on September 8 at the Union Grounds, 21–11, in a match called after four hours and eight innings by darkness. Victories over the

Union prisoners at Salisbury, N.C., ***drawn from nature by Act. Major Otto Boetticher; lith. of Sarony, Major & Knapp. This celebrated image was published by Goupil in 1863.***

Union, 20–5, on September 24, a game in which the losers were compelled by late withdrawals to play eight-handed, and over the Mutual on October 6, 18–10, closed the Eckford's unbeaten run for 1863. Amid the congratulations on its great unbeaten run, the Eckford may have been startled to see the suggestion, in the *Sunday Mercury* on October 11, that it should therefore retire from further championship competition, as it could never exceed its success of 1863.

Concluding Acts

Intercity visiting resumed, as the Athletic travelled to Princeton to return the earlier visit of the Nassau club. The collegians, after a loss to the Athletics in Philadelphia in May, 29–18, defeated the Philadelphia champions on their home grounds on September 26, 29–13. Considerable whining appeared in the *City Item* on October 5 about the conditions the losers endured in the latter game. Three starters, including captain Captain Moore, were absent; no provision had been made by the Athletic for pregame food, so that they played on empty stomachs; and, most notably, the vagaries of the Nassau's grounds: "No one but a topographical engineer could describe that ground. To get to first base you ran up a hill, and then down to 2nd base, up to 3rd base and home base. The right field played at the top of a hill, the centre field at the bottom, and the left field in a gully."

The Nassau then tried their luck on the less interesting fields of Brooklyn, arriving on October 19 and playing four games in four days. After posting wins against the Resolute, Excelsior, and Star clubs, none championship contenders, they took on the Atlantic, and were defeated, 18–12.

The Athletic spread-eagled a competitive field in Philadelphia much diminished by the war — they took two games from the Keystone in September and apparently received no other challenges. They enjoyed a trip to Altoona to play a friendly match with the inexperienced Mountain Club, sizzling the inexperienced hillmen, 73–22. According to the *City Item*'s account of September 19, the Altoonans had the antidote for the epidemic of swift, wild pitching in the early 1860s caused by the success of Creighton: The Mountains' hillside, unfenced field, with home plate at its downhill end, sent balls passing the catcher down the hill.

The season concluded with a flurry of informal games, and attention turned to proposals for rule changes to improve the game for 1864. Praise in the New York and Brooklyn media in October for the Nassau pitcher, who relied on slow pitches with a great "twist," presaged the changes in pitching rules that would significantly alter play in 1864. Reporters, at least, were wearying of watching the four-hour games caused by wild, speed-ball pitching for which there was no penalty. The *Brooklyn Daily Eagle* on October 23 insisted that there was nothing for it but to count wild pitches as runs for the batting team, as in cricket. A wild pitch was defined as one that either bounced in front of home base, passed over the head of the batter, or was wide of the striker's line — that is, more than three feet to either side of home base — the latter to eliminate the practices of pitching deliberately wide and of pitching at the striker. The *Sunday Mercury* on November 8 supported the idea, as did the *Clipper* on November 28. The *Sunday Mercury* also listed a number of items found problematic:

1. The definition of a balk, felt to be in need of clarification.
2. The definition of a jerked pitch, on the grounds that pitches were being jerked without an actual touch of the arm to the side of the body, as the rule then stated was necessary.
3. Specification in the rules that baserunners must actually touch rather than "make" each base, as the existing rule stated.
4. Addition of a penalty for infraction of the rule requiring that the striker bat with one foot on the striker's line. Suggested: that any ball hit perpendicular to the ground off the bat when the batter has not so stood, be called fair.
5. A rule instructing umpires to not count as strikes pitches swung at for the purpose of "deliberately hastening the close of an inning," a practice related to the tendency of even the most gentlemanly teams to "play off."

In addition, the *Sunday Mercury* noted that adoption of the "fly game," the elimination of outs on struck balls caught on the first bounce, would again be considered, as it had at all previous conventions, and predicted, in a note of December 6, three days before the NABBP meeting, that this time it would pass. Under NABBP procedure, changes would be discussed and recommended (or not) at a meeting held prior to the convention by the nine-member Committee on Rules and Regulations, all New Yorkers except for H.T. Dusenberry, of Newark. A mix of players and club officials, the committee included representatives from most of the major clubs, the Atlantic and Mutual excepted, and did not at this point include the influential Henry Chadwick, ineligible because he had not yet joined a club and been named as one of its convention delegates as of the previous meeting in December 1862. During the 1863 season, he joined the Star Club of Brooklyn, was named a delegate, and was subsequently chosen for the Rules Committee for 1864.

The meeting of December 9 adopted all recommendations made by the Rules Committee. Though the suggestion of counting wild pitches as runs was not approved, three measures were taken to curb fast, wild pitching: a back line was added to the pitcher's position, ending the practice of taking a run-up to increase speed, as in cricket; pitchers were required to have both feet on the ground at the time of delivery; and, finally, walks, as described by Chadwick in the *Daily Eagle* on December 10:

> Should a pitcher repeatedly fail to deliver fair balls to the striker, for the apparent purpose of delaying the game, or for any other cause, the umpire after warning him, shall call one ball, and if the pitcher persists in such action, two and three balls, and when three balls have been called, the striker shall be entitled to his first base, and should any base be occupied at that time each player occupying them shall be entitled to one base.

The exception to the meeting's unanimous acceptance of the Rules Committee's action concerned the fly game, which, as with all previous attempts, was rejected, by a vote of 25–22. Chadwick, an avid proponent, stated in his *Daily Eagle* write-up that it was defeated by "muffin" clubs "whose fun the fly game would put a stop to altogether." The breakdown listed in the *Daily Eagle* of the voting, however, lists four of the six delegates from the New York championship contenders (Eckford, Atlantic, Mutual) and three of the four from the top Philadelphia clubs (Athletic, Keystone) as voting to retain the bound rule.

Summing Up

The *Sunday Mercury*, in its summary of the meeting on December 13, first noted that the disappointing attendance (28 clubs, compared to 32 in 1862) indicated that participation in the game was at least "not on the decline" after two years of civil war. The convention's action in dropping 29 clubs, one more than attended the meeting, from the rolls because of inactivity in 1862 and 1863 indicated, however, the scope of the war's impact. The *Sunday Mercury* applauded the effort to curb fast, wild pitching, stating, "All present were convinced of the absolute necessity of putting a stop to the swift and wild pitching in vogue," and particularly the intimidation of batsmen by throwing at them. Emphasis on speed also, in the *Sunday Mercury*'s opinion, prevented the maximum development of fielding skills, and made the positions of pitcher and catcher too onerous.

Reviews of the season appeared in November, and were unguardedly optimistic. The *City Item*, instead of supplying its own views, printed on the 14th a lengthy letter from a New York correspondent signing himself "A Looker On," for whom the season had been "quite a brilliant and successful one," while 1864 promised to be "one of the best and most flourishing seasons in the annals of the game." The *Sunday Mercury* weighed in on the 15th, proclaiming 1863 the best season of the past three — the war years. It emphasized the improvement in the game from year to year, noting, "It is true that base ball, in one sense of the word, has been played for fifty years past; but what is now called base ball was only introduced in 1858." With the rules changes anticipated for 1864, it added, "in a year or so more, we shall place in the game in a thoroughly complete and permanent position." For the *Clipper,* commenting in its issue of the 28th, the season had been, under the circumstances, "quite a brilliant one."

The war's impact, nonetheless, had been severe. In addition to diminished activity in New York City, Brooklyn, Boston, and Philadelphia, the widespread formation of clubs and beginning of match play in the west and in some southern states before the war came to a halt in most locales. The contributors to *Base Ball Pioneers 1850–1870* (Morris et al., eds., 2012) found interclub play on a regular basis continuing in 1863 only in Upstate New York and in Michigan's Lower Peninsula, including its inauguration that year at the University of Michigan. Other places, such as Baltimore, Washington, D.C., Altoona and Allegheny City, Pennsylvania, Chicago and Freeport, Illinois, St. Louis, and perhaps San Francisco, retained single clubs that relied on rare intercity visits for competition. In a far greater number of locales, from Minnesota to Louisiana and from Maine to Georgia, organized play apparently ceased. In the new sport's ability to survive to the degree it had, however, the fraternity could find reason to agree with the *Clipper*'s assessment, also in its review of November 28, of where the game stood:

> ... the success attendant upon the progress of base ball during the past three seasons of the existence of civil war, not only affords evidence of the great popularity of the game, but also of its complete establishment as a permanent American institution.

Abstract

Five seasons into its organized existence under the National Association of Base Ball Players, the version of baseball known variously as the National Association, Knickerbocker Rules, or New York Rules game continued to face the challenge in 1863 of surviving the Civil War. Further, no end was in sight as the year opened. The war had ended the game's spectacular growth of the immediate prewar period, and ended significant organized play in all but its core areas — today's New York City metropolitan area and Philadelphia.The present article recounts the course of the season, now 150 years in the past, a season in which both the game and the Union struggled to survive.

Note

1. Kirsch, G., 2003. *Baseball in Blue and Gray: The National Pastime During the Civil War* (37–41).

"A Puritan Sunday"
Base Ball and Blue Laws in Walla Walla, Washington

Terry Gottschall

The headline — "A Puritan Sunday" — appeared above the fold on the front page of the *Walla Walla Statesman*'s July 17, 1902, edition. The article described a successful campaign by Protestant pastors and temperance ladies to enforce Washington State's long moribund Sunday closing laws. The most disturbing line came near the end of the article: "Under a strict interpretation of the law, it is doubtful whether Sunday base ball playing within the city limits is permissible."[1] Although baseball had long served as the national pastime, Sunday baseball occasionally collided with an even older tradition — the puritan practice of enforcing Sunday closing laws, or blue laws — even in the early days of the new century. Accordingly, a revival of local puritanism in 1901 threatened Sunday baseball in Walla Walla, Washington. The incident — which came to involve Bibles, booze, and baseball — threatened two successive baseball seasons, produced a state Supreme Court decision, and gained nationwide publicity before Walla Walla fans of Sunday baseball could finally enjoy their favorite sport in peace.

Blue Laws and Baseball

Blue laws — local or state laws that required Sabbath observance and prohibited labor or closed businesses on Sunday — developed early in American history. Although Episcopalian Virginia required church attendance in 1610, historian Alexis McCrossen notes, "The designation 'blue laws,' which colloquially refers to those laws that regulate morality, suggests Puritan and Pilgrim influence."[2] Massachusetts, for example, banned Sunday labor in 1650, while the New Haven (Rhode Island) colony provided the term itself when it printed its theocratic code on blue paper in 1665. Additional blue laws prohibited the sale of liquor, leisure time activities such as horseracing and boxing, and even hunting on Sundays.[3]

Two circumstances — industrialism and immigration — soon undermined the Puritan Sabbath's ability to regulate "morality." With a six-day workweek, industrial workers saw Sunday as a day of recreation rather than a day of rest. Likewise, a new wave of immigrants brought with them the Continental Sunday when they arrived at Ellis Island.

Terry Gottschall teaches classical and modern European history at Walla Walla University, College Place, Washington. He divides his research time between local baseball history — his pioneer ancestors arrived in the Walla Walla valley by wagon train in 1865 — between 1867 and 1920 and German naval operations in Asian and Pacific waters between 1859 and 1915.

 DOI: 10.3172/BB.7.154

Thus, according to McCrossen, "Sundays were especially busy in [immigrant communities], for it was then that entire families went to drink beer, visit with friends, listen to music, and dance, just as German and others did in Europe."[4]

Baseball, as the national pastime, quickly experienced the same conflict. The National League banned Sunday baseball in 1878, even expelling the Cincinnati Red Stockings after the 1880 season for violating the policy. The always contrary American Association allowed Sunday games from its inception in 1882 until its collapse after the 1891 season. When the National League absorbed four AA teams in 1892, it allowed, but discouraged, the option of playing Sunday games. The American League allowed Sunday baseball when it began play in 1901. The National League eventually surrendered to the inevitable, allowing a full schedule of Sunday games by 1934.[5]

Blue laws, widely established but often ignored, occasionally ensnared individual baseball players. For example, the Ohio Supreme Court upheld the arrest, trial, and conviction of John Powell for playing Sunday baseball in May 1897. In *State v. Powell* (April 19, 1898), the Court rejected the argument that the law violated the state's constitutional separation of church and state. The Court concluded instead, "A law enacted for sufficient reasons of a secular nature, as the public health, cannot be held invalid because there is a variety of religious notion upon the subject."[6]

Walla Walla, however, had not had any problems with Sunday baseball before 1901. The professional Pacific Interstate League — Walla Walla, plus Pendleton, La Grande, and Baker City, Oregon — had played games on Sundays without criticism or opposition

NORTHWESTERN GAS & ELECTRIC COMPANY'S BASEBALL CLUB.
Playing in the Amateur City League of Walla Walla.

"Not infrequently has the city been represented by nines that would ... draw big crowds in cities much larger than Walla Walla." (*Up-to-the-Times Magazine, *1906)

during its only season in 1891. Nearby Milton, Oregon, eight miles south of Walla Walla across the state line, had briefly experienced a different past when an evangelical pastor had convinced the town council to prohibit Sunday games in May 1891. Popular opinion and the threat of a lawsuit, however, persuaded the council to reverse itself and restore Sunday games.[7]

The Garden City

Blue laws certainly seemed an outdated historical artifact when Walla Walla entered the 20th century. Founded in the verdant Walla Walla valley and incorporated in 1862, the town had quickly become the "Garden City of the Northwest" based on its fertile soil and long growing season. The 1900 edition of the Walla Walla *City Directory* asserted firmly that the town had outgrown its pioneer roots to become a modern, sophisticated, and commercial metropolis in the new century. Walla Walla served as the seat of the eponymous county, surveyed at 1,300 square miles and with a total population exceeding 17,000. Walla Wallans could enjoy an active civic life by joining one of many benevolent or fraternal organizations. An opera house and theater provided cultural activities, while two colleges yielded intellectual pursuits. Spirituality coexisted with sin as 14 churches competed with 31 saloons. Three newspapers — the morning *Union* (Republican), the evening *Statesman* (Democrat), and the weekly *Argus* (self-described muckrakers) — competed for readership and maintained lively political discussions. The Northern Pacific Railroad and the Western Union Telegraph Company linked Walla Walla to the outside world. The state penitentiary provided jobs and Fort Walla Walla, garrisoned by the Sixth U.S. Cavalry and the 10th Field Artillery Battery, contributed to the town's economy on monthly paydays.[8]

Baseball, which serves even more than literacy as the true metric of civilization, had existed in Walla Walla since 1867. An editorial in the *Walla Walla Statesman* in July noted, "There is scarce a one-horse town in Oregon that has not one or more base ball clubs. Cannot we have a base ball club at Walla Walla?" The challenge spurred the formation of two teams — the Excelsiors and Walla Wallas — who played a three-game match series later in the summer.[9]

Walla Walla baseballists established their first town team — the "Athletic Base Ball Club" — to represent the city against similar teams from nearby communities in 1880. The Walla Walla town team, which became an annual institution, played visiting teams on Decoration (Memorial) Day or the Fourth of July for civic pride and bragging rights plus an occasional side bet between members of the sporting crowd.[10] These teams quickly confirmed Dorothy Seymour Mills' and Harold Seymour's reference to town teams as "down-home baseball" that "evolved into an American institution meriting a place alongside such other symbols of America's past as the little red schoolhouse, the fervid revival meeting, and the old-fashioned Fourth of July celebration."[11]

The Walla Walla team proved a popular activity through the 1890s but began to decline by the new century. The 1899 and 1900 teams suffered particularly from ineffective management, irregular schedules, and small crowds. Since many Walla Wallans labored from dawn 'til dusk through a six-day workweek, many could only rarely attend games played on weekday or Saturday afternoons.[12]

Walla Walla cranks, plus a core group of players from the 1900 team, met to establish a more structured organization — the Walla Walla Baseball Association — in March 1901. Following the recommendation of 1900 team captain and shortstop Frank Buchet, the association recruited attorney John L. Sharpstein as manager for the 1901 season. Sharpstein had played shortstop for several local teams a decade earlier and continued to support Walla Walla baseball as a devout fan.[13] Sharpstein came from a well known pioneer family that had arrived in Walla Walla by wagon train in 1865. His father, Benjamin, established a successful legal practice and served several terms in the territorial legislature.[14] The younger Sharpstein apprenticed in his father's office and was admitted to the territorial bar in 1879. Like his father, John Sharpstein was no country lawyer in a one-horse town. He also served several terms as city attorney and state legislator and regularly pleaded cases before the state Supreme Court, yet still found time to play and watch baseball.[15] Sharpstein's appointment as team manager proved quite popular. According to the *Union*, "The baseball men say they made a find when they enlisted Mr. Sharpstein as manager of the team and all are enthusiastic and declare they will play ball as they never played before."[16] Ultimately, however, it was Sharpstein's legal acumen, more than his baseball skills, that would provide his greatest contribution to the team.

Manager Sharpstein immediately set to work on a consistent and expanded schedule for the new season. He made arrangements to play games against local teams (Whitman College, the penitentiary Mavericks, Fort Walla Walla), nearby teams (Waitsburg, Dayton) in the Touchet Valley, Oregon teams (Athena, Pendleton) across the state line, and regional teams (Colfax, Ritzville, Pullman) linked to Walla Walla by railroad. He also arranged visits from barnstorming professional teams from the Class B Northwest League (Tacoma, Washington, and Portland, Oregon) west of the Cascade Mountains. More important, Sharpstein observed Continental Sunday, scheduling these games for Sunday afternoons to allow local fans to attend without having to take time off from work or miss Sunday morning church services.[17]

Work also began on the team's Second Street Grounds situated between Oak and Pine on Walla Walla's north side. While Sharpstein paid the lease on the property that housed the existing ballpark, fans volunteered to roll the field, repair the bleachers, and construct a new, covered grandstand along the third base line. This latter addition would prove particularly valuable during Walla Walla's notoriously long and hot summer. According to one observer: "In this way it will be much better for the fans and cranks as this will be the shady side of the field and also the side which the wind blows." Sharpstein also solicited bids from local businessmen interested in running the concession stand that sold snacks, soft drinks, ice cream, and cigars. The team set admission prices at "two bits" — 25 cents — for general admission and an additional 15 cents for a grandstand seat.[18] Because the ballpark sat in the middle of a residential area, Sharpstein also requested that fans not bring "horns, bells, pans, or other noise creating device" to the ballpark.[19]

Opening Day came on Sunday afternoon, April 28, as Walla Walla hosted the Dayton town team from nearby Columbia County. A large and enthusiastic crowd attended the game at the newly refurbished Second Street Grounds and watched the home team defeat the visitors, 7–2.[20] Not every Walla Wallan welcomed the arrival of Sunday baseball, however. Several Protestant pastors had taken the opportunity during their Sunday morning sermons to denounce the afternoon game as a "desecration of the Sabbath."[21]

Local cranks nonetheless welcomed Sunday baseball. Sharpstein had scheduled additional home games on the first three Sundays in May. More than 2,000 watched Walla Walla defeat Athena (Oregon) on May 5. Another large crowd watched the home team beat visiting Colfax (Washington) on May 12 in a poorly played game: "Walla Walla and Colfax played ball on Sunday. That is both teams played with the ball. Part of the game was interesting, part was not."[22] Walla Walla won its fourth successive home game on May 19, defeating Pendleton (Oregon). The newspaper account did not note specific attendance figures but did cite another large, enthusiastic crowd: "They were all out and the 'rooters' rooted, the 'looks' looked, and the 'fans' fanned — and so did some of the players."[23]

Trouble in Garden City

Sunday baseball may have pleased Walla Walla baseball fans but it proved sacrilegious for Walla Walla puritans. Members of the Walla Walla Ministerial Union, who had already condemned Sunday baseball in late April, now prepared to denounce the practice through a series of coordinated sermons at Sunday church services on May 26. This led the *Walla Walla Union* to advise readers: "The Second Street Grounds is not the only place where baseball will be in evidence on Sunday."

The Reverend Lee Johnson, pastor of the First Methodist Episcopal Church, explained to the *Union* that Sunday baseball had a "demoralizing influence" on Walla Walla's youth. The abolition of Sunday baseball, Johnson argued, would eliminate a

With the City Amateur Baseball League, Walla Walla enjoyed a thriving baseball scene, especially in the years following the turn of the century.

major source of temptation and restore purity in the younger generation. He concluded, "The Bible says that the Sabbath day shall be remembered and kept holy and how are we to do that when we forget our sacred duties and devote the day to pleasure and selfish amusements?"

Sharpstein, as both team manager and baseball fan, defended Sunday baseball. He rejected ministerial charges that Sunday baseball undermined morals or led young fans down perilous paths. Instead, he assured the *Union*'s reporter that "there can be no harm nor crime attached to a clean, wholesome sport." He made a second argument, citing the concept of a Continental Sunday with games "played on a day which is advantageous to many who would otherwise never be permitted the privilege of witnessing a game." Since many fans could not attend weekday games because they worked a six-day week, Sunday baseball allowed them to enjoy the game with their families on a relaxed Sunday afternoon. He likewise noted that he had considered the issue of Sunday baseball when he scheduled games on Sunday afternoons rather than intrude on morning worship services. He even suggested a libertarian element when he noted that fans "maintain their right to amuse themselves as they see fit as long as they harm no one in so doing."[24]

The struggle over Sunday baseball prompted a facetious *Union* editorial:

> The ministers of the city have announced that they will preach against people attending Sunday baseball games. This should bring to the churches a liberal attendance of the "fans," for they should not hesitate to go and hear what is being said of them. But the fan is a very irreligious sort of a chap and it is doubtful if the ministers will get much of an opportunity to address him unless they go out to the ball grounds in the afternoon.[25]

Nonetheless, several members of the Ministerial Union did, in fact, render unto God when they censured fans and castigated the practice of Sunday baseball in their sermons on May 26. Pastor J.W. Compton, for example, denounced "Sabbath Desecration" at the Second Methodist Episcopal Church. The Reverend J.M. Morris of the First Christian Church condemned those who would violate the "sacredness of the Lord's Day and the laws of Our Lord." Austin Rice preached to his parishioners at the Congregational Church on "The Sanctity of the Lord's Day."[26]

The pastors likewise rendered unto Caesar when they denounced Sunday baseball as a violation of state laws. Blue laws had, in fact, existed in Washington since 1853, when the territorial Organic Act had proscribed anyone who boxed, raced horses, danced, or "disturbed" church meetings on Sunday. Successive territorial and state legislatures inscribed additional restrictions, including the sale of liquor and other commercial activities.[27] Walla Walla preachers confirmed these Sunday laws when they read relevant sections from *Remington and Ballinger's Annotated Codes and Statues of Washington* to their congregations. Section 7250, for example, prohibited "noisy amusements" on Sunday, which, according to the pastors, would classify baseball grounds in the same category as a "playhouse or theater, race-ground, cockpit, or game of chance." The pastors also argued that Sunday baseball operated as a business — the team charged two bits admission and sponsored a concession stand — which would therefore violate Section 7251 which made it "unlawful for any person or persons of this state to open on Sunday for the purpose of trade or sale of goods, wares, and merchandise, any shop, store, or building, or place of business whatever."[28]

As the pastors preached their reproachful sermons, they might have noticed that

The Walla Walla Athletic Club nine was also known as the Sharpshooters. Attorney John L. Sharpstein (center) was the club's manager. Captain Frank Buchet is kneeling to his right.

their admonitions echoed somewhat loudly in emptier sanctuaries. Sharpstein had coincidentally, if not conveniently, scheduled an away game at Dayton, seat of Columbia County thirty miles north, whose residents welcomed Sunday baseball. Temptation must have won out over sanctity as nearly 500 Walla Walla fans accompanied the team. A disappointed Walla Walla contingent returned home later Sunday afternoon, however, knowing that they had desecrated the Sabbath for no good reason. According to the *Union*, the contest became a "fizzle" when Captain Frank Buchet forfeited the game after protesting a baserunning call by the local umpire.[29] No written record exists but the returning Walla Walla fans may have compounded their Sunday sin even further when they sought solace from the afternoon's debacle in Main Street saloons.

The issue of Sunday baseball soon passed from pulpit to courtroom when the local chapter of the Women's Christian Temperance Union opened a second front in defense of Sunday laws in late June. The teetotaling ladies of the WCTU demanded that municipal and county officials specifically enforce Section 7250 that prohibited both liquor sales and "noisy amusements" on Sunday. According to the *Union*'s account, City Marshal W.S. Halley had briefly enforced this particular Sunday law in in 1895 in response to an earlier outbreak of puritanism. Popular opposition, however, had quickly convinced him to drop enforcement, returning Walla Walla to the status of a "wide-open town."[30]

The combined efforts of the Ministerial Union and the WCTU quickly bore fruit. County attorney Oscar Cain announced in July that he intended to enforce the Sunday closing laws beginning on July 14. He specifically cited the same state statutes read out by the pastors in May: Section 7250, "Places of Amusement to be closed on Sunday," and Section 7251, "Business Houses to be closed on Sunday." He warned that violators could face fines up to $100. The *Union* concluded that Cain's enforcement of the blue laws meant that Walla Wallans could "not even [purchase] a glass of lemonade." The article speculated further that Cain's reference to Section 7250, which proscribed "noisy amusements," could apply to baseball, threatening Sunday's scheduled game against a visiting town team from Ritzville, a wheat-farming community in central Washington one hundred miles away. The *Union* concluded, "How the present fight will terminate is a matter for the future to determine."[31]

Manager Sharpstein nonetheless notified the *Union* that he intended to play the game on Sunday as scheduled. He asserted strongly that Section 7250 did not apply to baseball. He specifically cited a 1900 decision by the Missouri Supreme Court—*Ex parte Joseph Neet*—which had specifically concluded, "A game of baseball is an athletic game or sport, a game of skill, and not a game of chance nor a game of a demoralizing tendency." The Missouri Court noted that baseball on Sunday was "neither *mala in se* nor *mala prohibita*—neither immoral nor hurtful to body or soul."[32] Sharpstein concurred, noting, "There are many in Walla Walla who believe there is not the least harm in witnessing a game of the national pastime on the first day of the week." Sharpstein contended, moreover, that the comparable Washington statute could no more forbid baseball than it could prohibit "chess, checkers, authors, or walks in the country." He advised the reporter that he intended to use the Missouri case as a legal precedent if Prosecutor Cain took action against Sunday baseball.[33] The *Union* suggested that Sharpstein's public defense of Sunday baseball in the face of possible prosecution would actually enhance attendance at Sunday's game, predicting colorfully that "there will be more people inside the grounds than there are flies in a cheap chop house when Mulligan stew is on the bill of fare."[34]

Sunday, July 14—Bastille Day in France—saw only minimal revolutionary activity in Walla Walla. In fact, with the exception of three Main Street saloons whose owners deliberately chose to challenge Cain's enforcement of the closing laws, downtown Walla Walla stood strangely quiet on Sunday afternoon. The *Union* described the day somewhat facetiously, "Ice cream parlors were closed, the soda fountain was stilled, the smoker looked longingly through the closed doors of the cigar stand or stood with his hands deep in his trousers' pockets and chewed the stem of his empty cob pipe, for it was Sunday and even the most hardened sinner was aware of it."[35] Meanwhile, four blocks north at the Second Street Grounds, Walla Walla defeated Ritzville, 2–0, as pitcher Pat Ryan struck out eight to win the shutout victory. The Sunday controversy may have actually failed to incite local cranks, or perhaps

Carrie Nation was the emblematic figure of the Temperance movement.

frightened them away, as a mediocre crowd, estimated at 875, watched an excellent game.[36]

Judgment Day arrived immediately for the desecrators of the Sabbath. Justice of the Peace William Glasford ordered the city marshal to arrest the three saloonkeepers who had violated the Sunday closing laws. Manager Sharpstein, though, remained momentarily immune from prosecution since Prosecutor Cain had made no decision, according to the *Union*, "in regard to the game of baseball played on Sunday afternoon."[37]

Glasford empaneled a six-man jury on Tuesday morning to try James Casey, proprietor of a Main Street saloon. (Casey, a passionate baseball crank, had managed the Walla Walla franchise in the Pacific Interstate League in 1891.[38]) Cain prosecuted, while Sharpstein, who had an obvious interest in Casey's acquittal, served for the defense. Cain called eight witnesses, each of whom testified that he had observed Casey serving alcohol in his saloon on Sunday. Sharpstein called no witnesses but chose to challenge the law on constitutional grounds. He argued that this particular blue law, which intended to promote the "better observance of Sunday as a day of worship," violated Article I, Section 11 of the state constitution which separated church and state. When the jury failed to reach a unanimous verdict after 30 minutes of deliberation, Glasford declared a mistrial and announced plans to try Casey with a new jury.[39]

Justice came swiftly on Wednesday morning, July 17. The second jury, which Glasford had handpicked, convicted Casey after deliberating only five minutes. Additional trials, equally brief, convicted the other two saloonkeepers, whereupon Glasford fined each defendant $99 and costs. Sharpstein, who defended all three defendants, promptly appealed the cases to Superior Court to test the constitutionality of the Sunday laws.[40]

Sharpstein then faced his own day in court. Justice Glasford charged him with playing a "noisy game" under Section 7250. Sharpstein promptly negotiated an arrangement with Cain and Glasford to stipulate facts and arguments in Glasford's court but then immediately transfer the case to Superior Court for a final decision by Judge Thomas Brents. Sharpstein confirmed for the official record that he had indeed scheduled and then managed the game against Ritzville on Sunday afternoon, July 14, but also formally contended that a baseball game did not violate Section 7250's prohibition on "noisy amusements." Although Sharpstein also acknowledged that the team had charged admission to the game and the concession stand had sold cigars, soft drinks, and candy, he argued that these activities did not constitute a business and therefore did not violate Section 7251.[41]

Before Brents could make a formal decision in Superior Court, the issue became more complicated. Dorsey Nichols, who operated a general store in nearby College Place, refused to close his store on Sunday July 21. Nichols, a member of the Seventh-day Adventist Church, believed that Sunday closing laws violated his religious liberty under the separation clause of the state constitution. Glasford ordered Nichols' arrest but immediately bound him over for trial by the Superior Court. Sharpstein, who again represented the defendant, noted that Nichols observed Sabbath on the seventh day, Saturday. If Nichols obeyed the law and closed his store on Sunday, Sharpstein argued, he would contravene his religious beliefs by formally acknowledging that Sunday "was the rightful day of worship." When another jury quickly convicted Nichols in Glasford's court on Friday July 26, Sharpstein again appealed to the Superior Court.[42]

Ironically, as Judge Brents considered his legal options in the various cases, Walla

Walla's weather succeeded where pastors and puritans had failed. The *Union* noted that only 150 fans had watched Walla Walla defeat the visiting Pendleton Woodmen on Thursday evening, July 25. The article attributed the small crowd to Walla Walla's summer heat, wondering "why people would persist in playing ball in such beastly hot weather."[43] Sharpstein concurred: "The weather has become so hot that the people will not turn out to see the games, and it is really an imposition to ask the players to go upon the field at this season of the year." He therefore announced that the Walla Walla town team would conclude its season and disband after a weekend series in Baker City, Oregon.[44]

Mother Nature quickly confirmed that meteorology, not jurisprudence, influenced Sharpstein's decision. The U.S. Weather Bureau's official thermometer on the roof of the downtown Paine building consistently registered 95, while street-level temperatures exceeded 100. The *Union* also noted, somewhat ironically, that a railroad section hand had collapsed from heat prostration while transferring ice from a refrigerator car to an icehouse.[45]

Sharpstein formally disbanded the team on July 29. Baseball fans marked the occasion by giving him a diamond stick pin to celebrate his leadership on and off the field. According to the *Union*, "The cranks and fans know they owe to John L. Sharpstein the most successful baseball season Walla Walla ever saw." Sharpstein himself distributed team profits, which amounted to nearly $1,000 after expenses (uniforms, equipment, travel, per diem), amongst the dozen players who had filled out the season's roster.[46] The *Union* marked the event with facetious, if sincere, sadness: "No more for another year will the minister be called upon to preach upon the desecration of the Sabbath day by the rooters. The fans are folded, the cranks have lost their handles — the season is at an end.[47]

Although the season had now ended, Judge Brents still needed to resolve the various legal issues involving Bibles, booze, and baseball. After lengthy consideration, he produced a split decision on July 31. First, he upheld the validity of Sunday closing laws as they applied to saloons, confirming the fines for the three saloonkeepers under both Sections 7250 and 7251. He then threw out Sharpstein's indictment, to the relief of local cranks, on the grounds that Section 7250's "noisy amusement" clause and 7251's commercial definition did not apply to baseball. Judge Brents announced his longest and most compelling decision in the Nichols case, declaring Section 7251 unconstitutional — except as it applied to liquor sales — on religious liberty grounds. "Church and state," he said, "are to be kept separate." He also declared the Section prohibitively flawed since it allowed drug stores to remain open but required the closure of Nichols' general store even if the two businesses sold the same "goods, wares, and merchandise." Based on these arguments, Brents immediately granted Nichols a demurrer to appeal his original conviction to the state Supreme Court.[48]

"A Puritan Sunday"

Sharpstein and Cain traveled to Olympia in December to argue the Nichols case before the Supreme Court. In the new year, soon after their return, talk again turned to baseball and the upcoming season. Based on the success of Sunday baseball in the 1901 season, and freed from any legal liability, Sharpstein announced that he would again

"Marching Through Georgia," a satiric cartoon by Louis M. Glackens for the cover of* Puck, *January 15, 1908. "What fools these mortals be" was the magazine's motto.

schedule Sunday afternoon games against the usual local, regional, and barnstorming opponents. Captain Buchet proposed and the team's directors approved a team name, the wonderfully alliterative "Sharpstein's Sharpshooters."[49]

The regular season began on a cool spring Sunday, March 23, as the Sharpshooters defeated the Operettas, a local team drawn from teenage employees of the Opera House. The *Union* reported, "There were no heroes at the initial baseball game of the season played at the Second Street grounds Sunday afternoon, unless those might be termed heroes who turned their overcoat collars about their ears and watched it through."[50]

As the weather and season warmed, Sunday baseball again proved successful in Walla Walla as the Sharpshooters played Whitman College, Fort Walla Walla, and nearby town teams. Barnstorming teams drew particularly good crowds to the Second Street

Grounds as 1,200 fans turned out for the Northwest League's Helena Wolverine in late April and an astounding 2,800 fans attended a game against the collegiate team from the University of California in June.[51] Walla Walla fans, as reported by both the *Union* and the *Statesman*, began to discuss the establishment of a professional league to include Walla Walla, Baker City, La Grande, and Pendleton. Sharpstein traveled to Pendleton on Saturday June 28 to discuss the issue with reps from the other towns.[52]

The Sharpshooters had just returned from a successful road trip to Spokane and Colfax when the Supreme Court announced its decision in the Dorsey Nichols case on June 16. In *State v. Nichols*, the Court voted unanimously to reverse Judge Brents' original ruling in July 1901, which had declared that Section 7251 violated the defendant's religious liberty. The Court's decision ignored any mention of religious liberty, ruling narrowly instead that "[t]he enactment of Sunday laws, requiring the cessation of labor on the score of the physical and moral well-being of society, is an appropriate exercise of the police power of the state."[53]

The *Walla Walla Statesman* announced the decision under the banner headline "A Puritan Sunday" on June 18. The article anticipated bad news for baseball fans, wondering if "Sunday base ball within the city limits is permissible."[54] The ruling could in fact have had immediate repercussions since Sharpstein had scheduled a game against the Pendleton Indians at the Second Street Grounds for Sunday afternoon, June 22. The home team even expected a large crowd of Oregonians to travel north by train to attend the game.[55]

The *Walla Walla Union*, equally pessimistic, asked rhetorically, "Can Sunday baseball be prevented under the law?" The article noted that the same interests that had opposed Sunday baseball in 1901—the Ministerial Union and its WCTU allies—continued to oppose it in 1902. In fact, according to the *Union*, the two groups intended to bring suit in Superior Court in an attempt to compel Prosecutor Cain to apply the *Nichols* ruling—which confirmed the state's authority to close business on Sundays under Section 7251—to baseball. The opponents of Sunday baseball also hoped to persuade Cain to appeal Brents' July 1901 decision in which he had refused to apply Section 7250's "noisy amusement" to baseball. Since the Supreme Court had reversed Brents' ruling in *State v. Nichols*, might the Court next decide to reverse his other decision, thus prohibiting Sunday baseball as a "noisy amusement" after all? In any event, the article concluded, "the baseball business is again being agitated," since the abolition of Sunday baseball would force the Sharpshooters, who could not subsist on weekday receipts alone, to disband.

The article also quoted a lengthy statement from a "prominent attorney," presumably Sharpstein, in response. "Baseball is not in any sense a game of chance," the attorney noted, "and baseball as played on Sunday in the city of Walla Walla is a game that is pure and free from contamination in any way as much as anything can be at any time." He rejected any attempt to continue to apply Section 7250 to baseball: "The baseball ground is neither a theater nor a playhouse, and it cannot be a cock pit." Even avid baseball fans, he argued, could not approach the noise produced by a "crowd of boys playing with a steam calliope [or] beating on tin pans."[56]

Baseball fans relaxed, momentarily, when Prosecutor Cain announced that he would not enforce the blue law for at least 30 days. At that time, he warned, he would enforce the law against ice cream parlors, bakeries, candy and cigar stores, and general merchandise stores. He did not mention baseball, however, in his list of required Sunday closings.

Cain also admitted that he personally regretted having to enforce the law but acknowledged that he "would have to do his duty."[57] (A critic could argue that Cain had a conflict of interest since he had played in a memorable baseball game, umpired by Judge Brents, in July 1899, in which a newspaper team had trounced county officials.[58])

The *Nichols* decision and its possible application to baseball came at a complicated time for Sharpstein and the Walla Walla team. Beginning with preliminary discussions in February, Sharpstein and baseball representatives from the Oregon communities of Pendleton, La Grande, and Baker City agreed on June 30 to elevate their semi-professional town teams to full professional status in the new minor Inland Empire League. The league scheduled a 48-game season to conclude in mid–September. (Walla Walla's hot summer weather seemed to play no role in the development of the new season, unlike in 1901 when meteorological, rather than legal, heat had compelled Sharpstein to disband the team!) Sharpstein calculated that the team's 10-man roster would cost $1,000 monthly with gate receipts — the ubiquitous "two bits" — providing 75 percent and stock sold by the Walla Walla Baseball Association at $2 per share to raise the remaining amount.[59] Would Cain view the new professional team as a business and therefore enforce Section 7251's Sunday closure on the new enterprise?

The transition to professional baseball came swiftly. Approximately 1,500 fans watched the amateur Sharpshooters end their independent season on Sunday afternoon, July 6, with a victory and a final 22–13 record against all opponents.[60] Four days later, on Thursday afternoon, July 10, the Sharpshooters, with a mixed roster of amateur and professional players, opened their new season with a four-game series at La Grande. Returning to Walla Walla to prepare for their home opener against Baker City, the Sharpshooters received good legal news. Prosecutor Cain announced that he would begin enforcing closing laws on Sunday July 20 as they applied to commercial business but would take no action "relative to Sunday baseball."[61]

Although the Sharpshooters lost three out of the four home games to Baker City, Sunday baseball at least proved profitable. The home opener on Thursday drew 600 fans, while 300 each attended the Friday and Saturday games, but 1,100 turned out for the game on Sunday afternoon. There is no way to calculate the motives of the Sunday fans but perhaps a few attended the game in the absence of Sunday shopping. Likewise, there is no record of whether the team's concession stand remained open on Sunday.[62]

Meanwhile, Byron Lutcher, who operated a West Main cigar and candy store, opened his business on Sunday afternoon to challenge Cain's enforcement of the blue laws. When Prosecutor Cain filed charges against Lutcher in Superior Court, Sharpstein argued in Lutcher's defense that Section 7251 did not intend to prosecute the sale of "ice cream and soda water." Based on the *Nichols* ruling, Judge Brents rejected Sharpstein's arguments, found the defendant guilty, and fined Lutcher $25.[63]

Even though Cain had already promised that his enforcement of blue laws would not apply to baseball, cranks suffered nonetheless. When the Sharpshooters played away games, the proprietors of Caswell's Cigar Store and the Senate Saloon, both on West Main, posted telegraphed reports on the games inning-by-inning. Although fans could still read the returns on Sunday, now posted outside the businesses, they would do so without the aid of alcohol or tobacco.[64]

Sunday baseball in Walla Walla faced one final but momentary legal crisis in early

September. A women identified by the *Union* as "spinster" Kate Hootman, whose backyard abutted the Second Street Grounds' outfield fence, filed suit against the Sharpshooters in Superior Court on September 4. She accused the team of "keeping and maintaining a nuisance" under Section 7250, alleging that playing games and drawing spectators to the site produced noise that was "objectionable to the residents of that portion of the city." Hootman had kept baseballs hit into her yard and had even fired a revolver into the air to protest the "noisy game" beyond the fence.[65] *The Sporting Life*, published in Philadelphia, gave the story national attention when it reported the incident under the headline "Sour on Base Ball."[66] Judge Brents, however, tossed the case because he had ruled in favor of Sharpstein in July 1901 and Cain had confirmed that ruling by refusing to prosecute in July 1902.

Conclusion as Epilogue

Although Sunday baseball in Walla Walla triumphed again against legal obstacles, other factors conspired to end the 1902 season prematurely. The Walla Walla *Union* announced sadly on September 10, "The Inland Empire League has gone smash." Financial problems — two-bits admission never produced sufficient revenues to support professional players in small towns — caused the collapse of the La Grande team on September 8 with four weeks remaining, forcing Pendleton and Baker City to disband their teams immediately. The Sharpshooters, who had a larger fan base and thus greater revenues, stayed together long enough to play a series of exhibition games during Fruit Fair Week in mid–September against the team's former amateur players. Sunday baseball returned annually in and after 1903 with town teams — variously nicknamed including the Walla Walla Wallopers and the Walla Walla Wonders — and professional teams that played in the revived Inland Empire League in 1903, the Class D Inland Empire League in 1908, and the Class D Western Tri-State League between 1912 and 1914.[67]

Blue laws, however, also continued. The Walla Walla Ministerial Union and the Walla Walla chapter of the WCTU briefly launched another attack on Sunday baseball in May 1903 but failed to rally much support.[68] The state legislature revised but confirmed Sunday closing laws in 1909. The legislature combined the earlier Sections 7250 and 7251 into a single section, 242, "Sabbath Breaking," in Chapter 249, of the Session Laws of Washington. Sunday baseball, however, again escaped the new section that referred to, but did not define, "noisy or boisterous sport." Washington voters ultimately overturned Sunday closing laws by referendum in 1966.[69]

Although he had performed admirably as both team manager and team attorney, Sharpstein decided to "retire" from active involvement in Walla Walla baseball in March 1903. Although he retained his position as one of the directors of the Walla Walla Athletic Club, he deferred managerial responsibilities to Robert ("Bobby") Burns. (Burns managed the newly named Scots in a short-lived professional league between late April and mid–June.) Sharpstein nonetheless continued to practice law and dabble in politics. He later served a term in the State Senate, ran unsuccessfully for lieutenant governor, and presided as Superior Court Judge from 1926 until his death in 1934 at age 78. Walla Walla baseball owes him eternal gratitude for his service on the field and in the courtroom.[70]

Abstract

Sunday baseball occasionally collided with blue laws — state or local laws that required businesses to close on Sundays — in the late 19th and early 20th centuries. Because of such blue laws, for example, Major League Baseball did not adopt a full schedule of Sunday games until 1934.

Local baseball often faced the same problem. One such example occurred in Walla Walla, Washington, in 1901 and 1902, when Protestant pastors joined with the local chapter of the WCTU to oppose Sunday games as part of a broader campaign against "noisy amusements" and liquor sales on Sundays. The conflict eventually led to the arrest of the town team manager — a practicing attorney — and to a state Supreme Court case that momentarily threatened Sunday baseball.

Notes

1. *Walla Walla Statesman*, June 18, 1902, p. 1.
2. McCrossen, A. 2000. *Holy Day, Holiday: The American Sunday*. Ithaca, N.Y. (10).
3. Laband, D., and D. Heinbuch. 1987. *Blue Laws: The History, Economics, and Politics of Sunday Closing Laws*. Lexington, Mass. (8, 30–31).
4. McCrossen 2000, 43.
5. See particularly, Bevis, C. 2003. *Sunday Baseball: The Major Leagues' Struggle to Play Baseball on the Lord's Day, 1876–1878*. Jefferson, N.C.
6. *State v. Powell, 58 Ohio St. 324, 40 N. E. 900* (Apr. 19, 1898), cited in Bevis 2003, 278–282.
7. *Walla Walla Statesman*, June 1, 1891, p. 3. See also Gottschall, T. 2009. "'Two-bit Baseball': Walla Walla and the Pacific Interstate League, 1891," *Base Ball* 3, 52–66.
8. See *Walla Walla City and County Directory, 1900–1901*.
9. *Walla Walla Statesman*, July 26, p. 3.
10. *Walla Walla Union*, May 17, 1880, p. 3; May 16, 1885, p. 3.
11. Seymour Mills, D., and H. Seymour. 1990. *Baseball: The People's Game*. New York (188).
12. See, e.g., *Walla Walla Union*, June 14, 1899, p. 3; May 12, 1900, p. 4.
13. See, e.g., Lyman, W. 1918. *Lyman's History of Old Walla Walla County*. Chicago.
14. "The Late Honorable B. L. Sharpstein," *Up-To-The-Times Magazine* 1 (Nov. 1906), 361.
15. Beardsley, A. 1959. *The Bench & Bar of Washington: the First Fifty Years, 1849–1900*, MSS., Seattle. Walla Walla residents honored Frank Sharpstein's civic accomplishments by naming a school after him in 1898, now the oldest functioning school building in the state.
16. *Walla Walla Union*, Mar. 29, 1901, p. 3; Mar. 14, 1901, p. 3.
17. Ibid., Mar. 17, 1901, p. 3.
18. Ibid., Mar. 29, 1901, p. 3.
19. Ibid., May 5, 1901, p. 3.
20. *Columbia Chronicle*, May 4, 1901, p. 5. The *Chronicle* did not cite attendance figures. Copies of the *Walla Walla Statesman* and *Walla Walla Union* no longer exist for April or June 1901.
21. *Walla Walla Union*, May 23, 1901, p. 3.
22. Ibid., May 14,1901, p. 3. See also, May 7, 1901, p. 3.
23. Ibid., May 21,1901, p. 3.
24. Ibid., May 23, 1901, p. 3.
25. Ibid., May 24, 1901, p. 2.
26. Ibid., May 26, 1901, p. 4.
27. *Code of Washington, 1881*. Olympia (172, 227, 351).
28. *Remington & Ballinger's Annotated Codes and Statutes of Washington*, vol. 1, *Codes of Procedures*. Seattle, 1910 (710–711).
29. *Walla Walla Union*, May 28, 1901, p. 3.
30. Ibid., July 11, 1901, p. 3.
31. Ibid., July 11, 1901, p. 3.
32. "Ex parte Joseph Neet," in *Reports of Cases Determined in the Supreme Court of the State of Missouri*. Columbia, Mo., 1901 (157: 529, 536).

33. *Walla Walla Union*, July 12, 1901, p. 3.
34. Ibid., July 14, 1901, p. 5.
35. Ibid., July 16, 1901, p. 1.
36. Ibid., July 16, 1901, p. 3.
37. Ibid., July 16, 1901, p. 1.
38. See Gottschall 2009.
39. *Walla Walla Union*, July 17, 1901, p. 1.
40. Ibid., July 17, 1901, p. 1; July 19, 1901, p. 3; see also July 20, 1901, p. 3. Sharpstein appealed Casey's conviction to the state Supreme Court on *habeas corpus* grounds. The court upheld the conviction *In re Casey*, Mar. 11, 1902; see *The Pacific Reporter*, 68: 185–187.
41. *Walla Walla Union*, July 19, 1901, p. 3.
42. Ibid., July 26, 1901, p. 3; see also July 23, 1901, p. 3.
43. Ibid., July 26, 1901, p. 3.
44. Ibid., July 27, 1901, p. 3.
45. Ibid., July 30, 1901, p. 3; Aug. 7, 1901, p. 3.
46. Ibid., July 30, 1901, p. 4.
47. Ibid., July 28, 1901, p. 4.
48. Ibid., Aug. 1, 1901, p. 3. See State of Washington v. Dorsey Nichols, Walla Walla County Superior Court, filed July 31, 1901, Case no. 4165.
49. Ibid., Feb. 13, 1902, p. 3; Feb. 15, 1902, p. 5.
50. Ibid., Mar. 25, 1902, p. 5.
51. Ibid., Apr. 25, 1902, p. 5; June 5, 1902, p. 2.
52. Ibid., June 27, 1902, p. 3.
53. *Reports of Case Determined in the Supreme Court of the State of Washington*. Seattle, 1903 (28: 628–639). The Sharpshooters swept a doubleheader from a Spokane team and then defeated Colfax in a single game.
54. *Walla Walla Statesman*, June 18, 1902, p. 1.
55. Ibid., June 18, 1902, p. 6.
56. *Walla Walla Union*, June 21, 1902, p. 3.
57. Ibid., June 19, 1902, p. 1.
58. Ibid., June 6, 1899, p. 3; July 25, 1899, p. 4.
59. Ibid., July 1, 1902, p. 5; July 2, 1902, p. 5.
60. Ibid., July 8, 1902, p. 5.
61. Ibid., July 16, 1902, p. 8.
62. Ibid., July 8, 1902, p. 5; July 19, 1902, p. 5; July 20, 1902, p. 5.
63. *Walla Walla Statesman*, July 21, 1902, p. 6; July 25, 1902, p. 8.
64. *Walla Walla Union*, July 24, 1902, p. 8; July, 26, 1902, p. 5; July 27, 1902, p. 10.
65. Ibid., Sept. 5, 1902, p. 1.
66. "Sour on Base Ball," *The Sporting Life*, Sept. 27, 1902, p. 1.
67. *Walla Walla Union*, Sept. 10, 1902, p. 1.
68. Ibid., May 5, 1903, p. 1.
69. Chapter 249, Section 242, "Sabbath Breaking," *Session Laws of the State of Washington, 1909*. Olympia, 1909 (963–964).
70. Beardsley, A. 1959. *The Bench and Bar of Washington: The First Fifty Years, 1849–1900*. MLS thesis, University of Washington (54–55).

Frank Merriwell
A Hero for a Bygone Era

Rob Edelman

"There have been only three characters in history who ever could call their shots with uncanny exactitude, Superman, Frank Merriwell and Babe Ruth."
—Arthur Daley, *New York Times*, April 28, 1947

"Only one man could have done, if not exceeded, what Derek Jeter did on that glorious day he entered the 3,000-hit club, the only Yankee ever to join. His name is Frank Merriwell, and by now time has dimmed his memory for most everyone except young Americans, who have no memory of him at all. When Jeter hit his momentous home run, I announced he had just done a Frank Merriwell, and the young fellow standing next to me yelped: 'Who the devil is Frank Merriwell? I never heard of him. Who does he play for?'"
—Sid Dorfman, *The Star-Ledger*, July 13, 2011

A century prior to Jeter's heroics, no true-blue American of any age would have been unfamiliar with Frank Merriwell. Indeed, Merriwell's roots as an iconic character in mainstream literature predate his very existence. They may be traced to the mid–19th century, and the rising popularity of the dime novel: inexpensive, largely melodramatic adventure tales featuring the exploits of detectives, cowboys, explorers, and other action heroes. What then followed was the emergence of a dime novel sub-genre: stories tailored to young boys that spotlighted the derring-do of humble-but-valiant lads battling clearly defined villains. A number of these focused on baseball. Zane Grey, a ballplayer and wannabe big leaguer in his youth, penned *The Short-Stop* (1909), *The Young Pitcher* (1911), and *The Redheaded Outfield and Other Baseball Stories* (1920). With an assist from ghostwriter John Neville Wheeler, Christy Mathewson "authored" a quartet of cleverly titled "Matty Books": *Pitcher Pollock* (1914), *Catcher Craig* (1915), *First Base Faulkner* (1916), and *Second Base Sloan* (1917). Another Mathewson volume, *Won in the Ninth* (1910), was described in its advertising as a "live story with live characters written by the man who knows more than any other about the men who are playing the game to day." Prospective customers were encouraged to "buy it for your boy ... but read it yourself."

Writing as Hal Standish, Harvey King Shackleford authored stories featuring the ball-yard (as well as non-sports) triumphs of Fred Fearnot, first introduced in 1898 in

Rob Edelman is the author of *Great Baseball Films* and *Baseball on the Web*. His books include *Meet the Mertzes*, a double biography of *I Love Lucy*'s Vivian Vance and fabled baseball fan William Frawley, coauthored with Edelman's wife, Audrey Kupferberg. His byline has appeared in *Baseball and American Culture: Across the Diamond, Total Baseball, Baseball in the Classroom: Teaching America's National Pastime*, and dozens of other books. He has been a juror at the National Baseball Hall of Fame and Museum's annual film festival. He is a lecturer at the University at Albany, where he teaches courses in film history.

 DOI: 10.3172/BB.7.170

Frank Tousey's *Work and Win: An Interesting Weekly for Young America.* The series continued after Shackleford's death in 1906, with George W. Goode inheriting the ghostwriting. Typical baseball titles include *Fred Fearnot and His No-Hit Game; Or, Striking Out the Champions* (1906), in which "Standish" casually notes, "All the batsman could get off Fred's delivery was an easy pop fly"; *Fred Fearnot at Second Base; Or, Winning Out in the Ninth* (1907); *Fred Fearnot and The Scrappy Nine; Or, Having a Peck of Trouble* (1907); and *Fred Fearnot and the Rival Players; Or, Finishing a Baseball Feud* (1908). The 14-book "Baseball Joe" series, marketed between 1912 and 1928, centered on the derring-do of "Baseball Joe" Matson, first on his town team and then in prep school, at Yale University, in the minor and major leagues (with the Cardinals and Giants), in the World Series, and on a world tour. The "Baseball Joe" books were a product of the Stratemeyer Syndicate, a publishing factory founded by Edward Stratemeyer, which produced a wide range of children's fiction. The series' author, Lester Chadwick, was a pseudonym, so named in homage to Henry Chadwick, the early baseball pioneer. Some of the "Baseball Joe" tales reportedly were penned by Stratemeyer himself, while others were written by the prolific Howard R. Garis, best recalled as the author of the *Uncle Wiggily* books.

But then, neither "Baseball Joe" Matson nor any other fireballing hero was as celebrated as Frank Merriwell, he of Fardale Academy, Yale, and the world beyond. When discussing Merriwell, however, it is essential to note that last-second game-winning clouts were but one of his talents. You name the sport, and Merriwell could master it. But young Frank was more than just a schoolboy jock. Much more. He was as decent and moral as he was physically adept, a valiant soul and bastion of fair play who stood for right against might yet would forgive a remorseful foe. He was a savior of damsels in distress who said the right thing and did the right thing—always. Indeed, Frank Merriwell was a role model for the generation of American boys who were coming of age in the earliest years of the 20th century.

Gilbert Patten, father of Frank Merriwell and "idol of a thousand boys."

The actual number of Merriwell tales differs from account to account. According to J. Randolph Cox, author of *The Dime Novel Companion*, 777 Merriwell books appeared in print. On March 25, 1934, the *New York Times* reported that they numbered "nearly 300." Two months later to the day, the paper noted that "1,236 books" featured Merriwell, adding that "their total circulation to date is approximately 123,000,000." In 1964, *Times* book reviewer Peter Lyon observed that the stories "sold in the neighborhood of 500,000,000 copies." These numbers are at once staggering and confusing. But what is without debate is that Merriwell was the centerpiece of the most popular juvenile narratives in American publishing history. In 1927, James M. Cain, in a *Saturday Evening Post* profile of the architect of the Merriwell stories, wrote of the character: "He was the idol of thousands of boys who kept book on him as closely as thousands of other boys now keep book on Babe Ruth."

The author of record of the Frank Merriwell yarns is Burt L. Standish. But Standish is a pseudonym. The birth name of the creator of a majority of the stories is George William (Gilbert) Patten: a wordsmith who is one of the key contributors to the development of the juvenile-oriented dime novel. Patten penned many tales, occasionally under his own name but more often employing a range of pseudonyms from Herbert Bellwood and Stanton L. Burt to Barry Tallyho, Julian G. Wharton, and William West Wilder, also known as "Wyoming Will." (Across the decades, authors used pen names for various reasons, from preventing the overexposure of prolific writers — which certainly was the case with Patten — to distinguishing between an author's fiction and non-fiction work and his or her writings in different genres.)

Burt L. Standish was Patten's best-known pen name. Between April 18, 1896, and March 6, 1915, a period of 986 consecutive weeks, Merriwell stories appeared under the Standish byline in *Tip Top Weekly*, a Street & Smith magazine that was hyped on its front page as "an ideal publication for the American Youth." (On August 12, 1912, it was renamed *New Tip Top Weekly*.) At its height, the weekly's circulation was in the hundreds of thousands: a success that never could have happened without the creativity and input of Gilbert Patten.

Patten was born in Corinna, Maine, on October 25, 1866. In his youth he enjoyed playing baseball, as did countless other youngsters of the time. He attended Corinna Union Academy, where his grades were poor. (Unlike his most celebrated creation, he never attended college.) Despite this lack of interest in education, Patten, who by age 14 had grown into a gawky, 115-pound six-footer, developed a predilection for reading — and writing. At the tender age of 16, he began selling his stories. Two of his initial efforts, *A Bad Man* and *The Pride of Sandy Flat*, both western tales, earned him $6 from Erastus Flavel Beadle of Beadle & Adams, a dime novel publisher; Orville J. Victor, a Beadle & Adams editor, would prove an enthusiastic supporter. In 1886, the publisher paid Patten $50 for *The Diamond Sport; or, The Double Face of Bed Rock*, which ran in *Beadle's Half Dime Library*, and he became determined to establish himself as a wordsmith. Over the next decade-plus Patten did just that, primarily authoring westerns for Beadle & Adams. Starting in 1889, he created a series with a female hero — Violet Vane — also published in *Beadle's Half Dime Library*. He also worked on a newspaper, the *Pittsfield* (Maine) *Advertiser*, and in 1888 started his own paper, the *Corinna Owl*, which was bought up by the *Advertiser* a year later. In 1890–1891, he managed a semi-professional baseball nine in Camden, Maine, and in 1895 penned a play, *Men of Millions*, which coincidentally opened — and promptly bombed — in New Haven.

Patten admittedly remained disinterested in scholarship, and his first stories were grammatically imperfect. Alice Gardner, a schoolmate, critiqued and edited this early work. The two were wed in 1886 and produced a son, Harvan Barr Patten, but separated in 1898. Then in 1900, Patten married Mary Nunn, a union that lasted 16 years. Two years later, he wed Carol Kramer. This third marriage reportedly was a happy one.

Patten's career was thrust forward in 1895 when Ormond G. Smith, the "Smith" of the Street & Smith publishing company — his father, Francis Shubael Smith, founded the concern with Francis Scott Street — proposed that Patten pen a succession of tales spotlighting a daring student athlete. On December 16, Smith wrote Patten that the "essential idea of this series is to interest young readers in the career of a young man at a boarding school, preferably a military or a naval academy. The stories should [be] American and thoroughly up to date." Patten responded with a sample story, which he concocted in four days, and on January 3, 1896, Smith informed the writer by letter: "We have just finished reading your manuscript story 'Frank Merriwell; or, First Days at Fardale,' which you submitted.... We are entirely satisfied with this story, and satisfied that you can do the work we require." Smith added that Patten "selected a good name for the hero of the story. It is understood that this name is to be one of the firm copyrights and trade-marks, just as Nick Carter is. Hoping that everything will be satisfactory and that this will be the beginning of a long and favorable connection."

So it was Patten who added to the mix the Merriwell name and personality. As he explained, "I took the three qualities I most wanted him to embody — frank and merry in nature and well in body and mind — and made the name Frank Merriwell." He added that the "Burt L. Standish" pen name evolved from one of his favorite stories, Longfellow's *The Courtship of Miles Standish*. And of course, "Burt" was in no way connected to "Hal (*Fred Fearnot*) Standish."

Frank Merriwell; or, First Days at Fardale became the first Merriwell tale to see the printed page. Content-wise, it was a model for future Merriwell bravado. Here, young Frank arrives at Fardale, a military academy he hopes to enter, where he immediately meets and takes on a "haughty, over-dressed" bully by the name of Bart Hodge. Hodge tries to embarrass Merriwell, who at the outset is presented as a "born diplomat" and "modestly dressed" lad with a "frank, open and winning" face. But the cruelly sarcastic Hodge is unable to rattle his prey and, before the end of the story, he becomes Merriwell's steadfast admirer. Another character central to the Merriwell tales is introduced here: Inza Burrage, a "dark-haired, red-lipped, jolly girl." Upon first spying her, Merriwell is instantly smitten and, in story after story, she is the damsel in distress who is rescued by the daring Merriwell. In the first such occurrence, Inza trips while trying to elude a "mad dog." Merriwell "gently picks her up and moves her to the side as he prepares to battle an obviously hydrophobic canine with a jackknife [do not envision a dog with a jackknife — ed.]."

What follows is classic Frank Merriwell:

> "What are you going to do?" panted Inza. "You are not going to fight the dog?"
>
> "Yes!"
>
> "He will kill you!" she screamed. "Remember that one scratch from his teeth means sure death!"
>
> "I know that!"
>
> "Then run — run!"
>
> "And leave you and these girls to be bitten by that beast! Not much! Better that he should bite one than a dozen."
>
> As the dog pounces, Inza stops panting. "What a brave, noble fellow he is!" her white lips whispered. "How terrible that he should give his life for me! How grand!"

Young Frank is destined to survive this ordeal — and countless others across the years. Meanwhile, the character became astoundingly popular with its target readership.

Mere months after his debut, the *Tip Top Weekly* circulation topped 75,000 with each issue featuring a new 20,000-word story authored by Patten. Initially, he wrote them in longhand and then on a typewriter; eventually, he dictated them to a typist. "It was a terrific grind at first, but I later became used to it," he recalled. "As I came to know Frank better I grew fond of him and I confess that I followed his adventures almost as breathlessly as the army of boys who admired him." Still, Patten was frustrated by his weekly routine. "I had no time to devote to careful writing," he declared. "No time to spend in searching for the proper word to express my meaning." For this reason, he admitted that his writing often was "verbose and sloppy." But no matter, because his publisher was "not paying for style" but rather was "buying stories that young readers would enjoy and buy."

While penning the Merriwell yarns, Patten occasionally authored other works. For example, under his own byline, he concocted *The Rockspur Eleven*, a football story, the first half of which was published in the debut issue of Street & Smith's *Popular Magazine* in 1903. Less than a decade later, also as Gilbert Patten, he authored a series of tales, published by David McKay of Philadelphia, spotlighting the derring-do of Clif Stirling, a Merriwellian hero. An ad appeared in the December 3, 1911, *New York Times* hyping *Clif Stirling, Behind the Line* as a "tale of school life; of manliness and unmanliness; of success and failure." This football-oriented story was a follow-up to the initial Stirling entry, a baseball tale titled *Clif Stirling, Captain of the Nine*, which was plugged by Jack Coombs, the Philadelphia Athletics hurler. "Boys, it's great," Coombs (or more likely an ad copywriter) observed. "I enjoyed it immensely. Will help a boy to overcome obstacles encountered during his career as an athlete."

As for Merriwell, Patten had the character completing his time at Fardale and enrolling at Yale. On his first night in New Haven, he is challenged to a duel by Jack Diamond, a quarrelsome fellow freshman. While this particular battle is averted, the two eventually engage in a 13-page-long fistfight. As his story progresses from week to week, the plucky

"As the beast pounced, Inza's white lips whispered: 'How terrible that he should give his life for me! How grand!'" Oh, to be Frank Merriwell!

Merriwell faces off against Yale's wealthy snobs and similar characters from other Ivy League bastions. At one point, however, in a seeming lapse of judgment, he and some of his pals pilfer a turkey from a turkey farm. But it quickly is revealed that Merriwell had in fact paid for the bird, leaving a $5 bill for the farmer.

Arguably his greatest accomplishment at Yale was his proficiency in any and all athletic activity — and in particular, in his work on the pitching rubber. Merriwell was famed for the "double-shoot," a trick pitch which curved twice between the time it left his pitching hand and crossed home plate. Patten concocted the "double-shoot" while on a trip to Boston, during which he was flustered by his inability to "conceive something new for Frank to do." He continued:

> Completely at a loss, I dropped my work one day and went to a baseball game, where I got a seat behind the catcher. A tall, lean, long-armed pitcher was on the mound, and he had a queer cross-fire delivery that bothered the batters. Shortly after I sat down he threw a fast high ball that curved sharply inward and caromed off the end of the bat, which the hitter had not removed from his shoulder. Down in one of the front rows, a farmerish looking man jumped to his feet. "I been watching baseball for twenty years," he cried, "and that's the first time I ever see a curve two ways on one pitch." Well, that was it! He had given me the idea for Frank Merriwell's "double-shoot" ... In future stories, Frank used that amazing and impossible double curve on dangerous batters in pinches, and over the country boys almost ruined their arms trying to throw it.

In a change of pace, Patten also had Merriwell briefly leaving school to toil on a railroad, deal with disgruntled workers, author a successful play, and trek to the British Isles. (At one point, one of his fellow Yalies rhetorically asks: "Is there anything that Merriwell can't do?") He eventually returns to school to complete his studies; after all, a young man of such all-around brilliance could not forever remain a college undergraduate. As Frank finished his senior year Patten added to the series a new schoolboy character, one fashioned to appeal to the younger brothers of *Tip Top Weekly* readers: Dick Merriwell, Frank's half-brother. Dick debuted in *Frank Merriwell's Surprise; or, The Contents of the Oil Skin Envelope*, published on July 13, 1905. Here, it is revealed that Charles Merriwell, Frank's widower father, had remarried and sired a son. Young Dick, a strong-willed chap, is mentored by Frank. They play baseball together, with Dick becoming as adept at pitching as his sibling. While Dick is immersed in his studies, Frank plays semi-pro ball and battles shady villains upon investing in a mining enterprise. When Dick is off from school — he attends and graduates from both Fardale and Yale — he and Frank play on teams that beat the Boston Red Sox and New York Highlanders. (In a letter published in *Tip Top Weekly* on January 5, 1907, loyal reader Barclay Turner noted: "Frank's game with the Highlanders was great. I wish Jack Chesbro or Al Orth, the curveless wonder, had pitched.") Other plotlines have Frank opening the Bloomfield Home for Wayward Boys in Upstate New York and purchasing a Wyoming ranch where he brings his charges during summer breaks. This scenery change allowed for the creation of western-oriented plotlines. Future stories also had Frank and (occasionally) Dick battling con men, bandits, rustlers, and other nefarious characters.

Ever-so-predictably, Frank marries Inza. (Elsie Bellwood, a second love interest, eventually weds Bart Hodge.) This led to the creation of a third gallant Merriwell: Frank Merriwell Jr., whose birth is cited in *Frank Merriwell's Son; or, The Mark of the Star* (published in *Tip Top Weekly* on June 9, 1906). Junior's childhood is recounted in *Frank*

Merriwell's Boy (October 7, 1911). In *Frank Merriwell, Jr.; or, The Camp on Wind River* (August 3, 1912), Junior first becomes a full-fledged heroic character.

Patten remained with the series until 1912; his final effort, published on September 7, 1912, is *Frank Merriwell, Jr.'s Close Shave; or, The Plot That Failed.* Other writers took over for the remainder of the run, including William Wallace Cook, Frederick Van Rensselaer Dey, Frederick R. Burton, John H. Whitson, and William Almon Wolff. By 1915, the popularity of the series was waning and its appearance in *New Tip Top Weekly* fizzled out; the final weekly story was *Frank Merriwell, Jr.'s Detective Work; or, In Peril of His Life.* By this time, Patten was pursuing other professional interests. Between March 10, 1915, and June 10, 1916, he assumed the *New Tip Top Weekly* editorial duties. He also edited and wrote for *Top-Notch Magazine,* another Street & Smith publication.

Immediately after their *Tip Top Weekly* appearances, many of the Merriwell tales were reprinted, adding further coin to the Street & Smith coffers. For example, between 1896 and 1901, Merriwell stories were grouped together and reissued in *Tip Top Quarterly.* Between 1902 and 1915, they were published in the *Medal Library* and *New Medal Library* anthologies. Some came out in hardcover dime novel form. After the final *New Tip Top* installment, various Merriwell sagas were seen in pulp magazines. In 1917, two compilations appeared: *Merriwell Baseball Stories* and *Merriwell Football Stories.* Further reprints came during the 1920s in what was known as the *Merriwell Series,* which later were reissued as the *Burt L. Standish Library* and the *Merriwell Library.*

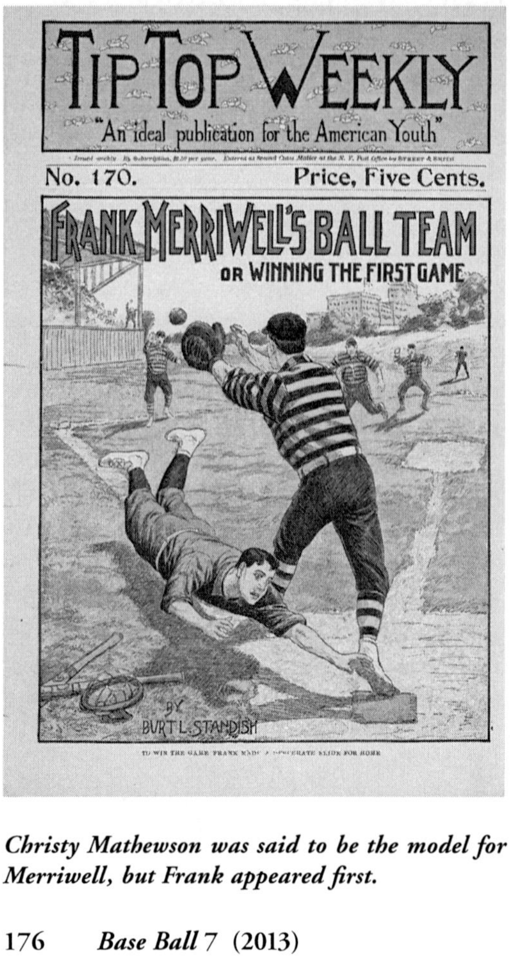

Christy Mathewson was said to be the model for Merriwell, but Frank appeared first.

In their day, Merriwell and his derring-do were a positive influence on countless illustrious Americans-to-be. One was Eddie Eagan, a national amateur heavyweight boxing champ, Olympic gold medalist, and chairman of the New York State Athletic Commission. Upon his death in 1967, the *New York Times* noted that Eagan "thrilled as a youngster to the dime-novel adventures of Frank Merriwell at Yale. He made up his mind that he would go there." And so he did, graduating in 1921.

In 1981, upon his election to the U.S. Presidency, Ronald Reagan listed *Frank Merriwell at Yale* as one of the five most influential books of his youth. The culture critic George Jean Nathan once observed, "For one who read Mark Twain's *Huckleberry Finn* or *Tom Sawyer,* there were ten thousand who read Standish's *Frank Merriwell's Dilemma; or Frank Merriwell at Yale.*" Other Merriwell admirers included actors (Fredric March); politicians (Woodrow Wilson,

Al Smith, Wendell Willkie, John W. McCormack); newspaper columnists (Franklin P. Adams); war correspondents (Floyd Gibbons); criminal lawyers (Jerry Giesler); sports editors (Dan Parker); boxers (Jess Willard, Jack Dempsey, Stanley Ketchel); and the likes of Christy Mathewson and Babe Ruth.

In the early 1960s, Edwin Foster Blair, a tackle on the undefeated 1923 Yale football team, recalled that a teammate who performed an extra-special gridiron feat would be met with a query: "Who do you think you are, Frank Merriwell?" The character even was admired by females. In 1951, Louella Parsons wrote in her syndicated newspaper column: "Shades of my girlhood! Frank Merriwell, whose adventures were read by every boy in America, were also read by this writer. I must say my mother never approved and I used to sneak the books from my brother, but what adventures Frank had!"

Still, by the 1920s, a hero such as Frank Merriwell was considered passé. His gallantry was decidedly old-school. A stereotypical college man no longer embraced 19th century morality, but instead was a Jazz Age creature who danced the Charleston and carried around a flask of gin. The popularity of the dime novel had been eclipsed by a relatively new and quickly evolving form of entertainment: the motion picture. In the movies, the emphasis on the Frank Merriwell–style American values that prevailed onscreen through the teen years was replaced by a worldly Big City sophistication. For after all, "How Ya Gonna Keep 'Em Down on the Farm (After They've Seen Paree)?" was more than just a hit song of 1919. It was a reflection of a changing era. And while the character of Frank Merriwell did not disappear into obscurity — far from it — he no longer was in vogue.

As the years passed, Patten kept up his writing career. Between 1914 and 1928, Barse & Hopkins published 16 Standish-authored books in what was known as its "Big League" baseball series. Four of the first five centered on one of his better-known creations: Lefty Locke, the central character in *Lefty O' the Bush*, *Lefty O' the Training Camp*, *Lefty O' the Big League*, and *Lefty O' the Blue Stockings*; the final title, *Brick King, Backstop*, featured a character from the *Lefty* stories. All were hyped in an advertisement in *The Publishers' Weekly*, which included a celebrity endorsement from Christy Mathewson. "I have read the books," reported Big Six, "and find them very enjoyable. Every 'fan' will enjoy the plots, as well as the clever base ball strategies." Follow-ups included *Lefty Locke, Owner*; *Lefty Locke Pitcher-Manager*; *Lefty Locke Wins Out*; *The Man on First*; and *The Grip of the Game*.

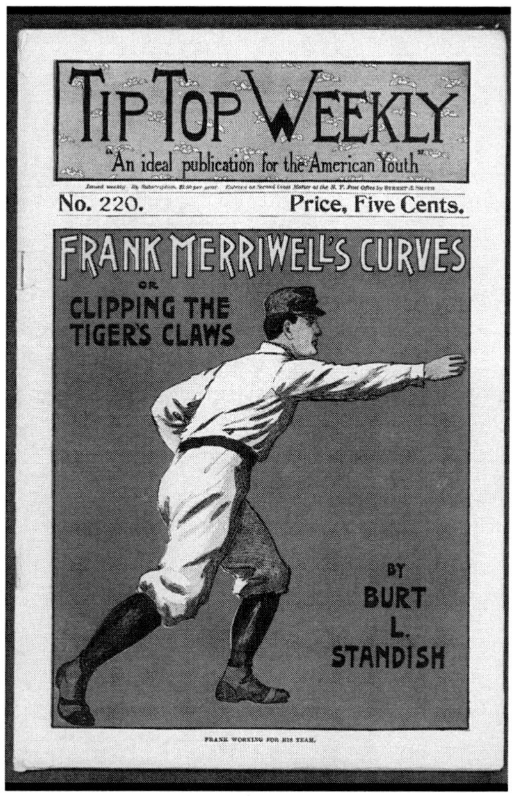

Merriwell stood for truth, faith, justice, friendship, duty, sacrifice, and strength ... and modesty.

"I think I was the first writer to make baseball more than incidental in his stories," Patten once observed. "At any rate, there was quite a while when I had the field almost exclusively to myself." But he never again earned the acclaim he enjoyed from the Merriwell series — and his long-fostering dream of penning the Great American Novel was never to be realized. Certainly, Patten was mindful of the impact of Merriwell. In 1932, in a survey of over 7,000 boys conducted by the Children's Aid Society, it was determined that Merriwell had endured as the most popular fictional hero of an earlier generation. And the character remained a viable commercial property — but only to a certain degree. In 1932, Patten reported that he was "modernizing" his Merriwell stories, which he hoped to republish. His goal was to "make the boys talk as boys do now" and add "some radios and airplanes for background." In an effort to hype the project, he observed that the original stories "were not well written. They were stilted, the boys never said 'won't' or 'don't,' always 'will not' or 'do not.' But they did have action, characterization and atmosphere.... Boys like good characterization just as much as they like action — perhaps even more." In 1933, John Levi Cutler, a University of Maine student, wrote his thesis on Patten. It was titled "The Dean of Dime Novelists and the Merriwell Saga; or, the Life and Career of William Gilbert Patten." Needless to say, however, there was no major Frank Merriwell resurgence in print — despite the fact that the Merriwell name was being farmed out to filmmakers, stage and radio producers, and comic book and comic strip authors. Briefly in 1928, a Patten-written strip, titled *Young Frank Merriwell*, was drawn by John Hix and marketed by the McClure Newspaper Syndicate. A second strip, *Frank Merriwell's Schooldays*, written by Jack Kofoed, drawn by Jack Wilhelm, and syndicated by the Central Press Association, appeared between 1931 and 1934. In 1940 the character appeared in four issues of Shadow Comics, published by Street & Smith, and years later Charlton Comics released four issues of *Frank Merriwell at Yale*.

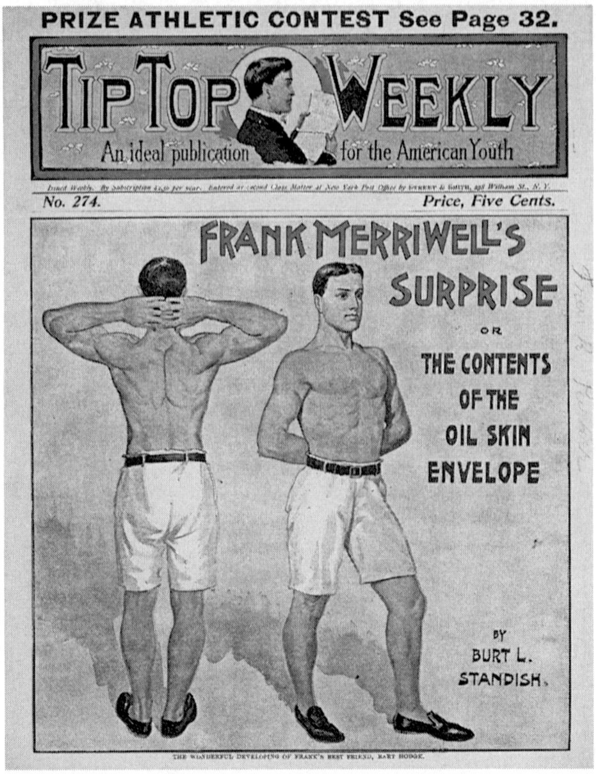

Patten's first story appeared on April 18, 1896. It was called "Frank Merriwell; or, First Days at Fardale" (dime-novel titles were always two-parters).

During the first week of April 1934, a host of performers and programs from the famous to the forgotten were scheduled for broadcast on the various New York–area radio stations. The more celebrated included Metropolitan Opera performers Lily Pons, Ezio Pinza, Rosa Ponselle, and Gladys Swarthout, as well as

"George Gershwin, Piano," "Bing Crosby, Songs," "Carole Lombard, Actress," "Ed Wynn, Comedian," "Fats Waller, Songs," "George M. Cohan, Songs," and "Harriet Hilliard, Songs," accompanied by the (Ozzie) Nelson Orchestra. The programs included *Amos 'n' Andy, Little Orphan Annie, Myrt and Marge*—and a 15-minute-long "sketch," titled *Frank Merriwell's Adventures*, to which Patten offered creative input.

This program featured Donald Briggs as Merriwell and began airing three times a week on NBC radio on March 26; its final broadcast came on June 22. Then on October 5, 1946, NBC-radio presented *The Adventures of Frank Merriwell* as a 30-minute-long Saturday morning kiddie show. Lawson Zerbe played Frank, while Jean Gillespie and Elaine Rostas were cast as Inza. By this time, even though the show offered listeners "a brand new series of stories," Merriwell was being marketed strictly as nostalgia. Each show opened with a description of the character as "an echo of the past, an exciting past, a romantic past: the eve of the horse-and-carriage, gas-lit streets ... the era of one of the most beloved figures in American fiction—Frank Merriwell...." These *Adventures* ran until June 4, 1949.

The character occasionally appeared on-screen. In 1910, Tip Top Films released *Frank Merriwell in Arizona; or, The Mystery Mine*, a two-reeler. (Patten himself was involved in the creation of two non-Merriwell films: 1915's *The Crown Prince's Double*, featuring Maurice Costello and Norma Talmadge; and 1923's *Temporary Marriage*, with Kenneth Harlan, Mildred Davis, Myrtle Stedman, and Tully Marshall.) In 1934, Patten initiated a court case against Superior Talking Pictures, a distributor of low-budget Westerns, which was planning to use the name "Frank Merriwell" in a series of short films. No such titles ever were completed. However, given his penchant for last-second bravado, Patten's creation was a natural as a movie serial hero—and so *The Adventures of Frank Merriwell* was the title of a 12-episode Universal series that played in movie houses in 1936. In its theatrical trailer, Merriwell is described as the "idol of a hundred million adventure lovers who have thrilled to his exploits and admired his *fine sportsmanship ... athletic prowess ... indomitable courage!*" Here, "Merry" (played again by Briggs) attends Fardale College (rather than Yale). At the outset, he belts a grand slam homer to lead his school to a come-from-behind 4–3 victory and then becomes involved with a "mysterious old ring that carries the secret of buried Spanish gold." In Saturday morning serial fashion, he is hurled through raging rapids; battles a wildcat, a circus lion, and an octopus; and faces other perils while demonstrating his athletic skills. The first and last episodes are, respectively, "College Hero" and "The Winning Play." Those in between include "Death at the Crossroads," "Descending Doom," "Monster of the Deep," "Between Savage Foes," "Imprisoned in a Dungeon," and "The Crash in the Chasm."

Then in the 1950s, scuttlebutt had it that a musical, to be titled *The Life and Times of Frank Merriwell*, was in the works. Henry Garson was penning the script, while Walter Schumann and Johnny Mercer were writing the music and lyrics. The word was that Phil Silvers would star (but presumably not as Merriwell), and the show was to be produced either on the stage or as an NBC-TV "spectacular." Nothing came of it. In 1966, the Theatre Company of Boston briefly mounted *Frank Merriwell's Last Race*, a play by Geoffrey Bush. In 1971, Frank and company sang and danced their way to Broadway—but not for long. *Frank Merriwell*, featuring music and lyrics by Skip Redwine and Larry Frank, opened—and closed—at the Longacre Theater on April 24. Monty Arnold, a longtime New York theatergoer who then worked in the Lincoln Center branch of the

New York Public Library, saw one of the show's seven preview performances. "It was awful," Arnold recalled over four decades later. "It was under-rehearsed. The highlight was when the bustle fell off the leading lady during the performance. Basically, we (in the audience) were laughing *at* the show."

By this time, the name of Frank Merriwell had long entered the lexicon of American popular culture, becoming a byword for sports stars who performed last-second heroics. Across the decades, Merriwell was endlessly referenced in headlines and cited by sports reporters and columnists. A perusal of articles published in the *New York Times* alone bears this out:

- "Frank Merriwell, alias Earl[e] Combs, jumped out of the story books yesterday and saved a ball game for the Yankees" (written by James R. Patterson; published on July 26, 1926).
- "Over in Flatbush ... the fans now refer to their favorite outfielder as Frank Merriwell O'Doul." The reason: "Happy-go-lucky Lefty ... has made more timely hits and great catches in the past two weeks than Frank Merriwell made in four dime novels" (John Kieran; August 12, 1932).
- "In a Frank Merriwell finish, Columbia scored four runs in the ninth to tie the game and then, behind by 9–7, sent three more across the plate in the twelfth to defeat Holy Cross, 10–9, for the first time since 1930 at Baker Field" (Allison Danzig; May 18, 1950).

Diamond heroes were not the lone athletes who were compared to Merriwell:

- "A Frank Merriwell finish in which Vannie Albanese, Syracuse fullback, scored a touchdown with a minute to play brought Syracuse a 7-to-3 victory today over Penn State before 12,000 fans" (unbylined piece; November 3, 1935).
- Footballer–war hero Tom Harmon is dubbed "a twentieth-century Frank Merriwell" (Thomas Haynes; November 19, 1944).
- On November 11, 1962, the paper ran the following headline: "Archie Roberts: Columbia's Answer to Frank Merriwell: Ace Sophomore Back Amazes Everyone by His Qualities."
- Boston College quarterback Doug Flutie is described as a "pleasant-faced, poised kid" who is "the second coming of Frank Merriwell" (Irvin Faust; December 2, 1984).

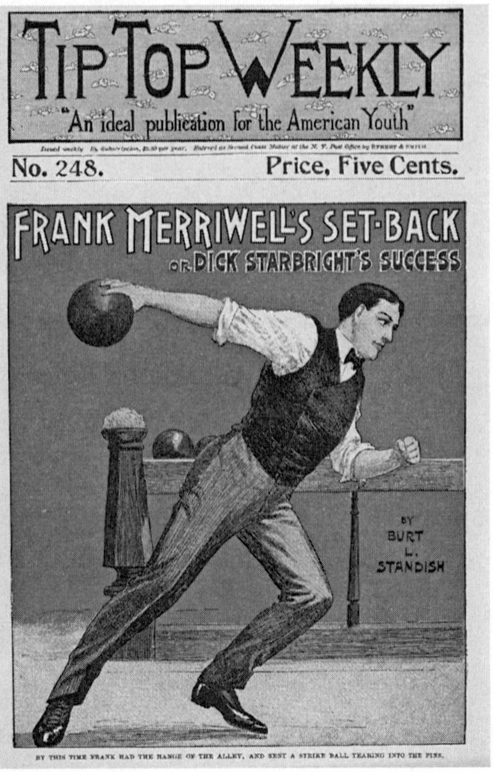

At first Patten was paid $50 for a 20,000-word story. At 5,000 per day, he figured, he could still do other work.

On occasion, Merriwell made his way into movie reviews. In his May 17, 1950, *New York Times* critique of *The Jackie Robinson Story*, Bosley Crowther observed that the "true-life story of Jackie Robinson ... is one which might have been written by the creator of Frank Merriwell, assuming that author had been conscious of the foul play of race prejudice." The character occasionally transcended sports-related reports. On December 16, 1938, the paper reported: "Santa's pack may be heavier this year, up-State business men agree today, but it will take a Frank Merriwell finish to bring the dollar volume up to par." Then on August 27, 1974, Alden Whitman described Charles Lindbergh, the celebrated flyer, as "the flawless El Cid, the gleaming Galahad, Frank Merriwell in the flesh."

Despite such references, the character remained a symbol of a prior age: a hero who was strictly of his time. By the late 1960s, life on college campuses was radically different from what it had been a decade earlier, let alone in the heyday of Frank Merriwell. In a February 28, 1967, *Times* article discussing the proliferation of pot-smoking at Yale, John Kifner began by asking: "Has Frank Merriwell been turned on?" Then in a piece, published on April 27, 1969, in which he explored the then-current state of campus turmoil, columnist Tom Wicker opened with a query: "Whatever happened to Frank Merriwell and Joe College?"

By then, the character's renown had long transcended that of his creator. In his later years, despite all his efforts, Patten was unable to generate a major Merriwell resurgence. He may have been considered a senior authority on the popular culture of the earlier generation. In fact, in 1931, he authored "Dime Novel Days," a well regarded two-part recollection published in the *Saturday Evening Post.* But more telling was his creation a year earlier of a new publication, *The Dime Novel*, which he hoped would spark a Merriwell revival. *The Dime Novel* had a one-issue run.

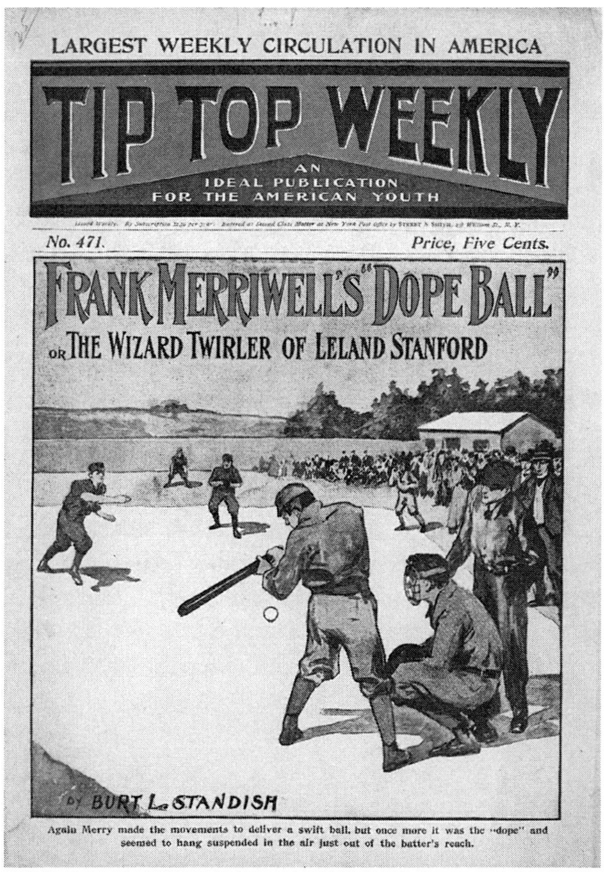

No, our boy Merry was not fooling around with Performance Enhancing Drugs.

Patten's third wife, the former Carol Kramer, passed away on August 21, 1939. According to the Associated Press, Mrs. Patten, 60, died at Overocks, the family estate in Camden, Maine, where "Mr. Patten often spent the Summer months when away from his literary activities

Formulaic stories, crude covers, implausible outcomes — we once dreamed of being strong and noble.

in New York." By all accounts, Patten never got over her demise.

At this juncture, the story of Gilbert Patten becomes the age-old tale of a writer who is not properly compensated for his work. Patten never shared in the profits that his stories reaped for Street & Smith. He was paid a straight salary for authoring them, earning no royalties on their sales or reprints. Initially, he received $50 per story; his highest Street & Smith payment was $150 per week, a healthy sum for its time but one that in no way reflected the profits earned by the publishing house.

This financial arrangement left him a man of modest means. In 1940, at the age of 73, he faced eviction from Manhattan's Hudson View Gardens, the four-room cooperative apartment he had owned for 14 years, for nonpayment of upkeep expenses. Patten was $400-plus in arrears, and requested a stay in the proceedings. "All I want is a moratorium until I can get the money together," he declared. Municipal Court Justice George L. Genung granted the delay. Patten's plight was highly publicized; several individuals who were strangers to the writer volunteered to stake him to the requisite funds. In the end, he sold the apartment for $3,000 and eventually moved into the home of his son and daughter-in-law in Vista, California, a San Diego suburb.

Patten still clung to the notion of reviving his most celebrated creation. In 1941, he penned one final Merriwell novel, titled *Mr. Frank Merriwell* and published by the Alliance Book Corporation. Here, the "modernizing" of the character involved his depiction as a middle-aged anti-fascist and anti-communist who fights for the underdog while retaining the high moral fiber of his youth. Murder, lynching, kidnapping, and a factory fire come into play in the story, and at one point Frank flogs a quartet of hooligans with a cane. "Are there enough middle-aged men, who cherish nostalgic affection for Frank Merriwell to provide a market for this saga of Frank Merriwell Grown Up?" asked the *Kirkus Reviews* critic. "Somehow, I can't see the creation of a 1941 equivalent of that market." The reviewer added that the book was "written in all seriousness, but [is] sure to be read, for the most part, with a blend of nostalgia and tongue in cheek." Needless to say, *Mr. Frank Merriwell* was no best-seller. Its sales reportedly were a mere 4,000.

Patten, 78, died in his sleep on January 16, 1945. In his *New York Times* obituary, it was noted that he "was for twenty years one of the most popular authors in the world. He also was one of the most prolific writers, turning out in his lifetime an estimated

40,000,000 words." Seven years after Patten's death, a group of Merriwell enthusiasts formed "Friends of Frank Merriwell," an organization dedicated to the perpetuation of the character's memory. The "Friends," whose minions reportedly ranged from a core group of between 20 and 50 to several hundred, were described in the media as "informal and loosely organized," with "its only headquarters [being] a corner table in the [Press Box] restaurant at 139 East Forty-Fifth Street [in Manhattan], where periodic meetings are held, and which also serves as a mailing address." In 1956, Joseph M. Graham, publicist for a New York–based insurance company and the organization's president, observed: "We compare what we used to read with what kids read today and we think we're the richer."

Then in 1964, Patten's heretofore unpublished autobiography appeared in print. Titled *Frank Merriwell's "Father": An Autobiography by Gilbert Patten ("Burt L. Standish")*, the 331-page chronicle was edited by Harriet Hinsdale with the assistance of Tony London and published by the University of Oklahoma Press. Its manuscript, which covers Patten's life through 1918, had been sitting in a crate in his son's house; his last years were recreated by its editors from his papers and via interviews with his contemporaries. In the book, Patten presents himself as a humble, friendly fellow and self-schooled writer who fully understood that he was no Mark Twain, Herman Melville, or Henry James.

Tellingly, according to Peter Lyon, who reviewed the book in the *New York Times*, it had for years "been impossible to find a Frank Merriwell story, unless perhaps in the Rare Book Room of a well-equipped library." So the question becomes: How well is he remembered *today*, almost a half-century after the autobiography's publication?

Indeed, what has come to be known as a "walk-off homer" might be described as a Merriwellian feat. But would such a reference be understood by 21st century sports fans?

Abstract

Frank Merriwell, the central character in a series of magazine stories penned between 1898 and 1915, was more than just a ballyard star who was famed for his last-second heroics. He was an icon and champion for American youth: an honest, fair-minded soul who battled snobbery and villainy — and also was the fantasy-world son that every loving parent wished they had. Merriwell was the creation of George William (Gilbert) Patten, writing under the pen name "Burt L. Standish." Decades after Patten penned the last of his Merriwell tales, the character remained a symbol of an earlier, more innocent age. However, while Merriwell's fame long outlasted that of his creator, he has in recent times lost most (if not all) of his instant name recognition.

Works Cited

Books

Cox, J. 2000. *Dime Novel Companion: A Source Book.* Westport, Conn.

Edelman, R. 1994. *Great Baseball Films.* New York.

Nolan, M. 2010. *Ball Tales: A Study of Baseball, Basketball and Football Fiction of the 1930s through 1960s.* Jefferson, N.C.

Patten, G. 1964. *Frank Merriwell's "Father": An Autobiography by Gilbert Patten ("Burt L. Standish")*, eds. H. Hinsdale and T. London. Norman, Okla.

Newspaper-Magazine Articles/Stories/Advertising

Boyle, R. "Frank Merriwell's Triumph: How Yale's Great Athlete Captured America's Fancy, or, Purified the Penny Dreadfuls and Became Immortal." *Sports Illustrated.* December 24, 1962.
Dorfman, S. "Derek Jeter pulled a Frank Merriwell with hit No. 3,000." *The Star-Ledger,* July 13, 2011.
Cain, J. "The Man Merriwell." *Saturday Evening Post,* June 11, 1927.
Godbout, O. "TV Show Planned About Merriwell." *New York Times,* May 9, 1956.
Griswold, J. "Young Reagan's Reading: 'I'm a sucker for hero worship." *New York Times,* August 30, 1981.
Holbrook, S. "Frank Merriwell At Yale Again And Again And Again." *American Heritage,* June 1961.
Kahn, E.J. "The Talk of the Town: No Bullies Or Toadies." *The New Yorker,* March 21, 1953.
Lefferts, B. "The Return of Frank Merriwell." *New York Times,* August 19, 1956.
Lyon, P. "Famous for His Finish." *New York Times,* August 2, 1964.
Standish, B. "Frank Merriwell; or, First Days at Fardale." *Tip Top Weekly,* April 18, 1896.
"(A letter from Kentucky.)" *Tip Top Weekly,* January 5, 1907.
"BARSE & HOPKINS FALL ANNOUNCEMENT FOR BOYS." *The Publishers' Weekly,* September 26, 1914
"Boys Today Doubt Alger Success Code." *New York Times,* February 3, 1932.
"Creator of Merriwell Is Fighting Eviction." *New York Times,* February 22, 1940.
"Delays Author's Eviction." *New York Times,* February 24, 1940.
"Frank Merriwell Hero In Court Case." *New York Times,* May 25, 1934.
"Frank Merriwell Rises From Ashes." *New York Times,* February 1, 1953.
"G. Patten, Created Frank Merriwell." *New York Times.* January 17, 1945.
"Merriwell Author Sells His Apartment." *New York Times,* March 9, 1940.
"Merriwell Stories Brought Up Top Date." *New York Times,* December 7, 1932.
"Mr. Frank Merriwell." *Kirkus Reviews,* March 3, 1941.
"Relaxation For An Author." *New York Times,* March 25, 1934.

Web

http://catalog.loc.gov/
http://freepages.genealogy.rootsweb.ancestry.com
http://john-adcock.blogspot.com/2011/10/frank-merriwell.html
http://www.booksonbaseball.com
*http://*www.comicvine.com
http://www.library.umaine.edu
http://www.thisoldradioshow.com
http://www.webstore.com/

Baseball Goes East
The 1876 San Francisco Centennials' Magical Mystery Tour

Angus Macfarlane

Baseball in San Francisco can be traced as far back as 1851, but as a meaningful, sustained, organized sport, it really began in 1866. Between 1866 and 1875 the San Francisco game experienced extreme ups and downs, finally bottoming out in 1872 as escalating interclub rivalries, win-at-all-costs mentalities, and on-field as well as off-field battles killed the game.

Following a year without baseball, it tentatively reemerged in 1874 with new players, new clubs, and, with the old troublemakers gone, an improved attitude. For the first time in a decade the game was free of conflict and controversy. Fourteen nines played 34 games in 1874. Although attrition reduced the number of clubs to 11 in 1875, there were 39 matches and prospects for an expanded season in 1876 seemed auspicious.[1]

The baseball news cycle typically began with a mention that the Pacific Baseball Convention was tending to administrative affairs at a January or February meeting, followed by reports of clubs electing officers and naming their starting nines for the new campaign. The preseason would begin in March, and by April or May each weekend would have a championship game. The season traditionally concluded at the end of November.

However, a researcher examining San Francisco's newspapers for reports of baseball activity in 1876 would find none of this and would be justified to conclude that the game had once again vanished from the scene.[2] Through July a mere four box scores — the year's total — appeared in the papers, three of them involving a new club called the Centennials. A fine-tooth combing of the papers would uncover a few tiny nuggets of baseball news that raised more questions than they answered.

What Happened in 1876?

The answer to this mystery is to be found in an article titled *The Centennials of Frisco* in the December 30, 1876 issue of the New York *Clipper*. It was a list of 44 games

---

After batting leadoff in the inaugural issue of this journal, **Angus Macfarlane** contributed a chapter on the early years of San Francisco baseball to *Base Ball Pioneers, 1850–1870* (2012). He continues to try to fill the chasm that is San Francisco's baseball history of the 19th Century while continuing to dabble in general San Francisco history. In addition, he is revisiting the career of Gavvy Cravath, hoping to do a book on the deadball era slugger.

DOI: 10.3172/BB.7.185

played by a club called the Centennials between April 20 and August 16, 1876. The first 12 were played in San Francisco and the next 32 ranged from Sacramento to Philadelphia. The accompanying text reads "The Centennials played in all forty-five (sic) games during the season of '76, winning 31."

The chronology of games, as noted above, lists 44 games: 29 victories and 15 defeats. Misprint or mystery? But, more importantly, *who were the Centennials*?

The first San Francisco baseball news since mid–November 1875 was this brief item in the *Daily Alta California* (hereafter *Alta*) of March 9, 1876.

> **The Centennial Base Ball Club**—The Centennial B.B. Club of this city has organized, composed of the strongest players in the State. They elected the following officers: T. Agnau, President; T. Brown, Vice-President; T. H. Gill, Recording Secretary; D. Ashley, Corresponding Secretary; R. T. Walker, Treasurer. The nine consists of the following gentlemen: Cullen, c.; Ashley, p.; Walker, 1 b.; Gill, 2 b.; Piercy, 3 b.; Curren, s.s.; Taylor, l.f.; Magenta, c.f.; Perrin, r.f.

The next day's *Chronicle* echoed the news, but neither report explained why the strongest players in the State had to be organized.

For whatever purpose they were formed, the designated Centennials were taken from two San Francisco clubs. The 1875 champion San Franciscos provided Walker at first base, Gill at second base, Piercy at third base, Curran (not *Curren*) at shortstop, and Taylor in left field. The 1875 cellar-dwelling Occidentals surrendered their battery of Ashley in the box, and Cullen behind the bat, along with center fielder Magendie (not *Magenta*) and right fielder Parent (not *Perrin*).

Also associated with the club (it was later learned) were Louis N. David, an antiquarian book dealer who was identified as "manager." and Clarence F. Townsend, an attorney, whose role and responsibilities were never specified. Centennial President T. Agnau was never referred to again.

Four of the chosen ones could be considered veteran ball players in that they were active before the cancellation of the 1873 season, while the other five were newcomers who began their careers after the baseball hiatus of 1873.

Foremost among the veterans was Andy Piercy. Though still a teen-ager (he would turn 20 in August) he could be considered one of the grand old men of San Francisco baseball.[3] His career stretched back to 1870 when he was a 14-year-old playing against men twice his age. He began with the Wide Awakes, who won the Pacific Base Ball Convention championship in 1871 by defeating the perennial champion Eagles in some of the hardest played contests ever fought between two mutually loathing rivals. Every year that there was baseball to be played, Piercy was holding down the hot corner for various clubs. In 1875 he was the third baseman for the San Franciscos.

The name John Curran first appeared in 1870 when he began to make a name for himself behind the plate, although he was chosen to be the Centennial shortstop. At 24 years old he was one of the older Centennials. He played for the Eagles and against Andy Piercy in some of the most intensely contested matches in early San Francisco baseball, but by 1872 he was Piercy's Wide Awake teammate. In 1875 he was the San Franciscos' catcher.

John Cullen, 24 years old, was the catcher for the St. Mary's College nine in the late 1860s and early 1870s. His first big-time mention was in September 1871 as catcher for the Libertys. He also caught for the Athletics in 1874 and 1875 before switching to the Occidentals.

Ed "Live Oak" (Live) Taylor was San Francisco's most beloved player of the early years. Born in either 1849, 1850, 1851 or 1855,[4] he first appeared with the Eagles in 1870 as an infielder, but he developed a reputation as an exceptional flycatcher during his seasons with the Eagles and Libertys. He played left field for the San Franciscos in 1875.

The newcomers included Delos Ashley, pitcher for the Occidentals in 1875 and John Cullen's battery mate at St. Mary's College. Unlike Cullen, Ashley did not immediately switch to big time baseball after graduating. Instead, he studied law in hopes of following in his father's footsteps. Ashley's ball-tossing career resumed in June 1874 with the Athletics. In June 1875 he switched to pitching for the Occidentals.

Another St. Mary's alum was Hypolite Magendie, who graduated in 1875. Still a couple of months shy of turning 20 when he was named a Centennial, his documented career is very brief; he was first mentioned in August 1875 playing second base for the Occidentals.

Twenty-two year-old Thomas Gill was a newcomer in more ways than one. Originally from Brooklyn, he arrived in San Francisco in time to play infield for the 1875 San Franciscos. Who he played for back east is another Centennial mystery. The *New York Clipper* box scores note that during 1873 and 1874 a *Gill* played for the Nassaus of Brooklyn at the same time a *Gill* played for the Arlingtons of New York. Whether there was one Gill playing for two clubs or an abundance of Gills can't be categorically determined, but in a May 13, 1876, item, the *Clipper* referred to "Mr. Thos. Gill, the old shortstop of the Brooklyn Nassaus."

Richard Walker and William Parent are complete unknowns. The first reference to Walker was in June 1875 playing right field for the San Franciscos. Parent's first mention was a week earlier when he appeared in left field for the Occidentals.

Undoubtedly news and information in 1876 was transmitted by means other than just newspapers. The purpose behind the formation of an elite nine was probably common knowledge in early 1876, but for the researcher that purpose is not learned until the *Chronicle* offered on April 27:

> **Centennial Base Ball**—An effort is being made in this city by some individuals who interest themselves in base-ball matters to complete arrangements for sending a picked nine of crack players to Philadelphia during the Centennial to take a hand in the grand international base-ball tournament. It is an indisputable fact that California contains a large number of excellent players, many of whom are so practiced that it is thought probable that California representatives might bring away a few of the laurels to be given at the Centennial match, and by people of base-ball proclivities it is ardently hoped that the programme of sending a few players east will not fail of consummation.

With that knowledge, the tidbits of baseball news in San Francisco's papers now make sense, but they beg the questions: What happened between the end of the 1875 season and the incredible announcement regarding the formation of the Centennials? When and how did the idea originate? Whose idea was it? How was it to be financed? How were the players selected? To what degree were Messrs. David and Townsend, who had never been mentioned in any San Francisco baseball-related context before this, involved? The answers are not to be found in any San Francisco publication, but the

Clipper provides the most important clue in a February 5, 1876, article titled "The Centennial Team From California," in which California was challenged to

> organize a representative baseball team from the clubs of California to visit Philadelphia during the Centennial Exhibition and test their strength as baseball players against the champion professionals of the East.

The *Clipper's* call to arms invoked the 1874 tour of the Boston and Athletic clubs "simply to show the Britishers how we play our national game" and concluded with "by all means let us have a California [team] in Philadelphia this Centennial year. Will Mr. Durkee and gentlemen of the crack clubs of San Francisco take this matter in hand?" [5]

Many questions regarding the formation of the Centennials will never be answered, but at least we have pinpointed the first domino to fall. The formation of the Centennials gutted San Francisco's top nine and significantly reduced the quantity of talent on the Occidentals, effectively wiping out the 1876 baseball season. However, enough local talent remained to arrange preseason matches for California's finest to test its mettle.

And here arises another mystery. Two different sources report two very different preseasons for the Centennials. City newspapers recorded matches on March 26, April 1, April 30, and May 28, all of which the Centennials won. With the exception of March 26, these reports included box scores and brief summaries.

The *Clipper's* year-end article, however, listed twelve Centennial games between April 20 and June 20 in which they were undefeated. Only date, opponent, and score were provided.

Adding to the confusion over their preseason record, *none* of the Centennial games listed in the *Clipper* summary correspond with *any* of the locally reported ones. However, the *Clipper* briefly noted in its weekly Short Stops column of May 20 that "[a]t San Francisco, Cal., recently the Centennial Club beat the Californias 24–7." And in the June 17 Short Stops it was noted that on May 28, in San Francisco, the Centennials defeated a picked nine, 25–9. These references are consistent with the locally reported outcomes, but they never appeared in the *Clipper's* end-of-year piece. Add one more Centennial mystery.

According to the record in San Francisco's newspapers, the Centennials played their first game, billed "a masquerade game," on March 26 against Mrs. Oates' Comic Opera Troupe, eking out a 24–23 victory.[6]

The Centennials' first legitimate competition came on April 1 against the Alert club, which finished a distant third in the 1875 campaign. Delos Ashley was the winning pitcher over O'Brien of the Alerts.

History and mystery become entangled over a match advertised in the *Chronicle* to be played on April 23 between the Centennials and a picked nine. There was no local follow up on this game, but the *Clipper* of May 13, 1876 reported an April 23 match between the Centennials and the Alerts, crediting Thomas Gill, the recording secretary for the Centennials, with providing the box score and game summary. Three thousand spectators witnessed the Centennials triumph 7–5 over the Alerts in "one of the finest games of ball ever played on the Pacific Coast," in which Delos Ashley held the Alerts to just four hits. Ashley's losing opponent was again O'Brien.

Inexplicably, this game was omitted from the *Clipper's* December summary.

Or was it?

According to the *Clipper's* summary, the Centennials defeated the Alerts by the same

7–5 score on May 16, not April 23. Misprint? Or mystery? Whichever, it wasn't the first, nor would not be the last.

On April 30 the Centennials' next opponents (according to the local papers) were the Californias, who gave the 1875 champion San Franciscos a strong battle for the title. This game featured the ubiquitous O'Brien in the box for the Californias. Four other erstwhile Alerts joined him on the so-called Californias. Once again Ashley prevailed over O'Brien 24–7.

Mysteriously, the *Clipper* records the Centennials defeating the Empires 13–11 on April 30.

On May 28, 1,000 people saw the Centennials play their final recorded warmup game against a picked nine, winning 25–9.[7] This time O'Brien was the Centennial pitcher while their regular ball tosser, Delos Ashley, did not appear in the game.

This was not just a baseball game, but also a farewell benefit for the Centennials,

> who are shortly to shake the dust of San Francisco from under their feet and travel Eastward to Philadelphia, where they go as a representative California Club, to participate in the coming matches at the Centennial Exposition.... The Centennials intend leaving June 15th on a *professional tour* (italics added), throughout the Eastern States, and expect to be away about three months.[8]

On July 1 the *Clipper* noted, "The advent of a representative California baseball team in the East is a fixed fact, the San Francisco ball clubs having adopted our suggestion to send a California nine East this Summer, as will be seen by the appended letter:

> San Francisco, June 15, 1876.
>
> Editor Clipper.—*Dear Sir:* The centennial year has brought together representatives of all States to encourage our national game. This has awakened an interest in the Golden State hitherto unfelt. A representative team of California will start on June 24 to make a tour of the Eastern States, it being the first baseball club that ever left California. All communication should be sent to the undersigned in care of W.A. Hurlbert, Room No. 5, 166 Randolph Street, Chicago, Ill.
>
> Yours truly, Louis N. David, Manager.

Between the picked-nine game of May 28 and their departure for Philadelphia on June 24, the Centennial roster underwent a radical change, as the San Francisco *Bulletin* informed its readers on June 24.

> The Centennial Club consists of Thompson, catcher; O'Brien, pitcher; J. Williams, first base; Keating, second base; Piercy, third base; Curran, short-stop; Taylor, left field; Gill, center field; Parent, right field, with Walker, Cullen and Ashley as substitutes. The short-stop, Curran, is Captain.

This is how the new roster compared with the first announcement of the Centennials:

First Announcement March 9	***Second Announcement June 24***
PITCHER: Ashley (Occidentals)	O'Brien (Alerts)
CATCHER: Cullen (Occidentals)	Thompson (Californias)
FIRST BASE: Walker (San Franciscos)	Williams(San Franciscos)
SECOND BASE: Gill (San Franciscos)	Keating (San Franciscos)
THIRD BASE: Piercy (San Franciscos)	Piercy (San Franciscos)

First Announcement March 9	***Second Announcement June 24***
SHORT STOP: Curran (San Franciscos)	Curran (San Franciscos)
LEFT FIELD: Taylor (San Franciscos)	Taylor (San Franciscos)
CENTER FIELD: Magendie (Occidentals)	Gill (San Franciscos)
RIGHT FIELD: Parent (Occidentals)	Parent (Occidentals)

The primitive state of San Francisco baseball reporting (which identified players by last names only) and the absence of any Centennial records leave us with no clues as to the identity of some of these truly historic figures.

Who Keating was is impossible to determine. The name can be traced as far back as 1868 to a Keating playing second base for the Eagles. In September 1869 a C. Keating played for the Eagles against the Cincinnati Red Stockings when they visited San Francisco. "Keating" continued with the Eagles in 1870 and 1871 when he was joined by "D" and "E" Keating. In 1874 C.J. Keating was named captain of the Alerts. Later that season he joined the newly formed San Franciscos. In 1875 C. Keating was the second baseman for the San Franciscos. Unfortunately we never learn his first name.

From other contexts we learn that O'Brien's first initial was "T," although his first name is never revealed. The first recorded appearance of O'Brien was in June 1874 with the Actives. In July he switched to the Mutuals. At the start of the 1875 season O'Brien was the pitcher for the San Franciscos but a month later he jumped to the Alerts.

The *Bulletin* thankfully provides Mr. William's first initial: J. That narrows it down a bit, but Williams was one of the most common surnames in early San Francisco baseball. A match between the Eagles and Atlantics on March 31, 1871 featured a plethora of players surnamed Williams: F. and J. Williams appeared for the Eagles while A., W., and J.B. each patrolled an outfield position for the Atlantics. In 1875 J. Williams was the shortstop for the San Francisco. The *Clipper* ultimately identifies Mr. Williams as "John" in an 1877 reference.[9]

In August 1874 Thompson — no first name or initial — is listed as catching for the Californias. In November the Californias were reorganized and Thompson was moved to shortstop, but at the end of the month he was catching again. In 1875 he began the season behind the plate, but was soon in the outfield.

On October 10, 1875 the *Chronicle* profiled the top clubs and their best players, some of whom would become Centennials, giving us valuable information on some of them.

Of the San Franciscos we learn:

> Curran, the catcher, is a veteran player and is generally conceded to be the best man in the state behind the bat, is very agile, a fleet runner, plays well on bases or in the field and is one of the best average players in the state.
>
> Taylor, the left fielder, and Piercy, the third baseman, are acknowledged to be the best players in their respective positions. Both are very active men, the latter being one of the fleetest runners in the State, a good catcher, short-stop or fielder, but is lamentably weak at the bat. Taylor plays well in any position and is the most reliable and effective batsman here.
>
> Walker at first and Gill at second base or center field are excellent players.
>
> Williams, the short stop, is built on the principle of a shot tower, and the experienced batsman who sees Williams unlimbering his joints and reaching for a ball, knows that if it is any less than fifteen feet from the ground, Williams' palm will stop it.

For the Occidentals comes this information:

> Ashley and Cullen, the pitcher and catcher[,] filled these positions in the Athletic Club last year and have played those positions together for years and become as good a pair in that line as there is in the State. They are good batsmen, swift base-runners and good players in every way.

For the Alerts:

> O'Brien, the pitcher and Captain[,] is one of the oldest players on the coast. He was drawn off from the San Francisco Club about a year ago to take his present position, and was as much an acquisition to the one club as a loss to the other. He is a strong, steady, untiring pitcher and by many considered the best in the state. He is weak at the bat and often displays too much temper and impatience for a good player, but he has his men well in hand, is looked up to as a leader by them and is the mainstay of the club.

Representing the Californias:

> The position of low comedian and right fielder is ably filled by an excitable young man named Thompson, who by his frantic bare-headed efforts to achieve the impossible furnishes infinite amusement to the spectators and players.

Whether their preseason record was 5–0, 12–0, or other, the Golden State's first baseball ambassadors (which included four future major leaguers: John Curran, John Cullen, Ed Taylor, and Andy Piercy) began their Eastern tour on June 24 with this hail and farewell from the *Chronicle*:

> Yesterday the Centennial Base Ball Club started for the East on their tour of contemplated field triumphs. Whether they will return as jubilantly as they started out remains to be seen, but there is every prospect, judging from the prowess they have heretofore exhibited, that they will make an honorable, if not brilliant record. It is confidently hoped and believed that the club will return with many hard-earned honors perched upon their banners.

Their first opponents on what would be a seven-week, 4,000-mile, 18-city and nine-state odyssey were the Amitys of Sacramento. As the team began its forgotten journey, Hypolite Magendie, the original Centennial center fielder, was left behind. With L.N. David and Clarence Townsend traveling with the players, they comprised a party of 14. It was very likely that a contingent of San Franciscans accompanied the Centennials to Sacramento to see their heroes play one last time.

Sacramento had a very dynamic baseball scene with Amity the leading club. On June 25, wearing their uniforms of white pants and shirts, red stockings, and a dark cap completing the ensemble, the Centennials defeated the Amity Club 34–9. Now history and journalism were on the same track; this was the Centennials' first match consistent with the *Clipper's* chronology of games.

Over the past two seasons a very cordial relationship had developed between the Amitys and San Francisco's clubs. In 1874 and 1875 teams from San Francisco visited Sacramento and later the Amitys returned the visits. Following the games the host clubs celebrated their guests at lavish banquets. There was no reason that it shouldn't happen this time and every reason that it should, given the historic nature of the Centennial's visit. Although made up exclusively of San Franciscans, the Centennials were still California's team.

Before they left San Francisco, Montgomery Street jeweler Col. Abe Andrews presented the team a gold badge in the form of a scroll surmounted with the Great Seal of the State of California. Valued at $40, it was to be awarded to the most recent game's best player. At the end of the tour it was to be permanently awarded to the Centennial with the best overall record.[10] Centennial captain John Curran was the first recipient. The postgame banquet, punctuated with numerous toasts to the success of California's representatives, would have been a fitting place to make the presentation. Unfortunately there was no box score, so we don't know what John Curran did to earn Col. Andrews' medal.

At the same time that the two nines were engaged in friendly combat, unknown to the outside world Lt. Col. George Custer and 700 men of his 7th Cavalry were fighting for their lives in Montana. News of Little Big Horn wouldn't reach the rest of the country for almost two weeks.

The *Chronicle*'s glorious bon voyage for California's diamond heroes notwithstanding, news of their games would be even slower in coming than word of Custer's fate, which brings up another mystery. The Centennials were gone for seven weeks and reportedly played 32 games, only a few of which received the briefest mention in their hometown papers. Why weren't the exploits of San Francisco's pride and joy reported with the same heady enthusiasm as their send off? The report of the Amity game would be the last word on the Centennials to reach San Francisco for a month.

Since there was no San Francisco newspaper correspondent traveling with the Centennials to make the telegraph wires sing with his dispatches praising their worthiness in victory and their nobility in defeat, did the job then fall to one of the players? Was it Ashley, the corresponding secretary? Or Gill the recording secretary? Or someone else?

If the Centennials kept journals or sent letters home, their whereabouts are unknown and the contents are lost. Fortunately the Centennial's road record, as reported in the *Clipper*, is now consistent with the reports in the local papers of the cities they visited. Thus, the reconstruction of their Grand Tour is possible, although only as brief snapshots taken from the perspective of the baseball writers of the various cities in which they played.

Despite the *Alta*'s characterization of their tour as a *professional tour*, the Centennials were strictly amateur players who had day jobs and were weekend baseball warriors. It is known that Delos Ashley and Andy Piercy came from families of means, but the others weren't so fortunate. Of the ones we know of for sure, they were single young men who had no families left behind unsupported. Perhaps the reference to "professional tour" might have to do with their expectations of financing the venture through a percentage of gate receipts and appearance money to cover travel expenses.[11]

The *Bulletin*'s send-off article of June 24 provided a glimpse at the team's early itinerary. After Sacramento their next game would be in Omaha, Nebraska on July 4. Then a game on July 5 in Council Bluffs, Iowa, just across the Missouri River from Omaha, followed by a game in Atlantic, Iowa on July 8. During their anticipated three-month tour, the Centennials' advance agent hoped to arrange games in Chicago, Cleveland, Detroit, Philadelphia, New York, and Boston. The *Los Angeles Herald* of June 25 wrote that the Centennials would play the White Stockings in Chicago.

The Centennials' Central Pacific train departed Sacramento at 8 A.M. on Monday, June 26.[12] It would be their home for the eight and a half days that it would take them to reach Omaha, 1,777 miles away. Their choice of the creeping crawler over the express train tells us that either they were in no hurry or were extremely frugal. First class express fare was $100 one way to Omaha and would take four days. Emigrant class, the choice of the Centennials, cost $45 and was the dry land equivalent of steerage class.[13]

The 60-foot long emigrant cars had seating for 48, were heated by wood-burning stoves and lighted by kerosene lamps. At one end of the car was the "ladies' saloon," measuring 3' by 5'. The "gents' saloon" at the other end measured 3' by 3'.[14] These cars were part of a mixed freight and passenger train. The average distance between stations was about seven miles. The express made better time bypassing the flag stops and freight sidings while the creeping crawler made every stop to pick up and drop off freight and passengers.

Three weeks earlier, as a grand publicity stunt, a train dubbed The Lightning Express made a record run from New York City to San Francisco: 3,317 miles in 83 hours and 15minutes. Of course the track was cleared the entire distance, and relays of fresh crews, coal, and water were available at regular intervals without delay. Sixteen train-setters paid $500 each for the experience, which included such luxury appointments as a gourmet dining car, a hotel day coach, and a sleeping car. Pulled by a powerful engine specially built for the run, the average speed was 40 MPH, topping a mile a minute along some stretches.[15]

The Centennials' train averaged a more pedestrian 8 MPH on the 19-hour, 155-mile leg over the Sierra Nevada to Reno, then just an outlier of Nevada's capital, Carson City, and the silver-mining boomtown of Virginia City. Reno was named for Major General Jesse Reno, who was killed in a Civil War battle. Ironically, a Major Reno had been involved in a recent battle. Arriving in Reno at 3:30 A.M., none of this mattered to the sleeping Centennials. Nor the fact that they were the first California baseball team to leave the state.

During the day, each car's 48 detainees sat in 12 pairs of facing bench seats — six pairs on each side of the car — two people per seat. At night the seats converted into double-bed sleeping berths for half the passengers. The other half slept in double "upper berths" formed by lowering the hinged sleeping platform from the ceiling and securely locking it into place. Each double berth — upper and lower — measured a comfy-cozy 5'9" by 3'3". After one night in these intimate confines, the "berth-mates" would be either best friends or worst enemies for life. There was no extra charge for these Spartan sleeping accommodations on emigrant class. Individual sleeping berths on the express trains cost $6 from San Francisco to Ogden and $8 from Ogden to Omaha.[16]

Andy Piercy, "the best general player on the Pacific Coast" (Clipper).

Sunrise on Tuesday, June 27 would find them crossing the cheerless and desolate Great Basin that comprised most of the Sagebrush State. Some of the Centennials may have obtained a copy of George Crofutt's *Trans-Continental Tourist,* a 169-page guide for the westbound traveler of what lay along the rail route.[17] The Centennials would have been flipping the pages from back-to-front as they chugged eastward. Approaching White Plains, Nevada, they might have read Crofutt's unflattering description of their surroundings on page 116:

> As indicated by the name, the plains immediately around the station are white with alkali, solid beds of which slope away to the sinks of Carson and Humboldt lakes. No vegetation meets the eye when gazing on the vast expanse of dirty white alkali. The sun's rays seem to fall perpendicularly down on this barren scene, burning and withering, as though they would crush out any attempt which nature might make to introduce vegetable life.

Sixty miles further east they came to Humboldt, one of a number of regularly-spaced eating stations where east- and west-bound trains stopped for 30 minutes to allow the passengers to eat prepared meals. The $1.00 meals at Humboldt were touted by Crofutt as being as good as at any station on the road. No meals were served on the train. Instead, passengers were advised to pick up provisions at stops along the way and to eat on board, but they were warned not to let the food sit for long or it would spoil.

With just primitive sanitary facilities, by this point the smell of food going bad in the packed cars would be unnoticed in the miasma of unwashed bodies.

In contrast with White Plains, Humboldt was described by Crofutt as an oasis in the desert. However, it was fleeting, as there would be no more trees to be seen till they arrived in Ogden, 460 miles away.

Thirty-nine miles east of Humboldt was Winnemucca, "population 500 and 90 buildings of all sorts." This was the transfer point for the 265-mile stagecoach route to Boise City, capital of Idaho Territory. Fare $50.00. Today that stage road is US Highway 95.

The wake-up call for Wednesday's breakfast would bring them to Elko, an eating station and, at the time, the home of the State University. At the start of day number three, the Centennials and everyone else on the train were fighting losing battles with sensory overload in the hot, crowded, noisy, smelly, poorly ventilated, swaying cars, as well as mind-crushing boredom and tedium exacerbated by the enforced inactivity of four dozen people crammed onto 500 square feet of floor space. Pacing up and down the 30"-wide aisles was not a viable option when everyone else had the same idea.[18]

After another full day they pulled into Ogden, Utah Territory at 8:20 A.M. on Thursday, June 29. At 895 miles from San Francisco and 1,033 miles from Omaha, Ogden was the transfer point between the Central Pacific and Union Pacific lines. It was also a railroad junction with the Utah Southern Railroad that ran to Salt Lake City, 34 miles to the south and to Provo, 40 miles further on.

Crofutt described Ogden:

> At this station the Union and Central Pacific Railroad Company have a union depot, large freight-houses, round-houses, machine and repair shops, and employ a large number of men. It is a regular eating station and a good restaurant is kept in the depot building, which is situated between the tracks.

The station was two miles from the city of Ogden. Ten miles to the west was the Great Salt Lake and to the east were the Wasatch Mountains. The Centennials undoubtedly used the nine-hour layover to stretch their legs and enjoy a relaxed breakfast and lunch while they read the *Salt Lake City Tribune*. The front-page news told of the Democratic Convention in St. Louis and the nomination of Samuel Tilden to be the party's standard-bearer against Rutherford B. Hayes in the presidential election. No word yet on Custer. Perhaps the Centennials found bathing facilities.

At 5:00 P.M. they were aboard a Union Pacific train winding through the Wasatch. Seventy-three miles east of Ogden they entered Wyoming Territory.

Their Friday morning meal stop at Green River received Crofutt's "not the best on the road" rating.

Night would be falling as the Centennials crossed the continental divide at Creston, 7,020 feet. This would not be their highest passage; that would come on the afternoon of the next day, 24 miles east of Laramie. After the train had huffed and chuffed uphill at a boiler-bursting average speed of 3.5 miles per hour for the past 90 minutes, they came to Sherman. Named after the tallest general in the Union Army, Sherman was the highest point on the rail line: 8,242 feet above sea level. At the time it was built it was the highest rail line in the world. From there they could clearly see Pike's Peak 165 miles to the south.

Thirty-three miles later they pulled into Cheyenne as the sun was setting behind them. The capital of Wyoming Territory, Cheyenne was a town that didn't exist before the Union Pacific surveyors arrived in 1867. It was also the exact halfway point between Ogden and Omaha. With 3,000 souls, "The Magic City of the Plains" was the largest town between Omaha and Ogden and a jumping-off point for the gold fields of the Black Hills of Dakota to the north. It was also the junction with the Denver Pacific Railroad to Denver 140 miles to the south where baseball in the Rocky Mountains was alive and doing well as evidenced by a game played earlier that day between the clubs representing the two territorial capitals. The Cheyenne Club "scooped" the Georgetown Club of Denver 26–9.[19]

Two hundred thirty miles and twenty hours from Cheyenne, they passed through North Platte, Nebraska, another town that existed only because of the railroad. Home to 1,500, a quarter of a century earlier it was home to no one. Simply called The Junction, it was the confluence of the North and South forks of the Platte River. This was the point where the Emigrant Trail crossed the Platte on the route from Independence, Missouri to South Pass in Wyoming, the easiest crossing of the Rockies for covered wagons. For the next 60 miles, between North Platte and Plum Creek, the east-bound Centennials — averaging 12 miles per hour — paralleled the west-bound route taken by the overland emigrants of the 1840s and 1850s who were happy to make 12 miles a day.

The Centennials weren't the first ball chasers to pass along this route to or from the west coast. In 1869 the Cincinnati Red Stockings came to San Francisco on these same rails, and in 1849 Alexander Cartwright came west on a wagon train. The persistent mythology associated with Cartwright's overland passage includes tales of him teaching or playing baseball with Indians, mountain men and soldiers in the prairie and mountains, but there is absolutely no proof that it ever happened.

In addition to the baseball clubs in Denver and Cheyenne, there were other stickmen who played the game across the great prairie and over the majestic mountains. On June 7, 1874, there was a baseball game at Ft. Abraham Lincoln, near Bismarck, Dakota Territory, between the Actives of L Company of the 7th Cavalry and a picked nine from nearby Lincoln.[20]

As the Centennials journeyed eastward, other nomadic Western baseballists had just been indelibly inscribed into American history, though not as frontier batsmen. This was the Benteen Base Ball Club. Captain Frederick Benteen was in charge of H Company of the 7th Cavalry under Custer. In 1873, while stationed in Nashville during Reconstruction, 54 men of H Company formed the Benteen Base Ball and Gymnasium club. Between 1873 and 1875, despite constant moves from Tennessee to Dakota to New Orleans and back to Dakota, the Benteens played baseball when circumstances and military duties permitted. They played 17 games against military and civilian nines, winning 12 and outscoring the opposition 464–230.

In 1875 the 7th Cavalry was posted to Fort Randall on the Missouri River at the border of Dakota Territory and Nebraska. In July they were sent to the Black Hills to remove gold prospectors who were trespassing on Sioux reservation land. While there, the cavalrymen played a team of teamsters, winning 25–11.

The last game the Benteens played was September 8, 1875, at Fort Randall against the 1st Infantry. The horse soldiers lost 12–7. The 7th then went up the Missouri River to Fort Abraham Lincoln. On May 17, 1876 they set off to locate and force the Sioux Indians back onto the reservation. In the Battle of Little Big Horn, four Benteen players were wounded and one killed.[21]

Snuggling into their sleeping berths on the night of July 1 after the long layover in Cheyenne, the Centennials fell asleep at 6,041 feet. When they woke up 100 miles later they had descended over 2,000 feet. Leveling out on the Great Plains, their rate of descent to Omaha was an imperceptible eight feet per mile.

The July 1 editions of the *Omaha Daily Herald* and *Daily Republican* confirmed what had been reported in the California papers when the Centennials began their journey — they would face an Omaha nine on July 4. Yet, for reasons never explained, the weekly *Atlantic (IA) Telegraph* informed its readers on June 28 to "expect a San Francisco club to play a match game on July 4"; the Centennials were originally scheduled to visit Atlantic on July 8.

Definitely another mystery.

A lot of time was spent looking at what passed for scenery on the skillet-flat and frying-pan hot Great Plains, but it was unlikely that any buffalo were seen. Over the past few years the vast herds had been slaughtered almost to extinction by sport hunters shooting at them from the trains. One year over 100,000 head were killed along the lines of the Union and Kansas Pacific Railroad alone.[22] In the winter of 1872, before the mass killings of buffalo began in earnest, Russian Grand Duke Alexis experienced the thrill of participating in a buffalo hunt with Buffalo Bill and Custer himself.[23]

Evening brought no relief from the day's triple-digit heat,[24] but it did bring a delightful surprise that was a summertime fixture east of the Rockies but unknown in California: lightning bugs.

On the final day, as the Centennials approached their long-anticipated destination and release from emigrant-class bondage, Fourth of July pyrotechnics started early. For hours the eastern horizon was a growing, menacingly dark wall lit by brilliant flashes. At 8 P.M., with Omaha still 20 miles and 90 minutes away, the train encountered the wall: a no-holds-barred Midwestern thunderstorm. Today's meteorologists would call it a giant super cell.

In Omaha, on the western edge of the storm system that covered the entire state of

Iowa, all the holiday banners, bunting and murals were destroyed. Twenty miles north of Omaha, Missouri Valley was hit by a tornado that unroofed countless buildings. In nearby Blair trains were blown off tracks. Hail the size of chickens' eggs up to seven inches in diameter bombarded the area causing property, livestock, and crop damage in the tens of thousands of dollars. Lightning killed a child. The Aurora, Iowa *Delta* called the statewide "hurricane" the most destructive storm to visit the state in years. Worst hit were northern and eastern Iowa where scores of lives were lost, mostly in flash floods and tornadoes.[25]

At 9:30 P.M. on Monday, July 3, 181.5 hours and 1,777 miles after boarding the train in Sacramento, San Francisco's finest had reached the end of the first part of their journey, but they were unable to revel in the simple pleasures of unfolding their joints, stretching their limbs, and breathing fresh air. They were under siege and they needed to find shelter.

Throughout the night the storm raged with all the terrifying splendor of nature unchained. Some of the westerners may have experienced earthquakes back home, but the multisensory assault of thunder bursting in air, the blinding hellfire from above, repeated too-close lighting strikes, wind, rain, and hail must have seemed like Armageddon.

Come the dawn's early light of July 4, Old Glory with it broad stripes and bright stars made appearances on homes, businesses, and public buildings as Omaha's 18,000 residents surveyed the post-apocalyptic scene and wondered if their Independence Day celebrations would come off. They were lucky. The torrential rain turned the dirt streets to bottomless mud, but property damage was light. As Omahans struggled to salvage their celebration, the *Daily Herald* of July 4 wrote that the Centennials would not play as previously announced, but would stop on their return to California later in the summer.

No mention was made of the game scheduled for Council Bluffs on July 5 as the West Coasters abandoned Omaha to celebrate the Centennial in Atlantic, a town of 2,500 fifty miles east of Omaha that billed itself as the Boss City of the Missouri Slope. The cities of Omaha, Council Bluffs, and Atlantic had baseball teams that played regular competitive matches against each other, so the Californians would not be facing country bumpkins unfamiliar with the game. Patriotic Iowans from miles around ignored the elements to pack the Cass County fairgrounds to cheer on their hometown heroes, the Troublesomes.[26]

Local pride was validated as the Troublesomes scored first with two runs in the bottom of the second inning. The visitors shook off their train-induced stiffness to take the lead with three runs in the fourth and fifth innings. The home team surged back with three in the bottom of the fifth to cut the deficit to one run. Single runs by San Francisco in the sixth and seventh innings made the score 8–5 going into the eighth. A Troublesome score was matched by the Centennials in the top of the ninth.

The weather was still holding as the Atlanticans came up for their final swings trailing 9–6. It seemed that the Pacific Coasters would disappoint the hometown crowd on the nation's hundredth birthday, but the local boys scored four times, and when the winning run crossed the plate the crowd's yells could be heard a mile away. Hats were thrown into the air and the Troublesomes were carried off the field on the shoulders of their deliriously jubilant friends. That evening the visitors were honored at a Centennial banquet given by the Troublesomes and their lady friends.

The *Atlantic Telegraph* credited the Centennials' agent for arranging the game, though it didn't identify him or elaborate on exactly *when* arrangements had been made. This mysterious, unnamed advance man would play an ongoing role in the Centennials' tour.

The following Centennials had the honor of representing California: Taylor, lf; Gill, ss; Keating, 2b; Parent, rf; Curran, c; Piercy, 3b; Williams, 1b; O'Brien, p; Thompson, cf.

The Centennials spent the night in Atlantic while storm-damaged tracks were repaired near Des Moines. The next day the humbled big city boys were confined for another 12 hours as a Chicago, Rock Island & Pacific train took them across Iowa to their next engagement in Davenport, a city of 20,000, on the Mississippi River. On July 6, the battle-scarred San Franciscans overcame 87-degree heat to defeat the Red Caps

Centennial Fun, ***a Frank Leslie publication, was a booklet of 48 pages filled with humorous drawings. The Centennial club's experience was not as amusing.***

23–9 before hopping back on the Rock Island line for the 140-mile overnight leg to the nation's fifth largest city: Chicago.[27]

Arriving on the morning of July 7, the Californians and the rest of the world received the first detailed news of Custer's Last Stand.

Front-page maps in both papers clearly showed the tracks of the Union Pacific Railroad south of the killing grounds. Although separated from the massacre by hundreds of miles and several days, the Centennials must have shared profound thoughts of what might have been.

While the Californians were crossing bats with the Iowa clubs, the Chicago White Stockings were dueling with the Hartford Dark Blues of Brooklyn for first place in the nascent National League. Two consecutive losses to the Brooklynites had dropped the Whites into second place, a half game behind the Blues.

On July 7 the *Chicago Tribune* gave a nice plug for that day's Centennial-Franklin game.

> THE CALIFORNIA NINE. The Pacific coast team of players will arrive here this morning, and will play the Franklins on the White-Stocking grounds at 3:45 this afternoon. The game will be an interesting one, and since the visitors are the first California team who ever came East, they should be encouraged. They will go East from here playing all the prominent amateurs and semi-professionals on their way.

A few hours after their overnight journey, California's best ball players found themselves in the friendly confines of the 23rd Street Grounds, the home of the Chicago White Stockings. It was a day off in the Chicago–Hartford series and the South Side field was available for their game against the Franklins, who had a 5–4 record.[28] Two thousand miles from home, San Francisco's finest were no longer the big fish in the small pond of Bay Area baseball. Now they were the new fish in the great sea of eastern baseball where they would be closely scrutinized and critically judged.

Playing in a blistering 93 degrees (30 degrees hotter than San Francisco's high reading for that day) the Centennials lost 5–4 in what the *Chicago Times* described as

> a game devoid of interest on account of weak batting on both sides. The fielding, however, was above average of *amateur* clubs and some really good work was done on both sides. [San Francisco had 11 errors to Chicago's seven.] The San Francisco nine is above the usual run of *amateurs* and especially in fielding, as they are quick in throwing to bases. Their great trouble was the want of a captain to run the men on bases. Taken as a whole, they are a good *amateur club*" [italics added for emphasis — author].

The lineup was the same as for the Atlantic game, though with some changes in the batting order.

The *Times* added a new Centennial wrinkle with: "This is their second defeat on their trip out of *seventeen* games which speaks well for them." According to the *Clipper's* account, this was their *sixteenth* game.

The Centennials were free on July 8 while the Whites and Blues resumed their series. Did the California amateurs watch that game? It's hard to imagine that they would travel so far, play on a major league field, and yet not see a major league game. Plus, if they still had intentions of playing the professionals, it would behoove them to scout their potential adversaries. Had they gone they wouldn't have been the only ballplayers from San Francisco at the grounds. Tom Carey, Hartford's shortstop, had played for the

Pacifics and Eagles in 1868 and 1869, most notably two games against the Cincinnati Red Stockings when they visited San Francisco in the fall of 1869.[29]

The western spectators would have seen baseball immortals Cap Anson and Al Spalding for the Stockings, and Candy Cummings, pitcher for the Hartfords, as they warmed up. Spalding, who would win 47 games in 1876, usually pitched for the Whites, but he opted to let Cal McVey take the box while he played left field. Candy Cummings, credited with inventing the curveball, had the day off, so the Californians missed seeing a grand pitching matchup. They did, however, witness some fine examples of what the *Tribune* called "scientific batting."

Ross Barnes, who had hit the National League's first home run on May 2 and who would win the league's first batting title with the astronomical average of .429, led off the top of the first. Expecting the right-handed striker to pull to left, Blues shortstop Carey, second baseman Jack Burdock, and center fielder Jack Remsen all joined Tom York in left field. In response to this unconventional alignment, Barnes contrarily hit to right.

Two batters later he was on third as Cal McVey came to the plate. Everybody knew what McVey would do and he did it: a perfect squeeze bunt down the first-base line to score Barnes. The White Stockings went on to win 9–3 to regain first place.

In Milwaukee the *Daily News* alerted its readers to the arrival of the Centennials with: "The West Ends announce that the San Francisco Base Ball Club, the Pacific Coast champions, will play an exhibition game in this city Wednesday next."

This was the first reference to San Francisco's picked nine as champions of any sort. Was it the advance man's doing?

During the 92-mile journey to Milwaukee the following day, the amateur Centennials became professionals — or so the Milwaukee papers would come to describe them.

The July 10 game against the West End club (who were 5–4) was umpired by Centennial Ed Taylor, usually the left fielder. The Milwaukee papers attributed San Francisco's 8–4 triumph to Taylor's making a number of controversial calls in favor of his team.

The *Milwaukee Sentinel* headlined their game account:

THE CALIFORNIA CLUB'S LEFT FIELDER
PUT UP TO UMPIRE YESTERDAY'S GAME.

————————

Where He Did More Than The Rest Of
His Club To Defeat The West Ends.

The *Sentinel* persisted: "The home club played against the umpire as well as the nine, that person working decidedly in the interests of the visitors."

The *Milwaukee News* concurred: "The rulings of the umpire, Mr. Taylor, a member of the San Francisco club, were from the start plainly in partiality to his own club."

While agreeing on Taylor's biases, the papers disagreed on the quality of the overall play. The *News* called it "a game of tolerable interest," while the *Sentinel* hailed it as "the prettiest game that has been played on the grounds."

If we are to believe the *Sentinel*, "The California Club is a strong one and played a better fielding game than the home club [San Francisco made seven errors, the West Enders 13], but their batting for the most part being weak." Both clubs had five hits.

To appease their hosts, the Centennials cancelled their previously scheduled July 11 game in Elgin to play another in Milwaukee.

The *Sentinel* fanned the flames with:

> Unquestionably today's game between the same clubs will be a red-hot one. With another umpire and a closer attention to business, the West Ends hope to get away with the ball tossers of the Pacific slope, and whether they do or not, the game will be well worth seeing. Both nines are on their mettle and will play to win. The grounds should be crowded. Game will be called at half past three.

The *News* advised its readers:

> The West Ends arranged for a second game to be played on the Wells Street Grounds this afternoon. On account of the expense which the members of the West End Club have been compelled to assume in order to get the members of the California club to remain over, which they have done at the cost of cancelling an engagement with the Elgin, Ill. club, the management of the home club announced that all members and all ticket holders at today's game will be charged the regular admission fee.

The Pacific Slope Champions were vindicated with a 12–4 victory. At the plate, instead of behind it, Ed Taylor had three hits and scored two runs. In the sixth he "hit nobly to left field, bringing Walker and Keating home and taking second."

The *Sentinel* snorted at the outcome: "The West Enders have better material than that which constitutes the *California professional club.*" [Italics added — author.] Nonetheless, the *Sentinel* brutally criticized the play of a number of West Enders.

During the game Centennial first baseman R.T. Walker injured his knee, but continued to play. Afterwards he would be out of action for a month, replaced by Williams, the center fielder.

The White Stockings were idle on July 12. The professionals routinely played the local amateur clubs and the Centennials had had hopes of engaging them since their tour began. Recent local precedence included:

- On July 7, an off day in the Chicago-Hartford series (while the Centennials were playing the Franklins in Chicago), the Hartford Dark Blues played the West Ends in Milwaukee.
- On June 30 the visiting Philadelphia Athletics also traveled to Milwaukee on an off day.
- In a four-day period following a series in New York, the White Stockings went 100 miles out of their way home to play in London, Ontario on June 19; travel 400 miles (undoubtedly by first-class express) to defeat the New York Mutuals at home the next day; travel to Milwaukee to face the West Ends on their home field on June 21; finally returning to Chicago and another victory over the Mutuals on June 22. Four games in four days in three cities, yet the National League leading White Stocking did not deign to play the "Pacific Coast champions" on their home turf.

After an arduous 287-mile train trip, the Centennials arrived in Detroit on July 13, the same day that the Aetnas, one of the city's top two amateur clubs, returned from a two-week trip to Pennsylvania and New York. The Aetnas had left in a state of disarray, with a dismal 2–6 record. They returned six games later "completely reorganized" according to the *Detroit Free Press*, which added "The Aetnas arrived home from its Eastern trip and if they did not win many games, they benefited from the experience." Silver-lining their 1–5 road trip, the Aetna manager proclaimed: "We didn't know anything about playing ball, but now we've got a boss nine." They also obtained three new players.

The Centennials settled in at the Cass Hotel on Third and Woodbridge near the train station and one block from the Detroit River. They would play at the Peninsular Cricket Grounds on Woodward Avenue, a mere 1.5 miles by Detroit City Railway from their hotel. With no more overnight, intercity train marathons for the next four days, they could rest, acclimate, and practice for what the *Free Press* termed the great baseball match on July 15.

For the comfort of the spectators, (and hopefully the visitors also) the managers of the grounds advertised that ice water was to be provided to mitigate the heat and humidity.

The Centennials brought their two-game winning streak to the grounds while the Aetnas brought a two-game losing streak. They also brought the players they had picked up back east. The new acquisitions made the difference for the Aetnas. Pitcher J.A. Sullivan, obtained from a Pittsburgh club, "dodgered" the Centennials with his curve balls, fanning 18. His dominance was so complete that the Centennials couldn't score till the last inning, losing 12–1 to the new and improved Aetnas.

The *Free Press* introduced the Californians:

> The visiting club is composed of quiet, nice-appearing young men, muscular and good ball players. In throwing and running bases they are particularly good, but it was evident that they had never had experience at batting curve pitching. Eighteen of the 27 outs by the California Club struck out on Sullivan's dodges.

In the seventh inning Centennial pitcher O'Brien was injured badly enough that he had to be replaced. No details were provided.

While the Centennials were in Detroit, their ever-efficient advance man had made arrangements for them to play in Rochester, New York. On July 15 the *Rochester Evening Express* touted that they would be in town on Wednesday, July 19. The next day the date was changed to July 20.

We don't know what the Centennials did during their day off on the 16th, but during the night they were undoubtedly marveling at something more impressive than lightning bugs and less destructive than Midwest thunderstorms. Along with hundreds of thousands from Maine to Iowa, they were watching an aurora display.[30]

After a day of rest the Centennials were back at the Peninsular Cricket Grounds, about one mile north of today's Comerica Park, to meet Detroit's other top amateur club, the Cass. Whatever injury O'Brien suffered, it wasn't serious enough to keep him from pitching. Also, he and the rest of the team must have adapted to the heat and humidity as they trounced the Cass 14–5 in 86-degree heat.

In a face-saving game report, the *News* attributed the Centennial victory to the Cass playing their worst at the same time the Centennials played their best.

Thanks to the *Free Press*, the Centennials regained their amateur status.

> Without exception the California Club can pass the ball to bases and run bases equal to any similar organization, not barring professionals, in the country. They do not hold the ball an instant, and they let it go swiftly and with an air of perfect confidence that it will be well handled at the other end of the route.

After the game the Centennials thanked their hosts and promised to return to Detroit on their way home. At the train station they paid their $7.25 fare for the 273-mile overnight trip to Erie, Pennsylvania, where they would play two games in two days.

For the next month the cream of California's ball chasers would play over two dozen games under the most adverse and trying of conditions. They would suffer daily *low* temperatures that were higher than San Francisco's *high* temperatures. Instead of being cooled and caressed by ocean fog and refreshing sea breezes, they would suffocate in oppressive humidity. Rather than play the customary one or two games a week, they would play five or six games a week with just Sundays off—with that day often being a travel day. And the endless travel would make their emigrant class creeping crawler ordeal to Omaha a joyride by comparison; often hopping on a train immediately after a game to rush to the next game in the next city, somehow managing to eat and sleep on the run. Only once would they enjoy two consecutive days of rest.

Another mystery: how did they keep their uniforms clean? Or did they?

When they arrived in Erie on July 18, the *Morning Dispatch* welcomed them as the Champions of the Pacific Coast. Considering what they had endured over the past 24 hours, the Champs did remarkably well against the 3–3 Keystones. O'Brien was showing no aftereffects of his recent injury. In fact, it was noted that he was demonstrating a facility with curves, but the Keystones' new hurler Phillips had a better "dodge pitch," retiring 10 Centennials on strikes. The *Erie Morning Dispatch* commented:

> [Phillips] pitches not an extra swift ball, but one that will deceive eight times out of ten. When the ball starts the striker would be sure it was coming where he wanted, but just as he nerves up to bat, the ball dodges away and just out of the reach of the bat.

Stumped by Phillips' curves, the Centennials trailed 6–2 going to the top of the 7th inning when they were gifted 6 runs by incredibly sloppy Keystone defense to take

The San Francisco Base Ball Club, photographed before their departure from the City by the Bay. Cullen, Curran, Taylor, and Piercy left their marks in the MLB encyclopedias.

a two-run lead. O'Brien gave up a single run in the bottom of the frame. After the Centennials went down in order in the top of the 8th, the *Morning Dispatch* recorded for posterity:

> In the 8th inning the Keystones secured three runs, making them two ahead. When Allen struck the home plate, tieing [sic] the game, he was loudly cheered by the spectators, and their enthusiasm knew no bounds when Talley and McCarty safely made the home.

The Centennials lost 11–8.

Evidently the advance man had visited Buffalo and liked what he saw so much that he arranged for the Centennials to play there. On July 18 the Buffalo *Daily Courier* wrote "the professional nine from San Francisco" would be in town on Thursday. But Thursday was July 20, a day they were scheduled to play in Rochester, 65 miles away.

The *Rochester Evening Express* serenely noted of the conflict, "A mistake somewhere."

The next day the Centennials suffered a Waterloo at the hands of the formidable Quicksteps of Wilmington, Delaware, a paid-nine powerhouse that would compile a season record of 51–3–1. Their 17–1 thrashing earned them this sympathetic passage in the *Morning Dispatch*:

> In justice to the Centennials it must be said that they are somewhat crippled, two of their best players are laid up and the remainder nearly played out with the fatigue of their long trip. What they need now is rest, but they are not likely to get it if they go further east.

Two of their best players are laid up. Do we have another mystery? Walker had been on the DL since injuring his knee in Milwaukee on July 11, but who else was "laid up"? O'Brien had been injured recently, but he was still playing. Might it have been Gill, the center fielder, who sat out the game? Based on the box scores, with the exception of Williams replacing Walker at first base, the lineup was stable and consistent at seven positions, with Ashley, Parent, and Thompson platooning in right field and the above-mentioned Gill missing the most recent game.

On July 19, unknown to the Centennials (who were probably quite chagrinned when they read the details in the August 5 issue of the *Clipper*) what was described as "probably the finest game ever played in California" took place in San Francisco on July 19 between a picked nine and a club called the Olympics. It was a 10-inning contest going to the Olympics 3–2.

After their 0–2 passage through Erie, the saddle-sore Centennials paid $3.90 to mount the stallion of steel's all-too-familiar saddle and gallop another 156 overnight miles to Rochester, bypassing Buffalo, to play two games. On July 20, 1876, they arrived.

The Centennials' advance man was doing a bang-up job, probably being responsible for the following in the *Rochester Democrat and Chronicle* of July 19:

> There is much interesting sport anticipated in the game tomorrow afternoon between the San Francisco club and the Rochesters. The former club is indeed a strong one and composed of skilled, experienced players. Their muscle is said to be of a high order and the prospects are good for a fine, exciting game.

It was at this point that the *Clipper* began their reports of the Centennials' tour with this new dimension to the ever-expanding Centennial mystery:

> **The Centennials of San Francisco**— Up to Friday, July 21, when they were at Rochester, N.Y., the secretary of the club informs us that they have won twenty games and lost five, but as he says the score book was lost, we are able to obtain the scores of but a few games so far played by them.

According to the *Clipper's* final account of their season, the Centennials were 17–7 on July 21, *not* 20–5. Might this be a case of someone cooking the books?

Apparently the Centennials had been scouted at the Keystone game in Erie. The *Evening Express* wrote: "The San Franciscos first appeared at the bat, Wamsley pitching for the Rochesters, it being thought the former could not hit curve pitching." Instead, the Centennials found "Snacks" Wamsley's curves to their liking and scored twice in the top of the first. Only a brilliant double play prevented them from scoring more.

For some unexplained reason, a player named White, who had never appeared in a Centennial game, was now their pitcher. Could it be that O'Brien was injured (or exhausted) and Mr. White was pressed into service? Delos Ashley certainly had the credentials to replace O'Brien, but his name didn't appear in the box score either. He had played in right field against the Quicksteps the day before, getting two of his team's three hits.

In the bottom of the first the Rochesters found White's offerings equally pleasing and evened the score. The Rochesters replaced Wamsley in the second with their regular pitcher, "Buckey" Wilbur, who held San Francisco scoreless and hitless for the next five innings while they scored eight runs off Mr. White to win 12–4. The *Evening Express* called it "a game not by any means brilliant on either side."

The *Democrat and Chronicle* was more charitable: "[The Centennials] played yesterday after riding all night from Erie, Pa., and it is a wonder that they played as well as they did."

This was a historic though unnoticed game for the Centennials. It was the 11th game of their Grand Tour, surpassing the 10 games played by the Washington Nationals on their 16-day western tour in 1867.[31]

The California boys derived no benefit from sleeping in non-moving beds that night.

Although they did a bit better the next day with O'Brien back in the box, Ashley in right field, and the mysterious Mister White gone from the lineup, they still somnambulated through the game, committing 17 errors in the first four innings to give Rochester six of their nine runs in a 9–6 loss. Nor did they help themselves at the plate, managing only four hits. Rochester could have played without an outfield as only one putout was registered beyond the infield. Rochester committed 14 errors, half of them in the seventh inning, which gave San Francisco three of their six runs.

The *Union and Advertiser* commented on some of the visitors:

> The catcher [Cullen] and first baseman [Williams] of the Friscos are fair players and their pitcher is a good man, but had better learn to throw and have it pass for pitching. [He] still keeps to the old fashioned style of pitching and consequently [is] at a disadvantage when playing against a club whose so-called pitcher throws the ball.

One interpretation of this advice might be that O'Brien was following the 1845 rule that "The ball must be pitched, and not thrown, for the bat," by which was meant that the ball must be delivered with the arm straight and swinging free from the body, with no bend to the elbow. By 1872, the rules had been changed to permit the pitcher to snap his wrist as long as he kept his hand, while in the forward motion, below the hip.

On Saturday, July 22, news of the Centennials flashed from coast to coast. On the East Coast the *Clipper* reported on the July 4 game against the Atlantic Troublesomes with a box score and the following description:

> CENTENNIAL vs. TROUBLESOME. The Centennial Club, semi-professionals of San Francisco, Cal., now on their way to Philadelphia, and playing the leading Eastern clubs by invitation, played the Troublesomes of Atlantic, Ia., July 4 in the presence of about one thousand persons. The game was one of the finest and most hotly-contested ever played in the State. It was noticeable throughout for the fine fielding of both nines, and the heavy and safe batting of the home club. The pitching of both nines was excellent and well supported.

On the West Coast, the weekly *California Spirit of the Times* reprinted a brief excerpt from the *Chicago Times* account of the July 7 Franklin game in Chicago, although incorrectly reporting it as being on July 8. A nine-line summary of the July 11 game with the West Ends was appended.

In San Francisco, the *Alta* and the *Chronicle* both mentioned a 14–4 Centennial loss to Rochester. However, the subscribers of the papers could conclude that these were two different games since the *Alta* wrote that the loss occurred on "Thursday," while the *Chronicle* reported the loss occurred "yesterday" [Friday]. In fact, there was no 14–4 Rochester game. On July 20, Thursday, the score, as reported by the Rochester papers and reprinted in the *Clipper* of July 29, was 12–4.[32]

Neither San Francisco daily paper made any mention of the nine other games played since the Amity contest of June 25.

On Sunday the 23rd the *Philadelphia Sunday Mercury* first noticed the Centennials:

> The San Francisco nine — under the management of Lew Davis [sic], an old member of the Philadelphias — will make their first appearance in this city on the 1st of August next, engaging in a game with the Athletics. The Californias will also play the Kleinz and Defiance clubs during their sojourn in this city.

After surviving a grueling stretch of five games in five days in three cities covering 429 miles, July 22 and 23 was a weekend of well-deserved rest for the rail riders. Before traveling 90 miles down the tracks to Syracuse, the iron horsemen presumably took advantage of the weekend to lick their wounds, rest their bodies and, perchance, wash their once-white uniforms.

Their arrival in Syracuse to face the Stars, a semipro team with a 25–8–1 record on July 24, marked one month on the road and the start of a daunting six-day stretch of six games in six cities spanning 300 miles. To the Syracuse press they were no longer the Champions of the Pacific Coast, but "The Boys from the Golden Shore."

Despite threatening weather, a fair-sized crowd turned up at Lakeside Park. The Stars scored two times in the first four innings while San Francisco could only manage two base runners in that span. In the top of the fifth Curran scored, but four unanswered Star tallies put the game out of reach. The final score was 8–3.

Once again O'Brien's pitching style was the subject of comment and criticism.

"O'Brien has an odd delivery of the ball and would be effective with greater care," observed the *Morning Standard.*

"The pitching of O'Brien is of the old order and San Francisco would find a vast deal less of field work if he should adopt the latter day style of pitching," pontificated the *Daily Journal.*

Both Syracuse papers generously called the visitors fair fielders [18 errors], and batters [five hits, six strikeouts]. The Stars, on the other hand, "did excellent fielding" [14 errors].

The next day's *Alta* wrote "Our Centennial Base Ball Club was beaten in a game in Syracuse yesterday by a score of eight to three." Clearly the technology existed on the West Coast to receive and report information in a timely manner, albeit totally lacking in detail.

Their next stop was Auburn, a short hop of 30 miles. A city of 20,000, it was world famous for over half a century for its penitentiary while its 5–2 ball club was just a fortnight old. The largest crowd of the Auburns' young season turned out to the improved grounds to see "The Gold Diggers." The grandstand was sold out and the overflow crowd stood behind ropes in the outfield.

The *Auburn Daily Advertiser* observed:

> Those who couldn't get in, or didn't want to pay the $.25 admission, took advantage of the economy seats in trees and on near-by rooftops as well as the tops of carriages parked along the fences, [behavior] that made the management's blood boil to see full grown men engaging in such niggardly practices. Some of them might better spend less money for beer and hoard up a quarter to pay their way in than to try to beat it in this disreputable manner.

The Auburns put on their finest fielding display while the *Daily Advertiser* noted

> The lads from the Golden State were outmatched both in fielding and batting. It was the best display of fielding which the home club has yet made [five errors]. The San Franciscos, on the contrary made [31 errors], and as the Auburns pounded their pitching very easily, the game was as good as won from the start. [Auburn led 5–0 after two innings.] The only point of interest as to the result after the fifth inning was whether [the Centennials] would make a run or not.

The visitors spoiled it with two unearned runs in the final inning, too little too late to avoid another Waterloo 14–2.

The Napoleons from the West spent the night of the 25th in Auburn before riding 80 miles to Elmira, home of Mark Twain, for a 3 P.M. match against a team from Ithaca. The *Elmira Daily Advertiser* reanointed them the Champions of the Pacific Coast "who are accounted a strong club."

Clearly Mark Twain was not writing copy, otherwise much would have been made of *The Champions* and their six-game losing streak during which they were outscored 71–24.

Incredibly the *Daily Advertiser* saw the contest as

> one of the most interesting and exciting games of base ball, and the best one so far as the score is concerned that ever was played in Elmira. The day was very fair and the announcement of the contest drew to the grounds a very large crowd. The game was a very closely contested one, the Ithacas keeping up their fine reputation both at the bat

and in the field, and the strangers gaining the sympathy and applause of the enthusiastic crowd by some very strong and close efforts.

A single run by Ithaca in the third was the only score till San Francisco tied it in the top of the eighth. Ithaca's three scores in the bottom of the eighth were almost matched by a two-run San Francisco rally in the top of the ninth, but its New York woes continued with a heart breaking loss.

Three different sources — the *New York Clipper*, the *Elmira Daily Advertiser*, and the *Ithaca Daily Journal*— agreed that the final score was 4–3. Each of their box scores, though, differed wildly in their statistics.

Another fact on which the papers did agree was that a player listed as Grace in the box score replaced O'Brien, who was shifted to right field.

We learn from the *Daily Advertiser* that the Centennials were doing well financially, "paying their expenses as they go" with plans to visit Boston and Philadelphia before returning home by the end of September.

However, we are grievously misinformed by the same paper which did not vet its source before reporting "They have played twenty-eight games since [Sacramento], losing but nine in all, and five of the last being of the number."

Correcting the record yet again, Elmira was San Francisco's 15th stop since leaving home and their record was 4–11. Quite a difference from 19–9, and way off the mark from the 20–5 record attributed to them in Rochester.

Game number 15 was another overlooked and unrecorded historic milestone by the Centennials. Two years earlier the Boston Red Stockings and Philadelphia Athletics had played 14 baseball games in England and Ireland.[33] That event had been dangled by the *Clipper* as motivation to form a California nine to go back east. The *Clipper* had succeeded and now the exemplar had been exceeded.

Unlike the mysterious Mister White, who pitched one game for the Centennials in Rochester and remained in Rochester, the enigmatic Mister Grace traveled with the Centennials on the 60-mile journey to Binghamton where he faced the Crickets (5–9–2).

In fact, Mr. Grace accompanied San Francisco to Elmira from Auburn, where he umpired the match.

It was not uncommon for a player to act as umpire. In addition to the controversial game umpired by Live Taylor in Milwaukee, the Troublesome match of the Fourth of July was umpired by R. Walker of the Centennials, the just-concluded Ithaca match was overseen by William Parent of the Centennials, and the present game was umpired by Mr. Walker.

However, it was unprecedented for an umpire to become a player.

The box score of the Cricket match contains another interesting tidbit: White was pitching for the Crickets. Could this be the same mysterious Mr. White who had pitched for the Centennials in Rochester?

No. The hurler for the Crickets had a vacuum-sealed alibi. According to the box scores published in the *Clipper* of July 29, when White was pitching in Rochester for the Centennials, White was the Cricket pitcher in Binghamton facing the Carbondales that same day. Therefore: two different pitchers named White. No mystery; merely a coincidence.

The mighty Crickets took the lead in the bottom of the second with a single run. When San Francisco scored two in the top of the third they had their first lead since their brief 8–7 advantage against the Keystones in Erie on July 18. They added to their slim margin with three more in the sixth and then held off a Cricket rally to prevail 6–5.

Unfortunately the sweet taste of victory was replaced by the acid reflux of defeat the next day in Wilkes-Barre, Pennsylvania, a coalmining town on the banks of the Susquehanna River. Despite a heavy drizzle, a large crowd gathered to watch "The Celebrated Centennials, considered the Champions of the Pacific Coast."

With Grace starting (and O'Brien in right), the game began with two Wilkes-Barre runs followed by a Centennial run. Both teams were scoreless in the second as the heavy drizzle turned to steady rain. The steady rain intensified in the third as Wilkes-Barre scored four times, answered by a single Centennial run.

Reminiscent of the Centennials' arrival in Omaha, the steady rain became a downpour in the fourth as the Wilkes Barres scored a deluge of runs off Grace. When Grace was replaced by O'Brien, who was untouchable in the top of the fifth, the downpour became a gulley washer. The Centennials prolonged their own misery (and everyone else's) by scoring three times in the bottom of the fifth. A merciful umpire called the game after five innings in favor of the home team, 14–5.

Counting only the "preseason" games documented in the San Francisco papers, and not those in the *Clipper*, this was the Centennials' 22nd game of the season, a record for San Francisco clubs. The previous high was 21 games by the 1875 Californias during a season that ran from March through November.[34]

The next game was in Easton, Pa., 50 miles to the southeast on the Delaware River. This was an appropriate stop for the Centennials; an Easton historical claim was that it was one of three cities in which the Declaration of Independence was first read in 1776 — the other two being Philadelphia and Trenton, New Jersey.

The paid turnout of just 300 Eastoners (in a town of 11,000) was not because the Centennials had been playing in smaller and smaller towns since Rochester. Nor was it due to the Centennials' mediocre record preceding them and the advance man being unable to put a good spin on a club that had lost all but one of its last 9. Nor was it because of the lukewarm welcome in the *Easton Daily Express*: "The San Francisco Club have been playing some very strong games during their Eastern trip."

It was simply because of a low fence that allowed people to watch the game for free.

To the *Daily Free Press*,

> the first three innings were attended by some very excellent playing on both sides from which it appeared that the game would be very close and hotly contested.

The *Daily Express* on the other hand, felt the game was

> devoid of interest on account of the many errors made by the home club, no less than twenty-seven being charged to them including muffs, wild throws, and misjudged fly balls which gave the visitors the game.

Notwithstanding having committed 14 errors, the visitors were termed, by the *Daily Express,* fine fielders who took in all the fly balls put up.

San Francisco began play as though they had something to prove, as Grace held the Eastons to two runs in the first four innings while the Centennials exploded for nine. In the seventh inning, however, Centennial fortunes turned as catcher Cullen was hit in the face by a foul tip. At this point San Francisco was facing a potential catastrophe.

Delos Ashley had not played in the last five games, Thompson had missed the past four, and William Parent had been absent for three games, all for unknown reasons. Walker, who was umpiring the game, was still injured as well. Thus, there was the grim possibility that San Francisco had no change players. With one eye swollen shut, Cullen swapped positions with center fielder Curran and spent the remainder of the game doing his best to keep his good eye on the ball. San Francisco won, 19–14.

Easton was 50 miles north of Philadelphia, but the Centennials' next stop was 50 miles to the southwest in Reading. They left immediately after the game, undoubtedly celebrating on the train and arriving in Reading on Saturday night. They rested on Sunday before facing the town's pride and joy, the Actives (35–21 for season). The Reading *Daily Eagle* didn't print a box or line score of the game, but it did have a good narrative.

> The [Centennials] are in good condition, considering the miles they have traveled and the number of games they have played. The veterans from the Pacific Coast had heard of the Reading giants as far west as Omaha, but never supposed they were made up of the material they yesterday encountered.

The *Daily Eagle* noted,

> [Despite a recent rain that left the field heavy and soggy] at practice the visitors showed up exceedingly well. A stranger would have selected them as the favorites as far as their batting and catching were concerned before the game.

The Centennials validated that positive assessment in the top of the first with a "neat double play" to harmlessly quell a bases-loaded and no-outs threat by the Actives.

> Up to the third inning the game was close and promised to be interesting, but the visitors fell to pieces and were completely demoralized.... Their two pitchers were hammered hard and their outfielders lost their spikes and plates running over the hills and chasing the ball.

The 17–0 final score was the worst drubbing of their tour. San Francisco had just four hits. Nary a Centennial got past second base.

In the absence of a box score, we don't know the status of Cullen and his swollen eye, or if the absent Ashley, Thompson or Parent made an appearance. But we do learn from the *Daily Eagle*:

> A specialty of the visitors is a prize for batting. A very heavy gold badge will be given to the player having the best average for the season. The man who makes the most hits in a single game wears it until another makes more and then he wears it until somebody beats him. Their left fielder [Taylor] won it at Easton, and yesterday made two clean hits and still has it. Today they are booked for Philadelphia.
>
> They are a gentlemanly lot of ball players and they received frequent applause from the thousand people who witnessed the contest. The players are in good condition considering the miles they have traveled and the number of games they have played.

The Centennials' Philadelphia schedule was published in the July 29 issue of the *Clipper*. On August 1 they were to play the Athletics and the Kleinz club the following day.

The July 30 issue of the *Sunday Mercury* announced the travelers' impending arrival in the City of Brotherly Love:

The San Francisco Centennial nine will arrive in this city next Tuesday [August 1], and on the afternoon of that day will play against the Athletics' Reserve-nine, the professional team being engaged elsewhere we regret to state. On Wednesday [August 2] the Californians play the Kleinz and on Saturday [August 5] the Campbell Club will meet the visitors. Our citizens are assured of a series of interesting games, and the enterprise and pluck of the visitors should be rewarded by a large attendance.

On August 1, the journey that was launched by the *Clipper*'s challenge nearly six months earlier had reached its destination and the Centennials' days of endless travel and restless nights were over. However, their arrival in America's second-largest city (with a population of nearly one million, Philadelphia had more people than all of California) was not the newsmaking event that their arrival had been in so many other cities and towns where they were treated like visiting royalty. In Philadelphia they were just another team, and not the only Centennial Club in town; there was a Philadelphia Centennial nine.

It was impossible for the Philadelphia press or the *Clipper* to report on all of the amateur and semiprofessional baseball activity in the metropolitan region. Previously the Centennial games generated detailed reports and/or comprehensive box scores in the local press, but once they landed in the big pond of East Coast baseball, the largest ripple that they could expect to make was a generic box score and a line or two of comment. In the *Clipper*, many reports were one sentence long, and three Centennial games were never noted except in the *Clipper's* December summary.[35]

Their first game in Philadelphia was not against the Athletics, or their reserve nine, but against the Campbells. A consolation was that they played on the 25th and Jefferson Street Grounds, the home field of the Athletics.

Grace started his sixth game and O'Brien was in right. Apparently Cullen was fit enough to catch. Playing center field and batting cleanup in place of Gill was a new player named Wynn. A 2–0 Centennial lead in the top of the third became an insurmountable 5–2 deficit in the bottom of the inning that ended with a 10–5 loss.

The next day, normalcy returned when the California nine faced the Kleinz. It was all hands on deck as the original Centennials reported for duty: O'Brien was hurling, Ashley was in right, Gill was back in center, Grace was gone for good and Mister Wynn, the mysterious one-game wonder, was no more.

With all the pieces back in place, the Centennials scored four runs in the top of the ninth inning to defeat the Kleinz 7–4. This game, also played at 25th and Jefferson, was a stellar pitching performance by O'Brien. Starting for the first time in seven games, he allowed no earned runs, gave up just four hits, and struck out five.

As with Mister White, we'll never know who Mister Grace was, or how he came to be a Centennial, but we may be able to explain Mister Wynn, Gill's one-game replacement in center field.

The Morse Code for **GILL** is: ***G*** [——.] ***I*** [. .] ***L*** [—] ***L*** [—]

The Morse Code for **WYNN** is: ***W*** [.——] ***Y*** [... .] ***N*** [—.] ***N*** [—.]

More than likely Wynn was the creation of a careless telegrapher or inattentive transcriber rather than a real person.

The Centennials' 13–8 victory over the Frank Brown club on August 3 generated neither a box score, nor a line score, nor a narrative; just nine words in the *Clipper*: "They also defeated the Frank Brown Club, scoring 13–8."[36]

August 4 was a day off that did not involve traveling, so we may assume that the Californians did what some 10 million Americans (nearly one in four) did that summer in Philadelphia: they went to the Exposition. Fifty cents admitted them to the 285-acre site in Fairmount Park along with 45,000 other daily visitors who beheld 250 exhibition buildings. Among the tens of thousands of exhibits they beheld were the new technological marvels the telephone, the electric light, and the typewriter.

An exhibit they could not have overlooked was the Sawyer Observatory. At 300 feet tall, it was the tallest structure in the United States at the time. Visitors could ride a steam-powered elevator to the top for a panoramic view of the site. Down at ground level was the right arm and the torch of the Statue of Liberty. To keep cool and hydrated as they strolled the grounds, they probably sampled a new treat: ice cream soda.

If visitors were at all interested in trains and locomotives, the Baldwin Locomotive Works of Philadelphia, the nation's oldest and largest manufacturer of locomotives, had a display of its products.

The highlight of the day was Professor Samuel King's afternoon balloon ascension. At 4:49 P.M. the Professor's 75-foot tall, 56-foot diameter balloon lifted off from the Exposition Grounds with 11 passengers and a cage of carrier pigeons. A pigeon-delivered message reported that the balloon easily reached an elevation of more than one mile.[37]

The next day the tourists faced the Campbells again, this time reversing the earlier outcome with a 10–6 win.

Another day off preceded a 25-mile trip to Wilmington, Delaware, to face the Quicksteps. This was the amateur counterpart to the professional juggernaut that crushed them 17–1 in Erie on July 19. As in the Easton game, this contest was two games in one.

The well-known and deservedly popular club, the Californias of San Francisco (sic)[38] led off with O'Brien scoring in the top of the first. The Quicksteps doubled the ante with two in the bottom of the inning, but the Centennials redoubled it with four in the top of the second frame to take a 5–2 lead. Over the next three innings the Centennials doubled their run total to take the lead at 10–7.

But then a Quickstep pitching change in the top of the sixth silenced the Centennial bats and energized the Quicksteps' clubs. The Delawareans scored eight in the bottom of the sixth on their way to a 19–10 victory.

There was no box score, but the *Wilmington Morning Herald's* lengthy narrative included:

> The catchers (there were two of them) for the visitors had quite a number of errors and passed balls, which enabled our boys to get in a lot of unearned runs. The fielding of the California Club, at the start and all through the game was excellent, and but for a few glaring errors the playing might have been called brilliant.... The batting on both sides was considered as being heavy ... the Californias made 11 base hits, while the Quicksteps made 14.

The *Clipper's* schedule of upcoming games had the Centennials playing the Chelsea Club in Brooklyn on August 8, but instead of visiting America's third-largest city, they played the Defiance club in Philadelphia. The *Clipper's* entire account was: "...8th, at Philadelphia, San Francisco vs. Defiance 11–6."

The next day the Campbells and Centennials faced each other for the rubber match. Walker's name appeared in a box score for the first time in a month. Both teams scored four in the first inning and two each in the ninth inning. The difference was single runs scored by "the team from the Pacific shore" in the second and fifth innings to win what must have been a thriller, 8–6.

On August 10 they crossed the Delaware River to take on the Eurekas in Camden, New Jersey, the ninth state of their tour. Their 20–0 "Chicago" of the Eurekas was their third consecutive win, a first on this trip. That milestone game was memorialized in the *Clipper* thus: "10th at Camden, N.J., San Francisco vs. Eureka, 20–0."

Their streak continued the following day in West Chester with a triumph over the Brandywine. It was also their 14th win since leaving San Francisco, bringing them to .500 for the tour.

According to the *Clipper* summary the Centennials returned to Philadelphia to face the Frank Brown club again on the 12th, achieving their greatest offensive output in a 27–6 demolition. But, except for that reference in the December summary, there is no record of the game.

Likewise, it is only the *Clipper* summary that notes their next victory on Monday against their doppelgangers, the Philadelphia Centennials, allegedly winning their sixth in a row, 10–7.

In what might have been the last game on their Grand Tour, the boys from the West Coast finally got to play a National League team: a California baseball first. For two hours and ten minutes their long-deferred dreams were realized as they battled the Philadelphia Athletics at the 25th and Jefferson Street Grounds. This game was not immune to its share of Centennial mystery. The *Clipper* and the *Sunday Mercury* differ on when it happened. The *Sunday Mercury* published a box score and a 12-line comment of the game reportedly played on Wednesday, August 16. The *Clipper*, on the other hand, in its only reference to the game in its December summary, has it taking place on August 15.

Both agree that the amateurs lost 17–6.

The Californians surrendered 13 runs before they managed one of their own, but they could claim a moral victory over the final four innings by outscoring the Athletics 6–4. The Centennials muscled up against pitcher Ezra Sutton, who usually played first base, getting 12 hits and forcing the outfielders to work in making 10 putouts. Walker got three hits off Sutton to win the gold medal for that memorable game.

The dream ended on August 18 with the disbanding of one of the most remarkable unknown nines of the 19th century. The only report was in the *Clipper*:

> The San Francisco Base Ball Club of California, after a successful tour (in games but not financially) disbanded August 18 at Philadelphia. They have won 24 games and lost 11. All the members being in good circumstances at home, left for California on the 21st.

Once again there is a major discrepancy regarding their record. Thirty-two road games were cited in the *Clipper* summary, and their record for those games was 17–15. If the *Clipper's* record is expanded to include the preseason games reported in their summary, the Centennial record for 1876 was 29–15. Taking into account only the preseason games reported in San Francisco's newspapers, they were victorious in all four, making their verifiable record 21–15. Incorporating the mysterious victory over the Alerts on April 23 (as reported in the *Clipper* of May 13), another possible tally is 22 wins and 15 losses.

And then there are the three problematic Philadelphia games — all victories — cited in the *Clipper's* December summary for which there is no documentation. Without proof of these wins, the record slips to 19–15 for the year and 14–15 for the tour.

News of the team's breakup was never reported back home. Instead, the *Chronicle* of August 27, clearly confusing the Philadelphia Centennials with the team they sent off with best wishes two months earlier, gave the results of games that were played after the California nine had called it quits, or which were clearly in conflict with real games they had played. The Centennials did not stop at Detroit and Atlantic, Iowa as they had promised. Nor did all the players return home. John Curran was signed by the Philadelphia Athletics for the final three games of the 1876 National League season. He remained back east for the 1877 campaign, playing with the Brooklyn Chelseas of the League Alliance.

Likewise, Thomas Gill remained back east. The name Gill appeared periodically in box scores of games played at Brooklyn's Prospect Park in 1877.

On October 7 the *Clipper* posted the final averages for the Centennial tour as provided by Mr. Gill. Keating, despite batting in the sixth or seventh slot for most of the tour, led with 37 base hits in 30 games for a 1–7 hits per game average.[39] Gill also had a 1–7 average, knocking 31 hits in 24 games. The winner of Col. Andrews' badge was never revealed.

The December 24 *Chicago Tribune* had the penultimate word on the Centennials in the Centennial year: "The Centennial Club of San Francisco this season won 30 games and lost 15. Expenses were $2,186 and the Club was out only $135 at the end of the trip East."[40]

Half of the Centennial dozen did not appear on a San Francisco diamond in 1877. As mentioned, Curran and Gill remained back East. Taylor didn't play in San Francisco that season, but later that year he played two games for the Hartford Dark Blues of the National League. He subsequently joined his Centennial teammate John Curran on the Brooklyn Chelseas.

There was no mention of Parent, Thompson, or O'Brien. Either they did not return to San Francisco or did not play any more baseball.

C. J. Keating suited up with the San Franciscos again, while former San Franciscos Richard T. Walker and Andy Piercy jumped to the Eagles. Delos Ashley, John Cullen and "left-behind" Centennial Hyp Magendie became Athletics.

John Curran's big league career was three games and out with the Athletics. Live Taylor's career would include two more trips to the bigs: 24 games with the National League Troy Trojans in 1879 and 41 with the Pittsburgh Alleghenys of the American Association in 1884.

Andy Piercy would play two major league games for the Chicago White Stockings in 1881.

John Cullen would be the last Centennial to make the big time, appearing in nine games in 1884 for the Wilmington Quicksteps of the Union Association.

The last of the Centennials to appear on a baseball field was the indefatigable Andy Piercy. In 1931, at the age of 75, he was one of the honorees at a Seals Stadium old-timers celebration. The final link to baseball's forgotten Grand Tour died on December 27, 1932, taking some incredible memories with him to the grave.

Abstract

Prominent among early baseball's epochal events are the richly documented and horizon-expanding Grand Tours of the Brooklyn Excelsiors in 1860; the Washington Nationals in 1867; the legendary Cincinnati Red Stockings tours of 1868–1870; and the 1874 tour of England and Ireland by the Boston Red Stockings and the Philadelphia Athletics. In 1876 there was another Grand Tour that was so poorly documented that there is no single chronicle of that event. Consequently it was immediately forgotten and has been lost to history ever since. This is the story of that forgotten Grand Tour.

Acknowledgments

I am everlastingly grateful for the assistance of SABR members Brock Helander (Sacramento Chapter); Mark Vatavuk (Forbes Field Chapter); Priscilla Astifan; Ed Morton (Connie Mack Chapter); and Richard Hershberger (DC-Bob Davis Chapter). Without their help the cracks and gaps in this narrative would have been wider and deeper than they are.

Notes

1. All references to baseball games played in San Francisco are based solely on reports in the local newspapers.

2. San Francisco had five major daily newspapers in 1876: *Chronicle*; *Examiner*; *Daily Alta, California* (*Alta*); *Call*; and *Bulletin*. For the timespan of this article, only copies of the *Chronicle*, *Alta*, and *Bulletin* are available.

3. Various sources give either November 1854 or August 1856 as Piercy's birthdate. His death certificate lists the August 1856 date.

4. Taylor's birthdate is listed as February 3, 1851, on baseballreference.com. At his death, the five daily San Francisco papers listed two different ages: *Call* (02/21/88), *Bulletin* (02/21/88), and *Chronicle* (02/22/88) reported Taylor being 38 years of age at death (year of birth 1849 or 1850); *Examiner* (02/20/88) and *Alta* (02/21/88) reported his age at 33 years and 16 days (date of birth 02/03/1855).

5. "Mr. Durkee" is John Durkee, a pioneer San Francisco baseball player who participated in the first fully documented game in San Francisco in 1860 with the San Francisco Base Ball Club (later Eagles). When his playing days ended he became the President of the Pacific Base Ball Convention, which oversaw the amateur game in San Francisco into the mid–1870s.

6. The *Philadelphia Sunday Mercury* also reported on the match in its April 4, 1876, issue, giving the Centennials second billing: "Mrs. Jas. A. Oates' Comic Opera Troupe played a game of base ball last Sunday week in San Francisco. The two nines were dressed in masquerade costumes, and the novelty of the match attracted a large assemblage."

7. The *Clipper* lists four more games beyond May 28: May 31, June 7, 14, and 20.

8. *Alta*, May 27, 1876. A week later (June 4, 1876, p. 3) the *Philadelphia Sunday Mercury* advised: "A picked nine of California base ball players will shortly visit the East, leaving San Francisco on or about the 16th inst."

9. *New York Clipper*, Feb. 17, 1877, p. 870, "The Game in California."

10. *San Francisco Chronicle*, June 25, 1876, p. 1.

11. During their tour the Centennials were at various times referred to as amateurs, semiprofessionals, and professionals. The *Clipper* had a special category for them: "Gate Money Amateurs," i.e. those who charged admission to their games. In a mini-editorial on April 21, 1877, the *Clipper* wrote: "Gate Money Amateurs: ... clubs which, while claiming to be amateurs, practically transform themselves into professional players by sharing gate money on enclosed grounds.... If they are legitimate amateurs, they should play on free grounds."

12. On June 27 the *Sacramento Daily Union* wrote: "The picked-nine ... left for the east yesterday morning." According to http://CPRR.org/Museum/Travellers_Guide_10–1878.html the only eastbound train leaving Sacramento in the morning was designated "mixed," departing at 8 A.M.

13. http://cprr.org/Museum/Ephemera/CP-UP_Timetable_1881/index.html

14. All passenger car dimensions from White, J. 1978. *The American Railroad Passenger Car*, vol. 2, p. 470. See also: http://cprr.org/Museum/Car_Builders_Dictionary/_car_builders_dict_195.html

15. http://cprr.org/Museum/Car_Builders_Dictionary/_car_builders_dict_197.html

16. San Francisco *Chronicle*, June 1, 1876, p. 3; June 4, 1876, p. 8.

17. Williams, H. (ed.). 1877. *The Pacific Tourist: Williams' Illustrated Trans-Continental Guide* (p. 13).

18. Crofutt's guide was replaced in 1877 by Williams' 296-page guide.

19. *Frank Leslie's Illustrated Newspaper* described the conditions in emigrant class in its February 9, 1878, edition: "What [is to be said] of the ordinary passenger-car, wherein the working-men and working-women — the miners, the gold-seekers, the trappers and hunters traveling from one station to another, and the queer backwoods folk who have left their log homesteads in Wisconsin and Michigan and Illinois to cross the trail of the sunset — do congregate, and are all packed like sardines in a box? It is a pathetic thing to see their nightly contrivances and poor shifts at comfort; the vain attempts to improvise out of their two or three feet of space a comfortable sleeping-place for some sick girl or feeble old person, and the weary, endless labor of the mothers to pacify or amuse their fretted children. Here and there some fortunate party of two or three will have full sway over a whole section — two seats, that is to say — and there will be space for one of them to stretch his or her limbs in the horizontal posture and rest luxuriously; but for the most part, every seat has its occupant, by night as well as day, a congregation of aching spines and cramped limbs. The overland journey is no fairy tale to those who read if from a way car!"

20. *Rocky Mountain News*, July 2, 1876, p. 4.

21. *New York Clipper*, June 27, 1874, p. 99, "Base Ball in Dacotah." The Actives won 17–10.

22. Anderson, H. 1970. "The Benteen Base Ball Club: Sports Enthusiasts of the Seventh Cavalry in Montana," *The Magazine of Western History* 20.3, 82–87.

23. Williams 1877, 62.

24. Ibid., 37–38.

25. Unless otherwise noted, all weather, temperature, and meteorological data are from *Annual Report of the Chief Signal Officer to the Secretary of War for the Year* (July 1876–June 1877).

26. Council Bluffs *Non-Pareil*, July 6–7.

27. In the *Atlantic Telegraph*'s June 28 report of a San Francisco club on its way to Atlantic, there was also mention of a 21–10 victory by the Troublesomes over the Council Bluff Quicksteps and the editorial boast: "The Troubs make it a rule to win every time."

28. Both the *Davenport Gazette* and the *Democrat* only printed the score of the game. No details, line score, or box score were provided. This was the second game that did not have a box score. For the tour, there were 19 complete box scores and one that lacked positions but was otherwise complete.

29. At the end of the baseball season, as it did with the Centennials, the *Clipper* published the season results of various clubs. Not all of the Centennials' opponents had their record printed. Those that did are mentioned.

30. In 1879 Carey was playing for the White Stockings. Following the conclusion of the season, the White Stockings came to San Francisco. On October 20, 1879, the *Chronicle* profiled the first major leaguers to visit the city. Of Carey the *Chronicle* wrote: "Carey, the shortstop, is an old Californian, having played ten years ago with the pioneer Eagles of this city." An examination of old box scores uncovers "Carey" playing third base for the Pacifics in 1868. In 1869 "Cary" played left field and caught for the Eagles. When the Cincinnati Red Stockings came to San Francisco in 1869, an Eagles player identified as "Carey" by the *Chronicle* and "Casey" by the *Call* faced the professionals, accounting for three of the eight Eagles runs in two games with two doubles.

31. From "Report of the Chief Signal-Officer," p. 385: "ATMOSPHERIC ELECTRICITY — Auroras have been observed on the following dates: that of the 16th being generally visible in the northern sections of the country extending from Maine to Iowa."

32. See: 19cbaseball.com/tours-1867-washington-nationals-tour.html

33. The *Clipper* correctly reprinted the box score of the July 21 game in its July 29 edition (p. 139). In its December summary, however, the *Clipper* incorrectly listed the score as 13–4.

34. See: 19cbaseball.com/tours-1874-world-base-ball-tour.html. Additionally, five cricket matches were played on that tour.

35. As reported in San Francisco papers.

36. The only Philadelphia paper that provided baseball news that I was able to access was the *Sunday Mercury*.

37. Also listed as "Frank Brower" according to the *Clipper* (Aug. 12, 1876, p. 155).

38. *Philadelphia Times*, Aug. 5, 1876, p. 1, "Up in a Balloon."

39. *Wilmington* (Del.) *Morning Herald*, Aug. 8, 1876.

40. Based on 20 box scores published between July 5 and August 20.

Author Index

Brunson, James Edward, III. "'He Drinks, Gambles, and Plays Baseball on Sunday': Walter L. Cohen and the Louisiana Colored Sporting Fraternity, 1875–1889." 4.1: 96–111.

_____. "Henry Bridgewater's Black Stockings of St. Louis, 1881–1889." 1.2: 12–27.

Carle, Bill. "Half a Century of the Game." Rev. of *Orator O'Rourke: The Life of a Baseball Radical*, by Mike Roer. 2.1: 100–102.

_____. "Nuggets." Rev. of *Major League Baseball Players of 1916: A Biographical Dictionary*, by Paul Batesel. 2.1: 99–100.

_____. "A Story Worth Telling." Rev. of *Three Finger: The Mordecai Brown Story*, by Cindy Thompson and Scott Brown. 3.1: 122–123.

Carney, Gene. "Eddie Cicotte on the Day that Shook Baseball." 3.2: 99–104.

Casway, Jerrold. "Baseball's Hibernian Collaboration." 3.2: 67–75.

Casway, Jerry. "Last Note." Rev. of *The Great Encyclopedia of Nineteenth Century Major League Baseball*, by David Nemec. 3.1: 118.

Dyte, David. "1845.4. Baseball in Brooklyn, 1845–1870: The Best There Was." 5.1 *Protoball Special Issue*: 98–102.

Edelman, Rob. "The Baseball Film to 1920." 1.1: 22–35.

_____. "Baseball on the Boards." 4.1: 4–19.

_____. "Baseball, Vaudeville, and Mike Donlin." 2.1: 44–57.

_____. "The Busher Speaks." Rev. of *You Know Me Al: A Busher's Letters*, by Ring W. Lardner. 2.2: 117–119.

_____. "Electric Scoreboards, Bulletin Boards, and Mimic Diamonds." 3.2: 76–87.

_____. "For the Record: The Movies, Eight Men Out and Historical Accuracy." 6.1: 102–108.

_____. "Lost (and Found) Baseball." 5.2: 23–37.

_____. "Mysteries of the Mighty Casey." 4.2: 40–51.

Felber, Bill. "Two Hall of Famers Speak: New First-Person Narratives by Willie Keeler and Kid Nichols." 4.2: 12–30.

Franks, Joel. "From Honolulu to Brooklyn: The Journeys of the Hawaiian Travelers." 2.1: 5–16.

Frutchey, Jim. "Anson's Gift of Primary Source Material." Rev. of *A Ball Player's Career*, by Adrian C. Anson. 5.2: 98–99.

_____. "Scranton Times Coverage of the 1906 New York State League Champions Led by Moonlight Graham." 4.2: 52–58.

_____. "Remembering the Chief." Rev. of *Chief Bender's Burden: The Silent Struggle of a Baseball Star*, by Tom Swift. 2.2: 121–122.

Gerlach, Larry R. "The Bad News Bees: Salt Lake City and the 1919 Pacific Coast League Scandal." 6.1: 35–74.

Gómez, César González. "March, Conquest, and Play Ball: The Game in the Mexican-American War, 1846–1848." 5.2: 13–22.

_____. "A New Perspective on Mexican Baseball Origins." 1.1: 64–72.

Gottschall, Terrell D. "'Two-Bit Baseball': Walla Walla and the Pacific Interstate League, 1891." 3.2: 52–66.

Haupert, Michael J. "Take Me Out to the Ballgame: The Pursuit of Pleasure and Profit on the Ball Field." 4.1: 28–43.

Hershberger, Richard. "The Athletic and National Clubs and the Early National League." 2.2: 63–74.

_____. "Baseball and Rounders." 3.1: 81–93.

_____. "The Borderlands of Professionalism: Cooperative Clubs and the Formation of the National League." 1.1: 103–118.

_____. "The Evolution of the 'Perfect Game.'" 4.2: 31–39.

_____. "'The New Marlboro.' Match Base Ball Co.' of 1863." 4.1: 87–95.

_____. "A Reconstruction of Philadelphia Town Ball." 1.2: 28–43.

_____. "A Voice Crying in the Wilderness." Rev. of *Ball, Bat and Bishop*, by Robert Henderson. 5.2: 107–109.

_____. "1821.5. New York Mansion Converted to Venue Suitable for Ballplaying: An Early Sighting of Baseball Clubs?" 5.1 *Protoball Special Issue*: 58–60.

_____. "1831.1. The Olympic Ball Club of Philadelphia." 5.1 *Protoball Special Issue*: 77–80.

Higham, Harold V. "King of the Pitchers." Rev. of *Fifty-Nine in '84: Old Hoss Radbourn, Barehanded Baseball and the Greatest Season a Pitcher Ever Had*, by Edward Achorn. 5.2: 99–101.

_____. "Witness to and Participant in Early Professional Baseball History." Rev. of *America's National Game: Historic Facts Concerning the Beginning, Evolution, Development and Popularity of Base Ball, with Personal Reminiscences of Its Vicissitudes, Its Victories and Its Votaries*, by Albert G. Spalding. 3.2: 126–127.

Hise, Beth. "1744.1. 'How Is It, Umpire?' The 1744 Laws of Cricket and Their Influence on the Development of Baseball in America." 5.1 *Protoball Special Issue*: 25–31.

Miklich, Eric. "1857.1. Nine Innings, Nine Players, Ninety Feet, and Other Changes: The Recodification of Baseball Rules in 1857." 5.1 *Protoball Special Issue*: 118–121.
Millen, Patricia. "1863.11. On the Battlefront, the New York Game Takes Hold, 1861–1865." 5.1 *Protoball Special Issue*: 149–152.
Milner, Andrew. "In the Beginning." Rev. of *Baseball (1845–1881): From the Newspaper Accounts*, by Preston D. Orem. 4.1: 118–119.
_____. "Their Baseball Lives." Rev. of *The Complete* New York Clipper *Baseball Biographies: More Than 800 Sketches of Players, Managers, Owners, Umpires, Reporters and Others, 1859–1903*, compiled by Jean-Pierre Caillault. 4.2: 123–124.
Morris, Peter. "'A Motion as Near Flying as Any Human Being Could Attain': The 19th Century Umpire as Sprinter." 2.2: 18–25.
_____. "The Mountaineers Are at It." Rev. of *West Virginia Baseball: A History, 1865–2000*, by William Akin. 1.2: 124–126.
_____. "Non-Primary Colors." Rev. of *Baseball in Philadelphia: A History of the Early Game, 1831–1900*, by John Shiffert, and *Before the Curse: The Glory Days of New England Baseball, 1858–1918*, by Troy Soos. 2.1: 108–110.
_____. "Sporadic Baseball, Episodic Book." Rev. of *Base Ball on the Western Reserve: The Early Game in Cleveland and Northeast Ohio, Year by Year and Town by Town, 1865–1900*, by James M. Egan, Jr. 3.1: 121.
_____. "'Why Shouldn't We?': The Scandalous Elopement of Abraham Lincoln's, Granddaughter and Minor League Pitcher Warren Beckwith." 3.2: 21–30.
Nemec, David. "The Union Association: An Unexpected Last Stop." 3.1: 44–52.
Newman, Timothy, and Bruce Stuckman. "They Were Black Sox Long Before the 1919 World Series." 6.1: 75–85.
Nucciarone, Monica. "Sowing Johnny Appleseeds of Doubt." 3.1: 53–66.
Payne, Marty. "'The Undesirable Position': Umpiring in the American Association, 1882–1891." 1.2: 104–114.
_____. "1858.46. Diffusion of the New York Game in Maryland." 5.1 *Protoball Special Issue*: 127–131.
Perkins, Greg. "The Cincinnati Game: Townball in Cincinnati, 1858–1866." 2.2: 35–46.
Pomrenke, Jacob. "'Call the Game!': The 1917 Fenway Park Gamblers Riot." 6.1: 5–16.
Rowe, Gail. "Baseball's Creation Myths." Rev. of *Baseball in the Garden of Eden: The Secret History of the Early Game*, by John Thorn. 5.2: 104–107.
Ryczek, William. "1854.9. William Van Cott Writes a Letter to the Sporting Press: December 1854." 5.1 *Protoball Special Issue*: 111–113.
Schaefer, Robert H. "Bizarre Base Ball Bats." 2.2: 75–82.
_____. "The Creation of a Legend: Germany Schaefer's Called Home Run." 5.2: 38–51.
_____. "The Legend of the Lively Ball." 3.2: 88–98.
_____. "The Postseason Play of 1902." 1.1: 56–63.
_____. "The Wiman Trophy, and the Man for Whom It Was Named." 1.2: 44–55.
_____. "1858.2. The Changes Wrought by the Great Base Ball Match of 1858." 5.1 *Protoball Special Issue*: 122–126.
Seymour Mills, Dorothy. "Ladies at the Bat." Rev. of *Baseball Before We Knew It: A Search for the Roots of the* Game, by David Block. 1.2: 122–124.
_____. "A Story with Endless Fascination." Rev. of *Buying the Black Sox: How Baseball's Cover-Up of the 1919 World Series Fix Almost Suceeded*, by Gene Carney. 2.1: 106- reviews GENE CARNEY'S Burying the Black Sox 106–108.
Simon, Tom. "A Federal League Fest." Rev. of *The Federal League of Base Ball Clubs: The History of an Outlaw Major League, 1914–1015*, by Robert Peyton Wiggins. 3.2: 127–128.
_____. "The Wonder Team in the White City: U.V.M. at the Intercollegiate Base Ball Tournament of 1893." 4.2: 79–120.
Steinberg, Steve. "Horace Fogel: The Man Who Knew (and Talked) Too Much." 6.2: 33–50.
Tholkes, Robert. "Not Likely to Flourish: A Survey of the New York Rules Base Ball Season of 1862." 6.2: 22–32.
_____. "'We Hope They Will Not Be Disappointed': A Survey of the New York Rules Base Ball Season of 1861." 5.2: 5–12.
_____. "'Your Valuabal Paper': Baseball Correspondence in the *Sunday Mercury*, 1859–1860." 4.1: 44–58.
_____. "1860.6. The *Sunday Mercury* Summarizes the 1860 Season." 5.1 *Protoball Special Issue*: 136–138.
Thompson, George A. "1805.4. An Enigmatic 1805 'Game of Bace' in New York." 5.1 *Protoball Special Issue*: 55–57.

Notes

NOTES

NOTES